JoAn,

Merry Christmas
1984

Allan

I Stand Corrected

I Stand Corrected

Corrected

More On Language from
WILLIAM SAFIRE

Times
BOOKS

Published by TIMES BOOKS,
The New York Times Book Co., Inc.
130 Fifth Avenue, New York, N.Y. 10011

Published simultaneously in Canada by
Fitzhenry & Whiteside, Ltd., Toronto

Library of Congress Cataloging in Publication Data

Safire, William, 1929-
I stand corrected.

Includes index.
1. English language—Usage—Addresses, essays,
lectures. I. Title.
PE1421.S22 1984   428'.00973   83-40090
ISBN 0-8129-1097-4

Designed by Giorgetta Bell McRee/Early Birds

Manufactured in the United States of America

84 85 86 87 88 5 4 3 2 1

To Frances Julius

INTRODUCTION

Who elected you?

"Who in this country decides on what is and what is not correct in English usage?" asks Olga Marx of New York. "Who, for instance, gave his blessing to omitting the *m* in the accusative form of *who*? Who shortens *looking out of the window* to *looking out the window*? Who approves of *It looks like it's going to rain*?"

Miss Marx, who is 89, observes that it was Prof. Brander Matthews of Columbia University who taught her that *It's me* should be accepted, because it fulfilled the function of the French *C'est moi.* "Incidentally, he wouldn't let me audit his course, not so much because he didn't like women, but because—so he explained to me—he couldn't lecture properly unless he tilted back his chair and put his feet on the table or desk in front of him, and that—he'd been taught—was an impolite way to confront females."

With that aside aside, Miss Marx confronts the issue: "In France, it is the Académie française who (that?) regulates usage; in Germany, the accepted German both in form and pronunciation is that spoken on the stage: *Bühnendeutsch.* Who or what is our arbiter of what is or is not acceptable in English?"

I am tempted to respond with a cool "Me." Or, if you prefer, "I am." (I do not have to point out that, in rhetoric, pointing something out while denying you are pointing it out is called "paraleipsis," "preterition," or "apophasis.") But her question is serious and better phrased than the usual "Who the hell elected you King of English?" protests in my file marked "Final Authority."

For centuries, a titanic tug-of-war has been going on among users of English. The struggle is between the prescriptivists (those who say *tug-of-war* is the proper name of the game) and the descriptivists (those who say *tug-o'-war* better describes the way the name is spoken by most people). The first group, called Language Snobs, insists that the language of the past is correct and should be followed, and the second group, or Language Slobs, wallows in solecism and holds that any language used today is destined to be the brave new word of the future. English teachers are generally in the prescriptivist bunch and see themselves as clinging to the ramparts in heroic defense of the rules of clarity and precision in the native tongue, while lexicographers are usually in the descriptivist crowd, portraying themselves as scientific recorders of the reality of the living, growing language.

As Mort Sahl used to say, "Is there anybody I haven't offended?" Ordinarily, my trick in portraying both sides in this debate as crazed extremists is to position myself as the voice of sweet reason; however, in this case, my purpose in setting the two sides at each other's throats is to sharpen and intensify the argument.

Because it is essential that the titanic struggle go on. (Avoid sentence fragments.) The purpose of language is understanding between person/person, person/animal, person/machine, and machine/machine. (I knew I'd find a use for the virgule.) To accomplish that purpose of communication, the Slobs have to win a few. "Mistakes" have to become "correct" through wide usage and general acceptance, as the users of lingo do their thing. *I could care less* is a shortening of *I could not care any less,* which seems to be the opposite; yet the short form is understood and the long form would be regarded as the sort of thing a visiting Martian might say. Thus, the short form has become colloquially correct, and I could care less what mail comes in about it. In this instance, the Slobs seem to have won; but I do not hear the phrase used this year as much as last, and in the long run—if the phrase atrophies from disuse—the Snobs will triumph.

At the same time, the Snobs must win a few. For example, the mixing together of words of different languages in a single phrase is incorrect (just as *mixing together* is redundant). H. L. Mencken, the darling of American lexicographers and certainly no Snob in the study of what he called the American language, objected to the phrase *per year.* As Mencken put it, "Even Congress, which is an ass, always uses *per diem,* not *per day."* If you like Latin, you should say *"per annum";* if you prefer English, say "a year." I shall take that to heart when shelling out three dollars an hour, or *per horam,* to my own kin for mowing the lawn.

The Slob has his role to play in this struggle: testing the perimeter with *parameter,* enriching and enlivening the vocabulary with new slang, stretching the grammatical rules with a more natural "It's me." The Snob has the opposite role with equal billing: resisting change that obfuscates and "befuzzes," holding fast to the orderly structures that make the language easier to learn, forcing the new to earn its way into the dictionaries by running a gantlet of ridicule and puckered faces. (The Slobs run a *gauntlet,* which is a glove.)

The sensible Slob knows when to quit: Farewell, *I could care less.* The sensible Snob knows when to flee the ramparts: Hail to thee, *contact* as a verb for "get in touch with."

The New York Times has for several years referred to the government of Nicaragua as "Sandinist." Recently, this directive went out to editors: "Starting immediately, let's please use the Spanish form of the word *Sandinista(s),* no longer the English form *Sandinist(s).* This is an exception to our usual practice of using English forms for the names of political parties and movements. In this case, the exception reflects widespread popular and diplomatic usage." The bearers of standards fought the good fight, but there comes a moment when the *prescriptivista* becomes the *descriptivista*.

To those middle linebackers of linguistics who grimly warn that "Winning is the only thing," the lover of language replies, "Playing is the only thing." The healthy growth of English needs the laxity of the Slob and the rigidity of the Snob. Vogue words and innovative usage will win or lose in the marketplace of the living tongue; Al Haig is winning with the adjective *nuanced* and losing with his nonce verb in "Let me *caveat* you on that, Senator."

Now to Miss Marx's question: Who decides who wins? The answer is not universal, but personal. For myself, I decide. I look at the challenging usage, check around to see what the other usage mavens have said, apply my own standards, put it on a back burner, stir it now and then, and come forth with my decision. In the eternal tug-of(o')-war, I grab the rope in the position of round-heeled prescriptivist, happy to stand on the burning deck but not after all the others have fled. I am my own Final Authority; the Académie américaine, *c'est moi.*

You don't accept that? You prefer to think it through yourself, do your own research, arrive at your own conclusion about whether it should be *out the window* or *out of the window*? Wonderful! You have just become your own Final Authority. Write a column; astound your friends; correct your associates who say "data is," and enjoy your newfound solitude. If you care about the language you use and are moved to influence others to write or speak more clearly or colorfully, you are eligible to join either side of the rope in the game between the Keepers of the Flame and the Worshipers of the Native Speaker. Welcome; we can use a few more players.

You will find yourself leading the life of the open mind. Pushing 90, Olga Marx knows how to keep the language vital: "Write about Black English sometime, a fountain of youth for our language. *If I'da knowed then what I knows now, I wouldn't have did what I done* and *fixin' to bloom* and *You can't never guess a man* and *mosying along* and *runnin' her big mouth as usual* and *calls herself makin' a soup* and a spate of delightful etceteras."

I Stand Corrected

absent, *see* the present absent

accent on the Caribbean

The scene is the Roosevelt Room of the White House, filled with pictures and plaques of the two Presidents Roosevelt, across the hall from the Oval Office. It used to be called the Fish Room, after Secretary of State Hamilton Fish, but visitors kept looking for the aquarium, so the name was changed during the Nixon administration.

Hunched around the long table are a passel of pundits, being briefed on the President's "Caribbean Basin Initiative" by Special Trade Representative William Brock, Assistant Secretary of State Thomas Enders, and a little guy from the National Security Council whose name I missed.

I went straight for the jugular, pointing to an obvious dichotomy in the administration's approach: How come the S.T.R. pronounced it "Cari-BE-an" and State said "Ca-RIB-ean"?

"Both are correct," said Secretary Enders instantly, taking the classic State Department position, which always holds that no disagreement exists and nothing ever represents a change from the previous statement.

"Tomorrow I get to say 'Ca-RIB-ean,' and he has to say 'Cari-BE-an,' " replied Mr. Brock, more relaxed and capable of greater political insight under severe questioning.

Although both are correct—even the State Department gets it right now and then—the preferred pronunciation is "Cari-BE-an." The word comes from an Indian people—the Caribs—with the accent on the first syllable, sounding much like "Arabs." In the fifteenth century, members of the Cariban tribes dominated northern Brazil and the north coast of South America, and were in the process of taking over the Greater Antilles when the Spaniards arrived and intervened.

Christopher Columbus heard them called *carib* in Haiti and *caniba* in Cuba; their propensity for eating their enemies led to the word *cannibal*. In both cases, the accent was on the first syllable; later, the Caribs were also called the Caribees, making a great case for preferring "Cari-BE-an." (Curiously, *cannibal* has always had its first syllable accented, although it seems to me that *caNIBBling* would be a more graphic verb than *CANnibalizing*.)

Having caused so much confusion at the briefing, I did not feel up to questioning the term *initiative*. That word was chosen by Mr. Enders because its meaning was narrow enough to fit into a more comprehensive approach to be labeled later. The diplomat evidently preferred *initiative* to the mundane *plan*, the tentative *proposal*, or the already-used *beginning*. And surely for this reason, too: The only adjectives that go with *initiative* are *bold* and *new*. Who ever heard of a timid old initiative?

Regarding the accent's placement in "Caribbean," the comparison of "Carib" to "Arab" seems not to show what you want it to. Observe:

AR-ab	*Ar-AB-i-an*
CAR-ib	*Car-IB-be-an*

which leaves CAR-ib-BE-an more or less in limbo. (Whoever heard of the AR-a-BI-an Desert?)

I think Car-IB-be-an is more mellifluous (and I don't mean MELL-i-FLU-ous.)

> *George A. Brewster*
> *Queens Village, New York*

I was surprised to learn that the Nixon administration changed the name of the Fish Room in the White House because people kept looking for an aquarium. I suspect that the real reason was that President Nixon is, as everyone knows, a cod-fearing American.

> *Marshall E. Bernstein*
> *Roslyn, New York*

If "Caribs" sounds much like "Arabs," why doesn't "Caribbean" sound much like "Arabian"?

> *Linda E. Soloway*
> *New York, New York*

I was pleased to see that you took on the great CariBEan vs. CaRIBBean controversy. This is a question to which I devoted no small amount of time when I came into this job a year and a half ago, and it continues to come up. Let me add that pronunciation of place names in that area is a constant problem. How many people up here know that newly independent Antigua is pronounced as if it has no "u" or that the island of Nevis is spoken of using a long "ee"? Not to mention the constant confusion between the Dominican Republic and the island nation of Dominica (Do-mi-NEE-ca).

But to get back to the point, I must tell you that the preferred pronunciation you gave for Caribbean is not, based on my experience, the one used by most West Indians (not "Caribbeans," please). A local example of someone using the CaRIB-Bean option is the Barbadian envoy here, Ambassador Skeete. The question we come down to, then, is whether we base our pronunciations on the norm in the country or the area we are pronouncing, or whether we go our own way. When the area in question is populated by fellow English speakers, this is indeed a problem. One I will leave you wordsmiths to ponder.

> David P. Wagner
> Country Affairs Officer/The Caribbean
> International Communication Agency
> Washington, D.C.

i disliked your glib reference to cannibalism. aren't you familiar with w. arens' the man-eating myth (oxford u. press, 1979)? he finds no acceptable substantiation for any account alluding to cannibalism. what does emerge clearly is the usefulness to the imperium the attribution of subhuman traits to a conquered people can have. the perpetuation of such slander can only be considered racist. as we contemplate a caribbean policy, harboring the intellectual fantasy of anthropophagy can hardly be appropriate.

> sunny salibian
> cambridge, massachusetts

I haven't gone back to Fernández de Oviedo or any other of the Spanish chroniclers to see if they say anything about how the Caribs themselves pronounced their moniker—the testimony would most likely be imprecise at best. However, those who brought the word into the European languages were Spanish-speakers, and I doubt very much that they pronounced it like "Arabs." As you know, the Spanish form of the word is "ca-RI-be," so, if we are going back to origins to determine pronunciation, I think that "Ca-RIB-ean" would be more defensible. Note that the Spanish form of the word's other principal derivative also stresses the middle syllable—caníbal.

But I'm afraid there is little logic in the way foreign words pass into English, even without the complication of an American aboriginal language. (That's why it doesn't distress me to have to say, or try to, "Cari-BE-an.") The whimsy, or maybe perversity, of the transferral process is well illustrated by the French lingerie *and* femme. *The former, which ought to have a palatal* a *sound (even if not nasal) is pronounced "LAHN-ger-y," whereas* femme, *which ought to have the AH, is pronounced with a palatal* a.

I will be glad to support your support of "caNIBBling," but if we can't lick "finalize," what can we hope to do with "cannibalize"?

Frank M. Duffey
Chapel Hill, North Carolina

---

acuity vacuity

President Reagan's personal physician, neurosurgeon Daniel Ruge (pronounced "roo-gee"), can out-jargon any jargonaut among the Reaganauts.

After examining the President recently, he issued what most journalists called "a clean bill of health," but included this sentence to befuddle the layman: "Previously documented decrement in auditory acuity and visual refractive error corrected with contact lenses were evaluated and found to be stable."

I'd hate to be a druggist trying to read his passive prescriptions. That translates as: "As I noted before, the President is hard of hearing and needs glasses, but neither of these ailments is getting worse."

Decrement is not a dirty word; it means "decrease." Its use enables some doctors to be able to be understood less and charge more.

I think the main problem with President Reagan is that his personal physician is attempting to correct the decrement in auditory acuity with contact lenses.

Abraham L. Halpern, M.D.
Port Chester, New York

You wrote: "Its use enables some doctors to be able to be understood less and charge more." The words "to be able" can surely be eliminated from that sentence, as they duplicate the meaning of "enables."

The sentence is awkward and, worse, wastes valuable copy space. As a newspaper reporter, I am all too aware of how much at a premium such space is.

When you are redundant, not only do you repeat yourself but you say the same thing twice, as I'm sure you know.

> Dan Holly
> New Brunswick, New Jersey

You can't be in the vanguard of language usage if you insist on remaining in the rearguard of pharmacolingo! The word druggist *went out years ago, along with the soda fountain. The current word is* pharmacist.

> Thelma C. Hilibrand
> Cherry Hill, New Jersey

advertising, *see* bloopie awards

airlinese, *see* winged words

all that jazz

The word *jazz* is probably the greatest contribution of American slang to the world's languages. Where did it come from and what did it originally mean?

"One lady asked me if I danced the jazz," goes a 1909 gramophone record, cited in the *Oxford English Dictionary Supplement*. The word in its earliest printed citations also meant a form of syncopated dance music, or the ragtime music associated with American blacks.

Another theory exists. In a 1927 issue of the *Journal of Abnormal and Social Psychology,* a social scientist suggested: "The word *jazz* . . . used both as a verb and as a noun to denote the sex act . . . has long been common vulgarity." Three years before, a music magazine, *Etude,* had hinted at it: "If the truth were known about the origin of the word 'Jazz' it would never be mentioned in polite society. . . . The vulgar word 'Jazz' was in general currency in those dance halls 30 years or more ago."

That's the present state of the etymology. Now along comes Jill Shelley, of New Canaan, Connecticut: "May I share with you a very exciting discovery? This is an early reference (in 1831) to the word *jazz* used exactly as we might do today —and by no less a grandee than Lord Palmerston."

Miss Shelley enclosed a page from Jasper Ridley's life of Palmerston, Prime

Minister of England in the mid-nineteenth century, adding: "You've described the feeling when someone who loves words runs across a find like this, and you were right—it's intoxicating."

In a chapter on the Belgian crisis of 1831, historian Ridley quotes this private letter from Palmerston: "I am writing in the Conference, Matuszevic copying out a note for our signature, old Talley jazzing and telling stories. . . ."

Wow. I zipped the evidence off to Robert Burchfield, chief editor of the Oxford dictionaries, known to wordsmen as "Superlex." His reply: "Your Miss Shelley is the third person known to me who has wondered whether Lord Palmerston, inexplicably, knew about *jazz* . . . their wonderment is surely in vain.

"If Palmerston's word has been read correctly by Jasper Ridley," writes Mr. Burchfield—adding, parenthetically, "(historians can never be trusted in this respect in the end)," and, oh, will he hear from the historians—"it must be an isolated Anglicized spelling of French *jaser*, 'to chatter, to gossip.' "

The zesty lexicographer from New Zealand neither equivocates nor jazzes around: "The word *jazz* roared into written English near the beginning of the present century, not earlier (see Volume 2 of my *Supplement to the OED*). The handful of scholars qualified to investigate the matter say that its origin is either unknown or dirty, probably the latter."

And that's that. Maybe. (You may fire when you are ready, Ridley.)

As a former teacher of French language and literature for 42 years, I was fascinated by the possible French origin of the word JAZZ *from the French "jaser" to chatter—to "buzz buzz." I went to my old Albert DAUZAT,* Dictionnaire étymologique *(1938) which says:*

> JASER (XIIe s. Adam) onom. V. GAZOUILLER. Dér. jaseur, jaserie (XVIe s.)

In other words an onomatopoeic word "to chatter" as we would say "buzz buzz" first used by medieval writer Adam de la Halle in a 12th century poem. It says "See gazouiller" which turns out to have first been used in 1316 by J. Maillard and which is a Normandy-Picardy form from the same root as "jaser."

My old H.L. Mencken, The American Language, *1937, p. 189, gives:*

> *"Websters New International" says that* jazz *is a Creole word, and probably of African origin, but goes no further. The Oxford says that its origin is unknown, but that it is "generally said to be Negro."*

Creole is a type of 16th and 17th century French of the Caribbean and of Louisiana. Perhaps there was some combination between the French Creole "jaser" and some obscure African word the Black musicians of New Orleans put together to make jazz.

Elizabeth Maxfield-Miller (Mrs. Miller)
Ph.D. Radcliffe-Harvard 1938
Concord, Massachusetts

Although the origin of jazz seems not yet pinpointed, I was surprised you made no reference to Creoles, to Louisiana, to New Orleans, to nineteenth-century brothels there.

The Britannica World Language Dictionary, *1959 edition, refers to the Creole word jass, meaning coitus, suggesting its origin in the brothels of New Orleans. H. L. Mencken's* The American Language *also refers to the Creole word for sexual intercourse. The* Harper Dictionary of Contemporary Usage, *1975 edition, defines the Creole word as "sexual motions involved in certain dances of African origin."*

In light of the available information, I wondered why the emphasis was on Prime Minister Palmerston.

Milton Horowitz
Jackson Heights, New York

It is to cry.

You read William Safire. He's talking about Jazz. Talking about jazz and not mentioning Scott. Can you imagine?

"The word jazz in its progress toward respectability has meant first sex, Then dancing, Then music." How's That for succinctness? That's what F. Scott Fitzgerald wrote in "Echoes of the Jazz Age" in The Crack-up. *Scott, the father of the Jazz Age. He gave it its name. It is to cry.*

Franklin Mason
Baltimore, Maryland

Dear Bill,

A quibble on jazz, which I believe is somewhat older than your column suggested. The Dictionary of Americanisms *refers to a 1926 article in* American Speech *saying Lafcadio Hearn found the word in use in New Orleans in the late 1870s or early 1880s (Hearn was living in New Orleans from 1878–1887). I don't have the complete works of Lafcadio Hearn in front of me (and doubt if all his newspaper pieces have been collected), but that's one possible indication of an earlier date, if indeed the cite exists. Also Jelly Roll Morton said he used the word* jazz *as early as 1902 (in Alan Lomax's* Mr. Jelly Roll, *taken from tapes at the Library of Congress): again this recollection may not be true, but is a second hint of an early date. Also* jazz *music is supposed to have started with poor blacks teaching themselves to play on band instruments left behind by the Civil War (i.e., 1864) winners and losers—that's one major theory, though no one has ever explained to me why those army marching bands left their instruments behind! The word* first *definitely seems to have meant "to speed up, make or become more frenetic," then spread to sexual use, and from there to the music use (in the whorehouses where jazzing went on in the rooms above and also at the piano or on the bandstand below)—in fact, some believe that white Chicago musicians called the music* jazz *purposely, in order to give it connotations of the whorehouse, as music not fit for decent white ears.*

The interesting difference between the expressions all that jazz *and* all that jive *(both meaning nonsense, bunk, lies, exaggeration) is that* jazz *meant music before it meant nonsense but* jive *meant nonsense before it meant music. Jive, meaning nonsense, seems to have appeared in Chicago around 1921 (as a black term) and then in 1928 two jazz records appeared using* jive *in their titles:* Cow Cow Davenport's State Street Jive *and* Louis Armstrong's Don't Jive Me, *the word* jive *then slowly becoming associated with a form of jazz and coming to mean swing music by 1937. Thus jazz music came before jazz talk, but jive talk came before jive music. (We all say that* jazz *probably has African origins, but no one has ever found an African word that is similar;* jive *may simply have been a pronunciation of* jibe.)

> Regards,
> Stuart *[Stuart Berg Flexner]*
> *Editor in Chief, Reference Department*
> *Random House, Inc.*
> *New York, New York*

Dear Bill,

The correspondence about Palmerston fascinated me and I write to tell you that Burchfield is quite certainly right. Indeed I'm surprised that what he wrote you was so tentative.

Members of the more privileged sector of the English upper class of Palmerston's time reached their young manhood while the French court was still in existence. Palmerston was also a Whig, and until the Revolution, the French were fashionable among the kind of Londoners who revolved around Devonshire House. The ladies of Devonshire House, particularly, had a way of scattering French words through their conversation, and even converting French words into English words. You can see the kind of thing I mean in the volumes of Greville's diary dating before he and England were both Victorianized; for

Greville commonly used a whole series of words like Palmerston's "jazzing" for "jasant."

I haven't time to do the necessary research this morning, but if you look at the diary, you will find a good many of these old conversions. Offhand, however, I only remember a description of life at the country house of the Duke of York, whose racing horses were trained by Greville. Among other things, Greville noted "the ton is polisson, and the talk tends towards polissonerie." I'm not quite certain I've quoted correctly; but this is near enough. It means that in the Duke's house, lewdness was acceptable and lewd jokes were common conversational currency.

Yours ever,
Joe [Joseph Wright Alsop]
Washington, D.C.

Note: Now that I have looked up my sources, I find that I made a foolish mistake. Palmerston was a "Canningite Tory" (that is, "liberal Tory" in modern jargon) rather than a Whig; and he only left the Tory party when the Canningite wing of the Cabinet broke with the Duke of Wellington in 1828. I thought him a Whig because he acted with the Whigs thereafter; and also because he spent a good part of his early mature life with the Whig grandees. Then, too, he had a Whig grandee's wife (and the sister of Lord Melbourne), Lady Cowper, first as his mistress of many years and then as his wife for many more years.

Greville's exact quotation about the atmosphere in the Duke of York's set in the early 19th century, which I have now looked up, was: "The men with whom he lives most are très-polissons, and la polissonnerie is the ton of his society."

J.A.

an ad is born

A bunch of admen are sitting around brainshowering—a mild form of brainstorming—and one of the laid-back layout men goes, "How about we use the dictionary?" A word man glowers: "I only use the words I know." "No," goes the artistic type, "I mean graphically—put our copy line in the form of a dictionary entry, you know, with all those accent marks and funny names in italics." "Parts of speech," murmurs the copywriter. "I like it—nice intellectual overtone, but you get to repeat the meaning for the buyers."

And lo! An ad is born. When the unoriginal idea is executed correctly, the ad works and the cause of lexicography is unharmed; perhaps some adwatcher may be moved to buy a dictionary, too, since language seems to be in vogue. But when the idea is botched, the only thing to discuss is whether to hyphenate "red-faced."

"Here's a half-page error," observes Sid Goldberg, executive editor of United Feature Syndicate, sending along a display advertisement from Neiman-Marcus. It is the largest-type mistake of the week.

"Last call/" begins the message, with a virgule because that seems to be the latest way to end a line. Then comes the "dictionary" copy: "(lâst, läst) *adj.* (kôl) *v.*"

Wrong. Not even the most famous store chain founded in Dallas can market an adjective modifying a verb. Adjectives modify nouns; adverbs modify verbs, adjectives, other adverbs, and even whole clauses and sentences. But do not take that stricture as permission to change the line to: "(last) *adv.* (kol) *v.*" because that seeming match-up of adverb and verb would be in error: *call* in "last call" is not a verb. It's a noun, as in "puts and calls" or "hog call," and its modifier must be an adjective. The right way to do it is: "(last) *adj.* (kol) *n.*"

If I am mistaken, Neiman-Marcus will present a thunderingly chic correction of my correction in its next ad, presumably under the heading "last *(adj.)* laugh *(n.)*."

Here I sit at my typewriter, red-faced.

It seems that our error has caught the attention of every grammarian in the country. From the lowliest retired schoolmarm to the sixth page of Section 6 of the February 14 edition of "All the News That's Fit to Print."

I assure you, Mr. Safire (and I hope you pass the word to Mr. Goldberg), that "call" as a noun is not an endangered species in this country. It has its champions from Pittsburgh to Podunk. From New York to Neenah. I know—because most of the responses to our ad landed on my desk.

But it wasn't till our regular morning brainshower today that your editorial was pointed out to me. It is gratifying to see that "call" has friends in high places.

We promise. We promise not to manhandle it again. And the next time one of our laid-back layout men (Beverly, perhaps) suggests, "How about we use the dictionary," we may even try it.

> Ed Taussig
> Copy Chief, Neiman-Marcus
> Dallas, Texas

and yet . . .

"Boeing has an estimated $3 billion to $4 billion riding on the success of two new planes," opined Peter Grossman in *Financial World* magazine, "—the 757 and 767—neither of which has yet to fly."

When Peter Samuel of Australian Consolidated Press sent this clip along with his scrawled emendations—"neither of which has yet flown, each of which has yet to fly, neither yet having flown"—I knew this was a case for Robert King, conservative dean of liberal arts at the University of Texas at Austin, a world-class double-negative hater.

Here is Dean King's explanation why "neither of which has yet to fly" is grammatically incorrect: "You start with the fact that English never, never allows double negatives: 'I don't have no money' is definitely, unarguably wrong. Now, *yet* followed by the infinitive implies negation *(OED* II.2.c.); in other words, 'The plane has yet to fly' means 'The plane has not hitherto flown,' and *yet* is effectively a negative element."

"So," concludes the somewhat prescriptive Dean King, who has been known to attribute the decadence of the French to their love for the double negative,

" 'The plane has yet to fly' is a negative, and putting any additional negative element in there makes it a double negative, which is WRONG! Thus, you can't say, 'The plane has not yet to fly,' and you can't say, 'Neither plane of which has yet to fly.' Q.E.D."

He suggests: "And neither plane has yet flown." Let the roundheels of descriptive usage rage about idiom and the shifting sands of time: Dean King is RIGHT. I don't like no double negatives either.

I don't like no double negatives, neither. You and Dean King are surely right to render the phrase about the airplanes "neither plane has yet flown." And despite its popularity as a Black idiom, the double negative in "I ain't got no money" is simply wrong.

And yet . . .

There are at least two very precise instances in which use of a double negative is required. The first is in logic, where both the Law of Non-Contradiction ("If A, then not not-A") and the Law of the Excluded Middle (If not not-A, then A) use double negatives. The latter of these Aristotelian "laws of correct thinking" is, indeed, the basis for eliminating double negatives in propositional linguistic use. When my computer hits two "no's" in the same proposition it automatically—and correctly—produces a "yes." If I am not not going to the store, I am, in fact, going to the store.

The second exception to Dean King's claim that "English never, never allows double negatives" concerns propositions in which a two-value logic ("X" is true or "X" is false, and never the twain shall meet) is just not adequate to a description of the fact. Typically, this occurs when we try to describe a somewhat ambivalent state of mind. (Pardon me, I think I hear the Squad Squad at the door!) If I say, "I am interested in what happens to Mr. Stockman," you understand me. Alternately, if I said either, "I am not interested in what happens to Mr. Stockman," or "I am uninterested in what happens to him," you would again understand me. But you would also understand me if I said, "I am not uninterested in Stockman's fate." I'm being a little tentative by using such an expression, and I'm implying that I might well become interested if you wrote up a good column on the matter. "He was not unhappy at the result" doesn't say that he was pleased with the outcome, but only that he was willing to live with it.

So-called "British understatement" also uses the double-negative speech form habitually, leaving it to the context or vocal inflection to indicate whether a tentative or a positive implication is to be drawn. "I do not exactly not like her" may be meant either ironically ("I'm madly in love with her") or as an indication that I'm almost grudgingly prepared to see her again in hopes of coming to a more definite attitude.

A membership card in the Linguistic Irregulars would not be unwelcome.

Craig L. Stark
Montclair, New Jersey

Dean Robert King's argument against the use of the word "yet" in the Boeing article you dissected does not fly. At least in my humble opinion.

Rather than being an "effectively negative element" as he termed it, "yet" in the usage described fulfills a very important function, in that it signifies something that has not happened, but is very definitely anticipated.

This implication that the action or state that is not at the moment but will soon be, the temporal modification, characterizes "yet's" unique and valuable role.

For example, neither "Are you ready?" "Not yet" nor "Have you seen the movie Reds?" "No, I haven't yet" is a double negative. On the contrary, they effectively communicate the transitory nature of the negative.

Thus, "the 757 and 767—neither of which has yet to fly" or put another way, not one of which has flown as of this writing, is not incorrect, but is, at least in terms of the sense conveyed, both accurate and comprehensive.

Mark Silveira
Portland, Oregon

Just like you, Mr. Safire, I don't like no double negatives and I don't never use no double negatives neither.

Now for a deathless comment. It emerged suddenly, many years ago, from the lips of a colleague, now deceased, whose speech was often liberally sprinkled with double negatives. Perhaps you will enjoy unscrambling it or you might submit it to one of your linguistic mavens: "Don't let no one do you no favors, then you won't owe nobody nothin'."

Emanuel Freund, M.D.
Haverstraw, New York

Dear Bill,

I don't think your Texas dean has got hold of the right end of the stick. If "yet" is "a negative element," then "Neither plane has yet flown" contains a double negative, which you say he deprecates.

The point is rather that "yet" (like "still," "already," and phrases to the same effect) are adverbs of time, which by their placement and idiomatic use describe situations as past or future. If a plane "has yet to fly," what makes the statement negative is the indication that its flying lies in the future; it doesn't negative its ability to do so. Oddly enough, "neither of which has yet to fly" means that the happy prospect applies to neither plane = both have flown. If Dean King were right, the common answer "not yet" would be an illiterate double negative.

Yours,
Jacques [Jacques Barzun]
Charles Scribner's Sons
New York, New York

Dear Bill,

I am disappointed with my friend Bob King's account of "neither of which has yet to fly." Bob fails to point out a peculiarity of yet that is highly relevant here, namely that while it is normally a "negative polarity item," i.e., requires negation (or one of a few other things that serve in its stead, e.g., an interrogative structure), in the expression be/have yet to it is not a negative polarity item:

> *The 757 hasn't/*has yet flown.*
> *The 757 hasn't/*has flown yet.*
> *Has the 757 flown yet?*
>
> *The 757 has yet to fly.*
> *The 727 had yet to fly when Air Kuwait placed an order for 50 of them.*
>
> *The manuscript isn't/*is finished yet.*
> *The manuscript is yet to be finished.*

I think be/have yet to *is simply a survival of the older sense of* yet *as "still" (not a negative polarity item), which remains in many modern dialects (e.g., the Scottish English of which I now retain only a fragmentary command) but otherwise is felt as an archaism except in* be/have yet to, *in which it remains alive, though restricted to formal registers. The Peter Grossman quote involved simply a blend of two uses of* yet, *the ordinary negative-polarity use and the* yet *of* be/have yet to, *and has nothing to do with negative spreading.*

With best wishes,
Jim [James D. McCawley]
Department of Linguistics
University of Chicago
Chicago, Illinois

Note: "Stigmata" such as *, ??, and ? are devices by which linguists indicate abnormality or deviance of examples (in decreasing order of the deviance that they indicate).

anti-ethicist

Daniel Patrick Moynihan, who invented welfare reform, is the most articulate of senators; he has been known to ghostwrite for his own speechwriter. That reputation for literacy caused his constituency to thump typewriters in fury upon receipt of his newsletter, in which he concluded: "I would especially welcome comment about this adventure into newslettering."

Lettering is a legitimate verb, and an honorable line of work for people who paint legible signs, but *newslettering* is new. One of Senator Moynihan's former Harvard colleagues, Prof. James Q. Wilson, has shared his displeasure with me:

"I am no doubt being captious by suggesting that *newsletter* is not a verb in even the most progressive (i.e., illiterate) dictionaries," thunders the great political scientist. (*Thunder* once was not a verb.) "But such is the Senator's influence and felicity of style that the word will soon be part of common discourse. Alas. If my good friend, the Senator, continues to newsletter me, I shall ask my post office to deadletter him."*

While he was at it (I get a great many two-part letters), Professor Wilson lodged a linguistic complaint against Patricia Harris, who found time before her departure as secretary of Health and Human Services to require universities to create Institutional Review Boards to approve research that receives H.H.S. funds. Each board, ordered Mrs. Harris, must include one nonscientific member: "For example, lawyers, ethicists, members of the clergy."

The freshly minted *ethicist* irritates Professor Wilson. "Does one ethicize? Ethicalize? Ethicate? Note in passing that ethicizing, or whatever, is not something done by lawyers or clergymen. I long suspected as much."

My new neoconservative pal in Harvard attached a copy of a useful booklet entitled *Urbababble,* published by the Parkman Center for Urban Affairs, 33 Beacon Street, Boston, Massachusetts 02108, which spoofs the lingo of those urbane people in the city business. (For example, the adjectives *key, critical, crucial, important, vital, underlying* are inextricably linked with *concern, question, problem, area, determinant, dimension, factor.*) But the cliché that caught my eye —one used even more often than "inextricably linked"—is *broad gauge.*

Whence *broad gauge?* This harrumpher of a phrase is used by high-domed academics and Big Picture businessmen to mean "Don't bother me with details, I deal with Policy." The *Urbababble* etymology: "From the seven-foot gauge established by the great 19th-century civil engineer Isambard Kingdom Brunel for his Great Western Railway. Final conversion of the G.W.R. to standard gauge was completed in 1892. . . . It is interesting to contrast the achievement of Brunel in iron, stone and concrete with the more illusive achievements of *Broad Gaugers* in the contemporary urban sphere."

Broad-gauge thinkers (the hyphen is needed when the phrase is turned into an adjective) are the types who come up with *social safety nets* and *workfare.* I'll newsletter that over to Moynihan and every other ethicist I know.

Now, finally, I must write. No past item in your magazine column cut to the core of my fervor for correct grammar, my professional integrity, or my notions of journalistic honesty as did your approving quotation of James Q. Wilson's disdainful comments about "ethicists." First, the grammatical point: even if the freshly

---

*See "newsletterer."

minted "ethicist" is (or ought to be) a legitimate English word, nothing whatever follows concerning a verb that denotes what "ethicists" do. Do scientists scientize? Do physicists physicize? Physicalize? Physicate? Do journalists journalize? And what do political scientists do? So much for Professor Wilson's unperspicacious remarks.

Of course, Professor Wilson is not merely railing against what he (falsely) perceives to be the illegitimate entry of words into the English language. His chief intention is to disparage what the term "ethicist" denotes. And that disparagement, in turn, follows from his political views: "ethicists" are the soft underbelly of overstaffed and unnecessary Congressional Advisory Boards, and National and Presidential Commissions. But what does the term denote?

Although I prefer to be referred to as a moral philosopher, since that phrase accurately reflects my area of academic expertise, I am now often called an ethicist, and more frequently, a "bioethicist." I can no longer object to a term increasingly used by both professionals and the public to describe my own work and that of many colleagues from the field of philosophy and from religious studies and theology, who do research, writing, and lecturing on topics in applied ethics (especially medical ethics or "bioethics"—also a newly minted term).

Living language should follow new roles, occupations, and circumstances that develop in society. "Astronaut" is now a perfectly respectable term (was it 30 years ago?) and "ethicist" is becoming one also. What Mr. Wilson, and you too, I discern, really deplore is not a new term that denotes a new professional role, but rather, the intrusion of that role into the affairs of traditional ruling powers in the public and private sectors. Moynihan is, of course, a politician, and no doubt a "bleeding-heart liberal," in your view. But that does not qualify him as an ethicist, contrary to your attribution.

Ruth Macklin, Ph.D.
Associate Professor (Bioethics)
Albert Einstein College of Medicine
of Yeshiva University
Bronx, New York

Does an ethicist ethicize, asks Professor James Q. Wilson of Harvard, as if to belittle that noun. Do physicists physicize, one might ask in return. Do, for that matter, romanticists romanticize? Do socialists socialize or realists realize? Do organists organize? Most -ists don't seem to -ize at all. So, on that score, an apologist for "ethicist" is not about to apologize.

You describe "ethicist" as freshly minted. After reading Jim Quinn's book, you might have learned. The OED Supplement gives citations dating to 1891 for that word. Surprisingly, "ethicize" not only exists but has an even longer recorded history, beginning with an 1816 citation.

Despite this reproof, I am an avid Safirist and even Safirize on occasion myself.

As for other pop grammarians, however, I'm no Newmanalist, and I never ever Simonize.

Richard Veit
Associate Professor, Department of English
University of North Carolina
Wilmington, North Carolina

I read with interest your excerpt of James Q. Wilson's letter in which he questions the term "ethicist." I have never understood why this term should puzzle anyone; if we have physics and physicists, why not ethics and ethicists? (Perhaps the intent is to deny that ethics, generally defined as the systematic study of morality, is a meaningful focus for professional academic inquiry. Or the intent may be to decry the "expertizing" trend in American life, based in the idea that only experts have anything worthwhile to say about whatever it is that they are experts on.)

In any case, there is an academic field of study called "ethics," and the people who practice it are "ethicists." In Britain they are more likely to be called "ethicians" (by analogy with physicians?). There are, depending on the sources of the moral values they employ and to some extent their methods, philosophical and theological ethicists. These should not be confused with "moral philosophers" and "moral theologians," respectively. Both moral philosophy and moral theology have their own traditions and are significantly different from contemporary philosophical and theological ethics. Finally, if I have to choose one of Professor Wilson's terms for what an ethicist does, it would be "ethicize"—certainly not "ethicate" or "ethicalize." Most ethicists of my acquaintance simply describe their work as "doing ethics," though this phrase gives me goosebumps.

James T. Johnson
Professor, Department of Religion
Rutgers University
New Brunswick, New Jersey

"Ethicist" is not "freshly minted," but has been used for years in the academic community and elsewhere in referring to practitioners of moral philosophy. So ancient is its pedigree that "ethicist" is cited in the OED, *and has apparently replaced the older "ethician."*

Further, and presumably even more devastating to the irritated Professor Wilson, the verb "ethicize" is also found in the OED, *and in modern dictionaries as well* (Webster's International, *2nd Edition;* American Heritage Dictionary*). It means "to discuss ethics, to speak or write on morals"* (OED).

Contra Professor Wilson, we may note in passing that lawyers or clergymen could, without violating the parameters of their own or anyone else's profession, ethicize. However, in citing ethicists as a profession separate from lawyers and clergymen, Mrs. Harris was merely following normal usage which recognizes ethics as a branch of philosophy entitled to recognition, and specialists, of its own.

Richard P. Hall
Summit, New Jersey

Why should an ethicist have to ethicize if an economist doesn't economize? Just because a sociologist does, unfortunately, sociologize? Such istifying was not Ms. Harris's doing but has long existed in the Academy, where no one would suspect that a mere suffix could turn anyone into an activist or a protagonist. "-ist" confers status and expertise, probably borrowed from such hard scientists as physicists and chemists. (Political scientists left that trail clear.) A philosopher or historian is too established to need such assist. But the more newly arrived classicists, Islamicists, medievalists, anthropologists, comparativists do. If the practitioners got there first, then add insulating syllables, as in buddhologist. Just to make clear that Professors are experts and not professors, there are now, though still rarely, theologists. But you will have to explain why there is no term for the expert in English language and literature, professor or otherwise. Can you resist Englishist?

James E. Dittes
Chairman, Department of Religious Studies
Yale University
New Haven, Connecticut

Dear Bill,

What is it that rankles people like Professor James Q. Wilson? Does one person's unfamiliarity with a term make it taboo? Ethicist is not "freshly minted." It has been in continuous use for at least ninety years. The fact that it may not be on the lips of every racetrack tout or Harvard professor does not invalidate it. It has been an entry in Webster's New World Dictionary *since 1970, and ethicize, with citations in the OED going back to 1816, was an entry in the first (1953) edition of our book. Patricia Harris's use of ethicist is at least as justified as Professor Wilson's use of progressive to mean "illiterate."*

Yours,
David [David B. Guralnik]
Vice President and Dictionary Editor in Chief
Simon & Schuster New World Dictionaries
Cleveland, Ohio

anti status quo

Have you noticed the way the British use the long *i*—pronounced "eye"—in words like *missile, futile,* and *fertile,* and we do not? At the same time, have you noticed the way we have recently been using that long *i* in *anti-, quasi-,* and *semi-,* while the British do not?

Ralph Goodman of New York noticed, and wonders why the "eye" vogue is rampant in the United States. That's hard to figure: Maybe Burt Reynolds, in the movie *Semi-Tough,* gave it a push. Or perhaps the diphthong—that sound that slides from one vowel to another, like *oy* or, in this case, *ai*—was given a boost by the coinage of *quasar* from *quasistellar* in the mid-1960's.

Sol Steinmetz, the big diphthong man at Barnhart Books, suggests that the explosion in the 60's of *anti-* words in which the prefix was followed by vowels may have started the eye-ing. *Antiestablishment, antiauthoritarian, antiinsurgency, antiimperialism* were words widely used: "Since the contiguous vowels in the unstressed syllables tended to blend with each other and obscure the prefix," posits Steinmetz, "it may have become useful or necessary for clarity's sake to replace the short *i* vowel (pronounced 'ee') of *anti-* with the readily available long, gliding variant *ai* vowel."

Having thus turned from "antee" into "anteye," the "eye" sound continued even when the prefix was followed by a consonant, as in *antitrust* or *anti-Semitism.*

Which is preferred, "antee" or "anteye"? Neither (pronounced "neether" or "nyther"). I'm more of a roundheels on pronunciation than on any grammatical or semantic question. Although I will resist a pronunciation of *liaison* as "lay-i-zon"* for a few years, I'm not antee-anteye anymore.

*See "Reaganese."

aspic, *see* do you speak aspic?

attorney, *see* we wuz robbed

ballpark figure

First up, baseball is a rich source for metaphors. How many expressions owe their origin to the game that started as "rounders" in England, became "the New York game" in the 1840's, and was spread across the United States by the New York and New Jersey regiments during the Civil War? I don't have even a ballpark figure.

Ballpark figure, however, stems from *ball grounds* and *ball fields* in the mid-nineteenth century, to *baseball park* in the 1890's, to *in the ballpark* around 1960.

"That's the windup," says lexicographer Stuart Flexner, who intends to demolish the Abner Doubleday myth in his next book. "Now here's the pitch: Our Random House dictionary citation files show the term first started out as *in the ballpark* (1962), as when talking about figures, estimates, etc., with 'I hope that's in the ballpark.' Then, in 1968, we first recorded *ballpark figure* from the *Seattle Times.*"

Evidently the ballpark was used as a microcosm: To be *in the ballpark* (even if out in left field*) was to be "in this world," just as to be *out of the ballpark* meant to be "totally out of play." Thus, an estimate—or "guesstimate"—that was adjudged within the range of reasonableness was *in the ballpark,* and a number of that sort recently became a *ballpark figure.*

Baseball terms were given wide circulation by the newspaper *baseball column* (1869), a creation of the *Brooklyn Union.* "Such columns," reports Flexner, "grew into the popular *sporting column, sporting page* and *sporting section* (created primarily for baseball fans) in the 1890's, then became known as the *sports page* or *sports section* in the 1920's."

Other baseball metaphors and their debut dates: *to keep one's eye on the ball,* 1907; *to be off base* (disrespectful, wrong), 1912, which was also the year that introduced *to have something on the ball; right off the bat,* 1916; *go to bat for* (to support or defend), 1928; *to play ball with* (cooperate), 1930; *to be in there pitching* and *to take a raincheck,* also the 30's. (The first raincheck Flexner has was issued in St. Louis in 1884; if you have an earlier one, send it to him. They'll never replay that game.)

We've come to the final inning. Time to head for the dugout.

*See "left. field."

Weingarten's An American Dictionary of Slang *shows 1882 instead of your 1912 for earliest usage,* to be off base. Oxford New English Dictionary Supplement *cites 1914 instead of your 1916 for* right off the bat. *For* take a raincheck, *you presume the 1930's, but Weingarten cites a 1929 quotation. Finally, on the expression* to play ball, *once again Weingarten strikes you out with a much earlier date. Yours is 1930 and his is 1902 (*OED Sup. 2 offers 1903).

David Shulman
New York, New York

*Let's drop reasonable*ness. *We can use -ability to make a noun out of any -able adjective except those which have their own noun forms, i.e.* capable, capacity; reasonable, rationality.

In education we have multiplied suffixes to our peril. Teachers with licenses (certificates) are called certificated personnel. What happened to simple speech? Or to certified?

Sondra Gordon Langford
Chatham, New Jersey

banshee workers

"We've been working like banshees," said Senator Claiborne Pell, Democrat of Rhode Island, "to try to get all the material we can." When this offbeat comment was featured on the front page of *The New York Times,* a keening wail went up from eager-beaver readers.

"Surely what the good Senator meant," wrote Timothy Childs of Norfolk, Connecticut, "was that they had been working like *beavers*! Banshees, as some of us know, are female spirits who keen, or wail, in Gaelic folklore, to announce the impending death of someone. Wailing banshees will not improve the quality of debate in our august upper house."

"I can just see them," writes Alyce Edwards of West Islip, New York, about the senators, "working like banshees and howling like beavers every minute!" She adds fancifully: "I think Senator Pell meant that they were working like a tribe in Africa—the Bantus—and the females are doing the work."

A banshee (accent on the first syllable) is, as described above, an Irish-Scottish spirit known for the noise it makes in prophesying death. The origin is the Irish *bean,* woman, and *sith,* fairy. However, Senator Pell is not alone in using the simile to illustrate *work* rather than *wail:*

"My husband has used the phrase *like a banshee* to connote frantic activity," snitches Judy Long of Carlstadt, New Jersey. "He says, 'I worked like a banshee all day.' I've argued the use of *banshee* with him repeatedly. . . . Imagine his glee, therefore, when he read Senator Pell's quotation. What is the reason for this change? And is it something that can be stopped?"

No, I suspect that *working like a banshee* is a euphemism for *working like a bastard.* Although *working like a beaver* has a long history for those of us who let a simile be our umbrella, the image of the hard-working beaver—chewing away on logs and twigs to build his dam—lacks force. A beaver's essential quality has become eagerness; and no longer is the beaver the epitome of furious activity. Enter the banshee, previously known for the ominous racket she made, to substitute for *bastard* and do the metaphoric work of the beaver.

A banshee which has long stationed itself outside my office, and who devilishly calls Pell "Mel," insists that wailing is hard work: "You know what it takes to howl all day? It's dispiriting." Evidently the banshees have tired of bewailing their outcast state and have hired public-relations counsel: Now they're becoming famous for their work ethic. Not surprisingly, beaver lovers are howling.

I thought surely your correspondents would have made the same assumption I had made on reading Senator Pell's "working like banshees." Strangely, no one seemed to feel that what he meant was "working like coolies." Isn't that the standard phrase—or perhaps I should say wasn't it? It is a bit dated. (Of course, the Senator may have used a similar-sounding word in order to avoid any implication that he was anti-coolie.)

Oh. Incidentally, if you were harking back to [Shakespeare's] Sonnet #146: one doesn't bewail one's outcast state, one beweeps it.

Constance Cunningham
New York, New York

You doubtless have a bagful of mail by now informing you that the Bantu, far from being a single tribe in which the "females" do all the work as Alyce Edwards alleges, are a very large group of African peoples living in such widely separated countries as Cameroon, Kenya and South Africa, and practicing a considerable variety of working customs. The congressional males to whom Ms. Edwards compared the Bantu may find her remark amusing; I suspect many hardworking

Bantu men would not. It is regrettable that such a slip found its way into your pages.

Peg Hausman
Providence, Rhode Island

The beavers howl, the banshees wail,
protest letters flood the mail.
"Safire made a serious error,"
whisper editors in terror.
"A banshee who," "a banshee which,"
William Safire's latest glitch.
He who uses "which" for "who"
deserves the banshees' loudest boo.
More power to the Tampa dame,
Safire's grammar is a shame!
Language is not William's art,
may his column soon depart.
I will miss not reading you,
even with a "which" for "who."

David Toren
New York, New York

Can't comment on the Scots' reason for substituting "Banshee" for "bastard" in the phrase "running like a . . ." However, "running like an (Irish) Banshee" metaphorically describes extraordinarily frenetic effort if the phrase originated in the 1840's. During that decade, when dispossessed and starving Irish peasants were indentured and loaded into the holds of cargo vessels sailing to America, tens of thousands died of disease, fever and starvation during the crossings. This required the death-signaling Banshees to work at a furious pace. Those able-bodied survivors of the previous night had to dispose of the expired bodies over the side. They had to "work like Banshees" to keep apace with the Banshees.

Joseph L. Kelly
New York, New York

bartenders' terminology, *see* **behind the stick, booze talk, chasers, cocktail talk, taking it neat, taking it straight**

baseball, *see* **ballpark figure, left field**

basis basis

In an introduction to an earlier compilation of these columns, I wrote that "my cap is reverently doffed to Executive Editor A. M. Rosenthal, whose idea it was to thrust me into the language dodge on a weekly basis."

"The word *basis* in that sentence," objects Stefanie Woodward of Salt Lake City, "is meaningless, and strikes a direct blow against conciseness and brevity. What's wrong with *weekly* or even *every week?*" Not only would that form save two or three words, the shortening would avoid error: "It is very difficult to do anything on a weekly basis," she continues, citing five definitions in an un-abridged dictionary of *basis,* not one of which includes the *on a basis* form. "If you write at regular intervals, you should say so, or use *regularly.* If you want to get more specific, say 'hourly,' 'daily,' or 'weekly,' but please don't say 'on an hourly, a daily, or a weekly basis,' unless you're talking about linear independent vectors or some such thing."

She's so right that she's wrong. True, "on a [whatever] basis" can be turgid: "I make corrections on a case-by-case basis" is not as crisp as "I make corrections case-by-case." In that case, *basis* is an extra word, used lazily, the way many sloppy speakers use *in terms of* or *vis-à-vis* rather than take the trouble to recast their sentences. And it is true that poor stylists also use *on the basis of* when they mean *by*—"Don't judge a book on the basis of its cover" might be a sentence for the magazine that S. J. Perelman called *Regurgito,* in which articles were padded for less-than-lasting interest. Such usages are on a periphrastic basis.

But the sentence I used sounded right to me, and I didn't know why; in such a fix, I bucked the letter on to David Guralnik, Simon & Schuster v.p. and dictionary editor in chief.

"Stefanie Woodward's attempted emendation of your sentence would not convey the precise meaning of your present unambiguous formulation," this rex of lex replied. "Rosenthal did not thrust you into the language dodge weekly."

Precisely; no editor likes to make the same decision every week. Mr. Guralnik noted that the sentence "He was paid on a weekly basis" may have the same denotation as "He was paid weekly," but the first form connotes something more: "The latter sentence could be used of a casual, even whimsical act, but the former clearly implies a regular, structured practice. Semantically, that use of *basis* is a metaphoric extension of the primary sense of the term (in *Webster's New World Dictionary,* 'the base, foundation, or chief supporting factor of anything' upon which something is structured); that is, the method of payment—or article preparation—is based on, or put on a base of, weekly disbursements or submissions."

The lexicographer lauds Stefanie Woodward for needling the unabridged dictionaries to give this common usage its fair lexical treatment. Since she concluded her note with "Don't think I'm trying to be a wise guy," Mr. Guralnik adds this pertinent distinction: "Don't call Stefanie Woodward a 'wise guy,' not if you want to remain on a friendly basis with her—to my mind, a less intimate relationship than being friendly with her would be."

Mr. Guralnik's analysis of "on a weekly basis" demonstrates that brevity may not always lend itself to unambiguous interpretation. In light of your remarks on conciseness, Guralnik's concluding comment—" . . . if you want to remain on a friendly basis with her—to my mind, a less intimate relationship than being friendly with her would be"—is worthy of inclusion in Perelman's periphrastic periodical. "A less intimate relationship than being friendly with her" says it all and is a more parallel construction. The intimacy of the two relationships is compared; the introduction of the verb form creates a clause where merely a phrase will do. I do, however, wish to remain on a friendly basis with Mr. Guralnik—to my mind, a less intimate relationship than being friendly with him.

Louis Montesano
New York, New York

You hyphenated "case-by-case" when it stood in front of "basis," since otherwise the reader loses his way in the modifier before getting to the word modified. In the following line this reason is lacking, so you should have written simply "case by case."

Frank Y. Gladney
Urbana, Illinois

bbl., *see* roll out the bbl.

beauty part

A confusing new word is smarming itself into the language, corrupting fashion pages and curdling the milk of human kindness in the hearts of wordsmen.

The word is *creme.* Estée Lauder offers "European Bust Conditioning Creme," Germaine Monteil advertises "Super-Moist Line-Stop Creme," and Chanel presents "Milk Bath Creme."

As gently applied in those usages, *creme* means "cream," an English word that is probably akin to the Latin *chrisma,* an unction for anointing.

Why not, then, say "cream"? Because the French word for "cream" is *crème,* and the use of the French spelling adds a little romance and pizazz to the name of the product.

Why not, then, spell the word the way the French spell it—*crème,* with an *accent grave* over the first *e?*

Unctuously, some cosmetic executives murmur about the difficulty of getting American typesetters to use accents over letters. That excuse could use a splash of astringent: Red-blooded typesetters stand ready to circumflex their muscles.

Some French firms, such as Carita, reject not only the spelling, but the idea of cream, preferring liquids; but at Chanel, Catherine D'Alessio, the firm's president, observes smoothly: "When a product's French name includes the word *crème*—'Crème Douce,' for example—Chanel uses the appropriate accent. But since *crème* is a word that the cosmetic industry has borrowed from the French and Americanized, we don't feel there is any need to put the accent on a product's English name."

With candor, Arlene Ritz, an Estée Lauder spokeswoman, asserts: "The decision to drop the accent from 'creme' in our advertising was made by Mrs. Lauder herself. She wanted it dropped to indicate that the creme was for facial use rather than something to eat." (Presumably, people have been eating "cold cream" with a spoon, not realizing it was for facial use.) "Dropping the accent was then extended to include treatment products as well as facial products. Additionally, it connotes a sense of luxury."

Ah, now we're getting deep down past the dead-cell layers to lavish on the essentially moist truth of it all. *Cream* needed toning up, and *crème* was too tony.

The cosmeticians wanted a word that sounded like *cream* and looked like *crème* —simultaneously familiar and ritzy.

One reason that Estee (I've just dropped her accent) Lauder and the others have deaccented *creme* is, I suspect, to introduce confusion into the word's pronunciation. The way to pronounce the French word *crème* is "krem," but the way to pronounce the nonword *creme* is "kreem"—unless you feel like pronouncing it "krem," in violation of both English and French rules of pronunciation.

Here's the beauty part: The cosmeticians now have it both ways. Sophisticated customers will read *creme*, think of the French "krem," and say either "kreem" or "krem"; Rosie O'Grady will read *creme*, think "cream," and say "kreem."

Granted, there is a tendency in English to drop discriminating accents— those *grave* or *aigu* marks that point the way to pronounce a letter in French. The Saturday matinee has dropped its accent and retained its long *a*. David Guralnik at *Webster's New World Dictionary* reports that *divorcée* is becoming *divorcee*, and *née* has become *nee*, though both are pronounced with the original long *a* (nee, née, nay). For a word crossing into another language, dropping an accent is no big deal—unless the result is confusion, and then it is a big deal indeed.

Cookbooks remain true to proper French: Crème Sénégalaise and crème brûlée carry that delicious little soupçon of an accent over the first *e*, and the reader is thus directed to pronounce it "krem." Elizabeth Pearce at *Gourmet* magazine says, "Our policy is to print all accents." *Olé!*

The merchants of youth have produced a word that is neither French—for without the *accent grave*, the word is not French—nor English, which already has the word spelled another way. *Creme* is an abomination, conceived in pretension, sired in affectation, borne with lifted pinkie, and brought up to be deliberately ambiguous.

Without getting emulsional about it, I think we ought to give *creme* a rinse. If we do not hold the line against sagging standards, what other sagging will follow? We have nothing to smear but smear itself: Hoi polloi, honest and forthright, will plunge their fingers into the simple English *cream*, while the correct *accent grave* will be *de rigueur* for the *crème de la crème*.

Apparently you are not a food junkie since you missed the more insidious uses of creme—"Creme-Filled" Twinkies *and* "ice creme" *(née ice milk), both denoting an absence of real cream in favor of a sugared concoction, both contributing (for the last 40 years) to my present incarceration.*

> Ben Moskowitz
> Pittsburgh, Pennsylvania

I found it objectionable that Rosie O'Grady was used to connote a lack of sophistication. Let it suffice to say that it was unnecessary to use a representative ethnic name for the sake of the comparison.

Carol Ann Murphy
Jackson Heights, New York

You have a paragraph repeating a murmur of an attempt to blame the lack of accents on "typesetters." Now a typesetter is "one who sets type," as is a "compositor." The terms date and refer to the setting of metal type. In this process accents are not separable from the letter, except for quite large sizes of type, and even then separate accents can hardly be used with lowercase letters, unless they are way way up above the letter, or well below it.

And you need 22 accented letters, lowercase, just for the common languages of French, Spanish, German, and Italian; over 50 for the majority of roman alphabet languages, and of course the same number for the capitals, so they all take up quite a lot of space in typecases.

The basic problem is the existence of the proper accented letter from the typefounders, or the proper matrices for Lino or Mono typecasting machines. As a printer from handset type, I can testify that in this country there are a lot of typefaces that never did have any accented letters, and today, with so few typefounders left, it's pretty hard to get any at all.

The fact is that many printers simply never bought accents—the typesetters might well have used them, if the copy had called for them, if they had existed, and if the printing establishment had bought them.

With more modern computer photocomposition processes, the question remains —how many fonts actually have the accents for the machine or computer operator to use? True, with offset printing one could put in the accents by hand before photographing the page, but this would not be the job of the actual machine operator (who might erroneously be called a compositor).

J. B. Hatcher
Minneapolis, Minnesota

I agree that cream is okay and crème is acceptable (although somewhat pretentious except in a legitimate French context) but that creme should not be allowed to rise to the top.

I was puzzled, however, by your use of the word "smarming" as if it meant "worming": "A confusing new word is smarming itself into the language . . ." I've heard smarmy used as an adjective by women to describe men by whom they were strongly put off (turned off). As such, it conjures up an image of an unctuous, insincere man trying to insinuate himself into a lady's good graces. (Can a woman be smarmy? The word doesn't seem to apply somehow.) Webster's Third International *gives as synonyms to the verb "smarm," to smear, gush, or slobber, none of which seems to fit your use of the word in your column.*

So tell me, is "smarming" now being used in the United States as the equivalent of "worming"—i.e., is "smarming" smarming its way into the language?—or is it a Safire neologism? If the former, it would be a shame, as "worming" is a perfectly good word and it would be a pity to dilute the meaning of "smarmy" as greasy or oily (it even sounds greasy and oily). If the latter, I recommend it be filed as a nonstarter.

Jeffrey H. Lite
Kano, Nigeria/ Department of State
Washington, D.C.

Please give Estée Lauder back her accent aigu! *She's "Es-tay" to her public. So you see, she really needs that delicious little soupçon of an accent. To close friends, she's "Es-tea"—and now that you know her better, you may want to say "Estea," too.*

Evelyn H. Lauder
Corporate Vice President, Estée Lauder
New York, New York

Well, you certainly milked crème for all it is worth.

Karl Felsen
Albany, New York

beefing up phrases

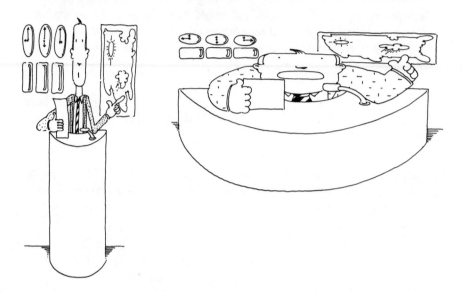

It may seem easy to coin new words and catchphrases, but the trouble is that somebody has usually beaten you to it. The same goes in spades for boosted coinages, those expressions that play on famous phrases: After *Iron Curtain* came a bunch of assorted draperies, of which *bamboo curtain* is the only survivor, and after *third world* (out of Charles de Gaulle's *tiers monde*) there was a rush on *fourth world.*

Out of *broadcasting* came, quite naturally, *telecasting,* on the theory that television, rather than broads, was being casted. That casting construction has been used again: "Cable's lines are breaking up that old mass media of mine," I wrote recently. "The admen call it 'narrowcasting.' " The *Speechwriter's News-letter* last month reported that the A.F.L.-C.I.O. was setting up a Labor Institute for Public Affairs "to explore satellite use and narrowcasting."

Bernard Ritzinger of Moline, Illinois, calls the latest casting "a new one on me" and envisions strange usages like "Cable News Network narrowcaster Daniel Schorr said . . ." He wonders who came up with it first.

I have been lying in wait for this query. Thanks to David Gibson of Hamlin, New York, I have in hand a publication called *Transactions of S.M.P.E.* for the year 1927. In this little-read item put out by the Society of Motion Picture Engineers, John B. Taylor of the General Electric Company described the transmission of speech over a beam of light, and wrote: "The demonstration of music in a beam or pencil of directed light has been called 'Narrow-casting' in order to invite comparison and contrast with the parallel art of broadcasting."

So come up with your "windows of vulnerability" to play on your "windows of opportunity," and your "postcourse correction" to deride the proposed economic "midcourse correction," and your "truly greedy" to play on your "truly needy." Let us all coin to our hearts' content, but beware any claim to originality.

Tiers monde, *I believe, is the coinage of French agronomist René Dumont. The next question: why did he use the archaic form of "third," tiers, as in the monastic hour of tierce, rather than the modern* troisième? *Stumble upon a pamphlet of Abbé Sièyes during the French Revolution,* Qu'est-ce que c'est le tiers état? *You of the fourth estate will recognize the origin of his term for the 95% of the people who Sièyes argued had no part in government, and find Dumont's model.*

Then the late Barbara Ward invented a fourth world to differentiate the truly needy from the resource-rich developing countries. (The First World is the West-plus-Japan, or the Trilateral Commission bloc, while the Second is under Communist control.)

Any more to conquer?

Ellen Rosenberg
Professor of Anthropology
Western Connecticut State University
Danbury, Connecticut

You wrote that "television, rather than broads, was being casted." I suppose when Caesar said alea jacta est, *he really meant to say "the die is casted."*

M. Angeles
Hato Rey, Puerto Rico

The late John B. Taylor (1875–1963) was my father, and I was of course interested by your reference to him. I do not know Mr. David Gibson, or how he came to have the information you utilized on "narrow-casting."

My father was a research engineer (M.I.T. 1897) at the General Electric Company in Schenectady from 1903 to approximately 1935. He was closely associated with better-known scientists in the research laboratories there, such as Steinmetz, Whitney, Langmuir, Coolidge, and Hull. His work with "narrow-casting" generated considerable publicity when he was taken aloft in the dirigible Los Angeles, *wherein he trained a searchlight beam on a receiver at the General Electric Company, which beam was the carrier of music and speech broadcast simultaneously over radio station WGY. Earlier he had devised what*

I believe was the first portable radio receiver, by wrapping the receiving antenna around an open umbrella and attaching earphones to a miniature receiver on the umbrella handle.

He was a very precise man, both with words and in habits.

Telford Taylor
New York, New York

behind the stick

The person dispensing drinks from behind a bar is called a *bartender*. Customers who are fond of the archaic call him *barkeep* or *innkeeper*. A clumsy bartender is called a *shoemaker;* one quick and capable is a *mechanic*. A woman tending bar is a *barmaid,* and there is relatively little pressure for *beverage attendant* ("On what airline?" sneers one barmaid) or *barperson*. *Bartendress* is silly; *waitron* has been a neuter-gender suggestion.

"I hate being called a barmaid," observes J. Fialla Gamsu of Waterhole 3, Saranac Lake, New York. "How can one as ravaged by time and demands for drinks as I be called a maid any longer? I prefer to be summoned by the subtle nonverbal communication of eye contact, the lonely tinkle of cubes, the eloquent gesture of the empty glass, the searching look as hand goes to pocket. . . ."

Other female bartenders have different tastes. "I have had people watch me pour drinks for five minutes and then ask me, 'Excuse me, are you the bartender?'" writes Betsy Kates of White Plains, New York. "My name is not *waitress, sweetie, honey, cutie,* a *whistle,* or a *snap*. You can call me *miss, excuse me, bartender, when you have a chance* (five of the sweetest words a customer could speak), or even *young lady,* or, sure, *barmaid* is acceptable. But I paid my dues to make it this far in the ranks: Let me be addressed accordingly. Or best of all, you could ask me my name and I'll be glad to tell you."

A bartender works *behind the wood, behind the mahogany,* or *behind the stick,* the last referring to "the beer-tap lever used to draw draught beer," according to Alan Catlin of Schenectady, New York, who calls himself a *professional barperson.* He adds that the phrase is metaphoric: "Wherever you work, you are 'behind the stick,' whether there is one or not."*

May I offer "BAR-TENDERNESS" without a trace of chauvinism, but only gentle-manly regard.

> John Crosby
> Professor of Geography
> California State University
> Fresno, California

better than never

"What is the accepted cutoff point," asks Reed Alvord of Hamilton, New York, "in using the phrase *the late*—e.g., 'the late George Apley'? Quite patently you wouldn't use 'the late Grover Cleveland.' It is the constant companion of obit fashioners, though how do they know when to quit?"

The purpose of saying "the late," as in "her late husband," is to tell the listener, "He's dead, you know." I would not use the form with famous people: "The late Anwar Sadat" insults the listener, who should know that President Sadat died. This is not a rule; some people use the phrase in a reverential whisper, to pay respects to the subject.

For names not household words, and in a medium whose readership is not likely to be familiar with the vital signs of the subject, "the late" is used for about ten to fifteen years after death.

The New York Times Manual of Style and Usage says: "Use *the late* only in reference to a person who has recently died." That "recently" has a lot of "give" in it. It adds: "Avoid a redundancy like this: *She is the widow of the late John R. Doe.* And do not fall into this error: *Only the late Senator opposed the bill.* He was not then deceased."

*See "booze talk," "chasers," "cocktail talk," "taking it neat," and "taking it straight."

Some years ago, when being shown the Palace at Jodhpur by the Maharajah's a.d.c., I made some comment which elicited the following reply—

"Oh, this was not built by His Highness, who is still at school in U.K. This was built by late, late, His Highness."

To wit, grandpa.

Angus MacLean Thuermer
Middleburg, Virginia

In discussing the phrase "the late" I'm surprised you didn't mention the one case where the phrase really makes some sense to me: English nobility. You have the present Lord so-and-so and the late Lord so-and-so. Same name—different people. The late Lord so-and-so retains his title until the present Lord so-and-so dies and takes it over.

David Scott
Venice, California

beyond compare

When anyone asks a stand-up comic, "How's your wife?" the answer is an automatic gag: "Compared to who?"

That is a double solecism, and sexist to boot. *To whom* is the obvious correction (the only way *whom* is used anymore is as the object of a preposition) but the less apparent mistake is *compared to.*

In a political column, I charged that the new chairman of the Senate Foreign Relations Committee, Charles Percy of Illinois, "had been a pussycat compared to Brezhnev," as portrayed in cables describing their Moscow meetings.

In his stentorian voice, and in a Nixonian construction, my old pal Chuck
responded: "I am not a pussycat." This prompted a savage right-wing political
savant to dub him and his ilk "percycats." In the midst of this teacup contretemps came a clear message from John Radosta of *The New York Times*'s
sports department about *compare:*

"What you mean here is *compared with,*" wrote my colleague, "to denote
difference, or contrast. *Compared to* is used to express similarity. My favorite way
of remembering the distinction is to quote Shakespeare's 'Shall I compare thee
to a summer's day?' "

I feel more lovely and more temperate already. The distinction is not a nitpick,
but a useful way to sharpen a word's meaning (I prefer *way to sharpen* to *way
of sharpening*). *Compare TO* puts two things in the same category, and likens
them; *compare WITH* sets them up next to each other for an examination of
both differences and similarities.

If you want to emphasize the way you are placing one thing in opposition to
another for purposes of comparison, use the verb *contrast.* Now you are into a
new kettle of prepositional fish.

Contrast, as a noun—emphasis on the *con*—usually takes *between:* There's
quite a contrast between Secretary of State Al Haig and Chuck Percy. But
contrast as a verb—emphasis on the *trast*—takes *with:* After you've finished
comparing dovish Chuck Percy with his dovish predecessor as chairman, Frank
Church, contrast Percy with Haig. Now, if you want to go all the way, turning
Al and Chuck into implacable opponents, use *contrast TO;* contrast Percy to
Haig. That's also phrased: "Percy, in contrast to Haig . . ."

Got that? The *to* in *compare to* is a weaker comparative than the *with* in
compare with, but the *to* in *contrast to* is a stronger comparative than the *with*
in *contrast with.*

I have plunged deeper into the preposition proposition than I intended. Suffice
it to say that compared to *contrast with, contrast to* offers the same differentiation
as *compared with* does to *compared to.* Writers who refuse to come to grips with
that are pussycats.

*You did an excellent job of comparing "compared with" with "compared to,"
"contrast with" with "contrast to," and "contrast" with "compare." You were
especially effective in comparing the weaker "compare to" to its counterpart,
"contrast with," and the stronger "compare with" to its counterpart, "contrast
to." If only you'd ended that fine section of your column one paragraph earlier.
Perhaps you realized after the magazine went to press that you incorrectly used
"compared to" (when instead it should have been "compared with") in beginning*

the second sentence of your last paragraph. You meant, of course, that compared with "contrast with," "contrast to" offers the same differentiation.

Robert L. Harris
Summit, New Jersey

Please share with your colleague John Radosta my overflowing thanks for demolishing a bugbear that has haunted me for years: the difference between compare with *and* compare to. *Page 87 of my Fowler's* Modern English Usage *is soiled with fingerprints left by my repeated appeals for help. Useless; it didn't stick. Now I need never turn there again.*

May I, in gratitude, offer a few similar crutches for the grammatically lame? They are elementary mnemonics, and I have found each of them useful:

Continuous, continual. *Your heart beats continually; a river runs sinuously and continuously.*

Supine, prone. *Prone is face-down; sUPine is face-up.*

J. Bryan III
Richmond, Virginia

For a moment I thought that I had caught you using "anymore" affirmatively. You wrote ". . . (the only way whom *is used anymore is as the object of a preposition). . . ."* Webster's Third *says that "anymore" is used only in a negative context or in a statement with a negative implication. Your sentence has the negative implication that there are ways in which "whom" is* not *used anymore. Therefore, I cannot fault your usage, but it did take me a moment to get comfortable with it.*

I grew up in central Illinois with a mother who was very sensitive to the neighbor's use of that word in an affirmative context, as in "We go to the movies a lot anymore." Many people of my acquaintance have denied that this affirmative usage actually occurs. It most certainly does; I have heard it for years, thanks to my mother's tuning of my ear.

Henry H. Swain, M.D.
Ann Arbor, Michigan

biosphere, *see* overload inoperative

bloopie awards

Time once again for the Bloopies, those coveted awards to the advertising industry, bestowed annually on the most creative copywriters and laid-back layouters by the Academy of Academic Academicians. ("What do you mean, 'Once again'?" a member of the redundancy-spotting Squad Squad is bound to write. "Why not just 'again'?" Because sometimes I like to use yet another intensifier, that's why.) The envelopes, please:

■ The Elizabeth Arden "Millenium" Award for misspelling goes to the Happy Legs division of Spencer Companies for its classic "100 percent natural linen jodphur." Macy's department stores also like this spelling. The Indian city of Jodhpur, home of the riding breeches after which the jodhpur was named, is appalled (as are many people in Nepal); but man's spelling must exceed his grasp, or what's a jod phur?

Runner-up: United States Steel, with "these indispensible materials." Snorts Louis Stone of New York: "Inexcusible!"

■ The Sine Qua Non Latin Bronze Helmet for unintended ossification to Philanz Oldsmobile, of Rochester, New York, for its "No Gimmicks, This Is A Bonified Sale!" (A more traditional popularization of *bona fide* would be *bonafeeday.*)

■ The Ultragreatest Superlative Flowerpot to the Helmsley Palace hotel in New York, for claiming its grand entrance to be "most unique," which is whiter than white and twice as dry as other uniques.

■ The Scrambled Parts of Speech Golden Egg to the Schick Super II people for their razor-blunt use of *macho* as an adverb in "get macho close," combined with their slicing of the noun *sharpness* to adjectival size although still in its noun meaning, with "custom honed to the ultimate sharp."

■ The Overused Adjective of the Year Incredible Award, which last year went to *natural*, goes to Taylor Lake Country Wines for calling its wine "honest," thereby casting aspersions on the competition's crooked, pocket-picking wine. Tied for this distinction are producers of "honest" yogurt and the publisher of an "honest" love story. (We will let no adjective go before its time.)

■ The Inhumane Society Gold Toothpick for the most delicious classified ad goes to the English-language *Mexico News*, Mexico City, for: "Doberman. Easy to feed; will eat anything. Especially fond of children. Write: David Stry, Cuernavaca 1228, Morelos."

■ The Eat-Anything Doberman Collar for the unprovoked rapine of innocent verbs to Procter & Gamble's High Point coffee, which "has the hearty, robust flavor to decaffeinate the ones you love." Shares this year's award with the Campbell Soup Company, for "the soup that eats like a meal." (Other choices available to the Campbell copywriter included "the meal that eats like a soup," and "the eats that soup like a meal.")

■ The Freedom-from-Agreement Laurels wreath to Pan American World Airways, for "Here's four great ways to tour a great country. Britain." (And here are one way to punctuate. Badly.) First runner-up was Citibank, a subsidiary of Citicorp (the *y* has disappeared from "First National City Bank"), for "How APS was able to take off on their own again with help from Citibank." Second runner-up was the Longines-Wittnauer Watch Company, for "Someone close to you is hoping for a Longines. Don't disappoint them." The writer was afraid of writing "him" for fear of losing sales to women, and did not want to write "several people close to you" for fear of making the buyer seem like a libertine. In desperation, he came up with the world's most honored dodge.

■ The On-Your-Toes Punster's Engraved Anklet to Bloomingdale's on Lexington Avenue in New York, for its panty-hose ad urging wearers to "go the whole color gamut" and giving its address as "59th and Legs." Not a bloopie, but worthy of heel-clicking.

■ The Baldfaced Prevarication Statuette to Coat Tails for "We make our clothes in a wide variety of styles and fabrications." Next to the singular use of *pant*, which has been hosed down from *pants*, and of *shirtings* (as in "I'd give you the shirtings off my back, Muffie"), the fashion industry has taken to the use of *fabrication* when it means *fabric*. *Fabrication* is a euphemism for a lie, and, yes, a wide variety of lies is available.

■ The Unnecessary Euphemism of the Year Dental Plaque to the Kimberly-Clark Corporation for its campaign to "Bring Wellness to Your Life." Evidently *wellness* is the new word for *health*, which some of us did not know has acquired a pejorative invocation *(sic)*. Get wellness soon, Health.

■ The Leave-Bad-Enough-Alone Kicked-Away Fumble (a deflated football) to T.W.A. for running this correction: "The Trans World Airlines ad featuring Florida which ran on Jan. 7, 1981, contained an omission."

■ Finally, the Red-Faced Pundit of the Year Golden Thumb to the promotion department of *The New York Times,* which ran a fine-looking picture of its right-wing thumbsucker with the copy line: "Week after week he takes you behind the news for a hard look at why things sometimes turn out the way they do." Writes Joseph Harriss of the Washington office of *Reader's Digest:* "The fact is, things *always* turn out the way they do."

And so they do. As they say at Citibank, subsidiary of Citicorp, who knows *y?*

I must protest the decision to give the Kimberly-Clark Corporation the Unnecessary Euphemism of the Year Dental Plaque for allegedly improper use of the word wellness. *You equate wellness with health. They are not interchangeable. Have you ever been in ill wellness? Health is a continuum ranging from illness to wellness. By promoting wellness those of us concerned with health (both good and ill) hope to decrease ill health or illness by preventive measures such as dietary counseling, physical fitness, stress management, etc. Although I have a healthy respect for your expertise in language, I am compelled to note that while health does not signify illness, neither does it specify wellness unless used in its adjective form.*

Wishing you no ill will or ill health,

Fran Grogan McGlynn, FNCS
Scranton, Pennsylvania

"Wellness" is a verbal abomination heaved up by pushers who are trying to foist something they call "holistic medicine" on an innocent public. "Holistic" comes from a Greek root meaning "whole"; "holistic" health apparently aims for a more sublime state of well-being than just plain old good health.

The promoters of "holistic" health include a few physicians disaffected from the orthodox path, but most are hyperactive trendies who babble of "options," "lifestyles," and "alternatives."

Contrary to your impression, "health" has not acquired a pejorative flavor, but merely suffers the curse of familiarity. As you know, if you want to sell an old idea (health) as something new, you have to conjure up some new verbal wrappings. Ergo, "wellness."

Warren W. Smith, M.D.
Columbus, Ohio

You reflected on the term "wellness," speculating that it is a circumlocution to avoid pejorative meanings in the word "health." Quite the contrary. I am sad to report that the preventive medicine types have been joining the two words in hyphenated wedlock for some time, as "health-wellness." More recently, I find this rendered as "the health-wellness concept." As near as I can make out, they are trying to differentiate between health—a state of not being sick—which results from curative medicine, and health which results from being basically well all along. As one might imagine, this distinction is terribly important to the "public health" fraternity, who never really cure *anyone.*

George R. Berman
Yonkers, New York

Your comment on Kimberly-Clark's understanding of the word wellness *is quite correct in my judgment. However,* The Oxford English Dictionary *wouldn't support Kimberly-Clark, nor would the founding father of wellness, Halbert Dunn, M.D., who left medicine to embark on his fifth career: wellness!*

Wellness can be imagined as a line parallel to a health/sickness continuum, because it is a reality distinct from health and sickness, capable of coexisting with either.

I am quite aware of the usage you decried. While it exists, it does not seem to be widely accepted except by health care deliverers who are always eager to find a new way to package an old product. Wellness promoters familiar to me across the country view the word as much more than a synonym for health.

Be well!
John J. Pilch, Ph.D.
Milwaukee, Wisconsin

Dear Bill—

Here I am out in the middle of the Atlantic with only the scantist of reference materials, but both my English dictionary and my French-English dictionary support my belief that the riding breeches named for Jodhpur are not a jodhpur, but jodhpurs. Also, though some advertising copywriters don't seem to believe it, there is no such thing as a trouser or a slack.

Incidentally, the French-English dictionary defines jodhpurs as culotte de cheval.

Sincerely,
Clifton Daniel
Point O' Woods, New York

blurb time

"You taught me language," snarled Shakespeare's Caliban, "and my profit on't / Is, I know how to curse."

If you want to give a good knowledge of contemporary cussing to a loved one in this holiday season—starting with "Bah, humbug!"—you might try *Slang and Euphemism,* by Richard A. Spears (Jonathan David Publishers, $24.95). He tracks "humbug" to "bugbear" and otherwise does a nice job of cataloguing oaths and slurs. *Language of the Underworld,* by the late David W. Maurer (University Press of Kentucky, $30) is more scholarly, but should be enjoyed from Jolly to Molly (Joliet, Illinois, to Mobile, Alabama, in the argot of underworld place names).

Hugh Rawson's *A Dictionary of Euphemisms and Other Doubletalk* (Crown Publishers, $15.95) is handy for Pentagonians searching for another word for *bomb* (they've devised *device*), and shows how the word *frank* is a fig leaf for *dirty talk* among swingers and *continuing differences* among diplomats. Rawson's dictionary is weak on etymology but strong on "barnyard epithet," and at least does not cost an arm and a leg (the lowest meanings of *arm* and *leg* can be found in Spears's work and will not be defined here).

Turning from slang to standard speech, the best Christmas present for the liberal-arts college student is *On Writing Well* by William Zinsser (Harper & Row, $8.95), and the best present for incipient businessmen and professionals is *Writing for Results* by David W. Ewing (John Wiley, and the publisher doesn't put the price on the book, which is publishing for no results). In each case, demand the second edition; both writers had a chance to fix their mistakes. A useful, handy new pocket guide to usage is *The Writer's Hotline Handbook* by Michael Montgomery and John Stratton (New American Library, $3.95).

The perfect present for a person already hooked on language is *American Speech,* a quarterly magazine published by the University of Alabama for the American Dialect Society. Did you realize that *creative* has gained a meaning of "fraudulent"? Or that *trip* was first used in its drug sense in a play written in 1957? Such four-a-year fascinations by the likes of I. Willis Russell and Peter Tamony can be bought for $12 from *American Speech,* University of Alabama Press, P.O. Box 2877, University, Alabama 35486.

The last word in linguistic newsletters is Laurence Urdang's *Verbatim, the Language Quarterly,* delightful and fun (using *fun* as an adjective), which costs $7.50 a year. (*Verbatim,* Essex, Connecticut 06426.)

Many of the above comments can be considered material for "blurbs." A blurb is an effusion, printed in an advertisement or on a book's cover, extolling the contents by a critic, a friend of the author, or, if worse (worst?) comes to worst, the publisher. (When Oscar Mayer visits Hebrew National, wurst comes to wurst.) I have often dreamt of supplying a blurb that goes: "The book can be put down but the author cannot."

Unlike *plug,* the coinage of *blurb* can be pinpointed. Gelett Burgess, a writer for *Smart Set* magazine, came up with an idea in 1907 for a way to tout a book: He drew a picture of a simpering girl on his book's jacket and said that his book was beloved by Miss Belinda Blurb. Our girl Belinda has never been busier: Unforgettable. Gripping. Luminous. The best linguistic gift since the gift of speech.

Although Messrs. Zinsser and Ewing may have had "a chance to fix their mistakes," I imagine they used the opportunity to correct them rather than to make them permanent.

The nonprescriptive dictionaries of today may give "repair" as one of the meanings of "fix," but your column is not the place where one expects permissiveness towards this colloquialism, and its use in this instance is particularly unfortunate.

Patricia K. Ballou
New York, New York

I have always had the impression that the word "fix" means to fasten or secure. I noticed in your column the use of the word with a meaning of alter or amend.

I don't think that the distinction is world-shattering at this time but if we can say that a writer fixes his words can we also say that one has fixed his tires?

J. R. McGregor
Dayton, Ohio

boll weevils whomp gypsy moths

The big news in Washington this summer was the triumph of the Reagan tax cut, and the hot political figure of speech was *boll weevil.*

A boll is the seed pod of a plant; a boll weevil is a sharp-beaked beetle (not nearly as cute as a June bug) whose larva destroys cotton plants and is therefore one of the South's biggest pests.

During the Eisenhower administration, a group of conservative Democrats led first by Howard Smith of Virginia and later by Omar Burleson of Texas took the name of the familiar bug and proudly applied it to themselves. "We were men of like minds," recalls Burleson. (Not to be confused by teenagers with "men of, like, minds"; commas can change meanings.)

When the Reaganauts recently needed votes in the Democratic-controlled House, this generation's conservative Democrats were not found wanting. One of the new men at the balance of power is Charles Stenholm, Democrat of Texas, who recalled yesteryear's use by Dixiecrats and put the boll-weevil label on today's conservative Democrats. He told a Lions Club in Roscoe, Texas, that the moniker was suitable because his group intends to stick around and keep the pressure on the leadership: "People have been trying to eradicate boll weevils for a long, long time."

Without success. The persistence of the hardy critter led some planters to diversify their crops, turning to peanuts along with the cotton. "The town of Enterprise, Alabama, erected a monument to the boll weevil," reports weevil-minded Jamie Clayton, press secretary to Representative Stenholm, "because it was the boll weevil that ultimately brought about a positive change in southern planting." She adds, with ominous symbolism, "It can be controlled, but not eradicated."

Not to be metaphorically outdone, a group of two dozen Frost Belt Republicans (the Frost Belt is where the sun never shines)—mainly from cities, and of the moderate (formerly "liberal") persuasion—came together and called them-selves the "Gypsy Moths." In Washington, insects are "in."

Coiner of the equally pesky label was freshman Representative Lawrence DeNardis, Republican of Connecticut. He told columnist David Broder that the gypsy moth is as much of a nuisance in New England and the Great Lakes states as the boll weevil is down South, and the term also had a political connotation: "The gypsy moth goes through a unique metamorphosis from worm to fly." He asked the Republican leadership not to let the group remain as worms but to let it fly with the other Republican highfliers.

Came the crunch, Democrats put pressure on the Gypsy Moths to defect from their Republican brethren, but the Moths stayed close to the Reagan flame. At the same time, Mr. Reagan swarmed all over the Boll Weevils, urging them to come across party lines to support his tax plan—which they did, solidifying a new coalition and bugging Speaker Tip O'Neill.

The verb most frequently used to indicate the triumph of the Boll Weevils was *whomp*—a mysterious locution that seems to have originated in *whip*, became *whup* or *whop*, and gained an *m* to become *whomp*. It appears to be a southern-ism, popularized by Al Capp in the comic strip "Li'l Abner," meaning "to defeat decisively," "to trounce." Combined with *up* (as in *whip up*), it means "prepare" or "concoct hurriedly," as in "I'll whomp up a batch of skonk's innards."

One "boll weevil" announced that he did not sell his vote—he just "rented" it. Where there was one vote rented, there must have been another—which seems to make President Reagan the lessor of the two weevils.

Ely Kushel,
Professor of Accounting
New York University
New York, New York

You may be aware by this time (through other letters from your readership) that the Supplement to the OED *gives a 1926* Blackwood's *citation for "whomp" referring to the loud outburst of an orchestra. I offer further evolutionary usage of "whomp." As the word has come to mean "bang" or "slap" (or as you point out, "to defeat decisively"), I refer you to the chant often heard in Tallahassee on Saturday nights from September through December: "Whomp 'em/upside de head/whomp 'em upside de head/ hey, hey, hey. . . ." Upon investigation, I have determined that this chant was imported into Tallahassee by way of Atlanta, being prevalent in the vicinity of Grant Field, also on Saturdays. Upon importation into the high Indian civilization centered on Tallahassee, this particular chant has been resuffused with its original orchestral inspiration. The "Marching Chiefs" of Florida State have their own musical arrangement which is played with "Whomp 'em." Ultimately, of course, the object is indeed to defeat decisively.*

This seems to create a full circle usage for the word, if indeed the orchestral derivative is genuine.

Jerry Holt
West Palm Beach, Florida

boniprops

"Can this be the same Richard Nixon," fumed the editorial writer of the Madison, Wisconsin, *Capital Times,* "who subverted the Constitution and avoided impeachment by a hare's breath?"

Such a fresh approach to the phrase *hair's breadth* is called a malapropism, after the character Mrs. Malaprop, in Richard Brinsley Sheridan's 1775 play *The Rivals.* A similar example is a BBC commentator's report on the arrival in Poland of a Soviet general "in a tight security blanket." The visitor could arrive amidst tight security, or even in a tight security net, but not sucking his thumb and clinging to his tight security blanket.

Most malapropisms involve the substitution of a word in a familiar phrase: "She hit the nail on the nose," or, to move the head, "She's head set against it." The amusement comes with a foreigner's misunderstanding of a word in a cliché: "I've got to get this off my shirt," or "a forlorn conclusion." Some malapropisms are mixtures of phrases: "I went after him hammer and sickle" and "Things always iron themselves out in the wash." The simple "I got it for a song" can meld* with "Don't give me that song and dance" to form "I got it for a song and a dance."

The best, and most sophisticated, malapropisms—more boniprops, because they are so good—are in the switches of single words within phrases. Lane Kirkland, president of the A.F.L.-C.I.O., admires the unconscious creativity of his European-born wife, Irena. These were three items I noted on a cocktail napkin after a drink with the Kirklands: "fuming at the mouth," "selling like fruitcakes," and my favorite, "naked as a jailbird."

Dear Bill,

My father, with that mixture of first-generation cultural and linguistic uncertainties, would often be more accurate in his observations than in his speech:

In one case, in a crowded diner when an indifferent and slatternly waitress was

---

*See "pre-emptive correction."

busier flirting with other customers than taking our order, he complained to me: ". . . she keeps hemming and whoring."

At another time when a married friend of mine—an active, but discreet, philanderer—bought a new stereo phonograph, my father commented: ". . . he just bought one of those new infidelity sets."

Just shows to go ya, bad language is often true reality.

> *Best,*
> *Ed [Edward Bleier]*
> *New York, New York*

At the risk of seeming too picky (which I am), your saying that the term malapropism *is derived from "Mrs. Malaprop" is like saying that* Caesarean section *is derived from Caesar's name, who was born by that method (assuming this is true)—rather than explaining that Caesar got his name from* caedere, *to cut. In any event, Mrs. Malaprop must obviously have received her name from the notion of "mal à propos," or inopportune.*

> *Danielle Salti*
> *Associate Editor,* Transaction
> *New Brunswick, New Jersey*

At a business meeting yesterday, the following malapropism was uttered by one of the participants in all seriousness (why "all"?):

"He certainly threw a wrench in the monkey works!"

It was a particularly apt unintended description of what had happened.

> *Stanley R. Weinberger*
> *Chicago, Illinois*

My wife is afflicted with this syndrome and it has made me turn my head more than once, the way you do when you know that a combination play has been made, that it is not quite right but you can't get the clue right away. Here are a few of hers.

1. *"I came out of the shower soaping wet!"*
2. *"I was so tired last night that I went home and went out like a log!"*
3. *"I love these old houses with their crooks and crannies."*
4. *"I needed that honey-dew donut like I needed a hole in the wall!" (Honey-dip?)*

> *Richard M. Senier*
> *Roslindale, Massachusetts*

In regards to malapropisms, I can see you've never met my friend Jane who goes to dances where the girls "stand around like wallflies" and shops at the store where they're doing "a landmine business."

> Barbara W. McLeod Biegner
> Chittenango, New York

On a bus one day I overheard a couple of ladies talking about one of their co-workers. "She comes pretty close, but she always says something wrong. I think she's a regular Mrs. Maladroit."

> Annabelle Quick
> San Antonio, Texas

When I was a working woman—way back in the 1930's—I was in the ladies' room, when another woman worker entered. She looked in the mirror and said, "I feel like the raft of God hit me."

> Lee Leclair
> Pico Rivera, California

My father-in-law has invented a few of his own—I guess we could call them "Pop-isms." Of note:
1. "It knocked the loop out of me."
2. "As happy as a pig in a poke."

> Charles R. Pegler
> Melville, New York

My wife, Melissa, creates words, involuntarily and despite a good education. It is with some hesitation that I write you and risk having any of her "garbledegook" loosed upon the public, but I'm hoping posterity will deal gently with her for she is otherwise quite civilized.

Our springer spaniel and I, upon arriving home after a hard day hunting pheasants in the rain, were labeled "dishempled"; apparently neither disheveled nor rumpled was adequate fully to describe our appearance.

To refer to my first paragraph, a small dinner party we gave was broken up when certain statements by a local politician at the table were described as nothing but "garbledegook." I'm afraid she intended to say gobbledegook but garbled it. Unfortunately her word has more clout.

Our teen-agers do not play loud music and generally raise a ruckus in our

recreation or rumpus room; not at all, these things take place in the "runcus room."
To spend an evening on the town is to go out and "rouse around."
An argumentative discussion among convening housewives is a "coffee clash."
One of our sons, who has an annoying penchant for making puns, got off a particularly bad one; his guilty simper was promptly called a "shmirk."
She once accused John McEnroe of making "unenforced" errors because he was playing "laxadaisically."

Edward Palmer
Albany, New York

Some time ago, at a staff meeting, my friend referred to an executive who is always in a hurry to get things done. "You know him," he said. "He's always going like a horse afire." It was conceded that a horse afire would indeed be moving right along. Later on during the same meeting, again referring to that same executive, he said, "Well, he likes to change streams in the middle of the river." But then, wouldn't you if you were on a horse afire?

At another meeting, hastily called to deal with a snafu that had occurred somewhere in the planning of a large-scale trade exhibition, he found himself halfway between screwed up and awry, and ended up intoning solemnly: "Something has gone ascrew!" Despite the giggles, everyone knew precisely what he meant.

Steffan Aletti
Editor, American Jewelry Manufacturer
Radnor, Pennsylvania

Malapropisms? My mother has a friend who has a medical condition that she calls a Hialeah hernia. We assume, perhaps incorrectly, that she means hiatus hernia, but maybe not. It's fascinating to think how one gets a Hialeah hernia. Heavy Exacta tickets? A big win on a lucky day?

Nan M. Irvin
Rensselaer, New York

bonker mentality

A false and malicious rumor flew around Washington a few months back suggesting that our secretary of state was off his rocker, or had flipped his lid, or did not have both oars in the water. These are expressions to denote mental instability; *The Washington Post* went to great pains to check out the rumor, and I dutifully reported that its reporters had found that Mr. Haig was definitely not bonkers.

"You got that from a source near me," said Ben Bradlee, executive editor of *The Washington Post.* "You know how I know? I always use the word *bonkers.* Good word."

In this connection, Patricia K. Tsien of New York writes, "Some people maintain that you have in fact said that Mr. Haig is 'bonkers.' The word is not in my dictionary of slang."

The word (like *crackers*) is from British slang; Eric Partridge guessed that it was a navy expression from *bonk,* the noise made when somebody is bopped on the head; *Webster's New World Dictionary* suggests it may be echoic, akin to *bomb.* (All etymologies of this are speculative.) British upper-class school slang often added *er* to slang terms, such as *rugger* for Rugby and *starkers* for stark naked.

What is known is that *bonkers* was British armed-forces slang, probably from the 1920's, made more general after World War II; its original meaning of "tipsy, drunk" changed to a more general "dotty, crazy." The word was given wide circulation in the British general election of 1964, when Quintin Hogg said that anyone who voted for the Labor Party must be bonkers. The Britishism traversed the Atlantic and became embedded in American slang in the 1970's, along with *loo* for lavatory and *on holiday* for on vacation.

Let me assure Miss Tsien that our secretary of state is in no way crackers, dotty, or doolally, as the British would say; in American slang, he has both oars in the water, even if his vocabulary needs occasional snake-checking.

You mention not having "both oars in the water" as a term for crazy. I first heard this in Waco 3 years ago and thought it was just another local, Central Texas expression. I submit another you may or may not have heard. If someone is "spaced out" or not "with it" for some reason, he is said to be "cruising with his lights on dim"!

Martha K. Grant
Waco, Texas

I grew up in Cheshire (UK) and was greatly influenced through my formative years by cotton-mill argot and Lancashire traditions emanating from Manchester, which was the closest large city. A phrase which I came across in 1946 or '47 related to "getting the bonk." I believe this still retains currency today in the particular sport in which I encountered it, that of cycling. One could become well and truly bonked, or really catch the bloody bonk, or have a bad attack of bonk. Bonk was usually cured either by plain rest, or better by food or beer—thus the best fix for an attack of bonk was a good nosh and a pint, or some tea and butties, or butts. These latter being carried slung across one's back in a butty bag, or musette, or even in a bonk-bag! We never traveled without a plentiful supply of butties—bread and marg with some sustaining filling. It is reasonably probable that a thorough examination of Beatles culture would turn up these same expressions, although I do not have such a ready knowledge of this resource.

In short, "bonk" is exactly the state of "watery-knees" presently characterized as "hitting the wall," medically associated with lowered blood sugar during athletic endeavors.

Keith M. Gardiner
Flushing, New York

Can't help but take exception to the assumption that "bonkers" may have root in Navy circles relating to the sound made by hitting someone over the head. "Bonk!" Afraid your guy is way off there. Almost made me as sick to my stomach as when I overheard a so-called "military expert" expounding in a bar one day about the origin of "shavetail" having to do with some arcane initiation rite for brand-new 2nd lieutenants actually having the hair shaved off their rear ends. God!

A thorough check with circles Navy, high up for that matter, namely my son and classmates at Annapolis due to graduate this month, discloses that the term for hitting someone over the head is not "bonk." Non, no, and negative! It is "thud" or "thwack," not "bonk." Now "bonk" may have come from the Batman comic strip, but not from the Navy. And "crackers" may have root in "thwack" because you cannot go around calling people "thwackers" so maybe . . . But I digress.

Your date of the early 20's and military usage of "bonkers" is correct. It started with the British colonization of India and the resulting crack Indian regiments that have distinguished themselves on so many a battlefield. Due to the native Indian's peculiar pronunciation of the word "bank" as "bonk" and their initiation into the dull and unimaginative world of the Bank of England, their use and meaning of the term for someone running around not quite "all-put-together" as "bonkers" puts a pretty descriptive and accurate cap on the matter.

John R. Shelter
Verona, New Jersey

Eric Partridge's guess about bonkers is about half right. For at least half a century, the unrulier kind of English boys have collected the shiny brown inedible nuts of decorative chestnut trees, and strung to form a rude kosh for "bonking" others' heads. In Britain, then, chestnuts are "bonkers," and so is anyone who doesn't believe this is why human "nuts" are "bonkers," too.

Andrew Charig
Pearl River, New York

booze talk

"*Mixers* are women hired strictly to make money for the house," says Elizabeth Hill of the Naked i Cabaret in Boston, "by drinking with the men. They're sometimes called hostesses." A *New York Times* colleague, Don Meiklejohn, formerly state beverage director of Florida, claims he learned about *spit cups* at a license revocation hearing: "A *mixer* sits with a customer and orders expensive champagne with a water chaser. The chaser arrives in a metal cup. A sip of champagne is seemingly followed by a sip of water. Actually the mixer, or stripper, is just spitting the champagne into the spit cup, or transfer glass. The tab soars and the stripper remains sober."

The *spit cup* must never be confused with *the cup*, which is the bartender's tip container, also called the *tip jar*, a rocks glass often placed near the cash register. According to Jack Murphy of New Paltz, New York, "Put this in your cup" is said by with-it tipping customers.

Bartender Edward Glanzberg of Tucson, Arizona, adds these terms familiar to those who work in bars but less well known to customers. "A *call drink* is any drink where the customer names the liquor by brand name; a *well drink* is any drink using the liquor of the house. 'What do you have in the well?' means 'What house liquor do you carry?'

"A *sleeper* is any money larger than the average tip left on the bar, which bartenders aren't sure is a tip or will be reclaimed; they put it on the back bar (not in the *tip jar*) until closing."

A busy bartender is said to be *buried* or *in the weeds*, and may be working on a *kamikaze* (cocktail in a shot glass to be gulped), a *Dusty Marty* (dry martini), or a deceptively innocent *iced tea* or *Long Island tea* (vodka, gin, rum, sometimes orange juice, colored by cola, very big in Tennessee).

A *twist* is, of course, a twist of lemon skin, but if you want a piece of lime, ask for a *squeeze*, which is more than you'll get from a mixer.

Although *stiff* is still used to mean a state of drunkenness (from the resemblance to a corpse rigid with rigor mortis), the word is more frequently used to describe one who refused to tip. Such deadbeats are also *shafties, diviners, short strokes, skels* (from *skeleton*), and *A.O.H.* (a corruption of *out of here*).

Terms for *drunken* are too mentionable to enumerate, but the latest include *wrecked* and *totaled* (from a car wreck that results in the total loss of the vehicle, and now used often to designate the reaction to a mixture of drugs and booze). *Power drinkers,* as heavy drinkers are now called, get *hammered, bulletproofed, buzzed, laid out, polluted, off nicely,* and *faced* (a euphemism for a scatological epithet). *Giffed* is a new locution, taken from T.G.I.F. (Thank God It's Friday). When someone is *stretched,* or has passed out, he is referred to as *tired* or *watching the ant races.*

"Let me congratulate you," writes Richard Reed of the department of anthropology at Harvard University, "for realizing the importance of a subject largely ignored by all but the anthropologist. . . . Due to Reagan's recent budget cuts for research in the social sciences, study in this area is more and more difficult."

That left-handed salute should go to bartending members of the Lexicographic Irregulars who have contributed herein to the sum of human knowledge, and not at taxpayers' expense. As Betsy Kates of White Plains, New York, concludes: "Always a pleasure." And as barmaid Lizzie Hill adds mysteriously: "After a rough night in the Zone, you'll hit the nearest diner and ask your waitron for a large regular coffee. Do you know what you'll get? Come to Beantown and find out. Bring some C notes. I'll peg you the instant you walk in."*

As a regular consumer of "ice tea," I must correct your description of its ingredients. An "ice tea" (not "iced tea") never contains orange juice. It always contains tequila and sugar.

> Jonathan M. Horn
> New York, New York

I believe that the word "skels," meaning deadbeat, which you state comes from "skeleton," actually comes from the word "skellum," a Scot word for "scoundrel." This word, with the same meaning of deadbeat, is also popular in police jargon.

> Wendy Brill
> New York, New York

Don't ever go to Tennessee to drink iced tea. It's very big on the East Coast too. The real iced tea is made with five white alcoholic beverages, and is extremely potent, and orange juice doesn't touch it.

*See "behind the stick," "chasers," "cocktail talk," "taking it neat," and "taking it straight."

Iced Tea: *Mix equal quantities of gin, vodka,*
white rum, Triple Sec and tequila.*
Pour two ounces of this mixture over
ice cubes in an 8-ounce glass.
Squeeze a wedge of lemon over it,
and fill the glass with Coca-Cola.

I make the "mix" in a half-gallon bottle and keep it in the fridge for visiting
emergencies.

Selina Swedrek
Laceyville, Pennsylvania

*You can omit the tequila without harming the taste, but the other four are abso-bally-lutely essential.

bopping along

The following bulleted items make up a fusillade of usage:
- "You have to be at your best, too," Farrah Fawcett told an interviewer three years ago, "—bopping along all the time, happy, upbeat, friendly."
- "You do not just bop off to China for a holiday," wrote Lorraine Davis in *The Passionate Traveler.*
- "Now we need a boppy ending," said a reporter for *People* magazine, interviewing Doe Lang, author of *The Charisma Book.*

Martin Joyce of New York City writes: "Have you noticed an increase in the rate of bopping in your neighborhood? As I sit here reading my *Village Voice,*

I read that Stanley Friedman, boss of the Bronx Democrats, in late October allegedly 'bopped down to the capital.' . . . What *is* all this jazz?"

Jazz is, of course, the immediate metaphoric source of the vogue verb *to bop*. "*Bop* is an intransitive verb of motion that is not just a New York trend," says Frederick Mish, editorial director of Merriam-Webster. "We have citations on it going back to 1966, but its use has increased substantially in the last few years."

The earlier use was a jazzman's imitation of a sound: I recently heard the gravel voice of Louis Armstrong on a 1930's record using the word as a noun meaning a type of music. Lexicographer Peter Tamony found a 1928 record using *bop* to describe a sound. *Bop, rebop,* and *be-bop* were onomatopoeic names for a complex jazz form using triadal chords: The second note was an octave higher and slightly ahead of the first and third, making a sound like *ta-dah, de-dum,* or *be-bop.*

Before jazz made the word its own, *bop* had a history of meaning a blow: "Dave the Dude," wrote Damon Runyon in his 1932 *Guys and Dolls,* "reaches across the table and bops One-Eyed Solly right in the mouth." That sense of *bop* as a blow, imitating the sound of fist meeting mouth, akin to *pop,* was recorded in a dictionary of Kentish dialect a century ago.

Here is where language does its magic: *Bop* started as a sound imitating a blow; then it was adopted by musicians to mean a beat, perhaps from a percussion instrument; then *bop* absorbed the lilting connotations of a piece of music in progress, and now fuses the sound with the music: To *bop along,* or *bop over,* means to go in a carefree, swinging style. (You don't just bop over to China—going there is serious business. As Farrah said, bopping along is happy and upbeat.) How's that for a boppy ending?

My son has brought home from boarding school the verb "boogie" as a synonym for "go energetically." It implies a local trip of some distance; and it is always used with the preposition "on," adding either "down" or "over," as in "boogie on over to the libe." True to its restless origins, boogying on down would seem to be more strenuous than, say, beetling on down (British parlance), and notably brisker than easing on down (current vogue).

Ann Schillinger
Mt. Kisco, New York

"Bop" is a noun in jazz usage. Bop evolved because of the intellectual and musical curiosity of a group of extremely gifted and adventurous jazzmen (Dizzy Gillespie, Charlie Parker, et al., circa 1944). They had become bored with the same old approach to jazz and the same, somewhat limited use of the harmonies and rhythms of the music. What they sought was more freedom of expression and wider horizons for their creative urge.

Some of the characteristics of bop—extended and altered chords (for greater note selection in improvising); dissonant harmonies; complex rhythms with an implied beat; extensive use of grace-notes and passing tones; and a cool approach to the playing of solos. It became more European as a type of jazz, was less reflective of the black musical heritage, and did not strive for the expressive characteristics of the human voice, as earlier jazz invariably had.

As to the genesis of the term—some attribute it to the be-bop often played by the drummer at the end of a phrase. More generally, it is felt to have arisen from a bastardization of the Latin arriba *(rebop, bebop, and, finally, "bop"). Arriba, of course, has sexual as well as musical connotations and means to go.*

Llewellyn Watts III
Hightstown, New Jersey

In 1978, I was visiting a classmate at the University of Kent, in Britain. It was the beginning of the term and we were invited to a number of "kick-off" festivities. At one of the dances, a bloke approached the two of us and asked, "Do you bop?" My friend and I looked at one another not sure what, if at all, to answer. The fellow then explained, "To bop: I bop, you bop, we bop. It's what they are doing," he added, pointing to the students who were jumping up and down in classic punk fashion. "Oh," we exclaimed, slightly relieved. "You mean dance."

I later learned at the University of Exeter that this meaning of the word was quite common in Britain. Perhaps it is another example where American English and British English are bopping along in two different directions.

Susan B. Lane
Darien, Connecticut

Dear Bill,

I'm not convinced about your "just bopping along."

First, let's not discard an obvious etymology, based on that old song line "When the red, red robin comes bob-bob-bobbing along"—just might be that "bopping down to Washington" means bobbing on down to Washington, that that use of bop, *at least, just might come from a pronunciation of* bob *(and since you took* bop *back to meaning a blow, note that the* OED *says* bob *meant to strike with the fist as early as c. 1280, so your original* bop, *hit, might have just been a pronunciation of* bob *anyway).*

As to bop *music, sure your bopping sound, scat word, even the rhythm suggest* bop. *BUT the original name for that music was* bebop *(1945) which then became* rebop *(1948). Now* bebop *and* rebop *could have easily come from the syncopated sound of the music, and perhaps did. Another very interesting etymology, however, is that it comes from the Spanish* arriba *(up). To Americans' ears and mouths this soon becomes* rebah, *then* rebop. *This may sound farfetched, and certainly did to me, UNTIL I heard Cuban, Mexican, etc. jazz musicians shouting* arriba! arriba! *to each other as they played—literally used by them to mean "go, man, go." Anyone who has heard this shout by Latin American or Caribbean jazz-type musicians must wonder about this as a very possible etymology (note that early bop bands often had Latin or Caribbean drummers or bongo players).*

Regards,
Stuart [Stuart Berg Flexner]
Editor in Chief, Reference Department
Random House, Inc.
New York, New York

Your etymology is questionable and your musicology flawed.

True, bebop was melodically, rhythmically, and to some extent harmonically complex but not because of "triadal" chords. (By the way, where did you get that word "triadal"? The correct adjective forms are "triadic" and "tertian.") The triad is hardly complex. It is, in fact, just about the simplest harmonic unit in all western music—jazz included. Indeed, no self-respecting bebopper would ever play a simple triad without flatting the fifth or adding a seventh, ninth, or augmented eleventh. What you describe as the second note in a "triadal" chord could not be played an octave above the lower note—that would simply make it the same note, just higher, and not part of a chord. That second note would have to be a tenth above for it to maintain the triadic relationship. What you've described only makes sense as a left-hand piano accompaniment pattern called "stride piano." But stride piano is not only much older than bebop, it is also a style that the beboppers specifically rejected. In short, your musical discussion makes no sense.

As for your etymology, you are in line with the majority view which treats the word as an imitation of a sound, but you missed one of the more interesting theories of the origin of "bop." Although the word appears first in the 1928 recording of "Four or Five Times" by McKinney's Cotton Pickers and several times thereafter, the use of the word to describe a specific musical style didn't begin until the 1940's. Jazz historian Marshall Stearns in his classic study The Story of Jazz *suggests that the word "bop"—originally "rebop"—has a Latin American genesis. At the beginning of his 18th chapter, Dr. Stearns, no doubt remembering the musical collaborations of Machito and Chano Pozo with Charlie Parker and Dizzy Gillespie in the early days of bebop, cites a Professor Maurice Crane and says: "The likeliest source . . . seems to be the Spanish expression 'Arriba!' or 'Riba!' (literally 'up'), which is the Afro-Cuban musician's equivalent for 'Go!' "*

Charles W. Freeman
Purdys, New York

The missing link in your history of "bop"—the change from a noun to a verb denoting some form of motion—lies in the mid-1950's, when the word was in use in rock and roll music as well as jazz. In rockabilly music, an early form of rock and roll whose most celebrated exponent was the young Elvis Presley, "the bop" meant both the music and the dance it accompanied, a souped-up lindy. The earliest citation of this form that I can find is in a song called "Crazy Legs," by Gene Vincent and the Blue Caps, which was released in 1956. The chorus of the song goes, "Crazy legs, crazy legs, bopping all over the floor,/do the bop, crazy legs, do the bop." Gene Vincent also recorded songs entitled "Bluejean Bop" and "Dance to the Bop."

Since there has been a revival of interest in this type of music in the last couple of years, it seems plausible to me that the use of the word "bop" to mean movement rather than music may have its roots in the sock hops of the 50's.

Cheryl Krauss
Brooklyn, New York

F.Y.I.:
Proper names are:
■ *Solid Ballot Square*
● *Bullet*

Joe Vesely
Jackson Heights, New York

I was surprised to read that the earliest citation available for the verb "to bop" goes back only to 1966 since "bopping" was the only way to walk for a number of the city's semi-toughs of high school age in the early 60's. To bop down the street was to walk with the chest and shoulders pushed out and pulled back with each step while simultaneously swinging the right arm behind the back, completing a full swing with every other step. While the hand was behind the back the finger would be snapped (optional).

For illustrative "bopping" see Richard Pryor in Stir Crazy *in the scene in which he first enters the jail.*

Bopping was meant to convey the message "Don't mess with me."

And let's not forget the song "Rockin' Robin," which begins, "He bops through the treetops all the day long. . . ."

Steven Paynter
Ridgewood, New York

bosky

Four stars are hereby awarded to Mimi Sheraton, *The Times*'s restaurant critic, for the year's most mouthwatering, double-entendred use of an archaic word.

"Set amid the bosky elegance of Washington's Embassy Row" was her beginning of a sentence about a hotel in the nation's capital. Bosky?

The formal meaning of *bosky* is "wooded," or "covered with bushes." "In this bosky wood," wrote George Peele in 1593, "bury his corpse." Sure enough, in Washington, the strip of old estates on Massachusetts Avenue known as Embassy Row is tree-lined, verdant with boxwood, and undeniably bosky.

The slang meaning of the same word, two centuries old, is "befuddled with drink; tipsy." Norman W. Schur, author of *English English,* speculates that "the meaning of 'dazed, muddled, slightly drunk' most likely came about from the idea that if you were wandering through the woods, you would probably be dazed or lost."

What a delectable confluence of meanings: Stroll down the shaded lane of Embassy Row some evening when the round of embassy cocktail parties is in full swing, and you will find yourself in the world's center of boskiness.

brunt, *see* butt out

bungie, *see* shlepper and bungie

burglary, *see* we wuz robbed

busjarg

"You have to have deep pockets to get in this business," Arthur Taylor, a cable-television executive, told *Women's Wear Daily,* explaining that heavy investment has to be made in cable long before profits can be seen. "Your ticket has to be punched before the train gets in."

I enjoy such zingy metaphors of business—flags running up flagpoles, cookies crumbling ("That's the way the Mercedes-Benz . . ."), and commuter-train conductors madly prepunching tickets lest they be caught unprepared for arrival at Profit Center, U.S.A. The expression "You've missed the boat" was replaced by "That train has left the station" and will one day be replaced by "That space shuttle has already started the countdown."

Less imaginative are the initials used in the argot of business. From the days of C.O.D. (cash on delivery) and F.O.B.* (freight on board), tradesmen have been creating jargon the easy way; so have soldiers, with *AWOL* (absent without leave) and S.O.P. (standard operating procedure).

Today's nonce abbreviations—sure to be dismissed by V.I.P.'s—include A.P.V. (administrative point of view, for people with narrow vision) and H.P.V. (holocyclatic point of view, pseudo-Greek for an appreciation of the big picture). More significant is C.E.O., for chief executive officer, a locution that seeks to answer the question "Who is really running things here—the president or the chairman?"

An abbreviation (not an acronym—it's still pronounced as a series of letters, not as a word) that has been catching on is C.O.B.—close of business. "I'll have that for you by C.O.B. Friday, chief!" I don't like it; I ran it up the flagpole and it didn't salute.

The hottest vogue word in business today is *positive*, a way of expressing hope briskly but not definitely. Will earnings go up? "I'm feeling positive about next year." If an H.P.V. C.E.O. isn't feeling positive these days, he'll have his hands in his deep pockets by C.O.B. Friday.

You referred to "deep pockets" in a statement made by Arthur Taylor. That expression is not uncommon in Virginia. For an old source, I turned to the English ballad "Little Musgrove" (Child #81). Those words are not present in the Child versions, but do appear in a form sung in Virginia. The scene is a duel as it began between an armed and an unarmed individual. See More Traditional Ballads of Virginia *by Arthur Kyle Davis, Jr., of University of North Carolina, 1960, p. 177, v. 14 and p. 180, v. 20. The stanza reads:*

> *"I have two glitteren swords,*
> *They cast me deep in the purse,*
> *You may take the very best one,*
> *And I will take the worst."*

Beverley B. Dunklee
Gloucester, Virginia

---

*See "fob watch."

butt out

Don't mess with Cleveland. Grace Kudukis, not the sort of woman to take lightly, has become head of Clevelanders for 100,000 Families, a stern-faced organization pledged to "take to task anyone who makes a negative remark about Cleveland."

Politicians and television comedians have already quailed before the wrath of this group; comic impressionist Rich Little apologized on the *Tonight* show for taking the city's name in vain.

"No person or city," declared Mrs. Kudukis, "should be continually the brunt of a joke."

Noting this, Madelaine Sutherland of New York writes: "Perhaps it isn't polite to say 'butt' in mixed company."

Right: A brunt is not a butt. A brunt is "the hardest part," perhaps from the burned remains of a fort after an attack. *To bear the brunt* means to receive the worst, heaviest, or hardest. One meaning of a butt is the thick end of anything; *buttock* is a related word, but in French, a *butte* is a mound of earth piled behind a target and may have given the word its meaning of target, as "the butt of jokes."

If this is taken to be derision in the land of cleve, make the most of it; I would rather bear the brunt than be the butt.

by any other name

Madison Avenue has ordered its copywriting regiments to eschew simple nouns in favor of nouns that require adjectives to describe the thing being advertised, thus giving an elegant, old-fashioned, Gatsbyesque feel to the copy.

"Sixty years of research and human engineering have given rise to a remarkable"—and here comes the item—"photographic instrument. The Pentax LX is a photographic instrument of such quality that it will exhilarate you. In your work. In your art."

We used to call those things *cameras,* from the Greek term for "vaulted chamber." Why is Pentax camera-shy? Perhaps for the same reason that the folks at the Dodge division of the Chrysler Corporation are calling their product "America's Personal Driving Machine."

We used to call those things *cars,* or *automobiles.* (In our art. In our copy.) Similarly, moviemakers (using photographic instruments that take pictures rapidly) have rejected the slangy *movies,* and have turned to *films;* of late, they are speaking in sepulchral tones of *motion pictures,* an early name of their product.

Only this morning, I climbed into my driving machine, stuck my photographic instrument into the limp-glove compartment, and drove past a motion-picture emporium on the way to my place of employment, where I plunked away at my type writing machine to produce this linguistic harangue. Love those mouth-filling throwbackisms.

cakewalking

"This is no cakewalk," said Transportation Secretary Drew Lewis about the air-controllers' strike. He was using a word that has come into sudden popularity in Washington.

When Director of Central Intelligence (not "C.I.A. Director") William Casey went to Capitol Hill to extinguish a firestorm of criticism, he used three figures of speech in rapid succession: "The bottom of the barrel has been reached," he said. "My life is an open book. This is going to be a cakewalk."

The first two are clichés, but the third is a delicious Americanism that had become a rarity until Casey rescued it. Far from being current spookspeak, it finds its roots in the Civil War: Richard Thornton's *American Glossary* defined it as "a walking competition among Negroes, in which the couple who put on most style 'take the cake.' "

The high-stepping "cakewalk" soon attracted musical accompaniment: The walk became a dance, and the word was immortalized in Claude Debussy's "Golliwog's Cake Walk." Soon the phrase came to mean "generally stylish"— Mark Twain called a Shelley biography "a literary cakewalk." By the turn of the century, the cakewalk—one word—was a stage dance, drawing on the fancy walking of the previous generation, as well as a mechanized promenade in amusement parks.

At some point, it became allied with something easy to do or a pleasure to perform. A cakewalker was someone having a good time; this was not to be confused with a "cake eater," or effeminate man, that derogation based on the preference of he-men for old-fashioned pies over fancy cakes.

While all this was going on in the United States, the British were using a similar expression to denote ease of accomplishment: *A piece of cake,* along with *cakewalk,* were expressions used by Royal Air Force pilots to describe missions against weak defenses. The British probably derived *piece of cake* from *cakewalk;* then the Americans of this generation dropped *cakewalk* and adopted the Britishism *piece of cake*—that is, until Bill Casey revived the earlier term to describe what he was sure would be an easy time before a Senate committee. That's how the language refreshes itself; nothin' to it.

In that secret "cakewalk" session of the Senate Intelligence Committee, Senator William Roth (Republican of Delaware) told Casey: "The Director of Central Intelligence must be like Caesar's wife—clean as a hound's tooth." The mixed metaphor drew a laugh in the committee room, and Casey waxed Roth with an apt: "In Washington, it's easier to be cleaner than a hound's tooth than it is to be above suspicion."

An interesting sidelight to your piece on (of) cakewalk is that the art form was alive and well as late as 1969 at the University of Vermont in Burlington. For fifty years, the U.V.M. annual winter carnival was called "Cakewalk." In addition to the requisite ice sculpture competition, dances and dating, a cakewalk competition was held.

Two member teams, one couple from each fraternity, practiced for up to six months on a dance/acrobatic routine set to traditional music. The highlight of the festival, in fact of the entire academic year, was the Saturday-night cakewalk attended by thousands of people. The winning team became instant campus celebrities. Unfortunately cakewalk and the entire winter carnival fell prey to the 1970's. Part of the costuming of the contestants required the use of blackface. Rather than a tribute to a past art form, the cakewalk and costumes were thought of as an affront to Blacks (formerly Negroes). Thus, cakewalk now exists only in books, magazine columns and the memories of University of Vermont graduates.

Aaron Glauberg, D.V.M.
Millburn, New Jersey

For shame (I think)! You wrote as follows: "A piece of cake, along with cakewalk, were expressions used by Royal Air Force pilots. . . ."
I question your making adverb + preposition = conjunction. The along with phrase is essentially parenthetical and cannot legally pluralize the verb. It is my opinion that you must say "A piece of cake" was . . ." unless you use and.

George D. Vaill
Colebrook, Connecticut

Yesterday I took part in an actual cakewalk at the 75th annual reunion of the Kresge family at Gilbert in the Pocono Mountain area of Pennsylvania.
This type of cakewalk is well known to many people of eastern Pennsylvania especially among persons of Pennsylvania-German ancestry. This cakewalk has been a feature of the annual Sunday School picnics and family reunions for generations and works as follows: Women of the church or group bake and contribute layer cakes for the cakewalk. At the picnic or event people buy tickets to participate and they form in a circle of about 50 to 100 or so people and walk counter-clockwise (usually) to the music of a local band.

The band plays briefly and suddenly stops and the person closest to a predetermined spot wins a cake. The music starts again and the circle starts walking until the music suddenly stops and another cake is won. Another method was used at yesterday's Kresge reunion. It was similar to the above except that when the band music stopped, a wooden arrow or pointer was revolved in the center of the circle to point to the winner. I won two cakes.

I don't know how long this custom has been going on but as a descendant of these people I remember walking in a similar cakewalk at the annual Sunday School picnic of my grandparents' country church around 1920.

These Pennsylvania-Germans came to eastern Pennsylvania from the Palatinate in the early 1700's. I don't know whether or not this cakewalk idea came over with these people from Germany. I do know that if you ask almost anybody in the villages and small towns of Pennsylvania what a cakewalk is it would be described as I have above.

Jackson P. Serfas
Philadelphia, Pennsylvania

Caribbean, *see* accent on the Caribbean

carrotsticks

"There must be nuance," said Secretary of State Al Haig, explaining his nuanced, or nuancal, approach to United States–Soviet relations, "there must be a combination of incentives and disincentives—carrots and sticks, if you will."

If you will, like *so to speak* and *as it were,* gets you past most people, but there is always one *you* who will not. One such will-notter is Thomas C. Palmer Jr., assistant foreign editor of the *Boston Globe,* America's foremost carrot-and-stick watcher.

"My unresearched opinion is that the phrase *carrot and stick,*" writes Mr. Palmer, "comes from the 'Our Gang' comedy series' image of a carrot hanging from a stick in front of a horse or donkey that is pulling a cart. Therefore, the correct interpretation of a carrot-and-stick policy would be that it is a bogus incentive, a never-reachable goal that falsely motivates a person or thing.

"Nevertheless," continues the Bugs Bunny of carrot-and-stickdom, "the phrase

is most often used to mean a two-phase, or two-part, policy of incentive and threat
—the implication being that if the carrot doesn't bring about the required result
from the beast, the stick will.

"Can you address this sticky issue?"

The expression, believe it or not (good name for a column), is of relatively
recent origin. In 1895, the *Westminster Gazette* of London wrote: "Among other
carrots dangled before the electors last month was Bimetallism." Those carrots
may have referred to the vegetable or the roll of tobacco called by that name.
On the other side of the phrase, Theodore Roosevelt in 1900 quoted what he
said was a West African proverb, "Speak softly and carry a big stick"; *stick* was
soon the vogue word for *threat.*

But it is not until 1948 that we have a citation connecting the two images.
London's *Economist* wrote of "the material shrinkage of rewards and the lighten-
ing of penalties, the whittling away of stick and carrot." Since that time, there
has been a flood of usages, and the phrase is treated as if coined by Aesop along
with the fox and the grapes, and the hare and the tortoise.

Stuart Berg Flexner, editor in chief of the reference department of Random
House, says that the combination was successful because the carrot and stick
appealed to two basic emotions—greed and fear—simultaneously. "*To dangle a
carrot before someone* seems to date from 1895 and originally to have had political
use," he summarizes cautiously, "and the combination term *carrot and stick*
seems to date from 1948 and to still be used primarily in political context."

But he doesn't go too far out on the stick; nor do I. Somehow, *carrot and stick*
seems older. We can inform editor Palmer with certainty that even if the phrase
began with the offer of a bogus reward, it now has lost that connotation and
means a simultaneous offer of a reward and a warning. But we cannot say with
certainty that the phrase was minted as recently as 1948; on the contrary, it has
an older "feel" than that.*

*In 1943 (or '44—I do not have any handy reference) Benito Mussolini wrote
a booklet entitled* Il tempo del bastone e della carota *("The time of the stick and
the carrot"). At that time the meaning of the phrase, as described in your article,
was clearly accepted, at least in the Italian language.*

> C. Mazzolini
> Larchmont, New York

*Editor Palmer has his children mixed up: the dangling before a horse's nose of
a carrot tied to a stick was a frequent occurrence in the Captain and the Kids comic
strip which was around at least as early as 1940. While these Katzenjammer kids*

*See "trickle-down carrotsticks."

did their dirty tricks in the countryside, where horses were plentiful, I recall that Our Gang comedies were, to use some delightful academic jargon, in an "urban setting, situation or environment."

Jack Belck
Knoxville, Tennessee

Your intuition as to the etymology of carrots and sticks seems to have been right on, at least anent the carrot end of the stick. This is from Hackforth's translation of Plato's "Phaedrus" (230d6): "A hungry animal can be driven by dangling a carrot or a bit of greenstuff in front of it."

Matthew Chanoff
Bronxville, New York

The time has come, the walrus-mustachioed pundit said, to talk of many things: of carrots, sticks and asses, and origins and things.

The phrase was originally "a carrot on a stick approach" to a mulish ass or an assish mule. The objective was to dangle the carrot from a stick in front of the recalcitrant animal in order to lead it in the direction that the coercer wished it to go. There was no beating with a stick involved, and if the animal complied and accomplished the goal, perhaps he was finally rewarded with the heretofore unreachable carrot, but the stick was not a weapon, merely the instrument for dangling the enticement.

John Wright
New York, New York

carte before the horse

Any logical person reading America's menus would be alarmed at the plight of the onion, which apparently is in dire need of a breath of air: Some steak and almost all liver is offered "with smothered onions."

That's a cruel way to strangle an onion. But the transformation of the phrase *smothered in onions* to the meaningless gasp of *with smothered onions* illustrates a mindless pretension in menu writing.

Vegetables on *le menu du jour* are *fresh-frozen.* (Why *fresh-*frozen? Because they are not *stale-*frozen? No; the vegetable is frozen, not fresh, and "frozen when it was fresh" is just a way to make the nonfresh sound fresh.) *Fresh,* of course, is the adjective that menu writers reach for when they feel their writing going stale. *Freshly squeezed* is a legitimate modifier of orange juice, even when clipped to *fresh-squeezed,* because it says the juice is not out of a can, carton, or bottle—but what, in describing bakery items, does *oven-fresh* tell us? Did it really come fresh from the oven—or did it come in a truck from the bakery?

Restaurateurs who oversell their food put the carte before the horse. Edward Maas, of Lakewood, New Jersey—who eats at a local Burger King because he likes the sign that recklessly urges motorists to "Drive Thru Window"—sends along this J. C. Penny menu with munchy modifiers: "Dixie Fried Chicken—tender and juicy, gently coated with a seasoned batter then fried to a crunchy goodness. Served with fluffy whipped potatoes and garden vegetable." In menuese, there is no goodness but *crunchy* goodness, no vegetable but a *garden* vegetable, no salad but *crisp* salad, no bread but *crusty* French bread, and no rolls but *oven-baked* rolls, besmeared with no butter but *creamery* butter. In this munchy-crunchy land, *hearty* soup is served from *steaming* tureens, and all sandwiches are *oversized* (to be eaten in overstuffed chairs), sent out of *gourmet* kitchens by chefs in their designer aprons. All pies are *homemade,* and some are even baked on the premises.

In a classic study of the style of restaurant menus published in *American Speech* magazine, Ann and Arnold Zwicky of Ohio State University noted the prevalence of past-participle modifiers: "Among participles naming modes of cooking," they write, *"broiled* and *poached* seem to occur most often. Some menu participles—*married, kissed,* and *handcrafted,* for example—are not part of the vocabulary traditionally associated with cooking, but most are cooking words, often modified—*gently simmered, specially flavored, kettle-simmered, delicately broiled.* Some of these participles, like *topped* and *dipped,* are characteristic of advertisements." Some frustrated copywriters cannot leave any noun unmodified: From her retirement home in Redbank, New Jersey, Hester Rusk writes: "For utter inanity I think the prize goes to *cooked squash."*

Some modifiers get misplaced. *Spring leg of lamb* bothers Richard Orioli of Webster, New York, who wonders if it augurs "a leg for all seasons"; very few eating places offer leg of spring lamb.

Brief editorial comments abound. *Cooked to order* has a specific meaning of "not ready yet," with a secondary meaning of "you can say how well done you like it," though this is now expressed as *to correct doneness;* however, *broiled to perfection* conveys no information. David Ginsberg of Roosevelt Island, New York, claims he saw a macabre menu advertising "chef's own liver, cooked to perfection."

If you say "in point of fact" instead of "in fact," your mouth will water at crustless *toast points,* an uppercrust way of saying "on toast." (Try farm-fresh eggs, gently poached, on toast points.) Frank Shanbacker of the NBC Nightly News reports a *toast medley* singing at him from a Hyatt hotel menu: "This was not even something as exotic as a sampling of breads from around the world, but two slices of white bread fresh out of the toaster."

Remember spaghetti? Remember when your spouse or paramour used to say, "I don't feel like cooking; let's just have some spaghetti"? Now the only word on the menu is *pasta.* "For years I enjoyed eating macaroni and cheese, linguine, and a variety of other noodle dishes," reports J. William Kelley of Princeton, New Jersey. "The names themselves conveyed something of the pleasures to be found in repast. But now everywhere I turn all is pasta." Like a flour child, he asks: "I wonder where all the spaghetti has gone."

A few restaurant menus cling to unpretentious old words. In Mel Krupin's in Washington, the chopped steak, as the hash houses call it, is called *hamburger,* a word that originated in *Hamburg steak,* so called because Netherlands beef was shipped to Germany and France via the port of Hamburg. (I order Mel's roast-beef hash because the name is from the French *hacher,* "to chop," and has a vigorous second meaning of "a mess or batch.") At the Four Seasons in New York, Tom Margittai and Paul Kovi serve a "slaw"—not cole slaw, which is Dutch for "cabbage salad," but just "slaw"—a salad of shredded carrots, zucchini, celery root, and cucumbers, as well as cabbage. (The hashslinger's call for "a side of slaw" is thus rendered correct at the dishiest of eateries.)

Watch out for French, especially phony French, which is supposed to transform plain fare into *grande cuisine. Turtle soup au sherry* is surely self-mocking. *Broiled steak minute* is silly; if a French name is desired for a broiled minute steak, try *steak minute grillé,* or *entrecôte.* When the restaurant personnel cannot translate the menu, some have been known to insult the customers. "Some years back," recounts Ed Miller of Manhasset, New York, "I asked a waitress what the *soup du jour* was. She said, 'That's the soup of the day.' "

Even the French were gauche in the naming of dishes. "There are many clumsy efforts to be poetic in the naming of dishes," reports George Lang, author of *Lang's Compendium of Culinary Nonsense and Trivia.* "For example, *vol-au-vent,* one of the most common pastry shells, is supposed to be so light that during Louis XIV's time, his second wife, Madame de Maintenon (who founded the famed Cordon Bleu school to teach young girls the art of cooking), named the shell *'vol-au-vent'*—literally, 'flying in the wind.' "

Which breezily calls to mind a menu that Monique Pierredon, proprietor of "Le Steak" restaurants in New York, Washington, and Florida, sent along to show how one restaurateur in the Far West adds elegance to his friers: "Chicken Gordon Blue."

You left out two of my favorite menuese locutions: "apple pie à la mode with ice cream" and "roast beef au jus with juice."

We have a local restaurant that calls itself the Café Tazza despite my efforts to point out to the owner, as he was having his sign painted, that it really ought to be Café Tasse or Caffè Tazza, but not both.

My other favorite place has a "price fixe" dinner, but when I asked why, they told me they knew it was "prix fixe" but patrons kept pronouncing it "pricks ficks" so they changed it. Presumably the patrons now pronounce it "price ficks." Bon appétit.

Stephanie von Buchau
Larkspur, California

In many restaurants, a poultry dish has been christened "Half Broiled Chicken." Are these restaurateurs offering us half of a completely broiled bird or are they more interested in conserving energy and thus offering us an entire chicken which has spent only one-half of its allotted time in the oven? If the former, then perhaps the dish should be renamed "Broiled Half Chicken" and if the latter, perhaps "Half-Broiled Chicken." (Hyphens can provide so much clarity if used properly.)

Paul Golob
Rego Park, New York

In a restaurant at Cape Cod where we dined one evening, there was a large sign on a standing placard advising guests to "Wait for Hostess to be seated." We found the sign fascinating—since it implied that the hostess must be seated first!

It joins the signs we have found posted with instructions that are impossible to follow—like the one that looms up along the highway as you are driving alone, "Form Two Lanes!" You can't do that.

Peggy Carew
Nutley, New Jersey

Add hazards of restaurant French: Neighbor of ours, driving back from Florida, found on the menu of a motel restaurant: COCO VAN ROUGE.

Could also be a Dutch Apache, of course.

J. C. Furnas
Lebanon, New Jersey

You've touched one of my favorite subjects: ranch-*fresh eggs,* country *sausage, etc. How obfuscating.*

Some years ago, while stationed in Massachusetts, I was dining in one of New England's famous restaurants. The menu featured "prime western steer beef." The following evening I found myself in a fine restaurant in Seattle, where the menu heralded "prime eastern beef." (Note: not steer!) Why is it that beef is only good, or so it would seem, if it's been transported great distances? If I'm ever in New Orleans, I'll expect the beef to be from Canada!

John W. Darr
Cheyenne, Wyoming

One day when I asked what the soup du jour was the waitress became confidential. "Soup du jour is always the leftover from yesterday's soup. I'll see what it is today."

Robert Singleton
Portland, Connecticut

I think you misunderstand the cooking term "smothered onions." When done properly this method produces a transparent, soft and very flavorable onion garnish to dryer meats (liver & flank steak) and fish (tuna & mako). Unfortunately, many chefs and cooks too misunderstand this term and bury their dish with sautéed onions instead of highlighting it with "smothered onions."

SMOTHERED ONIONS

2–4 Spanish onions (sliced thin but not paper thin)
2 oz Butter
2 oz Dry white wine
       Chopped parsley
       Salt & pepper

In a pot over a low flame melt butter, do not let butter brown—add sliced onions —stir until onions are coated with butter—add white wine—cover pot—stir occasionally—cook until onions are transparent—let cool down.

After cooking meat or fish, heat onions in melted butter and sprinkle with chopped parsley—salt and pepper to taste.

A nice addition to this garnish is poached cherry tomatoes.

D. Franklin Eldi
Westhampton, New York

Please note that several restaurants in the Los Angeles area serve beef dishes "with a cup of au jus."

Charles R. Treuhold
New York, New York

No flour child you.

My paramour has just peeked at my underwear and reported the spelling to be J.C. Penney. Confirms my suspicion that money is always on a Republican's mind.

John Odoner
Jamaica, New York

Just when we Italian-Americans thought our compatriots were finally catching on to what spaghetti is—and isn't—along comes a criticism of the trend toward "pasta" on restaurant menus.

We have long been amused by "spaghetti" as a generic term for pasta or macaroni. Spaghetti is, of course, only one of a hundred or more configurations of this popular staple, others being fettucini, linguini, rigatoni, ziti, etc. Let's hear it for "pasta" on menus!

Joseph Sturchio
South Egremont, Massachusetts

Blaine Littell was in Kenya for NBC before independence. When he went back after Uhuru, he felt certain he would find a French restaurant in its capital city —no country which lacks such civilization being fit for the comity of nations.

Sure enough, he found one. On the menu was "Potage du jour." When he asked the waiter what it was, the waiter said that he didn't know but he would find out. A moment later he returned from the kitchen, beaming proudly, to announce: "Today, sir, the 'potage' is soup."

Thomas H. Wolf
Director of Cultural Affairs, ABC News
New York, New York

I am as you are an enemy of overwritten menus; unlike you I prefer fresh-squeezed orange juice to "freshly squeezed" juice. I think that like "newmown hay" and "newborn babes," "fresh-squeezed juice" belongs to a construction that far predates English grammar teachers' ironclad rules about adverb endings. English speakers and their progenitors probably ate "fresh-baked bread" or its earlier etymological/spelling variants for over 1,000 years before "freshly baked bread" ever came out of an oven. These forms are not "clipped," they just never grew any annoying shoots to be clipped of.

Raymond Foote
Portland, Maine

I began to study culinary terminology to understand and gain confidence in cooking, and now I'm attempting to sort out the chaos and misconceptions rampant throughout the entire culinary field. Those who write menus are seldom aware of basic language usage and often have misconceptions about the food they serve. And too many purposely mislead the public. I was therefore happy to see your tackling of today's out-of-hand menuese. At the same time I would like to suggest some additions and modifications to your list.

"Shrimp Scampi" is so common that the general public actually believes such a dish exists. I have been asked by many patrons whether the item I have listed as "sautéed shrimp in garlic and butter" is anything like shrimp scampi (scampi are commonly prepared this way in Mediterranean areas). These days I simply answer, "Yes, very similar, but I think you'll like this more."

"Rice Pilaf" is a virtual repeat of "shrimp scampi." The two are, fittingly, usually served together (I won't bore you with a long-inked dissertation on pilaf, or pilau, or pilaw).

Those diners who want a steak often order the "N.Y. Sirloin," a nonexistent cut. The loin of beef is divided into two parts, the short loin and the sirloin. Steaks cut from the short loin are the club, T-bone, and porterhouse. If the tenderloin is removed from the short loin, a strip loin (or shell) remains. The N.Y. cut steak is not a sirloin, but a N.Y. strip, or shell, or simply N.Y. steak. Kansas City may be used interchangeably with N.Y.

"Fresh-frozen" can be partially excused, if one considers that the other style is "cooked-frozen." Shrimp are available in either form. (Watch out for boasts of fresh shrimp in the Northeast. Virtually all shrimp arrive in New York in the frozen state.)

"Toast points" are generally regarded to be trimmed toast, cut into triangles, or points.

Truth-in-menu laws prohibit falsely advertising items to be homemade, so several restaurateurs will designate "home-baked" those frozen, ready-to-bake pies and breads so loved by the mass of out-eaters.

In the area of cooking techniques there is so much ambiguity of terminology that few people know what they are saying. James Beard likes to sauté slowly, though I find it impossible—I either sauté or cook slowly. Julia Child uses a whisk, and I a wire whip. Foreign cooks abuse the language, and their editors and translators seem not to understand cooking. Even Escoffier had trouble differentiating his own classifications—entrées and relevés, entremets and desserts, pâtés, gallantines, ballantines, and mousses. The effort to research, clarify, and inform may be in vain, but I think of all the fun I'm having in the process.

David D'Aprix
Ithaca, New York
School of Hotel Administration, Cornell University

Dear Bill:

Pasta is the abbreviation of pasta asciutta, which correctly indicates a dried noodle product vs. freshly made pastas which contain egg and have to be eaten freshly or must be frozen. The fact is that the tastemakers of the U.S.A. were gastronomic adolescents and misbehaved when naming dishes. Spaghetti is simply one of the hundreds of kinds of dried pasta dishes, and to call everything spaghetti would be like calling the category of seafood dishes shrimp, for instance.

Entrecôte is not a minute steak. The true entrecôte is a cut between the ribs which in French is called côtes. Entre-côtes is a precise description of this steak-type. In America, it used to be called a ribsteak, though one doesn't find this often on the menu.

Fondly,
George [George Lang]
New York, New York

Dear Bill:

Prompted by your recent column, and assuming you may have missed my last book of poetry, possibly also my first:

MY COMPANION ORDERS DINNER

(on reading a restaurant review)

*"To begin," she said, "I will have
trivial tripe with alabaster endive,
and three stalks of taut asparagus.
Then the flexible flounder,
and two Cote d'Azurs, medium,
with lucid leek and petulant parsnip,
a tensile turnip, a complacent tomato
and a baked preternatural potato.*

*"I will have the 'plat' plain
and two 'jours,' preferably
Tuesday and Wednesday."
Then with her head atilt
a little like a daffodil,
she said, "To drink
I will have the ambience cold,
and for dessert, a half decor."*

Gene [Eugene McCarthy]
Washington, D.C.

cash customers

"Citibank has coined a new and unnecessary word," Mrs. Winsome Adams of St. Albans, New York, wrote me. "In several branches, the bank has signs which state that no two-party checks will be accepted for 'deposit or encashment.' 'Encashment'? What is wrong with the old-fashioned word *cashing*?"

The wheels of the vaults grind slowly, but a vice-president of Citibank, Nathaniel Sutton, investigated the matter and reports: "We plead guilty on *encashment*. We did use it, but we didn't coin it. The British did. And two recent editions of *Webster's* are keeping the word alive and well." The word is listed in *Webster's Third* as a Britishism. "I believe the British are more fond of *encashment* than we are, but you still hear it all the time in banking circles."

Does Citibank endorse this pretentious import? "While the dictionary confers legitimacy, it does not confer appropriateness," said Sutton, caving in without admitting a bank error in our favor. "I agree with Mrs. Adams that *encashment* has a jargonish ring, and that *cashing* is simpler and more appealing." He then deposited his policy directive: "In fact, *encashment* is one of the taboo words we urge employees not to use in the communications seminars our department conducts. But as you know, portentous words die hard."

There! Even a big bank can kick the big-word habit without going through withdrawal symptoms. *Portentous,* by the way, used to mean "portending evil; ominous" and has come to mean "pompous; self-important," possibly because it sounds like *pretentious* mixed with *portly*—but there is poetic justice in that, since pretentiousness can be ominous. Hats off, Citibank; you have rung Mrs. Adams's register.

That makes two banks we've held up in this space (the first, Chase Manhattan, no longer advertises: "I've put the Chase behind me.") Next on the slick-Willie list is the Bowery Savings Bank, which has induced its spokesman, Joe DiMaggio, to say in television commercials: "Is there anyone who couldn't use a bunch of cash?"

Say it isn't so, Joe. Not "a bunch of cash." Having fought off the extreme of pretension, we are now challenged by the extreme of condescension. I'd hate to go to my local bank seeking encashment only to walk out with a bunch of cash. "Has our money become so devalued," cries Lewis Rappaport of Brooklyn, upset by Joe's jolt, "that it is equated with fruit?"

If *bunch* applied to cash is a Bowery bummer, consider a bunch of pomposity from another banking institution, the American Express Company. On its 1980 wallet calendar, these words appeared: "How and where to access service." When Paul Wolski of New Hyde Park, New York, complained to the Amex people about this corporate harrumphing, little did he realize that the company accessed complaints. On the 1981 wallet calendar, "How and where to access service" has been changed to "How to use it." The clarity! The grace! I wouldn't leave home without it.

Long before our money became so devalued that it was equated with a bunch of fruit, a bona fide capitalist talked of tossing bunches of cash around. In 1911, George Eastman (whose biography I am writing) had the directors of the Eastman Kodak Company set aside $1 million as a welfare fund for company employees. "The interest on this fund," Eastman wrote, "is to be used in relieving employes who need help, either on account of sickness, or old age, or any other cause. . . . In view of the fact that our earnings may not always continue to be as large as they are at present and that the age and number of our employes is continually increasing, I thought it wise to put aside a good bunch of capital. . . . "

Betsy Brayer
Rochester, New York

As long as you criticized Joe DiMaggio's financial advice to New Yorkers ("a bunch of cash"), I thought that you might have some suggestions for interpreting another baseball veteran's fiscal recommendations. Phil Rizzuto, one of Joe's old teammates, does commercials locally for the Money Store in New Jersey, a second-mortgage financing company. The slogan Phil has been repeating for over a year is: "New Jersey homeowners! Borrow up to $50,000 and more at the Money Store!" How can the phrases "up to" and "and more" both be used in a single sentence that is still expected to make sense?

Michael K. Brush
Yaphank, New York

caste party I

A pop antigrammarian admitted that he had difficulty calling a movie by its new, upscale name: film.

Many words indicate caste in our society, despite the homogenization of language by network sitcoms. Phyllis Martin, author of *Word Watcher's Handbook*, pulled a few examples together in *Writer's Digest*. The old, dated, poor words are listed as "minus" on the left, and the young, with-it, rich words are the "plus" on the right:

MINUS	PLUS
tuxedo	black tie
washrag	washcloth
bathing suit	swimsuit
cake of soap	bar of soap
clap	applaud
honeymoon	wedding trip
tease	back-comb

The liquid served with meat and potatoes that used to be called "gravy" has been upscaled to "sauce" in the high-rent districts. Imagine eating mashed potatoes and sauce!

I have thought of a comeuppance that is sometimes appropriate when someone uses "gourmet" as an adjective. When I am accused of being a gourmet cook, I insist that I have never cooked a gourmet. When a local department store advertised for sale a "gourmet cooker" I called the management to complain that one could never cook a gourmet in one of those things. They told me the appliance had been so labeled by the manufacturer.

Kay Grizzard
San Antonio, Texas

caste party II

Only fuddy-duddies go to the *gym*, or to the *drugstore*, or to *Europe;* the upscale (formerly hoity-toity) crowd goes to the *spa*, or to the *pharmacy*, or to the *Continent*. The truly avant-garde know that nobody who is avant-garde uses *avant-garde* anymore: They are the *trendies*, or the *cutting edge*.

If you think of yourself as *middle-aged*, life is passing you by; on the other hand, if you are in *midlife*, it is you who are passing life by. Similarly, if you are *divorced*, you may consider yourself *damaged goods*, but if you are *newly single*, you think of yourself as having been through a *character-building experience*.

Language has always revealed caste. A generation ago, Prof. Alan C. Ross pioneered "U" and "Non-U," and recently Phyllis Martin came up with a list of plus-and-minus words to suggest usage that separates the out-of-it from the on-top-of-it.

Lexicographic Irregulars have unearthed a trove of usages that show today's marks of separation.

A decade ago, the passé people would say *rich* while the with-it types would say *affluent;* now the passé say *affluent* and the with-its say *wealthy;* in the same way, there used to be a split on *davenport* and *sofa;* now the split is between *sofa* and *couch*. The *graveyard* was replaced by the *cemetery*, which is now prettified as the *memorial park*. People who used to say *phonograph* were tittered at by people who said *record player;* now they in turn are looked down upon by those who say *turntable*. Cock your ear: When was the last time you heard a young, rich-affluent-wealthy type use the phrase *railroad station*? Upper-class use is now *train station*.

When the *moral of the story* is the *bottom line*, the *fact of the matter* becomes the *reality of the situation*. You like *raw vegetables*? I'll take *crudités*.

You read the *Bible*? I study *Scriptures*. Are you carrying a *watch* in your *brief-case* to give as a *present*? I'm carrying a *timepiece* in my *attaché case* to give as a *gift*.

Here is what is happening around the house:

MINUS	PLUS
porch	deck
stove	oven
socket	fixture
coffee table	cocktail table
fish tank	aquarium
shelves	wall system
row house	town house

Outside, what used to be the *bushes* are the *shrubs*. Now step into the kitchen:

squeezer	juicer
coffeepot	coffee maker
washing machine	washer
dishwiper	tea towel

Poke your head in the closet:

bathrobe	hostess gown
trunks	shorts
sneakers	running shoes
pocketbook	handbag
stockings	hose

Sometimes the switch to classiness is an advertising euphemism, as in the change from *costume jewelry* to *fashion jewelry*, or, loosely, from *girdle* to *control-top panty hose*. Often the switch is simply to get away from the familiar: *rouge* becomes *blusher, perfume*—even perfume—becomes *fragrance*. (Perfume is for the poor.) *Pimples* are out; *blemishes* are in.

In religion, the upper crust takes *saved* and turns it into *born again;* the *Holy Rollers* are now *charismatics*. *Pride* goeth before a *hubris*, and if Emerson were writing his essay today, "On *Friendship*" would be "On *Relationships.*"

What is *dirty* to the seedy is *adult* to the preppie; what is a *pinky* to the plain is a *little finger* to the handsome; what gets Out people *mad* gets In people *hostile*.

And if your boss threatens to fire you, put him down with "You can't outplace me—I quit!"

With the exception of the gym-spa comparison in your first sentence, the first portion of your column on new versus old terms for the same things is fine. But your lists compare words that just don't have the same meanings.

Let's start with gym and spa. A gym is a large room used for playing basketball or training fighters, with locker rooms and showers attached. At a school, the building with such a room at its heart may be called a gymnasium and may also have an indoor pool, exercise rooms, offices and trainers' facilities. A spa has these things plus steam rooms, space for dance classes and similar activities, but no large room for basketball.

A porch is an open room attached to a house and may have a floor at ground level. If raised above ground, the floor may have space below it enclosed by a wall or woven wood which cuts off view of the space but admits air. Porches have roofs and may be enclosed by screen. A deck never sits on the ground, usually has the space beneath it open to view, and is almost never roofed. It may be without sides. A stove is an appliance which includes an oven. An aquarium may be a fish tank, but it may also be a turtle tank or arranged for other animals that need a damp climate but don't live in water—a relationship similar to a rectangle and a square. Similarly, a wall system may be shelves only or it may include closed cabinets, a desk unit, or space for hanging items.

A squeezer is designed especially to get juice from citrus fruits, and it may be a hand-held mechanical item or it may be electric. A juicer is normally electric, although I once saw a crank type. It can get juice from almost anything that has any water content. A coffeepot is for serving coffee. It may be electric and also make coffee, or it may be part of a silver service and intended for serving coffee made in something else. A dishwiper, in many parts of the country, is a husband or child.

My husband wears a bathrobe after he takes a bath. I wear a hostess gown when I'm a hostess, if I can't wear jeans, but it wouldn't be suitable for wearing from the bath. One is fashionable and the other is functional. Trunks are for swimming, while shorts may be for running or pulling weeds. Sneakers are for little kids and sometimes have Mickey Mouse or Spider Man on them. Running shoes are designed for running, but not for softball or tennis, while those of us who can only afford one pair may use sneakers for everything but work and the opera. Hose may or may not have panties on top; stockings never do. Believe me, there's a big difference between a girdle and control-top pantie hose, and I hope you never need to wear either.

Fragrance may be perfume, but it may also be cream sachet. Holy Rollers are charismatics, but members of other churches, even Catholics, may also be charismatics. A relationship may be friendship, but it may also be hatred.

Your idea is interesting, and it may also be true. People do choose to use words that seem more up to date than the words they used in the past. But I think you missed a bet when you failed to point out communication may be hindered when the two words don't mean the same thing.

Pat McCrossen
Albuquerque, New Mexico

MINUS	PLUS
stereo	sound system
Personnel Department	Department of Employee Relations
used car	predriven classic
operation (by a surgeon)	surgical procedure
sherbet	sorbet
on-the-job training	hands-on experience
thermostat	environmental control system

A quick glance at France provides some consolation in all this. At least we Americans do not resort to fisticuffs when our language takes on slightly more/less sophisticated words.

> Michael F. McCauley
> Oak Park, Illinois

I thoroughly enjoyed "Caste Party." It reminded me of a new "retailese" I've been seeing and hearing in the media; the new fascination with -wear.

Examples:

> eyewear instead of glasses
> footwear instead of shoes
> neckwear instead of ties
> swimwear instead of bathing suits

I realize that they're probably catchall words to cover, in the case of eyewear, glasses and contact lenses. But I have just become aware of a preponderance of these -wear words in the past year or so.

> Marilyn Plummer
> Austin, Texas

Boy, oh boy! are you behind the times!

Nobody who owns one larger than 8×10 says "deck" anymore; that's used by real estate types, reporters for house and garden magazines and "interior decorators." Those ahead of the crowd say "slats," as in "Shall we hit the slats?"

Your whole list of pluses and minuses is out of date. Just one more example: a "stove" isn't called an "oven"; it's called by its proper name in knowing households, as "Say, would you please switch off the Jennaire?"

> Irving D. Suss
> Professor Emeritus of English, Colby College
> Bradley Beach, New Jersey

The substitution of fragrance *for* perfume *is, I think, an intent to mask the fact that one is probably not buying* perfume *at all, but a less expensive form— say, cologne, toilet water, one of those solids that pass as* perfume, *or maybe even scented talcum powder. These days it seems that most perfume manufacturers produce an abundance of products all carrying the same name and all sold, or marketed, as it is now said, under the general heading of* fragrance.

It may be, then, that perfume *is really for the* rich/wealthy/affluent *and* fragrance *is for those who wish they were any of those.*

Lisa McCann
Palo Alto, California

Rich people (not the same as upper-class necessarily) say rich; wealthy *is not as rich as* rich. A sofa *has a back; there are some kinds of* couches *that do not. A* turntable *is only part of the* record player, *as an* oven *is part of a* stove *(very often). It may be interesting to explain your confusion in terms of the habit of one class to notice or stress one part of an object over another, but in any case you are offering as equivalents words which are not necessarily synonymous.*

You have other problems, too. A coffee maker *is a machine, while a* coffeepot *(preferably silver) is what an upper-class person would insist the coffee be put into before it is served. No really upper-class person has a* wall system; *if not entirely covered with bookshelves (as in a library, not a living room), walls are for wallpaper, paintings, etc., not* storage. *Your* town house *might be a* row house *(a* brownstone *only if faced with sandstone, not some cheap brick or more elegant wood facade) but you must also have a country house; if you have only one house, it is not your town house, just your house (never* residence *or* domicile*). A* bush *is not a* shrub; *perhaps it is not upper-class to notice nature very much but I believe the bush's branches start closer to the ground and a shrub is, well, less bushy, more like a tree. Certainly not* shrubs—shrubbery. *I believe a* bathrobe *has to be absorbent, while a* hostess gown *in terry cloth would be extraordinary.* Running shoes *are cut lower than* sneakers *and cost a great deal more. Upper-class people would avoid any that bear a bold name on them: people should not carry advertising. Even one's own initials are not always in good taste and to wear anything marked YSL for Yves St.-Laurent is foolish. Let Messrs. Gucci, Adidas, et al. buy advertisements in appropriate places. Even Gloria Vanderbilt shouldn't have Gloria Vanderbilt written on her butt. (It is perfectly correct to sew name labels into the clothes of children being sent to schools or camps where uniforms complicate the distinguishing of ownership.)*

A socket *is only one kind of electrical* fixture. *No one anyone would want to know says* memorial park *or* bottom line. *Even a* cologne *has a* fragrance *like a* perfume. Scent *is nice, if a trifle British; in any case, it is seldom required that we comment on how others smell, and in purchasing in person (in* fragrance delicto?*) one specifies by name brand, surely, while* perfume *then has a technical* *meaning (it is stronger than some other preparations). Mad means angry to the point of acting crazy; you can be* hostile *quietly, without fireworks. No upper-class person has ever been* born again. *But I notice you say "upper crust" there, and elsewhere you speak of on-top-of-it and with-it and out-of-it, which is probably the source of much of the confusion. Upper-class people are never with it; they are above it.*

I do not mean to go on and on about this, but now that I have had to resort to a second sheet (if only so that you will not receive an unsigned, anonymous letter), let me take a few more words to tell you that relationship *implies sexual* involvement *in most usages, while* friendship *does not (though* friend *is sometimes politely used in cases of adultery, homosexuality, and simple* shacking up *on a more or less regular basis). I cannot imagine that Emerson would have had any thoughts worth preserving on the subject of cohabitation neither blessed by the Church nor strictly legal.*

What a lot of carping on only part of one of your weekly stints! And one could go on: a pharmacy *fills prescriptions and a* drugstore *may not. . . .*

Leonard R. N. Ashley
Professor of English
Brooklyn College, CUNY
Secretary, International Linguistic Association
Brooklyn, New York

It is true that the "graveyard was replaced by the cemetery, which is now prettified as the memorial park." For your information and guidance, however, a marked distinction can be made between a cemetery and a memorial park. Classically, the former under most cemetery regulations allows for the deedholder/purchaser to erect a "standing" monument (formerly headstone) to identify a particular grave (formerly plot). Memorial parks, on the other hand, prohibit standing monuments in favor of flat markers. Hence, a memorial park takes on the look of a park and will be "prettified" when viewed from a distance. Consequently you were essentially correct.

Then too, as a member of the profession, I have witnessed many who "would not be caught dead without a frilled casket" with an equal number who would rather because of personal preference, needs, wants or desire. However I applaud you for using correct terminology, since caskets differ from coffins. The shape determines usage, not caste. Coffins themselves are shaped while caskets are primarily rectangular, although manufacturers present "urn units."

In addition, you may well have taken mortician *from* undertaker, *but my preference today would be* funeral director. *Similarly,* funeral homes, *not funeral parlors, exist today. (You see, not long ago many were "waked" in their own parlors, invariably attended by an "undertaker." And only within a span of several decades have funeral directors been entrusted to care for the deceased in their own establishments, many of which were converted from ordinary homes.)*

Charles P. Kuczynski
Bayonne, New Jersey

catty-corner

"A friend of mine from the Middle West," writes Marian Lindberg of New York, "insists that a structure diagonally across from another is *kitty-corner* to it. In response, I have protested and advocated use of *catty-corner,* a more mature expression." Both Miss Lindberg and her diagonal friend were distressed to see the term *cater-corner* in their favorite newspaper, and turned to their dictionaries: All three were listed. "Why the different formulations?" they ask, as if this were an advice-to-the-word-lorn column. "Which came first?"

You cannot throw a brick at the back-alley cat in *catty-corner:* The *cater* ultimately comes from the French *quatre,* and the word means "four-cornered," later coming to mean "diagonal" or "oblique." From a mistaken identification with cats, it was spoken of as *catty-corner* and *kitty-corner.*

Dr. Frederic G. Cassidy, director-editor of the *Dictionary of American Regional English* (the man from *DARE*), has made a study of the way we speak of the diagonal or the askew. "The odder variants include *cattybias, catty-cue,* and *catty-godlin,*" he informs me from his odd angle, "and a big new area is opened up by *catawampus* and its huge brood: *catty-wamp, kitty-wamp,* even *canky-wampus.*" New Englanders will not understand these regionalisms. In the South and West, *DARE* has found a synonym in *antigogglin:* "*Anti* clearly means 'against whatever is in line,'" says Cassidy, "*gogglin* has its older sense, referring to eyes that squint; people who squint don't see straight; they get things crooked, or antigogglin."

What does a pedestrian do when he wants to save steps by crossing a square diagonally? "The overwhelming answer," reports *DARE,* "was *You cut across*—that's all over the country. Next most frequent is to *go kitty-corner* and its variants, such as to *angle across* (Minnesota), *cut cabbages* (Missouri), *go kitterin'* (Wisconsin), *jay-hawg* (Texas), *bee line* (Massachusetts), *take a nigh cut* (North Carolina), *walk bias acrost* (Maryland)."

If you think Professor Cassidy's ideas are slaunchwise or skewhiffy, harass him directly at the University of Wisconsin at Madison, where he observes the rest of us going off half-cocked. "Nobody wants to go straight all the time," he philosophizes. "For the unstraight, everyday things we seem to feel a need for more lively language. As long as we're going to be crooked or diagonal, why not make it keywampus?"

I was pleased to read the quote from Professor Cassidy: "Nobody wants to go straight all the time." Having spent most of my adult life being gay, I could not be in fuller agreement with the professor. This raises two questions on language. What is the origin of the use of "gay," meaning a person who has a preference for same-sex partners? Secondly, why does The New York Times *not recognize the usage? Is it a question of perverse pedigree? This meaning of the word is used even by those morally righteous who wish to stone me to death as an expression of Christian love. If these purest of beings use the word, why not* The Times?

Michael S. Ptaszek
New York, New York

When I was growing up, about 60 years ago, the phrase my family used for "crossing an intersection diagonally" was "making a Dutch cut."
I do not know whether this originated in my mother's family (German descent, Buffalo, N.Y.) or my father's (English descent, Hudson Valley). I have speculated that this may have referred to slicing a loaf of bread on the bias. Perhaps it was even derogatory.

George M. Corney
Hilton, New York

My wife, a native of Killeen in Central Texas, uses the word antigoddlin *to describe the cattycorner position. It goes along with* gottsch-eyed, *meaning having one eye looking off in a different direction than the other. That's a little better-sounding word (to my ear) than* slaunchwise *or* skewhiffy.

Kerry Grombacher
Austin, Texas

Enjoyed the column on "catty-cornered" but you left out the best one, "Whee-whaw." I grew up with that usage. My husband, from 15 miles away, had never heard of it. It says it all, best!

L.J. Bucklin
Chatham, Illinois

Dear Bill,

A word I would sometimes hear as a boy in the mountains of Western North Carolina, where nearly everyone is Scots-Irish (as well as kinfolk), and go back forever, was "sygogglin" or "sygoddlin" (spelling purely phonetic), which was said of a barn or a house that had started to lean. It was "sygogglin" if leaning to the right and "anti-sygogglin" if to the left.

Perhaps a year ago I wrote "Any Questions" of Harvard Magazine to see if they could dredge up any derivation. The other day I got this response from F.G. Cassidy (attached), who I gather is also in touch with you. I send along his reply, for whatever use it may be in the treatment he reports you may be planning.

all best
Bill [William J. Miller]
Truro, Massachusetts

Mr. Edward Davis
Harvard
7 Ware Street
Cambridge, MA 02138

Dear Mr. Davis:

I have in the DARE files 41 responses in which antigodlin or similar forms were given. Both parts of the word furnish variants such as anli-, anni-, cutty-, skew-, and for the second part -goggly, -goggling, -gozlin, -waddling. Since I am sure we did not collect all the existing variants, some further combinations of parts of these must be in use. We also collected si-godlin, but not the combination of anti- and si- in the same word. Your correspondent has, therefore, a refinement of his own with barns leaning left and right. I wonder whether this distinction was ever regularly made!

The etymology is not clear but obviously anti- suggests against the vertical norm, si- is surely reduced from side, skew- is obvious, and cutty- is probably a variant of kitty- or cater- as before corner. They all suggest something out of plumb or diagonal or crosswise. The Scots-Irish origin is as good as any possibility and probably better than others, judging by the area in which these words are established in the U.S. The goglin/godlin part is the least clear.

F. G. Cassidy
Director-Editor, DARE
Madison, Wisconsin

cautiously optimistic

Whenever President Reagan was asked how he felt about the approval of his Awacs sale, he would reply: "Cautiously optimistic." Since that time, the phrase has been taken up by every politician in Washington.

The phrase could use a rest. It says: "I'm hopeful, but in case it doesn't work out, I was careful not to be too hopeful." A classic hedge.

Why is nobody ever *cautiously pessimistic*? Because pessimism, even when judiciously modified, is not upbeat and sunny, as statesmen are supposed to be. And *recklessly optimistic* might be interpreted as smug.

Just for a change, let's try *carefully hopeful*. Or go back to George Bush's "We have momentum." Or a nicely pompous "My confidence, though restrained, is abiding."

Is there hope for the demise of *cautiously optimistic*? You know what I am.

Cautious optimism has always been an attractive out for coaches who don't want to put themselves on the line for a number of reasons. Perhaps they are in fear of their jobs, or perhaps they want to lull the opposition into a sense of false security (I have always wondered why the phrase often is written "a false sense of security"; the sense is real enough: only the security is bogus). Horror of horrors: perhaps the coach just doesn't know (actually, none of them knows; perhaps he has no idea). It is, of course, a cardinal sin in the coaching profession to plead ignorance before the fact. After the fact, ignorance always serves as a handy excuse ("Well, if I'd known how bad his ankle really was").

Your alternatives might well serve a politician, but would not do much good for a coach. Obviously a coach can't be cautiously pessimistic. There are coaches, however, who are pessimistic. Instead of "caution," however, they are quick to add "It's a young team, and they might come along faster than expected. We have a lot of potential." That is optimistic pessimism, yet another classic hedge. Coaches are never "recklessly optimistic," not because it is too smug an attitude, but because they don't want to look like fools. A politician always has some time to recover from "reckless optimism"—he is serving a term of office. In professional sports especially, one can lose one's job overnight. There are exceptions, of course. Billy Martin was recklessly optimistic before his team got walloped in the playoffs. Athletes are allowed to be reckless. It was Joe Namath's reckless optimism that won Super Bowl III. "Carefully hopeful" just wouldn't sound right. I realize that the two words are synonymous, but hope carries with it a link with faith and an association with pure chance, while optimism implies some sort of inside knowledge.

"We have momentum" is only applicable in certain situations. If a coach is

making his 1981 pre-season declaration, and the team was 0–12 in 1980, the only momentum "we have" is descending. And while almost every coach is perfectly capable of coming up with "My confidence, though restrained, is abiding," it would go against the image.

Cynics might be surprised, but "cautiously optimistic" is not always used to hedge one's bets, classically or otherwise. Modesty (albeit sometimes false) plays a large part. A coach who has a team that has been undefeated for two straight seasons, and has every single player returning for a third, has a perfect right to throw caution out the door, but a sense of propriety often prevents him. Either that, or he wants his opponents to think that he's worried (he doesn't fool them one bit, but they do it too).

I cringe whenever I type a release quoting the coach's "cautious optimism." Sometimes I change it to "careful," but the optimism remains. It is, after all, what the word implies. I have been "hopeful" about the Red Sox for fifteen years, but I have ceased to be optimistic, and I am old enough to no longer need caution.

> Nick Noble
> Sports Information Director
> Trinity College
> Hartford, Connecticut

P.S. Would "optimistically trepidate" be legitimate? Probably not. However cautious a coach or a politician may be, they are always brave, and trepidation carries the implication of fear.

---

caveat admonitor

The warning industry, always wearing a frown, reveals its character in its choice of words.

"Put Stamp Here," directs New York Telephone in that corner of the return-mail envelope that used to say, "No Postage Stamp Necessary if Mailed Within U.S." The Bellmen add the admonition: "The Post Office Will Not Deliver Mail Without Postage."

The same warning by which a company transfers a former cost to the consumer is put differently by Citibank, the bank with the fishy *i* in the middle of its name: "Affix Postage Here," the bank says in a high-falutin manner, adding in the bureaucratic passive, "Unstamped Mail Cannot Be Delivered."

Big fights occur in Washington over warnings. In 1965, Congress passed a bill requiring cigarettes to be labeled: "Caution: Cigarette Smoking May Be Hazardous to Your Health." The Federal Trade Commission and the tobacco companies wrangled over: (1) *Caution*—should it be the tougher *warning*? (2) The conditional *may be*—should it be the flatly certain *is*? (3) *Hazardous*—doesn't *dangerous* sound more ominous? The F.T.C. won; although its officials disclaim authorship of the changed warning, attributing it to nameless, faceless forces in the Congress, the wording now reads: "Warning: The Surgeon General Has Determined That Cigarette Smoking Is Dangerous to Your Health." Kentucky congressmen insist that the wording came from the F.T.C.

The difference is semantically significant: *Hazard* is from the French *hasard*, a crap game; *danger* is rooted in the Latin *dominium*, from the absolute power of a lord and master to do harm. With a hazard, at least you have a chance.

The federal government has fairly intelligible standards to go by in the language of warnings. Among toxicants like caustic soda (we used to call it lye, but Washington attorneys hate that word), a 1 percent to 2 percent solution for cleaning whitewall tires must say, "Warning: irritating to skin and eyes." A 2 percent to 10 percent solution of sodium hydroxide, because it is corrosive at that level, requires "Danger" and "Harmful If Swallowed" or even "May Be Fatal If Swallowed." A weak oven cleaner, with 2 percent sodium hydroxide, says, "Danger, May Cause Burns," but a strong one, near 10 percent, must say, "May Cause Severe Burns." Over 10 percent, it has to say, "Poison," and "Causes Severe Burns."

Though deregulation is rampant in Washington these days, the warning business remains in good shape. Product-safety types are looking for ways to get around language, the way international traffic signers do, with easily understandable symbols: an eye spurting tears, a man holding his nose, a gravestone with "R.I.P."—even back to the old skull and crossbones, where warning labels all began.

Warnings may be arguable, but they must never contain double meanings. Patricia Morrissey of Pennington, New Jersey, sends along a matchbook cover from ShopRite supermarkets which contains the sensible advice "Close Cover Before Striking," but then adds a curious admonition that can only widen the generation gap: "Please Keep Away from Children."

I do not believe highfalutin *is, or ever has been, hyphenated in any of its forms (-ten, hifalutin, etc.).*

> *Martin E. Kennedy*
> *Lambertville, New Jersey*

Thanks for mentioning the "warning" which appears on reply envelopes, insinuating that the customer or client is going to try to cheat by failing to put a stamp on it.

This infuriating practice affects me like getting lye in my eye. I will not use such an envelope. Many of them have computer marks on them, which doubtless help the recipient in opening and tabulating the enclosures. I am especially happy to use my own envelope in these cases.

Among the businesses and government departments which use the insulting rubric are the IRS, the Veterans Administration, my landlord, Macy's, Gimbels and Bloomingdale's.

I try to give my custom to decent department stores, like Altman's and Lord & Taylor, whose reply envelopes are free of any such insulting implication.

Arthur J. Morgan
New York, New York

chancellor's ex-checker

British-born Alistair Cooke, who interprets America better than any foreign correspondent since Tocqueville, earned his language credentials as a graduate student in American linguistics at Harvard. Accordingly, he is alert to an affectation known to grammarians as "the subversion of the schwa."

The schwa is a symbol in the International Phonetic Alphabet that looks like an upside-down *e*. The schwa is the sound of the *a* in *ago*, the *i* in *pencil*, the *e* in *taken*—that neutral sound in an unstressed syllable that is best expressed in letter form as *uh*.

English likes to change the pronunciation of vowels in unstressed syllables to the schwa: the *a* in *czar* sounds like "ah," but the second *a* in *Caesar*—in an unstressed syllable—is "uh." That's not a mistake—that's the way we speak the language.

Speakers overly concerned with correctness, however, err in disdaining the schwa. Mr. Cooke deplores the pronunciation "of radio and TV announcers and commentators who have decided that English, like Spanish, gives equal stress to all vowels. So that the commonest of all English *spoken* vowels (the neutral "or"—in the International Phonetic Alphabet, the upside-down *e*) is being banished."

Mr. Cooke noted, as have so many of us, the new pronunciation of the name of John Chancellor, anchorman of NBC Nightly News. For most of his life, Mr. Chancellor was called "Chance-luh." (The last syllable is a schwa.) But Mr. Chancellor always pronounced it with three syllables and the *r*, making it sound halfway between "Chance-uh-ler" and "Chance-uh-lor." Recently, the NBC announcers have been saying "Chance-uh-lorr." This prompted Mr. Cooke to write his journalistic colleague a friendly note pointing out that the "lorr" was ridiculous, and that he might as well start saying "thee Senn-a-torr fromm Oak-la-home-ah."

John Chancellor gives me this explanation: "For years, we simply said, 'Good night.' It wasn't until NBC changed the format, and I began signing off with my name, that the announcers caught on to the way I always pronounced my name.

"As you know," says the literate anchor, "announcers like to pronounce every syllable. As a result, the emphasis became a little too strong on the last syllable, even for me. I've talked to them about it, and the situation seems to have been resolved."

Let's listen closely this week. If the NBC announcer comes down hard on the "orr," get out your bumper stickers: "Save the schwa!"

Let us hope that you will not be accused of advocating the display of "Schwa" stickers . . . which sounds perilously close to "swastikas"!!

> Michael Canavan
> Brooklyn, New York

Anent your remarks concerning the "inverted-e (uh)," may I say merely this: You're so schwave!

> Gi Gi Shermin
> Hollywood, California

chasers

A *chaser*—a glass of water or soda to chase away the taste of a straight shot— is also called a *rinse,* and is used negatively in an ecclesiastical metaphor: *without the blessing.*

"A chaser usually refers to a beer rather than soda," observes J. Fialla Gamsu, and other bartender members of the Lexicographic Irregulars have pointed to *a ball and a beer* as a frequent combination. But most differ with her on the nature of chaser: "Your order of bourbon, neat, soda on the side," responds Doe Firth of Alameda, California, "would be called *shoot one, soda back.* "

Soda on the side is usually eastern; *soda back* is western and southern. *"Back* means any plain drink served in a short highball glass or old-fashioned glass and usually not charged for," reports Edward Glanzberg of Tucson, Arizona. "If a bar charges for a back, it shows a lack of class."

"In New England," writes Elizabeth Hill of the Naked i Cabaret in Boston's Combat Zone, "you may ask for a *tonic back,* but you'd better specify tonic water or you may receive a cola, ginger ale, or Sprite. In New York you could request a *soda back,* but once again, you may get any random soda 'pop' the bartender squirts out. A *tonic* and a *soda* are the same thing, in different places. Specify!

"A *splash* is never served on the side," she adds. "It is splashed over a shot of liquor on ice in a rocks glass."

When a soda or other soft drink is combined with a shot of liquor, that is called a *mixed drink,* no longer a *highball.* However, *mixer* is insider talk for another activity entirely.*

In Butte, Montana, a water chaser is known as a "ditch." Also, water in a drink is known as a "ditch." It's common for someone to order "a Brandy Ditch" (brandy and water).

Another term for a drink here is "Early Sage." That, translated, is "Early Times and water."

> Hiram Shaw
> Butte, Montana

A new fad drink has emerged in the Lansing area. The Kamikaze is a drink that is mixed in the drinker's mouth. The bartender pours triple sec, vodka and chartreuse directly into the mouth and then shakes the head back and forth to mix the drink. I know this sounds ridiculous but I swear it to be true.

> Edna Minche
> Lansing, Michigan

Chinese fire drill

The phrase *Chinese fire drill,* which means "a state of frenetic confusion or wild disorder," has puzzled me for years. I remember working at the White House when nearly every day seemed like a Chinese fire drill.

Where does it come from? National slurs are common in English—from *Dutch courage* (drunkenness) to *Mexican breakfast* (a glass of water and a cigarette) to *the English disease* (stagflation)—and the Chinese need not feel put upon. Perhaps the mysterious derogation comes from the vocabulary of the open road: In the December 1962 issue of *American Speech,* Don Dempsey, a former traffic

*See "behind the stick," "booze talk," "cocktail talk," "taking it neat," "taking it straight."

officer in the California Highway Patrol, compiled a glossary of traffic lingo and defined the term as "an accident scene of great confusion, such as a school-bus or cattle-truck upset."

Dr. Gerard Dalgish of Barnhart Books says that when he attended Lehman College in New York City in the late 1960's, the term was applied to a collegiate prank in which a group of students would jump out of a car as it stopped for a red light, run around the car several times, and jump back in just as the light turned to green.

Sol Steinmetz, the neologistic hawkshaw, observes that "it is interesting that motor vehicles are involved in both of these usages. But the relationship between vehicular confusion and a fire drill is obscure. I suspect, however, that the term originated in a disparaging ethnic joke . . . implied in the facetious use of *fire drill,* which is a very orderly and practiced activity, to mean a condition of great disorder and confusion." Why Chinese? "In the 1950's, when the term apparently originated, the Chinese were very much out of favor in this country."

Stuart Berg Flexner at Random House pursues the Chinese angle: "During World War II, several terms appeared, especially among British troops, using *Chinese* to imply disorganization, noise and confusion. Thus a *Chinese attack* meant a noisy, badly executed attack; the *Chinese national anthem* meant any loud explosion, especially of a bomb or shell not close enough to be taken seriously; and a *Chinese landing* sometimes meant a plane crash. Why *Chinese* took on this derogatory meaning of confused or laughably unsuccessful I don't know—perhaps because English-speaking servicemen found the Chinese language and ways of doing things very foreign and confusing."

None of these wordmen is (yes, none is) happy with having to speculate about the origin of the phrase. If a member of the Lexicographic Irregulars can find a citation before World War II, or has another theory, it will be welcomed. Whenever this question is asked at a dictionary headquarters, it causes much disorganized scurrying about, which some Chinese visitors have taken to calling "an American fire drill."

The phrase goes back rather further than the 1950's, since I first heard it used in the Marine Corps. in the early 1940's by old timers who had served in the 1920's and 1930's.

The full expression was "f——ed up like a Chinese fire drill" and along with it went the following (doubtless apocryphal) explanation for the phrase.

In the days of voluntary, and forced, Chinese immigration (remember the verb "to Shanghai"?) a group of Chinese laborers were on a ship bound for some destination in the New World, the nitrate fields of Chile, American railroads, or some such destination, and fire drills were held on the ship. The coolies would dip buckets into the sea, pass them from hand to hand and finally pour the water over the side.

One day a real fire broke out on the ship and the emergency procedures went into effect. However, the smoke from the hatches grew thicker and thicker as the fire spread. Then, a shift in the wind cleared the smoke, and revealed that the Chinese were pouring the buckets of water over the side as they had been trained to do in the drill.

John E. Lane
Ex-Sergeant, USMC
Professor, History Department
Long Island University
Brooklyn, New York

It should be easy to find citations of "Chinese fire drill" before World War II because the term was already a cliché in the decade immediately after World War I among school children in Brooklyn.

"Chinese fire drill" had the same root as "Chinese handball," and the root, as all roots should be, was in the ground. There was a general belief that if you dug a hole in the ground and kept going long enough you would come out in China. From this, "Chinese" came to mean "opposite" (the opposite point on earth, where people walk upside down).

The variety of handball we played in the limited sidewalk space usually available between a building and the curb required that the ball hit the ground before hitting the wall. This was the opposite of the rule in what we called "regular handball," thus the name "Chinese handball."

A fire drill was considered, as you pointed out, the epitome of "orderly and practiced activity." Any highly disorganized activity would be a "Chinese fire drill," not because the Chinese would do it that way but merely because it was the opposite.

Warren H. Goodman
Ossining, New York

I don't have the answer to your question about Chinese fire drills. However, I have long understood the adjective "Chinese" in this context to be a slur and to mean cheap, discounted, unreal, not genuine, not the real thing, ersatz, etc. "Chinese home run" was a common term for a homer down either foul line (about 259 feet, as I recall) at the Polo Grounds. Can't prove it, but I'm quite sure I used to read it in New York papers well before World War II.

John C. Thomas
Wilmington, Delaware

The term "Chinese Fire Drill" was common in the U. S. Navy during the 1930's. My father explained to me that the term originated in the U. S. Asiatic Fleet during that time, when Chinese were employed as cooks, tailors, and common laborers by the river gunboats stationed on the Yangtze River.

All U. S. Navy ships, including the river gunboats, have frequent fire drills, and the loud alarm bells appealed to the Chinese hired hands, who apparently thought that the noise was the important part of the drill and would join in by banging on pots, pans, garbage cans, and so forth, instead of joining with the American crew in fighting a pretend fire. Hence, in addition to meaning "something in great confusion," it must also include "with great noise, and somewhat awry from the original purpose."

Lybrand P. Smith
Torrance, California

"Chinese landing" is an ethnic allusion for something done wrong. When a warship is anchored or moored in a harbor or river it swings around the moor with the tide or current, always heading into the flow like a weather vane into the wind. An accommodation ladder is swung out over the side amidships to receive boats. The top stage or platform of the ladder is forward at an opening in the rail, usually on the ship's main deck. The ladder, really a stairway, descends at about a 45-degree angle rearward or aft. A lower stage or platform is at the bottom. Here boats hook on and discharge or embark passengers.

When a boat "makes" the accommodation ladder it comes alongside heading upstream in the same direction as the ship. This gives the coxwain steering the boat much better control and is much more seamanlike. In the Whampoa River off Shanghai and elsewhere in the Far East the native bumboats and water taxis would come alongside by the most direct route from the shore. This direction usually was with the current and so would result in a difficult landing headed downstream towards the ship's stern with the current speed added to that of the boat. Ship's boats in emergencies or by other necessity sometimes made this "wrong end to" approach to the accommodation ladder and the coxwain's comrades would jeer him for having made a lubberly "Chinese landing."

Brooke Nihart
Colonel, U.S. Marine Corps (Retired)
McLean, Virginia

A "Chinese landing" was never a crash landing, but a useful maneuver for alighting in a crosswind. By lowering the upwind wing of the aircraft and applying opposite rudder, the aircraft is in what is technically known as a slip, and drift due to crosswind is canceled. If the slip is maintained to touchdown, the aircraft lands One Wing Low. (Terrible pun, but the truth.)

Erik A. Eriksson
Lt. Col. USAF (Ret.)
Hicksville, New York

A "Chinese home run" is one or more of the following: a home run hit off the handle of the bat; a home run hit to the wrong field, that is, to the opposite side of the ball park from that to which the batter ordinarily hits; a very high pop fly home run that just drops into the stands.

Richard W. Boehm
Minister-Counselor
U.S. Embassy
APO New York

Both my husband and I were brought up on the water on the North Shore of Boston, but our fathers (who taught us to sail) did not know each other and lived in different towns. We are in our mid- to late fifties and learned to sail in the late 20's and early 30's. A "Chinese jibe" was a jibe you did not expect! The sudden force could break a mast or smash your head! By a good jibe you pull the main in flat to minimize the shock as you change course.

Anne L. Seamans
Marblehead, Massachusetts

Eric Partridge, in A Dictionary of Slang and Unconventional Usage *(1970 edition), lists "Chinese Rolls-Royce" as World War I Royal Army Service Corps slang for the Ford truck (presumably Model T) they used. Partridge also dates the pejorative use of "Chinese" to at least 1880.*

It really shouldn't be necessary to contrive explanations for the use of "Chinese" as a "mysterious derogation." As you've said, national slurs are common in both the King's and "colonial" English, and "Chinese" in this sense is of a kind with "gook" and "slope" applied to other Asiatic-Pacific groups.

The Englishman and the American (et al.) were in China as traders and missionaries, not as colonialist conquerors, and they found native customs and native ways of doing business un-Western and un-Christian.

"The heathen Chinese is peculiar," Bret Harte wrote in 1870 (albeit in another context), and the Chinese version of any Western experience, therefore, must have been inferior and worthy of derision. I think it is reasonable to assume that it would

not have been the gentleman factor, but his military hireling, who coined the colorful, derogatory locutions—which, of course, brings us back, at a reasonably early date, to "Chinese" fire drills, Rolls-Royces and whatever.

> Warren I. Louder
> Master Chief Journalist, USN (Ret.)
> Indianapolis, Indiana

cocktail talk

A couple of heavyweight minds have taken issue with my etymology of *cocktail*. In a gin-soaked piece of barroom slang, "Taking It Neat," I peremptorily dismissed all other speculation to decide upon *coquetel*, dispensed by the New Orleans apothecary Antoine Peychaud around the turn of the eighteenth century. Mr. Peychaud created his own brand of bitters and served his concoction in a *coquetier*, or eggcup, from which sprang *coquetel* and then *cocktail*.

"The problem with *coquetel*," writes Arthur Schlesinger Jr. from his Albert Schweitzer Chair at the City University of New York's Graduate School, "is that it must have flowed up north from New Orleans very quickly in order to become common usage in the English-speaking United States three years after the Louisiana Purchase."

Professor Schlesinger cites an 1806 use in the Hudson, New York, *Balance*: "*Cock tail*, then, is a stimulating liquor, composed of *spirits* of any kind, *sugar*, *water* and *bitters*—it is vulgarly called *bittered sling.* . . ." From this and other evidence, Professor Schlesinger staggers to the conclusion, which he freely asserts is a guess, that the word is not rooted in French, but in English. From England.

Gordon Messing, professor of classics and linguistics at Cornell University, also rejects the *coquetel* theory. He reviews the bidding as recounted by H. L. Mencken in his first supplement to *The American Language,* which included *cock-ale,* a mixture of chicken soup and ale, or a mixture of spirits and bitters fed to fighting cocks, and *cock-tailings,* a mixture of the leftovers, or tails, of various boozes thrown together and sold cheaply. Professor Messing puts forward his own theory: In British horseracing, docking a horse's tail has a long history. *To cocktail* has a 1769 citation meaning "to shorten a horse's tail."

The Messing Theory of Cocktail Coinage holds that in England, a cocktailed horse meant one "functioning in the role of a thoroughbred but lacking a pedigree," and its meaning extended to humans, as "a would-be gentleman." The horsy set used "cocktail" as an adjective for "pretentious, but inferior."

Writes Professor Messing: "At this point, may we not utter a faint but still a triumphant cry of 'eureka'? . . . Nothing, then, could be more natural than that some regular customer for straight spirits, or some barman inclined to dispense only straight spirits, should look down his (British?) nose at an unusual new mixed drink and condemn it as a *cocktail* (short for *cocktail drink*). If I am right, this momentous snub would have been first administered to the original cocktail around 1800, and it was not recorded for posterity."

Stuart Berg Flexner, Random House reference-department editor in chief, sticks to his gins: "It comes from French *coquetier,* eggcup, and dates back to the 1790's when the French-born apothecary Antoine Peychaud dispensed tonics of Sazerac du Forge Cognac and his own Peychaud bitters in eggcups, the concoction (used as a tonic for good health) then being called, after its container, a *coquetier.*"

But what of Professor Schlesinger's 1806 citation in the Hudson, New York, newspaper? Before the age of steamboats, there was no upward navigation on the Mississippi River—doesn't that suggest that the Hudson Valley newsman was uninfluenced by French coinages way down yonder in New Orleans?

"Hudson, New York, was then a major river port with easy access to other Hudson River towns," counters Flexner, "and to New York City and the world. If *cocktail* came from its New Orleans French form in the 1790's, as we say it did, then the first 1806 cite from New York State does not seem unlikely to me."

When distinguished sources disagree, somebody has to assume the role of Final Arbiter. I come down on the side of *coquetier* to *coquetel* to *cocktail.*

A sodden thought: If you think this controversy is a waste of time, and believe that great minds should stick to elevated notions, consider the significance of the coinage: Were it not for this word, nobody could put on a cocktail dress, go to a cocktail party, put feet up on a cocktail table, listen to a cocktail pianist, or order a nonalcoholic, bitters-less shrimp cocktail. The word goes to the heart of our way of life and deserves sober second thought.*

*See "behind the stick," "booze talk," "chasers," "taking it neat," "taking it straight."

If I may be allowed to dip another oar into the roiled drink, I would like to suggest another origin for the word "cocktail." This is "cooked ale," which could be either a mulled drink or a distilled liquor. Distillers refer to their mash, or wort, as "beer," and the distilling process itself as "cooking," and ale, after all, is almost the same kind of wort.

The legend of Elmsford should not be ignored, either. This has it that a barmaid in that Westchester town stirred a drink with a feather snatched from a cock's tail because no other barware was at hand. Since this is supposed to have happened shortly after the Revolutionary War, it is entirely plausible: Westchester County (N. Y.) had been overrun by troops of both opposing armies, as well as roving gangs of freebooters, so the wonder is that even a few items of hollowware survived. Also, and more to the point, on the question of facility of dissemination Elmsford wins hands down over New Orleans.

James Fanning
New Canaan, Connecticut

Your column about the origins of "cocktail" reminded me about another drink with an obscure name. It's "Cold Duck," which some enterprising vintners in America have succeeded in promoting as a first-quality product.

My 83-year-old father, who started in the food and drink business at age 14 in Germany, snickers at this. According to him, the drink was originally a mixture of leftover champagne and burgundy, salvaged from banquet tables (maybe even glasses) and mixed together. It was called "Kalte Ende," which means "Cold End," and implied a chilled finish for the leftovers. Some wag apparently discovered that a change in one letter produced "Kalte Ente," meaning "Cold Duck." It started to appear on menus as such before World War I, according to Max (Dad), much to the delight of teen-aged hotel apprentices in Berlin, who served the now-respectable dregs to snobs at full retail.

David Thomas
Raleigh, North Carolina

I was somewhat surprised that none of the speculators on the origin and coinage of the word "cocktail" seem to be aware of early mention of the word in the works of Washington Irving and James Fenimore Cooper.

In his History of New York *(1806), Irving wrote, "The roaring roystering English colony of Maryland . . . lay claim to be the first inventor of those recondite beverages cock-tail, stone-fence and sherry cobbler. . . ."*

Van Wyck Brooks, in the first volume of his magnificent history of American literature (The World of Washington Irving), *notes that Irving "was mistaken about the invention of the cocktail. It is usually attributed to the original of*

Fenimore Cooper's Betsy Flanagan in The Spy—*an inn-keeper of Westchester County, New York."*

William MacAdam
New York, New York

---

cologne, *see* send in the colognes

---

compare, *see* beyond compare

---

courtesan, *see* good courtesanship

---

crafty crafting

"This is a plea against the dreadful word *crafted*," writes Joseph Alsop, the retired columnist. "*Crafted* is meant to imply that porcelain, glass, furniture or metal-work has been largely handmade by a skilled craftsman. This always is a lie, unless the thing described is one of the inferior peasant manufactures which are still cheaper than machine products.

"Even in the countries these things come from," continues Mr. Alsop, who must not be confused with columnist Joseph Kraft in this matter, "the work of the really skilled craftsmen is all but exclusively for the local rich, while the peasant work that is bought by American importers in large part depends on the worst products of American industry, whether very sleazy rayon, or tenth-rate aniline dyes, or whatever. No really superior handmade product has ever been described as 'crafted,' at any rate to my knowledge."

The noun *craft* is from the Old English word for "force," with the underlying sense of "the cramping of muscles during the exertion of strength." This led to its meaning as a trade, particularly a line of work requiring manual dexterity or a knowledge of mechanics; a *craftsman* was an artisan, and bore the title proudly.

Crafts became allied to *arts:* A craftsman had an artist's skill without his artistry. But the adjective *crafty* had an established meaning of "cunning, sly, and deceitful," and the positive sense of *craftlike* never found a home in the language. Recently, however, the noun *crafts* has acquired a status more honorable than simply "not quite arts."

With the rise of consumer interest in handmade items of clothing and jewelry, *craftspeople* have emerged, and many are willing to use *craft* as a verb: "The word *craft* is a perfectly good verb," says Robert Ebendorf, professor of art at the State University of New York at New Paltz, and a leading goldsmith, "meaning to make something by hand, or to assemble parts for a handmade piece. I would also use the word in connection with writing—I see nothing wrong with a 'well-crafted speech.' "

Not all craftspeople would go that far: Jan Maddox, who teaches art at Montgomery College in Rockville, Maryland, says: "I'd say, 'It was a well crafted piece,' not, 'He crafted that.' "

Now we come to the object of Joe Alsop's scorn: *craft* revived as a verb to mean "construct with skill" and used by advertisers to hawk the "hand-fashioned." Writes Alsop:

"The few remaining English tailors who cut their suits individually for their customers are called in England 'bespoke' tailors, and . . . you would be thought mad if you said that such a suit was 'crafted.' But I did see the word used in a flier advertising one of the Hong Kong tailors who provide sailors with a suit, a girl, and a room for the weekend as a package deal. So it goes. . . . A word that implies a lie ought to be automatically banished from the English language. Instead, *crafted,* which began as an advertising man's word, has now crept into ordinary English, including the august columns of *The New York Times.* "

Guilty. A Reagan speech was described in these columns (only last August) as having been "crafted by Peter Hannaford." On the editorial page, the new verb was treated warily by a writer conscious of its trendiness: "Upscale plazas contain boutiques, not stores. And boutiques contain designer clothes, not dresses, and pasta machines, not hardwares. In an upmarket," the overworked-over editorialist complained, "whatever isn't gourmet is imported or crafted."

The people who despise the sneaky new verb are legion: *"To craft,"* snarls Bertram Lippman of Coram, New York, "had its provenience in trade, in the mercantile world of advertisers, the same people who say 'weatherproof' when they would like to say 'waterproof' but dassent. It is intended by the uncouth to imply 'classy.' But it does not mean *handmade*. . . . Would you be pleased if your columns were said to be crafted by you?"

This column is individually worked, shaped, sculpted,* hammered out, and fashioned by a contented columnist who thinks *craft* is a useful verb meaning "put together with care and skill" and who intends to use it without shame. But —always mindful of Alsopian ire—not too often. And not to imply, craftily, "handmade."

I am a painter with a recent M.F.A. degree from Pratt Institute. In my small circle of friends, effete intellectuals all, any use of the word "craft" has negative overtones. In fact, mention of "craft" or "crafting" will get one glazed-over stares. "Craft" is beneath notice. Very occasionally, "craft" will be used in an overblown phrase, for public consumption, to mean "power" or "mystery," tinged as the word has become with sorcery in bohemian circles.

We say neither "It was a well-crafted piece" nor "He crafted that." We say "It's technically competent," or "He's an excellent technician." Other synonyms for the quality of craft include "well-constructed," "finished," "tight" (usually a negative), even "He plays a good end game." All these usages imply an artistic aesthetic that puts a great deal of emphasis on the initial idea or concept for a piece.

This word usage is held by those with Marxist sympathies to come from an identification with the worker class, but I find it easier to explain it by remembering how many of our parents are engineers, architects, and plastic surgeons.

CA Hiscock
Dover, New Jersey

". . . would like to say 'waterproof' but dassent." Seems to me the word is spelled "dassn't" from "dass not" ergo "dares not" . . . no?

Ralph Bookman, M.D.
Beverly Hills, California

*See "exculpation."

creme, *see* beauty part

crispy commerce

A document has been leaked to me by a mole in the Department of Commerce. It is a memorandum on stylistic preferences from Jean Jones, who is director of something called "the Executive Secretariat." (So that's what happened to the typing pool. Who wants to be the lifeguard at the Big Shot's Typing Pool?)

Miss Jones is my kind of executive secretary. She quotes her boss, Commerce Secretary Malcolm Baldrige, as one who wants prose "halfway between Ernest Hemingway and Zane Grey with no bureaucratese." Let us go across the river and into the riders of the purple sage:

"Discontinue using the following words," she adjures her co-workers, and lists *viable, input, image, orient, maximize, therein;* instead of *delighted, happy,* and *glad* she suggests *pleased,* and urges *ongoing* be replaced by *is in process* or *is moving forward.*

She then plays "The Killers" to writers of the purple prose: "Discontinue using the following phrases: *prior to* (use *before*), *subject matter, very much, share* (as in *share your concern*), *as you know, more importantly* (use *more important*), *needless to say* . . ."

I'm with Executive Secretariat all the way. (Could it be that a great racehorse has, in retirement, become a business leader?) Hats off to the Commerce Department's timely assault on stereotypes and bromides. At the suggestion of my colleague Ed Cowan, I am pleased to add only this: Discontinue *discontinue.* Use *stop.*

I am sending you a spoof version which circulated this department when the first style guide was issued.

Such idiotic and childish efforts as this style guide only serve to deepen the malaise and bring into question Secretary Baldrige's priorities and goals.

Best of Luck with this one.

A Commerce employee (disgruntled at that)

MEMORANDUM FOR: Department Heads
FROM: Ron
SUBJECT: Presidential Stylistic Preferences

Platitudes and self-righteousness are key factors when preparing a letter for the President.

Here are some guidelines:

*Use the precise word or phrase.
     Rifle (not "gun")
     Pistol (not "gun")
     Pillow (not "holster")
     Mommy (not "Nancy")

*Discontinue the following words:
     Food stamps
     Human rights
     Black
     Woman
     Liberal
     Democrat
     Senility
     Old
     Kennedy

*Discontinue using the following phrases:
     All we are saying is give peace a chance
     No nukes
     Make love not war
     Save the whales

*Avoid redundancies, such as:
     Old President
     El Salvador, Viet Nam

Ron says, "In short, halfway between the Old Ranger and the Gipper."

cc: Gene Autry
      Roy Rogers
      Trigger
      Mommy

cushy, *see* trendy cushy

cut a deal

"Ronald Reagan and Gerald Ford have cut a deal," announced breathless floor reporters at the Republican convention of 1980. The deal, if such it ever was, found itself uncut in a few hours, but the phrase *cut a deal* outstripped *make a deal* in vogue use.

Why *cut*? One school of thought holds that the phrase comes from cards: "Cut [the deck] and deal." But James Howarth, a studio manager at the Chappell music company in New York, suggests it has roots, or cuttings, in the music business.

"In the old days, two or three years ago," writes Mr. Howarth, "an aspiring record producer would *meet* with so and so, *do* a deal, and *cut* a record. Since the music business, like the film business, has become an environment where the deal is often more creative than the product, one would now *sit* with so and so, *cut* a deal, and *do* a record." (Evidently yesteryear's *to take a meeting* has become *to sit with*.)

Recording engineers, accustomed to "cutting records" (from a lathe cutting a groove in lacquer), use the verb *to cut* metaphorically. Reports Mr. Howarth: "I will ask the comptroller to cut a check for the amount necessary." Similarly, military and naval types will recall the cutting of orders, which probably stemmed from cutting a stencil.

That sense of *cut* could be applied to a deal: "I think it goes back to the graphic arts," suggests Thomas Turley of Harrison, New York. "When copy was finally decided upon, it was cut into a metal plate either mechanically or by chemical action. The product of this effort was known as a 'cut' as was the process itself, 'to cut a plate.' In that sense, *cut a deal* means reducing a contractual exchange to fixed terms, written or otherwise."

Maybe. Or perhaps the provenance is more providential: In the Old Testament, covenants were "cut," and oath takers were sometimes smeared with blood from sacrificed animals. In Genesis 15:18 and 21:27 the Hebrew *karath b'rith* can be translated as "cut a covenant." Abraham concluded a covenant with God by cutting sacrificial animals in half.

Rabbi Andrew Baker of the American Jewish Committee takes it further: "The covenant *(bris)* they made with each other was in reality a deal cut. It was no careless drop of the knife that caused Abraham's circumcision (and that of Isaac and Ishmael, as well) to be its visible sign, for the literal translation of the operative Hebrew phrase is 'to cut a covenant.' . . . One might even suggest that the *mohel* (ritual circumciser) of successive generations is a sort of Jewish notary public whose job it is to insure that a proper deal is cut. Though a *bris* may not be a big deal, a deal it surely is."

I have a hunch we've gone the extra *mohel* on this, which is the unkindest cut of all. My vote goes to coinage by the record industry, although I'm willing to sit with anyone and do an etymology based on other specific citations.

I believe that "to cut a deal" has its origins in the practice of the legal scriveners of pre-19th-century England. It was their custom to engross (copy) a contract in two identical counterparts (copies) on one piece of parchment. The parties to the contract would sign both counterparts, and the parchment would be severed by cutting a wavy line between the two counterparts. The wavy line would provide evidence that the two documents were indeed halves of the original parchment document. Each part of the contract became known as an "indenture" because of the wavy line which separated it from its mate, a term which has survived as the name of certain types of contracts. The process of separating the indentures would, thus, have become known as "cutting a deal."

Robert S. Schwartz
New York, New York

My vote for the coinage of the phrase "cut a deal" most definitely does NOT go to the record industry. In the first place, no one ever "cut" a record on lacquer. The process was, since the first recording was made by Thomas Edison, that a record was made, or cut, in wax. This was transferred to an electroplated stamping plate, and then stamped into lacquer, or a lacquer-like substance. Later the first cut was made on an acetate-coated aluminum disk, and then stamped on a disk of a vinyl-like substance, a situation which still applies.

But since the early fifties all original recordings have been made on tape, which requires no cutting at all. This tape can be added to, subtracted from, fiddled with, diddled with, endlessly changed until the resident genius is satisfied. It is at this point that most of the deals are made. So why not say "tape" a deal? After the deal is made the tape is then cut onto a master, which is made into the stamping plate mentioned above, and everyone's off to the races.

I am 100% behind the school that says the phrase comes from cards. As a young boy growing up in California fifty to sixty years ago I played a lot of non-money poker. We would get together, and someone would say, "Let's cut for deal." We all cut the deck, and high card was dealer. Cut for deal means let's cut and see who deals. The very word "deal" comes from cards. The phrases "dirty deal," "shady deal," "dealing from the bottom of the deck" all have to do with a crooked card player, as "fair deal" applies to an honest one. The phrase "cut a deal" could be interpreted to mean "Let's cut the deck and begin to deal."

Everett S. Crosby
Germantown, New York

cut the mustard, *see* mustard cutters

depart department

In a piece defending the widespread misuse of *miss not being*, I wrote: " 'I will miss not being in Congress,' said Representative Elizabeth Holtzman, as she prepared to depart Washington."

Andrea Brunais, a reporter for the *Tampa Times*, quickly responded: "Depart Washington? Where was she going to depart it? In the middle?"

Miss Brunais pointed to the *Associated Press Stylebook:* "Depart. Follow it with a proposition. 'He will depart from La Guardia.' 'She will depart at 11:30 A.M.' Do not drop the preposition as some airline dispatchers do."

Guilty. Not even a contestant for Miss Not Being of 1981 would claim common usage to support the dropping of the preposition from *depart*. The only time that the word should be allowed to stand naked in the language is in an evocative archaism, like "He departed this life." If you want to say "He departed hastily," use *left* instead.

"Instead of preserving the integrity of the language," chastises my Florida correspondent, "you are contributing to its corruption." She then adds the crusher: "Shame!" That's de part I like.

I tried following some linguistic advice that you offered via The Associated Press Stylebook.

Not only did it not work but it resulted in my receiving a severe beating at the hands of a female acquaintance.

The circumstances were these: I had a date with a lady friend that very Sunday night. I was anxious to have a good time because I was leaving on a long, boring business trip early the next morning.

As I was bidding her good night, it occurred to me that this was an excellent opportunity to apply your admonition in the segment entitled "Depart Department."

I simply said, "I'm departing at 7 o'clock tomorrow morning. May I sleep with you tonight?"

The beating followed. Never again will I follow "depart" with a proposition.

> *Milton Schorr*
> *Syosset, New York*

Dear Bill,

The AP Stylebook that Andrea Brunais cites errs in conflating two very different ways of omitting prepositions. The omitted preposition in "She will depart 11:30 A.M." doesn't have any particular relationship to depart *(I take it that the AP guru would be no happier with "We arrive 11:30 A.M." or "The class begins 1:30 P.M."). These examples illustrate an extension of something that English allows under a rather odd set of conditions, namely omission of the preposition from time adverbs. Whether omission of the preposition is impossible, optional, or obligatory depends on fine details of the way in which the time is expressed, and synonyms sometimes diverge from one another (e.g.* time *and* occasion*):*

He'll arrive in March.
*He'll arrive March.
He'll arrive on Tuesday.
?He'll arrive Tuesday.
He'll arrive (on) Tuesday morning.
He'll arrive in Paris (in) the second week of April.
He'll arrive in Paris (*in) next week.
He'll arrive in Paris (?in) the same week that I will.
>   *in which I will.*
On that occasion/*time, I felt uncomfortable. (At that time involves a different meaning of time*.)*
That time/*occasion, I felt uncomfortable.

Since there is no apparent generalization as to when the preposition in time adverbs is omitted, I don't find it surprising that there is some fluctuation with regard to when people omit it, and I don't see anything horrible in its omission in sentences like "She will depart 11:30 A.M.," since the time expression could be nothing other than a time adverb and there is no ambiguity as to what the understood preposition is when the adverb refers to a point rather than an interval of time. Perversely, the language not only tolerates but practically demands ambiguity in the case of expressions like next week that refer to time intervals: "He'll be in Paris next week" can indicate either that he will spend (the whole of) next week in Paris or that he will be in Paris sometime between Sunday and Saturday, yet the language does not allow one to use the prepositions that would remove the ambiguity:

*He'll be in Paris for next week.
*He'll be in Paris in/during next week.

The omission of from after depart is something quite different. The from is never omitted when depart has derived senses like the following:

He departed from his prepared text at several points.
They departed from their usual practice and allowed us to join them.

The core sense of depart is only loosely paraphrasable as leave, since leave but not depart can be used for temporary absences:

Don't leave the house for even a minute!
?Don't depart from the house for even a minute!
*Don't depart the house for even a minute!

One can leave persons, but one can depart or depart from only places:

John has just left his wife.
??John has just departed from his wife.
*John has just departed his wife.

("places" here must be interpreted broadly enough that milieus count as places, as in "John has departed from academia"). [By the way, the non-synonymy between depart and leave is good reason for me to be appalled at your suggestion that one should use leave instead of depart when there is no prepositional phrase: by following your advice, one loses a simple way of indicating that the absence is to be permanent and receives nothing to compensate for that loss. Are you the first person ever to object to "He departed hastily"?] For depart but not leave, the place must be one that the person had been at on a permanent basis, e.g. one can leave a room but not depart from a room. After this much rumination over depart, I ought to be able to put my finger on some difference in meaning between depart Washington and depart from Washington that proves that your original choice

of words in the item on Elizabeth Holtzman was correct, but so far all I've been
able to come up with is a vague feeling that omitting the preposition makes the
departure more permanent.

> *With best wishes,*
> *Jim McCawley*
> *Department of Linguistics*
> *University of Chicago*
> *Chicago, Illinois*

depression

When Alfred Kahn, Jimmy Carter's chief inflation fighter, used the politically taboo word *depression* in a statement from the White House, the economist was pounced upon by assorted communicators and soothing-sayers; as a result, the hapless but happy man pledged to substitute the word *banana* for *depression* in any future economic message.

Here we are, five years later, and many people fear a deep, full-fledged banana. In fact, some who write about the economy (an "economic writer" is a writer who uses as few words as possible) have broken the taboo: We are witnessing a boom in the outspoken usage of the word *depression*.

"I don't want to start a panic," Edward Yardeni of E. F. Hutton & Company told *The Wall Street Journal* (when Yardeni speaks, everybody panics), "but I think there's a 30 percent chance of a depression occurring."

This unabashed public use of the dirtiest word in economics led to its prompt adoption by the media. ABC's Sam Donaldson asked Senator Edward Kennedy if "we are going to tip over into a real bread-line depression," receiving the reply, "If you asked any auto worker out in Detroit, they would say that we are in a depression at the present time." Asked the same question, another potential Democratic presidential candidate, Robert Strauss, said, "We've got one foot in a depression in some sectors."

The tossing about of such a word is both political and linguistic news. When the word was flung at Franklin Roosevelt during the mid-1930's, he waggled a finger at opponents and told them not to speak of rope in the house of a man who had been hanged: "If I were a Republican leader speaking to a mixed audience, the last word in the whole dictionary that I think I would use is that word *depression.*" About that time, *recession* came into being, replacing the odious *depression,* a word that Henry Vansittart first applied to a slowdown in 1793, and that Aldous Huxley resuscitated in 1934.

Prof. John Kenneth Galbraith informs me that the word first used widely in this regard was *panic;* Karl Marx later preferred *crisis;* ultimately, a much softer term—*depression*—was chosen, so as not to panic the crisis-prone. However, the euphemism *depression* came to be remembered as the moniker for the terrible times it described, and thereby gained a fearsomeness of its own. "A depression," says Dr. Galbraith, "is something that in social memory has taken on the dimension of a disaster."

Since then, hard times have been euphemized as "rolling readjustments," "crabwise movements," and "extended seasonal slumps," but it seemed that linguistic order was just around the corner when the National Bureau of Economic Research defined a recession as "a recurring period of decline in total output, income, employment and trade, usually lasting from six months to a year and marked by widespread contractions in many sectors of the economy." Journalistic shorthand reduced that definition to "a two-quarter decline in gross national product."

In 1970, Dr. Sol Fabricant at the N.B.E.R. tried a refinement to describe a time when the economy grows at a below-normal rate: a "growth recession." But since *recession* had the connotation of downturn, Dr. Herbert Stein, then chairman of the Council of Economic Advisers, satirized it with this imaginary conversation:

STEIN: That's a handsome dog you have there, Sol.
FABRICANT: That's not a dog. It's a horse.
STEIN: But, Sol, it's so small.
FABRICANT: I know. It's a growth horse.

So we see how the stigma of hard times attaches to every euphemism designed to sweeten those times. But what about "a real bread-line depression," one that will—in the phrase Treasury Secretary George Humphrey used in the 1950's— "curl your hair"? Shouldn't the word have some specific meaning?

The Depression—capitalized, sometimes with *Great* added—refers to the panic, crisis, paralysis, and unemployment of 1929–33, sometimes merged with the follow-up slump of 1936–37. To define "a" depression—small *d*—calls to leading economists elicited these definitions, along with disclaimers of any predictions of disaster:

Alan Greenspan: "A depression is either a 12 percent unemployment rate for nine months or more, or a 15 percent unemployment rate for three to nine months."

Richard Rahn: "I would consider the country to be in a depression if there were a sustained, major drop in G.N.P. for more than one year, combined with unemployment well into the double-digit range for an extended period of time."

Arthur Laffer: "A depression is when an economy, through a sequence of degenerative events, finds itself literally on the wrong end of the Laffer Curve."

Robert Lekachman: "When unemployment touches 10 percent and stays there for at least a year."

From the man who fearlessly used the term before it became voguish—Prof. Alfred Kahn of Cornell—comes this definition: "In the real world, there is no clear line between recession and depression; there is a continuum. If unemployment is above 10 percent, and all the other requirements of recession are met —that is, if we have two quarters of consecutive decline in real G.N.P.—then we've got a depression."

bill—

al kahn, to my best recollection, was using "banana" in place of "recession," not "depression." just goes to show how far the language has been debased, with society now demanding a euphemism for a euphemism.

> *bob hershey,*
> *an economic writer*
> [The New York Times]
> *Washington, D.C.*

A recession is when your friend loses his job; a depression is when you lose your job.

> *Murray Illson*
> The New York Times *(Ret. '78)*
> *New Rochelle, New York*

---

disparadoes

It's always the same: *Disparate* is being used when *different* is meant. The high-domed *disparate* has worked its way into the Top Forty of Academic Voguisms, passing *quintessential, fragile,* and *resonant,* and may be on its way to challenging *perceived.*

Disparate (accent on the first syllable) has done to *different* what *one time* has done to *once:* It has shouldered aside a simple word and replaced it with a suitably off-beat one. *Wall Street Journal* writers have adopted it, sometimes correctly, and I misused it recently in writing of "such disparate souls as Anthony Lewis and I."

Difference is rooted in "carried apart," and means "not alike"; *disparate* shares a root with *separate* and most often has meant "unequal." I did not mean that fellow pundit Anthony Lewis and I were unequal: I meant only that we were markedly dissimilar. A more precise formulation about our differing views would have called forth *diverse,* meaning "conspicuously different," or *divergent,* "going off in different directions."

Disparate is misused when intended to mean "different as hell," or, as the kids say, "real-real different": Careful writers use it only to denote inequality, or an absence of any relationship. There is a distinct ("with a separate identity") difference between *different* and *disparate*—don't fuzz 'em up.

Disparate *is gaining over* different *in some contexts for a different reason. In sensitive contexts (such as your own "A. Lewis" example),* disparate *has a distinct edge over* different: *it implies* "virtually *different" (rather than "both different from someone/something else"). You should have left your sentence as is.*

Contrary to your assertion, disparate *does not imply any more inequality than* different. *However, as sometimes happens with derivatives, its derivative* disparity *does imply inequality quite strongly, and should be avoided when any dissimilarity etc. is intended.*

Miroslav Rensky
Brooklyn, New York

divers diving in

President Reagan's State of the Union address was noteworthy to writers because (1) the speechwriter, Anthony Dolan, was given a seat in the First Lady's section of the House gallery, the best treatment ghosts have received since the Kennedy presidency, and (2) the President took an unequivocal position on the *dived-dove* controversy.

"We saw the heroism of one of our young government employees, Lenny Skutnik," said the President, looking toward his wife's section of the gallery, where Mr. Skutnik stood, looking even prouder than Mr. Dolan, "who, when he saw a woman lose her grip on the helicopter line, dived into the water and dragged her to safety."

What is the past tense of *dive*? Does the verb follow the example of *drive*, the past tense of which is *drove*, or does it take the lead from *connive*, which moves to *connived*?

For the answer, place yourself in the water, awaiting rescue; when your rescuer swims up, ask him: "How did you enter this body of water?" He will surely reply, "I didn't think about it, I just dove in." That is the way most people talk; *dove* is common usage. If he says, "I dived in," you are being saved by a pedant and you should start composing your expression of gratitude with care.

Dove is, however, an aberration, almost a mistake, based on the past tense of *drive*. When you recite the present–past–past participle of *drive*, you say *drive-drove-driven*, but when you plunge into the same for *dive*, you do not say *dive-dove-diven*. If anybody said to me, "I have diven into the water to save you," I would thrash about wildly, hoping for a more regular rescuer. The past participle of *dive* is indisputably *dived*, showing that the odd past tense *dove* is a quirk of usage.

On a formal occasion, such as an address to the Congress, formal usage is called for: Thus, Mr. Reagan's use of *dived in* was correct. On informal occasions, such as rescues, or in metaphors like "He dove into a sea of controversy with the New Federalism," the more natural *dove* is correct. Each has its proper moment; I'm not a hawk on *dove*.

You are not alone in asserting that dived *is higher style than* dove. *Margaret Nicholson calls* dove *"colloquial" and Eric Partridge stigmatizes it as "dialectical" although he allows that it is merely colloquial in America. However, I think that you misstate the case when you argue that* dove *is formed by analogy with* drove. *Admittedly, the past tense* dove *should be accompanied by* diven *but* dive *is a child of two parents so it should not surprise us that one of its brothers resembles the mother.*

Dive *comes from Old English* dȳfan *(to submerge) and from Old English* dū-fan *(to dive). These words gave rise to overlapping Middle English* diven *and* duven. *The first gave us* dive *and* dived *and very likely the second gave us* dove. *(*Dūfan *is, in fact, a strong verb with past participle* dofen.*)*

I think you're right on a different score, though. Dove *could not have survived in modern usage without the help of the (false) parallel* drove.

Michael Engber
New York, New York

The paradigm dive dove *is not "an aberration . . . based on the past tense of* drive." *Both verbs were "strong" or "ablaut" verbs in Anglo-Saxon—that is to say, the past tense was formed by a change in vowel. Some of these verbs have become weak in modern English, such as* bide bided. *On the other hand, some verbs have both strong and weak forms:* shriven *and* shrived; molten *and* melted; swollen *and* swelled. *In addition, there are a few verbs that retain doublets with different meanings, such as* seethed *and* sodden. *Although most dictionaries prefer* dived *to* dove, *this is not for historical reasons.*

Andrew Mayer
Bethesda, Maryland

divers opinions

The Civil War (sometimes referred to as the War of Northern Aggression) goes on.

"I'm surprised you didn't look before you leaped into your discussion of *dived* and *dove*," writes Allan Metcalf of the American Dialect Society. "It happens to be one of the rare instances where variation in a verb form is a matter of geography uncomplicated by social class or degree of education.

"In the eastern states, at least, the northern form is *dove;* the southern form, *dived*," reports the dialectitian at MacMurray College, Jacksonville, Illinois. He adds: "Washington happens to be one of the few places where both forms are prevalent, so it's not surprising you'd come out with a different sense of the situation."

Excuse me for pointing out the self-hoisting petard you planted in your reference to me as a dialectitian. *We prefer the suffix* ologist, *logically enough, although*

sometimes an ician *is legitimately applied. But* Titian*? No, I think I'm more of
a dialect Rembrandt.*

Allan Metcalf
Jacksonville, Illinois

*In reporting the sound comment of Allan Metcalf, secretary of the American
Dialect Society, you called him a "dialectician." I suspect that Socrates, Hegel, and
Karl Marx, promoters of dialectic, might be offended at this usage. Two series of
words run as follows: the dialectologist studies dialectology in treating the dialectal
materials of dialect, while the dialectician studies dialectics in treating the dialectical materials of dialectic. Therefore Allan Metcalf should be called a "dialectologist." It is true that in journalese some night-club comedians have been called
"dialecticians," but this is a departure from the usage current in knowledgeable
circles.*

Allen Walker Read
Professor Emeritus of English
Columbia University
New York, New York

do you speak aspic?

A harangue of mine about the prevalence of *mode* in bureaucratic speech (we
are never merely haranguing, but we are in a haranguing mode) attracted more
examples of the language of aspic.

Ellen Weber, of the New York City Technical College, reports that a dean recently wrote this sentence to a job applicant: "As you probably know, the college and the state are not in what I would call a hiring pattern." A simple "are not hiring" no longer suffices; the offending academic is in a circumlocution pattern, taken from the airlines' "landing pattern."

Meanwhile, down at Cape Canaveral, the director of the Kennedy Space Center, Richard Smith, registered his shock in swaydo-technotalk at a strike by union employees: "I am shocked that the walkout took place," expostulated Mr. Smith, and then slipped into an aspic locution mode: "They put us in a surprise condition." Presumably, everything at the Space Center is in a certain condition of readiness, and "in a surprise condition" fits spaced-out speech rhythms more than the old-fangled "They surprised us."

In this language of aspic, the speaker jellies himself, or places himself in a jellied state: All places are "in the wherever *area,*" and all action takes place "in a whatsis *situation*" or stands "in a whosis *posture*" or "a closing-down *mode,*" "something or other in *nature*" or "in *character.*" It is enough to put a listener in an apoplectic situation condition area, purple in nature.

We can never learn the language of aspic—instead, we hang suspended in a learning *experience.*

doing my thing

A few nitpickers have chosen to challenge my etymology of *do your thing,* which led to *do your own thing.* In a piece called "Freaking In," I credited Ralph Waldo Emerson with the coinage, from his essay on "Self-Reliance" in 1841; doubters have written to complain the phrase is not in their edition.

Joel Myerson, professor of English at the University of South Carolina, whose forthcoming *Ralph Waldo Emerson: A Descriptive Bibliography* is eagerly awaited, can set us all straight.

These two sentences appeared in the first editions of his essays, both in America and England: "But do your thing, and I shall know you. Do your work, and you shall reinforce yourself." Then, in 1903, an editor got to work, changing "thing" in the first sentence to "work."

Why? It seems that in one 1839 journal entry, Emerson wrote "do your thing"; in another entry, and three times later, he wrote "do your work." Says Professor Myerson: "Because both readings appear in Emerson's journals, the editors of the Harvard edition of *Essays: First Series* (1979) have accepted the change from 'thing' to 'work' as by Emerson. I agree with their view."

O.K. Let's grant that Emerson was the sort who liked to rewrite his lectures and to cross his transcendental *t*'s; let's say that he wanted "do your thing" changed to "do your work." The fact is he wrote "do your thing"; it appeared in the first edition; that makes him the coiner. Nitpickers—do your work. I will do my thing.

In the thirteenth century in southern France, inquisitors questioned a very large number of persons, asking about heretics (Cathars or Albigensians and Walden- sians) they had encountered and in what circumstances.

The gist of the replies made in the vernacular was written down by a scribe in a kind of Latin; these were collected in inquisitorial registers. Some of these survive in the multivolumed collection of manuscripts, known as Collection Doat, *in the Bibliothèque nationale, Paris.*

In an interrogation on September 6, 1243, Jean Blanc of Hautpoul (Johannes Blanch) is recorded as saying that he had seen a certain heretic in a house and after the conventional greeting left the house to go to work.

The entry reads: ivit foras facere factum suum,—*"went outside to do his thing."* *It is in* Doat, *Vol. 23, folio 243.*

Walter L. Wakefield
Potsdam, New York

doing your own thing

In ascribing the derivation of *do your own thing* to Ralph Waldo Emerson (in "Freaking In" and "Doing My Thing"), I stirred a hornet's nest of Chaucer's *Canterbury Tales* enthusiasts. Among the citations, from "The Merchant's Tale": "Hoom to hir houses lustily they ryde, / Where as they doon hir thynges. . . ." From "The Knight's Tale": "Two fyres on the auter gan she beete, / And dide hir thynges. . . ." From "The Nun's Priest's Tale": " 'No dreem,' quod he, 'may so myn herte agaste / That I wol lette for to do my thynges.' "

Meanwhile, doing his own thing on early usages of locutions thought to be modern, Donald Kelley of New York City sends along *right on* as spoken by Anthony in Act III, Scene 2 of *Julius Caesar:*

For I have neither wit, nor
words, nor worth,
Action, nor utterance, nor
the power of speech
To stir men's blood. I only
speak right on. . . .

For not doing your homework in checking the spelling of a leading character in two of Shakespeare's plays, write 100 times:

Friends, Romans and countrymen, lend me your ears; my name is Mark Antony, or Marcus Antonius, as listed in the Dramatis Personae, but never Anthony, as it appeared in the column "On Language" in the Sunday Times. . . .

Solomon R. Kunis
Bellerose, New York

dollar sign, farewell

Have you noticed the way dollar signs have been disappearing lately? As the money supply goes up, the dollar-sign supply goes down.

Flip through the pages of this newspaper and look at the retail advertisements. It makes a satisfying noise and is instructive: Surreptitiously, more and more stores are dispensing with dollar signs.

"Pure cashmere, pure luxe by Ciao," advertises Lord & Taylor, concluding with this *arrivederci:* "Reg. 240.00, 167.99." And this from Bonwit Teller, advertising Bogatin blouses: "Jewel-necked, puffed at the shoulders . . . 70.00." To overcome the chafing of jewels on the neck, Bloomingdale's offers Max Factor's "Living Proof Skin Nurturing Concentrate, 9 vials, 35.00."

On the other hand, retailers from Cartier and Macy's use dollar signs in their ads, resisting the tide. What's going on?

"People know what we are talking about without the dollar sign," says Eleanor Koslossky at Bloomingdale's. "Besides, once you use it in an ad, you have to use it every time a price appears, and then you'd have dollar signs all over the place."

Bonwit Teller agrees with the practice, but for a different reason: "Ours was a visual decision not to use the dollar sign," says Grace Perez. "It is easier to see the prices without the dollar sign."

H'm. B. Altman has another reason: "We do not use dollar signs in our ads because the typeface that we use—'souvenir style'—has fat and ugly dollar signs," says Mary Irish, whose eyes smile only at slim, chic dollar signs. "Rather than destroy the looks of the ad, we simply don't use the sign. There is nothing pretentious about it."

Hah! The defensiveness of that explanation offers the clue we're seeking: Dropping the sign, the sign-droppers rightly worry, may be seen as an act of pretension, an aloofness to such crass matters as dollars, a whisper of price to those too refined to listen to such trifles shouted out in print.

"I suspect the elimination of the dollar sign is guided by an ill-advised sense of 'elegance,' " writes Claudio Campuzano, of New York City, "the same sense of 'elegance' that leads to the present use of so many euphemisms."

The stores which do use the crass, noisy, pushy emblem that signifies they sell goods for (ugh) money strike no poses of truth-in-labeling or assertiveness in the marketplace. On the contrary, Saks Fifth Avenue's Elaine Garefolo says, "Saks uses the small dollar sign because that is the typeface we have. There are no psychological implications." And Judy West of Wallachs (there are no male executives anywhere in retail advertising) illustrates the practicality of that company's choices: "It is our policy to use the dollar sign when we have an even-numbered item—that is, instead of the decimal point and following zeros. When there is a price with cents following the decimal point, then we do not use the dollar sign."

At Brooks Brothers, Mildred Schlesinger sounds like Brooks Brothers: "We use the dollar sign because we do everything the traditional way. I hadn't even noticed that the other stores had dropped theirs."

What does this split decision on dollar signs signify? Is it a space-age space-saver or an opulent-era op-out? I think Mr. Campuzano has a point. The absence of the dollar sign is a little la-di-da. It should not be so costly to a store's prestige to proclaim the cost of its wares, and it might even tell the international traveler something he needs to know.

The dollar sign itself, now derogated as fat and ugly by the unforgiving Mary Irish of Altman's, has its origin cloaked in controversy. A prevailing belief is that the sign is derived from a *U* superimposed on an *S,* with the bottom of the *U* worn off by time. This is almost surely wrong. So is the notion that it was invented by Thomas Jefferson when he proposed the dollar as the American unit of money.

One theory holds that it comes from an abbreviation of the peso. A more intriguing theory suggests that the "pillars of Hercules," symbols of strength and power, which appeared on ancient Tyrian coins, are the source of the sign. These pillars, entwined by a scroll, reappeared on Spanish "pieces of eight" and later became the symbol for both the peso and the dollar.

I think it is a graceful symbol, with ancient roots and a mysterious history, as beautiful and significant as anything else that appears in a retail ad. Besides, it helps the reader to know that the number the advertiser is whispering isn't the amount of zlotys that the purchaser is expected to pay.

Doesn't "amount" usually refer to quantity of an unstated measure? I believe common usage would dictate "number of zlotys" or "amount" or even "amount in zlotys," but not "amount of zlotys."

Kenneth Sax
Chicago, Illinois

*I thought you might be interested to learn that this and other items of punctuation are being put to use in computer programs. Certain characters, !, *, $, seldom appear in isolation, at the beginning of words, or in the case of the $, alone or without the numerals immediately following. This quality makes them extremely useful to programmers as immediate identifiers for program names, instructions, and so on.*

What may be of interest to you is the names that change in verbal shorthand for these characters as a result of their introduction in speech. "Exclamation point" becomes "bany," "asterisk" becomes "star," but "dollar sign," to my knowledge, has yet to acquire a monosyllabic handle. I have been using "buck" locally but don't particularly like it.

Michel Ridgeway
Cornwall, New York

For shame, oh, for shame! Before making Mary Irish sound like a pompous fool by quoting her on something she never said ("the dollar sign is fat and ugly"), could you not have read the first part of your column to discover what she did say ("the typeface that we use . . . has fat and ugly dollar signs")?

There's a whopping great difference there, no? (Perhaps like the difference between saying I have accused you of foolishly misquoting your own column and saying I have accused you of earning your living by misquoting fools. Or something.)

To say that Mary Irish has derogated the dollar sign as fat and ugly is a bald-or bold-faced lie, which raises a question: bald or bold? I rather like it both ways. But it's sloppy work, either way, and her reaction to your apology will tell us just how unforgiving Mary Irish really is.

Jim Butler
New York, New York

You are correct in raising the question as to the disappearance of the dollar signs —but you didn't go far enough! As a corollary to the dollar sign item the proliferation of the numerals 99 should follow.

Possibly beginning with the mass emigration into the United States circa 1880 the merchants conceived the ploy of persuading the foreigners who had not yet absorbed the nuances of American monetary system that an item priced at (e.g.) 89.99 was cheaper than a competitor's $90.00. (Note the absence of the $ sign.) Look at the pricing system today and you'll see the same implied presumption. It's as though today's merchants were of the same low opinion of their customers as their predecessors were of the immigrants a century ago!

I am probably the world's worst customer—I refuse to buy anything that has the exponent 99 attached to a larger whole dollar. I don't like to be considered naive or easily fooled. I realize I am a kook in this matter, so be it—some years ago I went into a piano store and selected one, asking the price. When the salesman said

499.99, I told him, "I'm going to leave and come right back. When I ask you the price of this instrument saying I want to buy it, if you say $500.00 you've made a sale." I did, and believe it or not the man COULD NOT SAY $500.00! He repeated that "it's only 499.99"!

A. F. Heffelfinger
Tucson, Arizona

You mention two possibilities about the origin of the dollar mark. You may be interested to know that the origin of the dollar mark has been researched thoroughly and is summarized in A History of Mathematical Notations *by Florian Cajori.*

Cajori demonstrates, at least to my satisfaction, that the origin of the dollar mark is the notation p^s for pesos. I think you were wrong to describe this possibility as a theory.

Cajori also mentions the pillars of Hercules theory but dismisses it along with other "flights of fancy."

C. T. Fike
Bronxville, New York

Double-A rating

Somebody in the National Collegiate Athletic Association is trying to push all of us around. The Sanhedrin of intercollegiate sports has whispered "86-Hup!" to at least one television network—a signal for linguistic dictation.

Watching a professional football game on CBS the other day, I heard an announcer giving a promotional plug for a collegiate game say: "N.C. Double-A. football! Wait a minute. We're supposed to say 'N.C.A.A.,' aren't we? O.K.— N.C.A.A. football!"

Nothing is wrong with "N.C.A.A.," each initial pronounced individually, nor is there anything wrong with "N.C. Double-A.," which is the way most people I know pronounce it. But there is a great deal wrong with any organization's issuing instructions to impressionable television continuity directors about the "right" way to pronounce two letters in succession.

"We do request that the networks use 'N.C.A.A.,' " admits David Caywood, the organization's public-relations director. "This is not a new policy. We do not call the networks every time an announcer says 'N.C. Double-A.,' or 'N.C. Two-A.' " "N.C. Two-A." was a new one to me, which I instantly put out of my mind lest I blurt out the wrong form on some television show, thereby corrupting the pronunciation of generations of Americans.

"The N.C.A.A. prefers to be referred to as the N.C.A.A.," says David Pickle, editor of the *N.C. Double-A. News*, "primarily for the sake of consistency. No formal rule. I believe that instructions to announcers for N.C.A.A. basketball are to say 'N.C.A.A.'—no memo, just an unwritten, understood preference."

At the networks, NBC and ABC press representatives say that any instruction to announcers to tilt against "Double-A." is news to them. But at CBS, Jay Rosenstein, director for sports information, says carefully, "The N.C. Double-A. has given us no *instructions* on the way to say its title." He emphasized the word "instructions," which mediamen hate to take. He then reverted to the impenetrable passive: "It is *understood* that the preferred use is N.C.A.A." Then out came the smoking pistol: "CBS Sports has instructed its announcers to use the preferred usage."

Hah! CBS Sports, which has just signed up with the N.C. Double-A., is eager to please the linguistic bureaucrats who are dribbling and lateraling with the American public's right to pronounce the same two letters next to each other with the idiomatic "double."

"It's the same as when Tony Dorsett indicated that he prefers his name to be pronounced 'Dor-SETT,' " the CBS spokesman offered in extenuation. "He didn't issue instructions that we have to follow, but since that is the way he prefers it, we pronounce it that way. Similarly, it is understood"—there is that passive construction again, as if orders come from never-never land, or double-never land—"that the N.C.A.A. has always been the N.C.A.A., and we, therefore, instruct our announcers to say it that way. Nobody from the N.C.A.A. gave anyone instructions of any kind."

Certainly the Dallas Cowboys' scatback Tony Dorsett has the right to ask that his name be accented on the last syllable, and courteous speakers will oblige. Similarly, Mike Taliaferro, a former quarterback, wanted to be known as Mike *Tolliver*, which is an age-old stretch of the pronunciation rules; nevertheless, announcers went along. I would draw the line at calling Joe Theismann "Sammy Baugh," however.

Organizations should tread very lightly when it comes to expressing "preferences" to other organizations seeking good financial relations with them. Somehow, preferences get translated into instructions, written or otherwise, and then broadcasters find themselves involved in a vast, dark conspiracy to denude the language of a simple pronunciation form. When a researcher of mine spoke to an assistant to fearless Howard Cosell at ABC, asking about the forbidden Double-A., the sportscaster's aide replied cryptically: "I realize it is a simple question that you are asking. But Howard decided that he did not want to respond to the question." H'm.

Dear Bill:

I seem to recall, coincidentally enough, that Joe Theismann was pronounced Joe Thee*smann at his advent to the campus at Notre Dame but as his prowess soon prevailed the drumbeaters arranged for it becoming* Thighs*mann so as to better associate with* Heisman, *of the trophy of that name.*

> Best to you,
> Pete [Pete McGovern]
> Westport, Connecticut

I suspect a more menacing or blackhearted basis for the "request" or "preference" by the N.C.A.A. that announcers avoid saying "N.C. Double-A." The N.C.A.A. aims to avoid confusion with the N.A.A.C.P. (National Association for the Advancement of Colored People), which is always pronounced "N. Double-A. C.P." The "Double A." usage immediately bounces the N.A.A.C.P. into the forecourt. However, it is the N.A.A.C.P. which should blow the whistle and claim personal foul. After all, it is the N.C.A.A. which is associated with recruiting scandals, placing universities on probation, and attempting to keep its members from being offside. The N.A.A.C.P. should seek to avoid confusion with the offensive fouls and blindside tackles associated with N.C.A.A. activities.

> Lewis A. Rappaport
> Brooklyn, New York

Does anyone remember that NCAA used to be NCAAAA (National Collegiate Amateur Athletic Association of America)?
In those days no one objected to "N.C. long A's."

> Robert C. Schnitzer
> Weston, Connecticut

Perhaps the reason "N.C. Two-A" was a new one on you is that you are too young to remember when the I.C.A.A.A.A. (Intercollegiate Association of Amateur Athletes of America) (or American Amateur Athletes or Amateur American Athletes?) enjoyed as much or more prominence in the collegiate sports world as the N.C.A.A. The I.C.A.A.A.A. generally was referred to as the "I.C. 4A," so it was natural for many writers and radio broadcasters to refer to the other organization as the "N.C. 2A," especially in speech. After all, you wouldn't want a radio announcer to struggle through "Eye-Cee-Aye-Aye-Aye-Aye," would you? "I.C. Quadruple-A" wouldn't do, either.

As for Mike Taliaferro's preference for "Tolliver" as the pronunciation of his name, my friend Rhea (pronounced Ray) Taliaferro Eskew, president and publisher of the Greenville, S.C., News and Piedmont, feels the same way about it. He has told me that the name is well known in the South and that "Tolliver" is its correct pronunciation. His son generally is called "Tolly," not "Tally."

Frank Tremaine
(Senior Vice-President, UPI—retired)
Savannah, Georgia

With regard to the NCAA, to hell with the periods, I belong to the Institute of Electrical and Electronics Engineers—the IEEE. And we all refer to it as the I-Triple-E.

I also belong to the International Association for the Advancement of Appropriate Technology for Developing Countries—the IAAATDC. Try rattling that off without getting bogged down in an endless confusion of AAAAAAAAAAAAA and it is understandable why I refer to it as the I-Triple-A-TDC.

I think that the NC-Double-A is trying to establish some sort of an intellectual image to divert the attention of everyone from the fact that they are making a lot of money off of educational institutions.

Ralph C. Walker
Dumb engineering professor
Bucknell University
Lewisburg, Pennsylvania

As I read Tony Dorsett's request to announcers as to how he prefers his name to be pronounced, I was reminded of poor Ben Oglivie of the Milwaukee Brewers, who almost never seems to get his name pronounced right. Practically every announcer calls him by the more common OgILvie rather by the uncommon Og-LIvie. I don't know if this is significant or not, but when Ben Oglivie played for the Boston Red Sox, there they did pronounce his name right. Either Oglivie

should go back to Boston (why they let him go I'll never know) or he should get
after all those announcers the way Dorsett did.

John Voulgaris
New York, New York

double genitives

I wrote about "Bernard Baruch, a friend
of Churchill's," and received this zinger
from Leonard Zahn of Great Neck, New
York: "Aha! At last! You've committed an
error that is seen every day in virtually
every newspaper. A friend of Churchill's
what?"

I tried it again with "a close personal
friend of Mrs. Reagan's" and got the same
objection from Sinclair Hoffman of Chicago: "Why have an apostrophe-s on Mrs.
Reagan's name? Would not 'a close personal friend of Mrs. Reagan' be better
and simpler usage?"

Supposing so, I tried it the other way, and quoted a letter from someone about
the word "friend": "I cannot be a friend, standing alone (unless I'm a Quaker),
but I can be a friend of John or Mary." In came a letter from Henry Morgan
of New York objecting: "Speaking of John, can one be a friend of him? Whatever
happened to 'a friend of John's'?"

O.K., let's take a position on double genitives. Not everybody does; the style
of *The New York Times* lets writers take their pick, except in cases where
ambiguity arises, such as "a picture of Churchill" versus "a picture of Churchill's."

Which is correct—a friend of Churchill, or a friend of Churchill's? The
Language Snob will insist that the *of* denotes possession, and the addition of the
apostrophe and *s* is redundant. In retort, the Language Slob will mumble that
this is an idiom of long standing and it is no business of the language purist's.
Some permissive nonslobs, like Mr. Morgan, point to the pronoun as evidence
that the *of* needs a little more help in possessiveness: You would not say "a friend
of him," but would say "a friend of his."

Both are correct; the double genitive is not so redundant as to make it the
target of the Squad Squad's. But readers of this column's do not trample over
members of their families to glom their hands on this page for such hedging.
O.K., so "friend of Churchill" and "friend of Churchill's" are both correct—but

which is better? Which adds to lucidity? You are not plowing through this prose to see with how much you can get away, but to discover the path of consistency and good taste, as befits a friend of Churchill.

That's it: friend of Churchill, no apostrophe, no *s*. For the past two paragraphs, I have been trying the double genitive form—"readers of this column's" and "target of the Squad Squad's"—and I don't like it. For pronouns, of course, it's the only way—nobody is a friend of me, and everybody is a friend of mine—but I'll let the nouns stand alone. Saves space, avoids misinterpretation in speech.

Got that, Henry Morgan? Become a friend of John. Let somebody claim to be a close "personal" friend of Mrs. Reagan. When in doubt, keep it short—that's the best way for readers of this column, and certainly for any friend of Churchill.

In discussing the double possessive you failed to note what it is that provides the driving force behind its use: the subconscious urge to imply plurality. The proof of this contention is that the double possessive is invariably used with the indefinite article, implying one of a class, never with the definite article, implying singularity. One may say "a friend of Harry's" but never "the wife of Harry's." ("A wife of the sultan's" is possible.) The first responsibility Harry undertakes becomes "the obligation of Harry," the second "an obligation of Harry's."

The above is offered as explanation, not justification. The double is an abomination of practically everybody's.

Victor Fox
New York, New York

(Your distinction is much too fine—any friend of Churchill's is a friend of mine.)

Arthur J. Morgan
New York, New York

If you had the ear you are always writing about, you would realize that "the target of the Squad Squad's" and "a friend of Churchill's" are not comparable. For one thing, the double genitive is used when the thing possessed is one of many. "The target" is clearly the only target. Similarly, "readers of this column" means all the readers. However, "a reader of this column's" would still be incorrect; a column doesn't have readers in the same way that Churchill has friends. The pronoun serves as a guide here; you would never say "a reader of its." Clearly, the possessor must be animate.

The double genitive is a very simple construction that nobody had any trouble with until somebody decided it was illogical. There are lots of things in the language that are illogical. If they work, why worry? And the double genitive works better than the "reform" you have now sanctioned. I cannot understand how you can say that letting the nouns stand alone "avoids misinterpretation in speech" after you have pointed out that "a picture of Churchill" means that he is the subject of the picture.

> *Christine Kindschi*
> *Copy Editor*
> *Austin, Texas*

One cheer (to preclude the censure of the Squad Squad) for concision in the matter of double genitives. But isn't there a distinction in meaning (not consistently observed in current usage) between "a friend of Churchill" and "a friend of Churchill's"? The latter seems close kin to what your high school Latin teacher called "the partitive genitive" or "genitive of the whole." "Jones was a friend of Churchill" simply states a fact without further predication. "Jones was a friend of Churchill's" states the same fact but further predicates that Churchill had other friends. Jones was one member of the class "Churchill's friends," and he is being singled out for some (here unspecified) reason.

I would defend your use of the " 's" in the phrase "a close personal friend of Mrs. Reagan's" on these grounds. You are singling out a member of a class that, presumably, includes many friends who are not close at all. Perhaps the distinction can be made clear in other ways, but it is real enough. In any case, "a friend of Churchill's" seems to mean "one friend out of the many Churchill had." The "out of" explicitly indicates the partitive construction.

> *Ron Macdonald*
> *Northampton, Massachusetts*

You were right to begin with! Why let the ignorant lead you astray?

> **Double Possessive:** *When the thing possessed is only one of a number belonging to the possessor, both the possessive and of are used.*
> *a friend of my brother's . . . a book of Ginn's . . . who, as a devoted friend of Darwin's, employed . . .*

I quote from Words into Type, *third edition (Englewood Cliffs, N.J.: Prentice-Hall, 1974), p. 360, but you will find this in other manuals of style and in the grammar books you held in your hands during your schooldays.*

May I point out that the less knowledgeable among your correspondents would never be received at the Court of St. James's if they referred to the "Court of St. James." There's no such place. If you don't believe me, check with the State

Department. Our government sends an ambassador not to England, but to the Court of St. James's, and said ambassador or ambassadress (Mrs. Armstrong surely knew her post) had better understand the honorable double possessive before presenting his or her credentials.

Frances L. Apt
Copy editor
Belmont, Massachusetts

Change the "of" to "to" and then "a friend to Churchill" is not awkward. Certainly no one would be tempted to say "a friend to Churchill's." What do you think?

Peggy Baird
Huntsville, Alabama

The Language Snobs, as usual, are wrong. Your instincts, as usual, were right. Perhaps I can give you enough ammunition to squelch the Squad Squad, snub the Snobs, and maintain your original correct position.

1. There is really no such thing as the "double genitive" in English.

"Of" has uses and meanings unconnected with its role in genitive constructions. The "of" in "one of the boys" or "several of my friends," for example, is partitive in meaning. It expresses the relation of a portion to its totality. A logical translation of the partitive "of" might be: "from among all." "One from among all the boys." "Several friends from among all my friends."

In a sentence like "a friend of Churchill's" the "of" is this partitive "of," not the genitive "of." It means "one friend (= a portion) from among all Churchill's friends (= the totality)." We normally dispense with either occurrence of the repeated noun: we say either "a friend of Churchill's" or "one of Churchill's friends."

The apostrophe and s are therefore not only not redundant, they are necessary. Because the "of" is not genitive, the apostrophe and s are our only indication of the "possessive" idea.

2. We might speak of "The friend of Churchill"—if he had only one. This would involve no partitive, no portion of a totality: the "of" would be genitive.

But we cannot say: "The friend of Churchill's." For, even supposing that the total number of his friends equaled one, the relation of portion to totality (required by the partitive "of") would be forfeited: with the, the phrase means "the total number of friends from among the total number of friends," which means nothing at all.

Thus the definite article (which here signifies totality: "the plays of Shakespeare" = "all the plays") can never be used in this construction. We cannot say, for example, "the son of Mrs. Ford's." If Mrs. Ford has only one son, we may refer to him as "the son of Mrs. Ford"; if she has more than one, we must say "a son of Mrs. Ford's." All of which explains why your sense of the language was offended by your test phrase "the target of the Squad Squad's." The problem is in the "the."

We do not say "a friend of Churchill," then, for basically the same reason we do not say "a brother of me" or "a column of Safire." Keep up the good words.

Russell Astley
Chairman, Department of English
Gallaudet College
Washington, D.C.

I would suggest that the language snobs and slobs get together on this issue and adopt a simple rule to the effect that if the noun following "of" can be tastefully replaced by its pronoun in possessive form, the noun takes the apostrophe, but that the apostrophe is not used with the noun where a substituted possessive pronoun sounds strange or awkward, such as readers of your column being referred to as "readers of its" instead of "readers of it" or a target of the Squad Squad being called "a target of its" rather than "a target of it."

Henry G. Coryat Jr.
Rhinebeck, New York

The double genitives which you mention are not really double genitives. One of them is a partitive. Another example of a partitive is:

> *It is an ancient Mariner,*
> *And he stoppeth one of three.*

The partitive "of" can be considered an alternative to the construction "out of." Thus, "a painting of Winston Churchill's" is another way of saying "one out of Winston Churchill's (collection of paintings)."

The remark that the double genitive construction is unavoidable with pronouns is not correct. In the phrase, "a friend of mine," "of" is partitive, and "mine" is a possessive pronoun, not the genitive of the personal pronoun "I."

The genitive form performs many functions, possession, derivation, and partition. This is so in other Indo-European languages. For example, in French the possessive construction and the partitive construction are identical, and in Russian the genitive case is used for the partitive. However, in many other languages the partitive and the genitive are quite distinct. The fact that a "double genitive" phrase may contain two genitive forms does not mean that their functions are duplicated.

J.M. Daniels
Toronto, Ontario

I liked what you said about double genitives, but I think that it is stilted or awkward English to say or write "to see with how much you can get away." Perhaps you tucked the with in after see just to have fun—that is, to bother readers like me. But if you weren't doing it for fun, I would like to urge you to let the prepositions fall where English idiom has long preferred them to fall—at the end. Actually they are often adverbial particles, not prepositions.

Many students of the English language would agree, I think, that "see how much you can get away with" is better English than "see with how much you can get away"—better in the sense that it is natural, more idiomatic. In writing, just as much as in speech, we should use idiomatic as opposed to unnatural-sounding English.

Richard K. Redfern
Bradenton, Florida

With the single genitive (a friend of Churchill) the focus is on the first party; with a double genitive (a friend of Churchill's), on the second.

We have in New Zealand various organisations such as "The Friends of the Museum." The implication, to my mind, is that these people support the museum (they contribute money) but that the museum, or its principals, do not necessarily know of the existence of each member.

Similarly with the organisation "Friends of the Earth": it implies that members are friendly toward this planet, but not that the planet reciprocates this friendship. If the organisation were called "Friends of the Earth's" the implication would be that the Earth, or this planet (presuming that in this context the terms are interchangeable) regarded these people as friends, and that their degree of friendship toward it was of relatively minor significance. The philosophical impossibility of proof of the second indicates the correctness of the title the organisation has chosen.

Again, "Friends of Britain" are those countries that regard themselves as friendly toward Britain; "Friends of Britain's" are those countries Britain regards as friends. The perspective from each capital may not necessarily be the same.

"A friend of Churchill" may be a person who never met him, but regarded himself or herself as supporting what he did. "A friend of Churchill's" has to be a person whom Churchill himself regarded as a friend.

The point is made clear by your illustration (no pun intended) of "a picture of Churchill" which may not have been in his possession and which he might not have been aware existed. With the apostrophe s, the emphasis swings to Churchill himself and makes it clear that it was a picture by another artist owned by Churchill. (If one were talking of a picture he had painted one would say "a Churchill picture" or "a picture by Churchill." In rare cases one could use the double genitive to denote a picture Churchill himself had painted, but I suggest this would be an unusual way of putting it, and would most probably be used only after discussion of other pictures he had painted.)

Your illustration of "a target of the death squad('s)" I regard as a red herring: the word "target" is inherently passive, and this makes the apostrophe s redundant.

You advise Henry Morgan to become a friend of John. This means that friendship toward John will emanate from Henry Morgan. If he were to become a friend of John's, that would imply that the friendship emanated from John. The degree of friendship from the other party is unknowable in each case from the context of the phrase: such friendships are often unequal—one man's friend is often the other's acquaintance.

> *Hugh Nevill*
> *Washington correspondent, New Zealand Press Association*
> *Washington, D.C.*

It seems to me that you miss a slight nuance between "a friend of Mrs. Reagan" and "a friend of Mrs. Reagan's." The question is not which phrase is better in general, but rather which of two slightly different meanings the writer intends in a particular case.

You're on the right track when you distinguish between "a painting of Churchill" and "a painting of Churchill's." In the second phrase, the noun modified by "Churchill's" is understood, and understood to be "paintings": "a painting of Churchill's paintings." The "of" here means "from among," as it does in "the pick of the litter," or "the cream of the crop." It's not, strictly speaking, possessive at all, as Latinists will recognize, but partitive. (In "a painting of Churchill," on the other hand, the "of" has the force it does in "love of country," or "a singer of songs": its object receives the action implied in the noun modified. Neither possessive nor partitive, but objective.)

"A friend of Mrs. Reagan's" ("of" partitive, "friends" understood) is therefore not redundant; it implies more strongly than does "a friend of Mrs. Reagan" (which is a possessive), that Mrs. Reagan has more than one friend, and therefore, to my ears at least, has a slightly more modest ring. (Your original phrase, "a close personal friend of Mrs. Reagan's," thus pulls both ways, and I myself would drop the " 's" there.)

The phrase with the " 's" also sounds less formal than the one without (the ecology group would never have named itself "Friends of the Earth's"), no doubt because of the missing noun after the possessive. Informally we might say, "I prefer Harry's cooking to Martha's," but in formal writing we would have to make it "to Martha's cooking" or "to that of Martha." The more formal equivalent of "a friend of Mrs. Reagan's," with its implication of plurality, is "one of Mrs. Reagan's friends," not "a friend of Mrs. Reagan" (compare "a painting of Churchill's," "one of Churchill's paintings," "a painting of Churchill"). There cannot be many languages capable of making such a subtle distinction with such admirable econ-

omy, and it would be a shame to abandon the possibility of doing so in English to wrongheaded purists.

Vincent Daly
Assistant Professor of English
University of Hartford
Hartford, Connecticut

Dear Bill,

Please do not let your good instinct for idiom be overruled by the simple-minded reasonings of people who have read little else than the daily paper. I refer to the "friend of Churchill's" question, which you decide against yourself and in favor of your ignorant critic. Are we going to hear you say: "a friend of me, who always sticks that big nose of him in matters that are no concern of him"?

Fowler says: " 'a word of Coleridge' is no more English than 'a friend of me.' " The of and 's together do not constitute a double genitive; the 's suggests the mutuality of the relation by implying Coleridge's friends, i.e. a friend of (among) C's collection of friends. So strong is the feeling that it has idiomatically extended to "that nose of his," where a collection of noses is an unlikelihood.

Listen moreover to Follett: one is able (by using the idiom) to differentiate between "a portrait of Sargent" (= his likeness) and "a portrait of Sargent's" (= a painting by him). Trust your Sprachgefühl*!*

Yours,
Jacques [Jacques Barzun]
Charles Scribner's Sons
New York, New York

"early on" and on and on

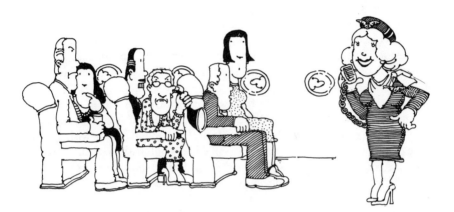

A "querulous query" came in from Paul Stone of Yonkers, New York, about the way *early on*—a Britishism—has caught on in the United States:

> *Early on they made me*
> *wonder*
> *Is it good, or is it blunder?*
> *When is "early," where is*
> *"on"?*
> *Should it be in the lexicon?*

Putting it more prosaically, is the *on* necessary in *early on*? Does it add to meaning or is it just an affectation and a redundancy?

I am sensitive to queries on *on*, because I once wrote, "Sometimes *off* is added on," and was rightly reprimanded with "Isn't just *add* sufficient?" That ticked me off: I had erred. There is a good place for *to add on*, and its noun form, *an add-on*—the proper place is where the meaning is "to heap on," or in noun form, a sudden addition or unexpected appendage; the *on* is then a particle, not a preposition. A simple addition requires no *on:* I should have written "sometimes *off* is added." That episode alerted me to the subtle change of meaning added by *on* (and not "added *on* by *on*").

"I maintain that the *on* does indeed add something to the meaning," responds James McCawley, professor of linguistics at the University of Chicago, who uses both *does* and *indeed* to intensify the expression of his judgment. "While *early* can be used in relation to any system for locating events in time, *early on* is restricted to earliness in relation to a 'course of events' that is being recounted."

In evidence, Professor McCawley points to the way *early on* is never used when referring only to clock times: One does not say "Alice usually gets up early on." On the contrary, *early* denotes a general time, and *early on* a place in a course of events—like the *on* in *on course*.

Another great student of *early on* is Dr. Frederic G. Cassidy, director-editor of the *Dictionary of American Regional English,* which has just received a needed infusion of funds from the Mellon Foundation. *Later on* came into use more than a century ago; *earlier on* came along fifty years later, and a back-formation, *early on,* appeared in Britain in 1928.

Cassidy puts forward a theory that parallel construction *(later on, early on)* triumphed over logic: "*Early* and *late* imply the sense of a stretch of time along which we mentally place events: a chronological continuum, if you wish, in which 'time marches on.' This logic seems acceptable enough with *later on:* It takes us from our position in the present to a position farther along the continuum (to the right, since our culture conceives time as moving from left to right), as *on* implies continuation of movement in the same direction. If we were strictly logical about it, then, we should say *earlier back* (in the time-stretch)."

But we do not; idiom's parallelism triumphed over logic, and *earlier on* beat back *earlier back.*

On wins other battles, too. When the flight attendant, née stewardess, sing-songs over the loudspeaker: "For those passengers continuing on, please do not deplane as we will be departing momentarily," she is right—you continue on a journey just as you continue your journey, so *continuing on* is correct. But if I were to begin the next item with *Continuing on,* that would be a mistake: This column is not supposed to be a journey, metaphoric or otherwise.

I would like to comment on the following sentence: "But if I were to begin the next item with Continuing on, *that would be a mistake: This column is not supposed to be a journey, metaphoric or otherwise."*

It seems to me that the word "otherwise" should be replaced by "other" since "journey" is here a noun and should be modified by an adjective ("other") and not the adverb "otherwise." I suppose that "otherwise" can also be used as an adjective to mean "different" or even "other" (see, e.g., Webster's Third New International Dictionary *[unabridged 1970];* Webster's New Collegiate Dictionary *[1977];* Oxford English Dictionary *[1977]). But some authorities object to this use of "otherwise" (see, e.g., W. Follett,* Modern American Usage *[Hill and Wang Publ. 1966] at 242–243 [or paperback ed. at 301–303]; H. Fowler,* Modern English Usage *[E. Gowers editor, 2d ed. 1965] at 425–427; M. Freeman,* The Grammatical Lawyer *[1979] at 239–240; E. Gowers,* The Complete Plain Words *[Pelican 1962] at 226–227 [or Pelican 1973 at 228–229]).*

I hope that with respect to the word "otherwise" you now will ask yourself how your column could be written otherwise (differently), otherwise (or else) I may be forced, sensibly or otherwise (without good sense), to write to you again.

Ronald David Greenberg
Associate Professor
Columbia University
New York, New York

I agree with Professor McCawley that early on *is restricted to earliness in relation to a course of events that is being recounted but I was startled to read that Dr. Cassidy believes that* later on *places the event to the right—"since our culture conceives time as moving from left to right." My notion was that we metaphorically conceptualize time as a moving object coming at us. Or we immerse ourselves in time and experience ourselves moving in or with time. I find some agreement with these ideas in a book that you would greatly enjoy. It is* Metaphors We Live By *by George Lakoff, Professor of Linguistics at Berkeley, and Mark Johnston, philosopher, University of Chicago Press.*

I am a practicing psychoanalyst in Pittsburgh and early on *I was in love with Ingrid Bergman. That was in the course of human events when a kiss was still a kiss and a sigh was just a sigh, as time goes by. At that time I didn't concern myself with such arcane matters but I don't believe that these poignant experiences were passing from left to right.*

Time is also a commodity to be used up. Up, of course, is good, more and rational. So that when time is used up we are irrationally and emotionally down. Dylan Thomas in his "a grief ago" plays with time. An hour ago or a year ago will do—but a grief ago? Someone in an analytic session said "two cats ago" and surely this was two griefs ago. The grief is embraced and sustained by two /a/'s so that one's enduring time is conflated with using time as some discontinuous commodity. The iambs hint at the fairy tales we heard when, early on, it ran: "Once upon a time there was a man who took a wife . . ." Sometimes a thing of sorrow is a joy forever—as time goes by.

Donald J. Coleman, M.D.
Pittsburgh, Pennsylvania

Your flight attendant should be told that the word "momentarily" indicates duration, not anticipation.

"Momentarily" means for a moment, *not* in a moment, *or "coming soon."*
You must be more careful in selecting your flight attendants.

Peter Briggs
Franklin Lake, New Jersey

I enjoyed the flight attendant's announcement: "For those passengers continuing on, please do not deplane as we will be departing momentarily." Although I suffered through deplane *and* as for *because, I found the flight attendant's remark on departure to be philosophically stimulating. The attendant doubtless knows that* momentarily *means* for a moment *and thus has claimed that departure lasts for only a moment. Except for the moment of departure, one either waits to depart or has departed. I hope that my next flight attendant is as intellectually provocative as the one in your column.*

André Barbera
Ithaca, New York

I find "When the flight attendant, née *stewardess, singsongs . . ." a subtle putdown of female flight attendants. FAs can be, and now are, of assorted genders. To this reader, who can't recall ever hearing a male voice referred to as "singsong," your gratuitous "née stewardess" appears derogatory.*

To add injury to insult, the illustration furthers the derogatory picture. (I'll give you some benefit of the doubt on the illustration, but assume you must take some responsibility for what Kimble Mead places above your column.) Take a good look, please. Don't the women passengers look slightly more mentally and physically handicapped than their seatmates? And isn't the flight attendant too obviously female?

Renee Lord
New York, New York

the eco-psycho connection

"To many," writes the *Miami Herald*, "a depression is what you take to a psychiatrist, not an economist." The depressive syndrome, according to the American Psychiatric Association's glossary, includes "slowed thinking, decreased purposeful physical activity, guilt and hopelessness."

Does the word *depression* form a subliminal bridge between the disciplines of psychology and economics? To find out, I interviewed the founder of the school of psychonomics, Dr. Sigmund Keynes:

Why do interest rates stay so high? "Irrational inflationary expectations. Lenders have been traumatized by years of negative real interest rates."

What is eroding the self-esteem of investors? "Budgetary jitters. They look at the projected federal deficit and they go——." (Shakes all over.) "We call this the Micawber Syndrome."

Some writers, like Leonard Silk of *The New York Times,* have called the present downturn a "Great Repression," induced by the repressive actions of the government—would you agree? "I like the term, as do all psychonomists and econotherapists. Repressions are followed by primal rate screams."

What phrases can we look forward to, as anti-inflationary psychology takes hold and a shared societal goal becomes interpersonal capital creation? "American Dream interpretation is a big new field, dealing as it does with double-digit envy," said Sigmund Keynes with a more-holistic-than-thou look. "Reduce the psychic income tax and—holistic macro!—we can end all kinds of depression with revenue therapy."

---

egghead

We may be on the brink of an etymological breakthrough.

Egghead—as a derogation of intellectuals—burst on the political scene in 1952, when Adlai Stevenson was running against Dwight Eisenhower.

The first columnist to use it was Stewart Alsop, who reported: "After Stevenson's serious and rather difficult atomic-energy speech in Hartford, Conn., this reporter remarked to a rising young Connecticut Republican that a good many intelligent people, who would be considered normally Republican, obviously admired Stevenson. 'Sure,' was the reply, 'all the eggheads love Stevenson, but how many eggheads do you think there are?' "

Years later, the gifted Stew Alsop revealed that the "rising young Connecticut Republican" was his brother John (not Joseph). *Newsweek* quoted the coiner describing the term to mean "a large, oval head, smooth, faceless, unemotional, but a little haughty and condescending."

The Democratic candidate tried to laugh the gibe off—"Eggheads of the world, unite," Stevenson said; "you have nothing to lose but your yolks"—but the word picture hurt him. Since then, however, hawkish academics have been able to describe themselves as "hard-boiled eggheads."

Now comes fresh evidence of an earlier usage from Mrs. F. B. Opper, of Le Rouret, France, who reads this column with a fine-toothed comb in the *International Herald Tribune.* (Why doesn't some grooming outfit come up with a snaggle-toothed comb?) She writes: "Unless John Alsop was writing editorials in Chicago shortly after the First World War, he did not coin *egghead.* " She directed me to the archives of the Toledo, Ohio, public library, where the papers of her grandfather, Negley Dakin Cochran, are stored.

For a measly three dollars, I was able to obtain a photostat from that library of a letter to Mr. Cochran from Carl Sandburg, the poet, who had worked for Cochran as a reporter on the *Chicago Daybook,* a tabloid published before World

War I. The typed letter is undated, but signed "Carl." The context indicates the year to be 1918:

"That letter of yours was like a slow strong southwest wind blowing the right rain for war crops," wrote Sandburg. "At Halsted and Madison last night I saw a thing I never saw in my life before. A movie of T.R. was put on the screen and there was not one handclap nor so much as a murmur or a grunt one way or another. Only discreet and curious silence. A Wilson picture later got a big hand, a regular storm."

Then comes the big find: " 'Egg heads' is the slang here for editorial writers here.—I have handed in five editorials on Russia and two on the packers, voicing what 95 percent of the readers of The News are saying on the cars and in the groceries and saloons but they have been ditched for hot anti-bolshevik stuff. . . . At that it isn't so much the policies of the papers as the bigotry and superstition and flunkeyism of the Egg Heads."

Sandburg embraced the vernacular; his reference to what people were saying "on the cars" meant what was spoken of on the trolley cars, and "man in the cars" or "man on the cars" was then more commonly used than "man in the street." His letter concludes with a sage observation about writing: "Since we got into the war I notice more writing like people talk. They are copping your style, which is no style at all and yet all style."

Neat trick, Mr. S.: ". . . reads this column with a fine-toothed comb . . ." You have either discovered a startling new multi-purpose aid to the visually handicapped or—Heaven help us!—were careless. You go over, scrutinize, examine with this instrument but don't read with it, even figuratively. My snaggle-toothed comb simply could not swallow this phrase, if I may be permitted to expand further the utility of that ubiquitous utensil!

L. Straka
Elmsford, New York

When someone says they received "a photostat" (small p) it immediately tells me that person is in the "over 50" ranks. And, I'll bet you a hot fudge sundae that you didn't get a real Photostat (capital P) copy of Mr. Sandburg's letter, either.

Why? Well, a little history is needed here. The word Photostat is still a registered trademark that was also the name of the former Photostat Company of Rochester, New York. That company was very successful in manufacturing and marketing their photographic copying machines during the 1910 thru 1950 era. These machines were fixtures in large businesses and in government offices where multiple copies of various and sundry documents were needed.

They were impressive behemoths, those older models. They represented the "high technology" of the day with their cast-iron framework, mahogany cabinetry and brass trim. Often, an entire room was dedicated to the use of the device. A "key operator" in those days held the key to the Photostat Room, and was a highly regarded, highly skilled technician.

Anyway, when someone needed a copy of, say, a deed or bill of sale or last month's sales figures, they would be off to the Photostat Room to get (what else?) "a photostat."

As a marketer of copying machines, the Photostat Company was a howling success. But, in protecting its trademark, it was something else again. Thus, a victim of its own success in making "Photostat" a virtual household word, Photostat—the trademark—is now found in some versions of Webster's Third *as, first, a noun meaning the device which makes copies and, second, a copy made by a photostat device.*

The lesson here was learned well by large companies like Xerox and Coca-Cola with trademarks to protect. These two giants spend piles of money on advertising campaigns and watchdog departments to make darn sure we don't "make a xerox" of anything and when we order "a coke" at our local ice cream parlor, we indeed get "The Real Thing" and not some other brown, fizzy liquid instead.

Now, since I mentioned ice cream, let's get back to my little proposition and your copy of Mr. Sandburg's letter. Unless that copy has a very smooth, reflective surface and is a bit tacky to the touch, it's not a Photostat copy. Real photostatic copies look and feel very much like black-and-white photographs because they use basically the same wet, chemical process on light-sensitive paper.

My guess is that your copy has been made by the xerographic process, which uses dry powder, electrical charges and heat to make an image on plain paper. It may have been made on a Xerox, IBM, Savin or other copier made by any of a couple dozen different manufacturers. But, it sure wasn't made on a Photostat copier.

And the Toledo public library doesn't have one, I'm told.

So, I guess it's O.K. for you "old geezers" to keep on calling your copies "photostats"—but only if they are made on honest-to-goodness Photostat machines.

Lavern L. Thompson, Jr.
Chelmsford, Massachusetts

Unfortunately, though I have contributed more than a thousand antedate citations to the Supplement to the Oxford English Dictionary, *I failed to supply anything at the time for* egghead.

To remedy the situation, you will find the clue in the statement by William and Mary Morris, Dictionary of Word and Phrase Origins: *"First used by Owen Johnson in one of his Lawrenceville novels and revived during the 1952 campaign of Adlai Stevenson."*

David Shulman
New York, New York

My compliments to you and to Mrs. F. B. Opper of Le Rouret, France, in the matter of running down the origin of the word "egghead." I guess that Carl Sandburg, a laudable predecessor, walks off with whatever laurels may be bestowed for originating the word, although I suspect that his letter which you quote was not given public currency until you included it in your column.

At the time that the brief flurry took place when my late brother, Stewart, wrote his column in 1952, some careful researcher in discussing the matter gave the credit (or blame) to Warwick Deeping, who published a novel in 1920 called Second Youth *in which he referred to "a little eggheaded pedant."*

For myself, I do not think that I ever claimed to have originated the word, although I suspect that had I not made the remark that I made to brother Stewart and had he not published it in the Alsop Brothers national column, the question of who originated the word would not be a matter of interest.

> *John Alsop*
> *Hartford, Connecticut*

encashment, *see* cash customers

enhance me, villain

The rise of *enhance* began in the 1960's with the need to spruce up monaural recordings for playback in stereo equipment. Salesmen called the static-erasing rerecording "enhanced sound"; sound engineers winced and called that a "quasi-technical term."

"The term *enhanced sound* has been around for the last ten years," estimates Almon Clegg of Panasonic, "and has been a generic term for the last three years. Our term for enhanced sound is *ambiance.*" Over at Sony, Mark Finer explains that sound is enhanced "with the use of different types of circuits that delay, in microseconds, the reception of the signal to the ears. This expands the stereo image. . . ."

After wowing the lexicon of the ambiance chasers (a punning coinage of Mrs. Muffie Brandon, now of the White House), *enhance* puffed itself up into the jargon of politico-military affairs. Instead of *neutron bomb,* which sounded threatening, we began to hear of *enhanced radiation weapons,* which sounded comforting.

In 1978, the Pentagon—entranced with enhanced—started to use the word in connection with the F-15's which were being sold to Saudi Arabia. The Carter administration pledged to the Senate that it would not sell "enhancements" to the Saudis. "At that time," says Pentagon spokesman Mark Foutch, "the enhancement weapons were fuel tanks that would extend the plane's range, and additional air-to-surface weaponry." (Air-to-surface weapons used to be called "bombs," but bombs are no longer mere bombs when they are missiles. A bomb is dropped; a missile is shot. A "smart bomb," which seeks its target, is still "dropped." An enhanced radiation weapon may be dropped, shot, or talked about a lot.)

But it was not until the word *enhance* recently came out of the mouth of majority leader Howard Baker in an economic setting that it can be said to have turned the hat trick in jargon use: "I'm willing to consider revenue enhancement in outyears," he said. *Revenue enhancement* is the gentle new term for *tax increase.* This is a double euphemism: Revenues are what the government shovels in, and taxes are what the taxpayer forks over. Since it is less painful to receive than to give, *revenue* sounds nicer; on top of that, *increase* is harsh—enter *enhance,* which lifts effortlessly off the ground. Pye Chamberlayne of U.P.I. radio said: "Nothing in life is certain except Negative Patient Care Outcome and Revenue Enhancement."

The word is rooted in the Latin for *to raise,* and came to English via Old French. In recent times, it has shifted its primary meaning from "to lift" or "to raise in value" to the current "to improve, to make more attractive." In the sixteenth century, however, it had a meaning which turned out to be prophetic: An enhancer was one who raised prices. Hugh Latimer, in a sermon before Edward VI, denounced the "money makers, inhaucers and promoters of them selves."

Dear Bill:

For all I know you may be too young to recall this, but the word "enhance" received hundreds of millions of exposures (as admen tot this up) in the 1930s on the Jack Benny program. The Jell-O commercials, jovially presented by Don Wilson, carried a quickly mumbled "artificially enhanced" as a shirttail to those "six delicious flavors." Since one could assume that only a relative few in Benny's vast audience would have any idea of what the phrase meant, this was deemed a safe way of keeping the advertising claim honest.

I agree, of course, that only in the last few years did the word bloom into the many-splendored euphemism it is today.

Cordially,
Mike [Michael Horton]
Brussels, Belgium

In 1953, Emory Cook, in Connecticut, issued records of music recorded by two microphones, one fastened to each side of a dummy head. These two channels were cut on separate bands on the disc and played back by means of a double-headed tone arm, each track being listened to by half of a set of headphones. These records were "binaural" (literally). Stereo tapes (c. 1955) and stereo discs (1958) were recorded by two (or more) microphones placed a much greater distance apart. Listening to the latter with stereo headphones was like having ears thirty feet apart.

Thus the word in your article should read "monophonic," not "monaural."

Mike Deskey
New York, New York

enjoy or else

A word about the "dining imperative," a crisp command that is evidently drilled into the working habit of every waiter and waitress in the land. The command is usually delivered in a flat tone intended to cow the customer: "Enjoy your dinner."

Perhaps this locution came into being because waiters grew irritated at taking orders and wanted to snap out an order of their own. A French waiter may say *"Voilà,"* a German waiter *"Bitte,"* and an Italian waiter *"Prego,"* but these terms mean "Here you are—in case you're too drunk to see what I'm setting in front of you, I'm making this innocuous noise." But American serving persons, barking their crisp (garden-crisp) command "Enjoy your dinner," are really saying "Enjoy it—or else."

I always answer, "I will if I like it. Enjoy your work." The feeling of triumph is worth all the hearty, kettle-simmered soup that gets spilled from the steaming tureens into my lap.*

"Enjoy your meal" need not be taken as an imperative; the subjunctive is as reasonable, milder, and can express the same sort of idea. The jussive subjunctive, if I recall correctly.

Consider: as a subjunctive, the message would be "I hope that / may you . . . enjoy your meal." The nefarious (derive that one!) "Have a nice day" makes

*See "carte before the horse."

little sense as an imperative, but some as a hortatory subjunctive. "Peace be to you"
seems a similar case.

As was said in Bridge on the River Kwai, *"Be happy in your work!"*

Wm. J. McKeough
Greenvale, New York

Did you know that when that same waiter returns in four minutes to ask "Is
everything all right here?" s/he is not really concerned with your sheepish smiling
nod (your mouth is invariably full) or even with seeming alert enough to merit a
tip? No indeed. If you say everything is fine at that point you are absolving the
management of any liability for rusty barbs on your fork or roaches in your fritters.

Keith R. Knox
Washington Island, Wisconsin

I, too, object to the command "Enjoy your dinner." I'd like to tell the girl she
can count on my doing just that, given the correct combination of quality and
service. Come to Cheyenne, Mr. Safire. Here the most common utterance from a
waitress is "There you go." She'll say it with the delivery of every item: the water,
the entree, the check. I can't help but wonder where I'm going.

John W. Darr
Cheyenne, Wyoming

etc.

In noting the mispronunciation of *et cetera* as "ek cetera" in "Tsk Force," I
defined the Latin phrase as meaning "and the rest." Joel Tall, of Washington,
sent this correction: *"Et cetera* means *'all* the others.' *Et al.* or *et alia* means
'the others.' "

I sit uncorrected. Edward W. Bodnar, S.J., in the classics department at
Georgetown University, passes along this assist: "The term *et cetera* in Latin
means 'and the rest,' 'and the other things.' It refers to things, not to people. 'And
so forth' is a good translation. *Et al.* can stand for either *et alii* ('and other
persons') or, less usually, *et alia* ('and other things')."

Since *cetera* cannot refer to people, according to Professor Bodnar, the rule
I would promulgate is this: *Et cetera* refers to things, *et al.* to people.

Solved. The next letter will ask how to pronounce *al*. The answer: Forget "all"; the abbreviation is for *alii*, and—just *inter alii*—should rhyme with alfresco, *al dente*, etc., and not Al Haig, Al Capone, et al.

You commented on the correct usage of etc. *and* et al. *With sure scholarship you managed to untangle use from misuse of those phrases. Towards the end of the article, however, you used the phrase* inter alii. *I shudder! Alii is the masculine, nominative plural of the word in question, and is the proper form in the phrase* et alii. *The word* inter, *however, is a preposition, and governs the accusative (or objective) case in Latin. The ordinary form of the phrase for which you were searching is* inter alia, *where alia is the neuter accusative plural form. An adequate translation is "among other things."*

Please keep delighting those of us who are lovers of language with your wit and your usually excellent scholarship, but be kind to an old Latinist's heart: let dead languages, like sleeping dogs, lie.

> *(Rev.) Alan J. Placa*
> *Merrick, New York*

When you compile your tally of indignant Classicists who write to you about your misuse of alii *to follow* inter *(which requires the accusative and not the nominative case), include me!*

Depending on the gender of the antecedent, there are three options:

> **inter alia**   *("among other [things]", when the antecedent is neuter)*
> **inter alias**   *(when the antecedent is feminine plural)*
> **inter alios**   *(when the antecedent is masculine plural)*

There must be a local Latin teacher whose proofreading could save you from having to retract your incorrect pronouncements on the Latin language.

> *Catherine Spotswood Gibbes*
> *Information Scientist*
> *Massachusetts Institute of Technology*
> *Cambridge, Massachusetts*

It must be one of your missions (or mischiefs?) to occupy the nation's unemployed classicists, as you regularly send them dashing for their styluses (not, please, "styli," or similar pedantry). A month ago it was some beef-witted etymology of "homosexual," today it is "inter alii." They used to say that if you know Latin you automatically know English grammar; however, it doesn't work—to borrow the hoariest of ablative absolutes—"vice versa." Perhaps it would be wiser to leave the learned tongues to the learned, if only for the sake of their apoplexies.

Peter Brodie
Stockton, New Jersey

As a regular reader and ardent admirer of your column, I was surprised to see the Latin preposition "inter" followed by the word "alii," which is either the genitive singular or the nominative plural of "alius." The Jesuits of Xavier High School and Fordham College always taught me that the preposition "inter" took the accusative case, e.g. "inter alios" or "inter alia."

Ad multos Annos,
Raymond X. Farley, M.D.
Manhasset, New York

euphemisms, *see* geezer power

even Stephen

The New American Library, which has changed its name to the acronymic NAL Books, ran this headline in its advertisement on the front cover of *Publishers Weekly:* "Only NAL Could Publish a Book That Even Scared Stephen King." (Mr. King, a master of suspense novels, provided a blurb for another horror show.)

"One might assume," writes Bruce Kenyon of New York, "that Mr. King was perhaps entranced, delighted *and* even scared, . . . bored, nauseated and *even* scared, . . . or perchance it was even Mr. King who was scared."

The nice NALies should watch out for the even Stephen. *Even* is a word, like *only,* that does its job in a sentence only when placed with precision. As an emphatic particle, *even* means "hard though this may be to believe" (just think —*even Stephen King!*) or it may be used as an adverb to intensify a comparison ("even worse"; "bored, nauseated, and even scared") but it cannot do both at the same time.

As for the floating *only,* that even troubles me. (No; make that read "that troubles even me," or "that troubles and even terrifies me.")

!

When an excited correspondent wrote, "Help!" he was using an exclamation point correctly. It would be incorrect to write, "Help."—unless it was in melancholy answer to a question like "What is it that the truly needy need, Mr. President?"

However, "I must get an answer before I go crazy!" strikes me as a misuse of the punctuation mark, which is strained and strident when used at the end of declarative sentences. The exclamation point can properly be used at the end of quoted sentences along with *he shouted* or *she screamed* or *it roared,* but in narrative prose it is being used to excess.

Around the corner, a new store has opened which calls itself "Plymouth!" and which has a sign in the window that hollers "Sale!" I have not entered that store for fear of being browbeaten by the salesperson. The only time *Plymouth* should carry such punctuation is in answer to "Halloo! On what rock is this ship about to founder and sink?"

"I am concerned about the proliferation of exclamation points I have noticed recently!" writes Dan Woog of Westport, Connecticut. "I've enclosed an example, from *The New York Times*!" The clipping enclosed was an advertisement from CBS Sports (that craven crew who dutifully call the N.C. Double-A.* the N.C.A.A.): "Today! 3 P.M. live! The Peach Bowl! Two teams that live and die by the forward pass, air it out in Atlanta's Fulton County Stadium!"

Comments Mr. Woog: "It seems to me when you have too much of a good thing, it's not good anymore! It loses its effectiveness! And people say, 'Big deal!' "

I salute the CBS copywriter's use of *air it out* to describe a game featuring much passing, but wish I could block his extra points (adding a late hit for his unnecessary comma).

Overstatement subtracts force from language. Before using an exclamation mark, ask yourself: Is this truly an interjection? Do I really want to make it look like a verbal explosive? If your answer is "Hell, no!" then—heavens!—avoid it.

On the subject of exclamation points: You may be interested to know that they are called "excitement marks" by schoolchildren in the primary grades. At least, that is in one Brooklyn school.

Arminé Dikijian
Brooklyn, New York

*See "Double-A rating."

As a self-appointed member of the Squad Squad from Cape Cod, all I can say is "Gotcha!"

You say: "Halloo! On what rock is this ship about to founder and sink?" For shame, sir. Mr. Webster says "founder" means "to sink," and I, as an avid sailor, have been taught this, too. Many landlubbers use "flounder," which is unthinkable.

Bob West
Harwich Port, Massachusetts

exculpation

In a peak of fit, I announced in a piece called "Crafty Crafting" that the newly voguish verb *to craft* would be used on occasion to mean "shaped, sculpted."

"The second of these words is widely used and by very good writers," writes Jacques Barzun, the nation's foremost usagist, in his tone of gentle reproof, "though strictly speaking it is a corrupt form."

Corrupt? "The true one is *sculped* or *sculptured.* The *t* belongs to the ending, as in *fixture.* I am curious to see whether you will have it *fixted.*"

You've parlayed your peak of fit into a freak of wit, primrose-pathed by Jacques Barzun.

Sculpt comes from the Latin perfect participle sculptus *(base sculpt-) of the verb* sculpere *(base sculp-), though* OED *calls* sculpt *a "ludicrous back-formation from* sculptor.*"*

In any case the t, *as in* corrupt *or* fact, *belongs to the participial base and not to the suffix* -ura *(-ure): cf.* fissure, figure.

Fixture (which J.B. cites) is anomalous: "Variant of obsolete fixture *(influenced by MIXTURE)"* Am. Her. Dic., *where* mixt- *is a regular participial base: cf.* cult *& culture,* rapt *& rapture, etc.*

Let me end with a plug for studying Latin as one guide through the maze, and do forgive the fit of pique.

John Van Sickle
Professor of Classical Studies and of Comparative Literature
City University of New York
New York, New York

Your column must have been written in the same peak of fit *in which you had earlier announced your decision about the voguish word "to craft." I read it all in a delight of transport, though I did wonder what mind of state you must have been in when you wrote it! But let me stop before an* envy of state *sets in, though not without rejoicing that the Spirit of Spooner Survives in Safire!*

B.S. Chandrasekhar
Department of Physics
Case Western Reserve University
Cleveland, Ohio

expectant

The emblazonment of misused sex terms across the covers of national magazines continues apace.

When the newly rejuvenated *Harper's* magazine was seduced by *courtesan,* its editor was justly subjected to excoriation by me. Now *Time* magazine has gone and gotten itself impregnated with error, and smack-dab on its cover.

"*Time*'s cover of February 22," writes Mary Kay Pennotti Byron of Tuxedo Park, New York, "maligns Charlie's poor angel Jaclyn Smith. How ungracious to call her an 'expectant actress.' No matter what they think of her talent, she is an actress by profession. And of all times to get her upset! Their cover clearly shows she's pregnant. I think an apology is in order."

In its cover story "The New Baby Boom," *Time* presented a tasteful photograph of actress Smith joyfully holding her hands on the baby developing in her body. The only problem was the caption: "Expectant Actress Jaclyn Smith."

Miss Smith is indisputably expectant—that is, she is expecting to have a baby. It is accurate to describe her as *expectant,* if that adjective is left to stand by itself, because the word has become the most recent euphemism for *pregnant.* It is less arch than the French *enceinte* and less flippant than Walter Winchell's *infanticipating.*

The managing editor of *Time* refuses to cave: "We went with *expectant actress,"* says Ray Cave, "because, according to our *Webster's Third New International Dictionary, pregnant* is the first definition listed for *expectant.* It is therefore not an incorrect usage."

I think the usage was conceived in error and borne in solecism. When you are an expectant mother, you are pregnant; when you are an expectant father, you expect to become a father; when you are an expectant actress, you expect one day to become an actress. *Expectant* means "pregnant" only when the noun following—spoken or understood—is *mother.* When the noun that *expectant* modifies is anything else—actress, heiress, magazine editor—the specific meaning of pregnancy vanishes and the more general "expects to become" takes over. When a woman knows she is pregnant, she is always expectant, but when she is expectant, she is not necessarily pregnant.

Hell, the permissivist might say, everybody understands that the phrase *expectant actress* accompanying a woman wearing a tentlike dress is intended to mean "pregnant woman who is an actress." Reply: If so, why not say "pregnant actress"? Why invite ambiguity?

As pundits, admen, and cinemactresses know, *Time* has coined many useful new words; *expectant* to mean only the state of pregnancy is not one of them. *Pregnant* is a beautiful word, no longer in the least taboo, denoting the carrying of incipient offspring; in metaphoric use, it encompasses more than its current euphemism. (Now, there's an expectant thought.)

Couldn't help but grin (not expectantly) when you mused aloud about who on earth could object to seeing the word "pregnant" on a magazine cover in the current, modern, with-it year 1982.

The answer is about a dozen of our readers who wrote us bristling notes after we ran a cover picture of Diana, Princess of Wales, with the legend "The Pregnant Princess" right next door. One of the letters was from an obstetrician (not mine, fortunately) who found the word much too tasteless and anatomical for the public prints.

Yup, it surprised me, too.

> Louise Lague
> Assistant Managing Editor, People
> New York, New York

I must take issue with your statement that the word "pregnant" is "no longer in the least taboo." This word is still forbidden in television commercials. If you watch commercials to any extent, you will discover that it is permissible to describe in revolting detail the symptoms of hemorrhoids, the condition of one's bowels (too much action or too little), and all manner of unattractive bodily secretions. But it is not permissible to say "pregnant."

One especially offensive commercial shows a pregnant woman said to be suffering from hemorrhoids. This ailment is discussed in depth, but the other actress in the commercial is made to say, "Since you're expecting, Sis, check with your doctor." To me, this is a reversal of real life. It's been a good twenty years since I heard anybody say, "Hey! You're expecting!" On the other hand, none of the people I know go around babbling cheerfully, in public, about their intestines.

I guess it's all a question of what one has to sell to the public, don't you suppose? Manufacturers can't sell pregnancy (yet), so they don't have to name it.

Rita Gilbert
North Salem, New York

Ray Cave, the managing editor of Time, *defends "expectant actress" on the grounds that "according to our* Webster's Third New International Dictionary, pregnant *is the first definition listed for* expectant. *It is therefore not an incorrect usage."*
Well, not exactly. My copy of Webster's Third *gives the following citation:*

one a: *characterized by expectation: Expecting, waiting . . .*
    b: *expecting the birth of a child [an expectant father];*
specif: *pregnant [expectant mothers].*

The verbal illustrations make perfectly clear how the adjective is used in this sense. Furthermore, Mr. Cave seems to be giving some weight to his assertion that this sense is the first *definition. Even if it were, which it isn't, such an assertion is irrelevant. The preface to* Webster's Third *states clearly that definitions are in chronological order by dated evidence and semantic development. There are no preferred definitions, as Mr. Cave seems to think.*
Maybe Time *needs an easier dictionary.*
As for "borne in solecism," that is a "borne" from which no columnist returns.

Annette H. Landau
New York, New York

"Expectant" actress, just as you so clearly argued, is wrong for Ms. Smith's caption. It, in fact, gives her "too little." "Pregnant" may, however, give her "too much."
"Pregnant," no matter how well documented by the adjacent photographic evidence, means or implies far more than "being with young, gravid." It also— fortunately—means "teeming with ideas, fertile, inventive"—as in "pregnant wit." On reading your various entries, I have sometimes felt like calling them "pregnant" in this sense. Would people be generally willing to call Ms. Smith a "pregnant actress" at this stage of her theatrical career, without at least some direct reference to a particular part that she may have performed (on stage) and in which she may have so distinguished herself? Hardly, I would say.
Moreover, "pregnant" also means "heavy with important contents, significance or issue; weighty; suggestive, potential." In this sense again, I find you occasionally deserving of the epithet at stake. But Ms. Smith?
Even if she has already merited such praise, heaping it upon her with ostensible

ambiguity on that Time *cover could invite more derision than admiration.*

The alternative meaning "suggestive" seems to be unable to relieve this undignified imbroglio, and the meaning "potential" may turn out to be the worst offender. Does it not suggest that she promises to become, or "expects to become" an actress, i.e., the very implication which was to be removed?

What to do?

H.M. Semarne
Saint-Paul, France

expeed, *see* spearing the mint

fashionese for fall

Fall fashion has pulled up lamé—that is, the metallic look has taken over. Ask for a "metal tape" and you don't know whether you're going to transport yourself into the frontiers of stereo recording or measure your hem.

These fabrics with an evil glint are part of the *Opulent Era.* (In fashionese, an *era* is a month or so; if it lasts a whole season, it is an *epoch.* The ultimate length of time—*age*—is not used in the fashion industry, but *ice age* aptly describes that time of life when a woman feels free to wear all her diamonds.) Although ostentating is derogated by *snob dressing, opulent* is a work-ethic word, from *opus,* "a work," which leads to riches. In this, fashion is once again leading politics, anticipating a return to the gold standard.

The Far East dominates the 1981 fashion lingo, Eleanor Lambert tells me:

Samurai flashes with short barrel coats, full pleated knee pants, side-fastened bodices, all held together with bold and chunky belts and jewelry. A Chinese costume exhibit by the Costume Institute at the Metropolitan Museum of Art boosted the *Manchu* tunic, an embroidered jacket with narrow rim collar and kimono sleeves worn over *rice-paddy pants* (narrow, cropped above the ankle), especially functional for those fashionable women who spend their days doing stoop labor in the fields.

Gothic describes soft, willowy clothes like those worn in the fourteenth century by young women being chased through secret passageways in castles. The *heroine dress* is romantic but dramatic, usually in white with embroidery and lace, and should not be confused with last year's *innocent dress,* worn by models on the verge of screaming. The opposite of the young, romantic look is called *Proustian* or *Edwardian,* which are sumptuous and sophisticated versions of the same period.

The new heroines are wearing what Lord & Taylor copywriters describe as *burnished brown.* The adjective usually means "polished," but perhaps this usage is taken from the French *brunir,* "to make brown." Ben Brantley of *Women's Wear Daily* reports *big sweep* is the phrase for huge shawls, *long and strong* refers to the silhouette of mid-calf skirts, and the *Sir Tom Jones look* calls up visions of milkmaids in full sleeves.

Whatever became of yesteryear's *occasion dressing,* which was the modern translation of "Sunday go-to-meetin' clothes"? It was replaced last year by *mood dressing,* and is now replaced by *attitude dressing,* which is said to "create an image of yourself," making a fashion *statement,* which is more of a throat-clearing. When successful, such an outfit becomes a *drop-dead dress,* which causes all those in the room entered to freeze in admiration or horror.

An unfortunate new term is *sweaterings,* which is to sweaters what *shirtings* is to shirts. Pants have not become *pantings* because that word calls up images of slavering hounds, but *trouserings* may soon be expected. I fear such participlization; horses should sweater while men perspirer and women glower.

Having read a few of your political columns, I can see why you prefer the "work-ethic" myth that opulence *is derived from* opus. *Alas, your etymology is as faulty as your political economy. Just as opulent wealth is more commonly inherited than earned, the begetter of opulence is not* opus *(labor) but merely more* ops *(wealth). The two words of course are not unrelated, but in word as often in fact, one must trace back several generations to find the connection—in this case, according to* Lewis and Short's Latin Dictionary, *all the way to Sanskrit. So if you are living opulently, it is probably because grandpa was already rolling in* opes, *and the last one to do any* opus *may have been his great-granddaddy.*

Gerard E. Lynch
Associate Professor of Law
Columbia University
New York, New York

A fine gentleman of our city, Albany, New York, has conducted a noble (which usually connotes unsuccessful, but which in this case has none of that) experiment in growing rice right here on the banks of the Hudson River. Mr. Ferguson grew up in Jamaica, W.I., where he became familiar with Chinese rice-growing methods, and when he came to this country, it came into his head that rice could be grown here. Through the good offices of the mayor of Albany and a professor in the agriculture school at Cornell he got the use of some land by the river and a lot of hybrid rice seeds from mainland China. What he has now is a lot of rice growing along the banks, and we are now in the midst of a harvest season.

I have had the opportunity to help him in this project not with any expert advice or land but rather with hand labor over the growing season. The harvest involves bending over, grabbing a fistful of rice root in the left hand, slashing it with a sickle with the right hand and stacking the bundle. This maneuver is executed in high large Tingleys for slurping through the muck and whatever else you don't mind getting splattered and sweaty. Rice-paddy pants don't make it, particularly if they are cut too high because they'll slip out over the top of the boots when you bend over and get wet, which mistake will allow water to trickle down into the boots. Pruney feet and worse ensue. A pair of corduroy hand-me-downs from a kid and a tank top are just fine for the purpose. Now I appreciate that the notion running through the person who goes for the shorter pant is that this operation is carried out in bare feet, but local custom prescribes boots. Do you think that that information will run like wild fire (not wild rice; that's a different kettle and/or grain) through the fashion industry? Do you envision telegrams being sent to various cutting rooms in fashion houses to lower the pants to coincide with the Albany rice-industrial formula?

Probably not a lot of your readers, female, have the privilege of practicing stoop labor in the rice fields so it is possible that this may be your only letter with this particular inside story. Thought you'd want to know.

> Ann Githler
> Albany, New York

---

five in a row

An item about queuing (or, as Americans trying to sound British would say, queuing up) called "Queuing for the Net" offers the chance to pass along this observation by Robert Amerson of Boston: "There is a word in the English language with five consecutive vowels: *queueing.*" (The most permissive dictionaries accept that it is a second spelling.)

If anybody comes up with a word containing six straight vowels, he wins the cigar. If more than one person responds, all the others will have to get in line (or on line, in New York).

I wondered when you would mention the great queuing-up controversy. It isn't a difference in geographical colloquialisms, as you implied. It's simple logic, as I've tried to explain to my southern friends. One doesn't get "in line" (in the middle of the line). If he did, he'd get static from everyone behind him. He gets "on line," i.e., on the end of the line. When people get on line behind him, then he's in line. Simple?

Joy Rubin
New York, New York

Apropos of the recent item in your column regarding words with many consecutive vowels, I might mention aye-aye, *a rather common lemur from Madagascar. If you find the hyphen in this word offensive, there are several other six-vowel possibilities, including my particular favorite,* Aiouea, *a genus of Central and South American plants.*
   It is a pity that English does not seem to have a word to denote someone who is being queued for (a ticket-taker, e.g.). The word queueee *would be a formidable, six-vowel specimen.*
   If one had nothing better to do, one might set oneself the problem of using the most consecutive vowels in a comprehensible sentence. An attempt to reach this goal is the following entry, a remark on Canadian natural history, featuring 31 consecutive vowels:
   Sequoia, aye-aye, ai,[1] o'o,[2] Aa,[3] *Aiouea,* aiaiai,[4] Euonymus *and* Parthenium *do not occur in Manitoba.*

Richard Larson
Urbana, Illinois

[1]*a two-toed sloth*
[2]*a Hawaiian bird*
[3]*a genus of orchids*
[4]*the roseate spoonbill*

You mentioned that the word queueing *has five consecutive vowels. Two other possibilities for interesting multivowel words come to mind. One is a variant spelling of* meow *(actually listed under the entry* miaow), *shown in the* Oxford English Dictionary *as* mieaou; *the form* mieaouing *is conceivable, giving you six vowels in sequence. The other possibility, which only has five vowels in a row, is* cooeyed *or* cooeeing, *the verb describing a call made by Australian aborigines.*

I suppose I will have to get "on line" with all the other correspondents (including those using "on-line" computations to try to come up with the answer!).

Keith Hollaman
New York, New York

I refuse to join the queueoid assemblage competing for the prize you offer for a word containing more than 5 consecutive vowels.

James Fanning
New Canaan, Connecticut

NO! NO! NO! 1000 × NO! "Queueing" absolutely does NOT contain five vowels in a row. It contains "a string of five letters which may be used to represent vowel noises." That's different, quite different.

It contains (a) a diphthong in the first syllable and (b) a short vowel in the second.

A word is a noise, not ink marks on a page.

Remember that old statement: "A word has as many syllables as it has vowels or diphthongs." According to that, our word has five syllables.

It's exactly like the fearsomely false claim that "facetiously" contains "all the vowels in alphabetical order." The word contains only two different vowels if you make the first syllable rhyme with "hat," or three, if you begin it with the vowel schwa (last vowel heard in sofa or first vowel in above). The second and fourth syllables contain the diphthong represented by /iy/, a short vowel plus the "off-glide /y/."

John F. Gummere
Philadelphia Inquirer & Daily News
Philadelphia, Pennsylvania

My colleague Professor Lou Katz of the Department of Electrical Engineering and Computer Science at the University of California–Berkeley and I used a PDP-11 and a program in a system called UNIX (a trademark of Bell Labs) to search the dictionary for sequences of four vowels.

While unsurprised by aqueous, guaiac, Hawaiian, lieue, Louie, *or* queue, *we were both overwhelmed by items like* euouae *and* Guauaenok.

Peter H. Salus
Professor of Linguistics and Dean
University of North Florida
Jacksonville, Florida

flaunt v. flout

Saving only the Supreme Court, the nine circuits of the United States Court of Appeals are the highest courts in the land. Ordinarily, the appellate judges are deferential to each other—with mutual respect slopping all over each other's decisions—but on one subject there is blood all over the floor.

The case at issue is *Flaunt v. Flout.* In defining *willfulness* in connection with violating a law, Judge Joseph F. Weis Jr. of the Third Circuit wrote: "Willfulness connotes defiance of such reckless disregard of consequences as to be equivalent to a knowing, conscious and deliberate flaunting of the Act."

Flaunt? Hardly. *To flaunt* is "to display ostentatiously"; *to flout* means "to show contempt for," akin to the noun *flute,* from the whistle of derision.

The brethren noticed. In discussing and rejecting the Third Circuit's definition of willfulness, the Fourth Circuit also zapped the Third's preference for *flaunt:* It put quotation marks around *flaunt* and noted that willful violations did not require "an intentional flouting of the Act."

In another case, the Ninth Circuit joined in the controversy, not only disagreeing with the willfulness decision but the flaunting thereof: It quoted the errant Third Circuit's *flaunt* and inserted after it in brackets the word *sic,* Latin for "thus," which means "precisely reproduced even though wrong."

The Third Circuit held its ground; in another case, Judge Weis wrote "flaunting the Act, or 'flouting it,' as some would say. . . . " Obviously, he thought those "some" who sic'd his *flaunt* were in error.

The Eighth Circuit weighed in next by quoting Weis on "deliberate flaunting of the Act" and inserting the word *flouting* in brackets after *flaunting,* as if to say, "This is what he meant to say." (For all these citations, I am indebted to Charles Hadden of Arlington, Virginia.) The Tenth Circuit then chimed in by putting *flaunt* in quotes.

I petitioned Judge Weis in Pittsburgh, where the Third Circuit sits: Is he the linguistic equivalent of "Turn 'em loose, Bruce"? *Arguendo,* is he flaunting his use of *flaunt* to flout convention? On what does he bottom his opinion?

Here is the judge's response:

DEAR MR. SAFIRE:

Some years ago Judge Learned Hand wrote, "[I]t is one of the surest indexes of a mature and developed jurisprudence not to make a fortress out of the dictionary. . . . " Nevertheless, when I am beleaguered by my colleagues who [sic]'d and ". . ." my use of that perfectly good word *flaunt,* I must take my station behind *Webster's Third.*

Before I wrote my second opinion defending the use of the word and mildly reproving my intolerant brethren, *Babcock & Wilcox Co. v. OSHRC,* 622 F. 2d 1160 (3d Cir. 1980), I sought support from the publishers of the dictionary. The editorial director responded by citing reputable authors and said, "[E]ven the writers who comment unfavorably on this use of *flaunt* indicate that it is widespread. For these reasons, the editors of the *Third* judge this use to be established in the language and entered it without stigma."

Much less charitable, I must say, is Thomas H. Middleton's reference to a possible etymological bond between the two words in the March 1981 issue of *Saturday Review:* "That would simply imply that *flaunt* has more than just a bonehead relationship with *flout.* It might be flout's illegitimate child and the flaunt-flout confusion becomes evermore understandable."

For shame! Do the flout forces know no limit to their campaign of vilification? Are you not aware that in a series of cases the Supreme Court has championed the rights of illegitimates to share in the benefits of our society? See, e.g., *Trimble v. Gordon,* 430 U.S. 762 (1977).

Will I give up on *flaunt?* By no means. Even at the risk of being labeled a loose constructionist, I shall stand my ground against what I consider to be a formidable assault on judicial independence. John Marshall withstood the attacks of Thomas Jefferson, and I trust that I shall survive my battle with the flout forces.

Respectfully yours,
JOSEPH F. WEIS JR.

P.S. I reserve the right to use *flout* if I choose.

As an attorney, I am almost willing to tolerate your ignorance regarding the number of federal judicial circuits. (There are eleven, including the United States Court of Appeals for the District of Columbia.) After all, you a-legal (take that, says an allegator) types can't be expected to know this sort of thing.

Edward S. Shipper, Jr.
Washington, D.C.

I am sure that as a jurist Judge Weis is well aware that widespread usage does not necessarily establish legitimacy.

He should acknowledge his error manfully and retreat from the field of battle gracefully, with the proviso, of course, that he be allowed, indeed encouraged, to flout his banner as he goes off.

Peter M. Coope
North Stonington, Connecticut

Not to my surprise, our exchange on "flaunt-flout" has done little to advance the cause of jurisprudence.

In writing to me after your article appeared in the Times, *one of my friends began, "My dear Lord Flauntleroy."*

A Philadelphia lawyer wrote, "As Jean Pierre Rampal might say, on reading the Weis-Safire correspondence, if you've got it, flaut it."

I received a note from a law school classmate asking, "Is the rumor true that you are going to be the principal flautist in the Pittsburgh Symphony's premiere performance of Webster's Third?*"*

I'm told that on Monday morning one of the trial judges in Pittsburgh leaned over the bench and exclaimed to a perplexed lawyer, "Mr.——, you will not flout the law in this courtroom. In fact, you may not even flaunt it."

Joseph F. Weis, Jr.
Pittsburgh, Pennsylvania

fob watch

"You must have received hundreds of letters by now," writes Mary Mae Tanimoto of Newton, Massachusetts, with distressing accuracy, "pointing out that F.O.B. means 'free on board.'" In a passage on abbreviations called "Busjarg," I had passed along a lifetime's misapprehension that the letters stood for "freight on board."

"The goods are to be put in the hands of the carrier," explains a spokesman for the American Trucking Association, "free of expense to the buyer, at the place designated." Thus, "F.O.B. Detroit" means your snazzy American-built vehicle is handed over to a shipper with all charges up to then absorbed by the seller—and all subsequent shipment costs are to be paid by the buyer.

What does *free* mean? To the trucking people, it means "free of expense to the buyer." Harry Hall of New York suggests it means "to free the seller of further responsibility. . . . Another concept is to advise the buyer who must pay for loading the merchandise. A similar term, but with a different meaning, is F.A.S., which means 'free alongside ship.' In this case the buyer must load it, or pay for loading."

According to the International Chamber of Commerce in Paris, "F.O.B. means 'Free On Board' . . . the risk of loss or of damage to the goods is transferred from the seller to the buyer when the goods pass the ship's rail."

I have difficulty with nautical metaphors. In a speech I once prepared for Senator Everett Dirksen, I concluded with "at last we have a firm hand on the rudder of the ship of state," to which some old salt replied, "If that's so, somebody is drowning and nobody is minding the tiller."

However, I reject a passel of nit-picks that my abbreviation passage stimulated.

AWOL means "Absent Without Leave" to me, not (as my colleague former company clerk Bob Hershey claims) "Away Without Official Leave." (Credit Hershey with knowing that his "service number" was not his "serial number.") And S.O.P. stands for "Standard Operating Procedure," not "Standing Operating Procedure," as various variants aver. (Some dictionaries say either is correct, but the dictionaries are wrong. *Standard* is standard.)

Coincidentally, the word *fob*—in the verb *to fob off*—has been shipped to me F.O.B. Los Angeles from U.C.L.A. professor Jascha Kessler. He notes an error in meaning by a book reviewer who wrote that "criticism, too, will have to be read closely. It should not be fobbed off as a secondary activity. . . ."

Fobbed off does not mean "dismissed" or "derogated" or otherwise waved off by people making pooh-poohing sounds. To fob off is to trick someone into accepting something of little or no value; to palm off, as one sells the Brooklyn Bridge. We must not fuzz the meaning of this valuable locution, from seventeenth-century thieves' cant, by confusing it with *slough off*, pronounced "sluff off." Nor can we permit forgetful writers to fob off phony explanations of initialese.

Quick: What does C.O.D. stand for? Cash on Delivery? Or *Collect* on Delivery? If the answer is not "Both," then I'll go AWOL.

According to Who's Who in America *you were barely twelve on Pearl Harbor Day and missed military service in World War II, whereas by the same source I was pushing 29 and spent a while in the active USNR in the military secretariat of the U.S. Joint Chiefs of Staff, where it was the U.S. Army, oddly enough, that awarded me a Legion of Merit (Legionnaire grade only).*

So it is understandable that you have missed the original meaning of S.O.P.

By Army usage—dating from peacetime latitudinarianisms—a colonel newly arrived in command of a regiment was entitled to issue his own Standing Operating Procedures; that is, to stand until he changed his mind or was succeeded by somebody else.

For a petty example: the colonel (if his cap visors and belts and holsters happened to be morocco-colored instead of tan) could order in his new S.O.P.: "Officers' uniform leathers morocco." Or vice versa, if he was a tan man.

This led to frets, of course, and as the war went on the petty stuff got wiped away.

You are probably right in your diktat "Standard is standard." But it didn't used to be.

John Tibby
Port Washington, New York

You described the word "fob" as seventeenth-century in origin. I was surprised at that since it appears in Shakespeare's Henry IV *parts one and two, and in his*

Coriolanus. *As I looked a little further, I noticed that the* OED *gives one example of the use of the word in* Piers Plowman, *dated to about 1387. The* Middle English Dictionary *notes several other uses of "fob" and derived forms all around the year 1400. It would seem clear that, while the word may have figured in the cant of seventeenth-century thieves, it was not they who gave it to the language. Langland and Shakespeare had made use of it before them.*

From all this snooping around some things more interesting than dating emerge. The Middle English Dictionary *suggests that the origin of the meanings associated with con games and trickery is itself benign. That dictionary records the use of the word to mean "froth, foam" and offers this line from a medieval recipe: "take the white of an egg and beat it well in a dish and set aside the* vobbe*(fob)" (my paraphrase). From "froth or foam" the word comes to mean trick or deceit.*

While we see one meaning in the verb, "to fob," Cunliffe in his New Shakespearean Dictionary *(1910) saw three distinguishable meanings in Shakespeare's use of that expression:*

1. *"to impose upon, 'put upon.'" Here his example is from* I Henry IV, *1, 2, "and resolution so fobbed as it is with the rusty curb of old father antic the law."*

2. *"to fob or fub off, to put off." Here the example is the Hostess' complaint that she has been "fub'd off, and fub'd off and fub'd off" by Falstaff (*2 Henry IV, *2, 1) With obvious delight Shakespeare makes the word not only a description of Falstaff's trickery but a pretty clear suggestion of other impositions he practices on the woman.*

3. *"to set aside by a trick." Here the example is from* Coriolanus, *a skeptical Roman burgher advises him, "You must not think to fob off our disgrace with a tale" (1, 1).*

The literary pedigree of the term suggests two observations to me. First, aren't we perhaps sentimentally prone to accept the notion that thieves create words and poets borrow them, when the reverse may be true, as it may be here. Secondly, by insisting on the one meaning of "fob off" as trickery, as you appear to do, don't we perhaps deprive ourselves of shades of meaning which are discernible to others?

We would tend to read each of Shakespeare's uses of fob in the same way. We would see the Romans suspecting Coriolanus of a trick, the Hostess as the victim of Falstaff's trick and Falstaff himself as accusing "old father antic the law" of playing a confidence game on resolution. These meanings seem to carry the connotations of "fob," but curiously seem to miss the denotations which Cunliffe sees. This, too, is a deprivation.

James H. McGregor
Assistant Professor, Comparative Literature
University of Georgia
Athens, Georgia

You seem to have misused F.O.B. again when you wrote that the word fob *"has been shipped to me F.O.B. Los Angeles from U.C.L.A. professor Jascha Kessler."*

In essence F.O.B. refers to the last destination to which the seller or shipper will send the item involved at his expense and from which point onward the buyer or receiver of the material has to pay for further shipment, if needed.

In this instance I presume the good professor placed the necessary postage on the envelope which carried his letter to you in Washington. Therefore, it might be more precise to say that his message was forwarded F.O.B. Washington.

> *Louis Kruh*
> *Co-Editor,* Cryptologia
> *Merrick, New York*

Many years ago, when I lived in Brooklyn, the Dodgers (then Brooklyn Dodgers baseball team) played at Ebbets Field in Brooklyn.

During the baseball game, if the bases were loaded with Brooklyn players, the radio announcer ["Red" Barber] would say "the bases are F.O.B.—Full of Brooklyn."

> *(Mrs.) Ann Meehan*
> *Shrewsbury, New Jersey*

You quote a representative of the American Trucking Association who supplied an explanation for you. Immediately thereafter, however, when you enlarge upon that explanation, you refer to the handing over of a vehicle to "a shipper," when I believe you mean, and should have said, "a carrier" (whether private or common). A shipper is that person (whether a real person or a corporate person) who ships goods via a carrier to a consignee.

> *Thomas P. Hackett*
> *Cheshire, Connecticut*

With respect to "S.O.P."—I was startled by your conclusion that standard is standard—for the following reasons.

E.S. Farrow, A Dictionary of Military Terms, N.Y. 1918: "Standing Orders— orders issued to adapt existing regulations to local conditions and to save frequent repetitions in operation and routine orders. . . . "

War Department, Dictionary of United States Army Terms, 1944: "Standard Operating Procedure. See Standing Operating Procedure." "Standing Operating Procedure, set of instructions giving the procedures to be followed as a matter of routine . . . ; standard operating procedure . . . Abbrev: SOP"

S.O.P. defined as standing operating procedure in editions through 1959. (In Naval use=senior officer present)

Henry S. Parker
Bethesda, Maryland

---

fort, eh?

Pronunciation is not my strong suit (I have to keep reminding myself to go to the mat on "impriMATur"), but I know the need to separate *forte*, pronounced "fort," from *forte*, pronounced "for-TAY." The pronunciation changes the meaning.

The one pronounced "fort," such as generals are supposed to hold, means "strong suit" (a bridge player's term) or "special accomplishment." My forte (single syllable) is capitalizing on my mistakes. The word comes from the Latin for "strong."

"For-TAY," however, takes an Italian turn: In that language the same Latin word came to mean "loud," the opposite of *piano*, which means "soft." "It is pronounced to rhyme with *sashay*," advises Jonathan Fuller of New York City, "as in 'He sashayed to the pianoforte and played *fortemente*.'" *Pianoforte* means "soft-loud," which shows that the instrument invites playing either way, in contrast to the harpsichord, on which the player is not encouraged to bang. (Unfortunately, *pianoforte* is pronounced either "fort" or "fortay," so forget it.)

Remember: Your forte (one syllable) is your strong point, which you can brag about in a voice that is forte (two syllables). As for the phrase *Hold the fort, for I am coming,* that was the title of a gospel song that immortalized William Tecumseh Sherman's slightly less inspiring message to the Union defenders at Allatoona Pass: "Hold out; relief is coming." (Sherman never said "War is hell," either—pithy statements were not his forte.)

Anent forte *and* forte, *here's a helper from an anonymous collection of "Epitaphs for Orchestra Members":*

> *Here lies one whose life was short, yea,*
> *It was* piano, *and he played* forte!

Marjorie Giafflin
Newfane, Vermont

There is no need to distinguish between pronounciations of "forte" because the word has one meaning: strong. Since the word did indeed come from the Latin fortis/forte, the Latin pronounciation should be observed, that being "FOR-tay."

In Italian, "forte" means strong, firm, hard. The definition of "forte" as "loud" is peculiarly musical and is not common usage in Italian. When Scarpia, for the benefit of Tosca, sings "piu forte" (more strong), he is admonishing his minions to increase the physical torture and not the conductor to increase the aural torture.

The bridge player's "forte" is his strength or strong point, and when the musician plays "forte," he plays with strength. I suggest that the pronunciation "fort" is preferred by would-be Francophiles who pronounce this Latin word using the French rules.

However, my whole case is destroyed if, according to the OED, we are both wrong and the word entered the language not from the Latin but from the French "forte" (fort) meaning strong. Nonetheless, my Latin and musical roots elicit the two-syllable pronounciation from me.

Jonathan Fuller's maladvice not withstanding, in Latin and Italian the word is pronounced "FOR-tay" as the accent always falls on the penultimate syllable in these tongues.

Finally, the musical instrument should always be pronounced "pianoFORtay" as the other way is simply wrong.

Italo Marchini
Upper Montclair, New Jersey

It seems to me that you have been led astray by Mr. Jonathan Fuller concerning the correct pronunciation of "forte."

I've been involved in music as a musician for nearly twenty years and for the past four years as editor of a publication, the Schwann Record and Tape Guide, *dealing with musical recordings—and I have never ever encountered before the rendering of forte as for-TAY. Obviously I have never met Mr. Fuller. It has always been FOR-tay. Arturo Toscanini said FOR-tay. Two of my musical colleagues speak fluent Italian and they say FOR-tay. I say FOR-tay.*

According to my copy of Cassell's Italian, the stress in "forte" falls on the penultimate syllable.

Paul Crapo
Belmont, Massachusetts

fortuitous, fortunate, *see* holding the fort, scaling the depths

fragging the fragments

Sentence fragments are littering the literate landscape.

Advertising copywriters are the worst offenders. I called attention to the overuse of this device a couple of years ago, in the only way some people could be appealed to. This way. In short bursts of scorn. Period.

Such revisionism in punctuation has not yet been stamped out. Presumably, some copywriters still cling to the belief that jerkiness equals punchiness, and have banished colons and dashes in favor of the period.

For example, a recent advertisement for my favorite newspaper reads: "We have entered a new age. The age of corporate clutter." The clipping was sent in by Charles Miller of New Market, Virginia, with this comment: "We have entered a new age. The age of the *Times* nonsentence." The advertisement concludes: "You have entered a new arena, but not as a spectator. As a player." In this new arena, English gets belted all over the ring. As a language.

The fragmented sentence style gets a fine going-over in "Off *The Wall Street Journal*," a hilarious parody by humorists Tony Hendra and Robert Vare. In a supposed ad by a distressed motor company for a "generic car"—an automobile with no name, the ultimate in stripped-down economy—the headline is "The Frill Is Gone," and the copy reads:

"We've got to cut costs. For your sake as well as our own. So we all got together and came up with a solution. We think it's the last word in American auto manufacture. The no-name car. No name, no chrome, no frills, no extras. Nothing. . . . If you're cold, wear a coat. If you're hot, take it off. You've got wheels, an engine, something to steer with, brakes and lights. Beyond that zip. Zero. Nothing. *And if nothing can't pull us through, nothing will.*"

That sort of spoof ought to get through to copywriters who cannot stomach a colon and to account executives who think readers like to live staccato lives. Which is all we can do. In the new arena. With the rest of the clutter.

frank and fruitful exchange

"The foreign minister and the secretary had a fruitful exchange of views," says the Official Spokesman.

The State Department correspondent jots down "fru," and asks, "Would you also characterize their talks as candid?"

"A full and fruitful exchange," says the Spokesman carefully, adding a new adjective, not the one the reporter suggested.

"You would not say 'full and frank'?" asks another member of journalism's ultracognoscenti.

The Official Spokesman never overtly rejects a word of art, but substitutes one of his own: "Forthcoming," he says finally.

Here is the key to that meaningful minuet. In spokesmanspeak, *fruitful* means: "It went pretty well. They got somewhere." *Candid* means: "They hollered at each other a lot and told each other where to get off." *Frank* is the diplomat's way of saying: "We did not agree on a thing." *Full* means: "It went longer than we figured, lunch got cold, the chef is miffed." *Full and frank* means: "It looks like war." *Forthcoming* means: "They actually made an offer, and we're thinking about it." Its opposite is *unhelpful,* which translates as: "Such crude interference could set back the cause of peace for decades."

Those are the old standbys in striped-pants vocabulary, which are sometimes adopted by politicians: When Senator Edward Kennedy left a meeting with President Carter, who had tried to talk him out of running for the 1980 Democratic nomination, the Senator called their meeting "frank but not unfriendly," using *frank* in its spokesmanspeak meaning of "argumentative."

Robert McCloskey, a veteran State Department spokesman now an omsbudding columnist, recalls describing meetings with a French term—*tour d'horizon* —which meant "wide-ranging discussion." He used that whenever reporters wanted to zero in on a particular topic, and he wanted to signal that "they talked about a lot of things, not only that." McCloskey also used *a good exchange* whenever he meant: "Ask me some more about it—I'm prepared to brief."

A newer locution in diplomatese is *Sherpa meeting,* an extension of the "summit" metaphor begun in World War II by Winston Churchill. A Sherpa is a member of a Tibetan people, living on the southern slopes of the Himalayas in Nepal, famed for mountain-climbing capabilities; Sherpa Tenzing was famous for participating in the first conquest of Mount Everest. In Sherpa meetings, diplomats prepare the documents for world leaders to sign at summit meetings.

Churchill was also present at the creation of a ringing diplomatic phrase when he said at the Guildhall in London, in the opening days of World War I, "The maxim of the British people is 'Business as usual.'" This was a defiant maxim, telling the world that not even war could interrupt the steadfast work of the British people.

In the generation between the wars, however, a curious conversion overtook the phrase: "No business as usual" was a sardonic Depression sign, and the once-proud slogan gained a meaning of smugness and complacency. And so it is today: "The United States has made clear," Secretary of State Haig told the Senate Foreign Relations Committee, as he recommended extraordinary measures to prevent Poland from going into default, "that we will not do business as usual with either Poland or the Soviet Union while repression in Poland continues."

You mentioned "a newer locution in diplomatese . . . Sherpa meeting, an extension of the 'summit' metaphor begun in World War II by Winston Churchill."

In fact, however, Churchill did not use that metaphor in World War II, and was not in a position for some years after the war to call for a "summit meeting." It was not until his Conservative Party was returned to power in the 1950s that he called (in 1955) for a "summit meeting" of the heads of the great powers.

During World War II, I believe, the summit meetings were called "Big Three" (or "Big Four," if De Gaulle was present, or "Big Five," if Chiang was present) meetings.

> *Bill Branche*
> *Buffalo, New York*

freaking in

Word freaks the world over owe a debt to Henry Blumberg of Little Falls, New York.

Up to now, one slang use of the word *freak*—to mean aficionado, maven, connoisseur, enthusiast—has been thought to be of recent origin. For a century, *freak* has been used to mean "abnormal," as in *freak show*, but it was not until the 1960's that *freak out* blossomed into drug lingo. From that, slanguicographers thought, came *speed freak* and *acid freak*. Wrote Richard R. Lingeman in 1969: "By extension one who is obsessed with a certain way of thinking, as in *political freak.*" And so on, until we came to *word freak* as used in the snappy lead to this entry.

Comes now Mr. Blumberg, a former district attorney of Herkimer County, a man given to perusing old trial transcripts. On page 3,161 of *People v. Gillette* (1906), as the defense counsel was summing up, this Dreiserlike passage appears: "Well, he got the boat. He had a dress suitcase with him and he had a camera. Evidently, from the evidence in this case, he was one of your Kodak freaks. . . . Wherever they go and whoever they see and whatever place they come to, they have got to have a Kodak along for the purpose of getting pictures."

That's the sort of citation lexicographers lust after: a certified copy of stenographic notes, showing a usage in context, proving beyond a doubt that the locution was current in 1906.

Now we'll all have to rethink our freakiness. Since *freak* as a noun meaning "crackpot enthusiast" predates the use of *freak out*, long entries in the *Oxford English Dictionary Supplement* will have to be supplemented and recast.

You don't think this is important? You think such concentration on minuscule (spelled with a *u*) matters is a waste of time? Mark my words—linguists yet unborn will be mulling over Blumberg's Discovery. I am proud to publish his findings in this space. Not since Safire's Discovery of the origin of *do your own thing** has there been such a leap forward in the etymological exploration of slang.

---

*"If you maintain a dead church, contribute to a dead Bible Society, vote with a great party either for the Government or against it. . . . Under all these screens, I have difficulty to detect the precise man you are. . . . But do your own thing, and I shall know you."

—Ralph Waldo Emerson,
"Self-Reliance" (1841).

Wrote I you before about a then presumed momentary lapsus syntaxis of putting predicate before subject. Thought I reformed were you. Or derived was the lapse from its context in your abhominable and sinister Rightist political column.

*See now I, however, two lapses in the chaste section "Freaking In." Begin two
paragraphs together:*

*Wrote Richard R. Longeman in 1969 . . .
Comes now Mr. Blumberg . . .*

*Despair I over reforming you politically, but hope I for your syntactic improve-
ment. Must consider you the reason why such word order is folly. Use we subject
before predicate, because is reserved the inversion for interrogatives, imperatives,
Hyman Kaplan, and syntactic chic-anery. Moreover, resides the linguistic principle
on applicability. Just as refuse we to honor "try and" for "try to," because has "try
and" no past tense, so wrong is your arsey-versey syntax because makes it a hash
of any sentence using the verb "to be."
Are you wrong.*

*Earl Miner
Princeton, New Jersey*

geezer power

A gang of curmudgeonaries has taken after me
for using the term *geezer*. I wrote about the
"geezer power" confronting anyone seeking to
change the Social Security system, and the reaction would be illustrated by cartoonists with
cane-shaking and ear-trumpet-brandishing.

"As Chair of the New York Gray Panthers'
Economic Task Force and a member of the
New York Congress of Senior Citizens," writes
Leo Hartman, who is a person in his own right
and not a chair, "I want to express my resent-

ment at William Safire's recent snide reference to what he calls 'geezer power.' "

"I resent being referred to by a punk as an old geezer," fulminates William Watkins of Birmingham, Alabama, adding ominously: "Don't get in my way."

More to the point, Mrs. C. Chachakis of Miller Place, New York, writes: "If I choose to join groups which will help me collect what I have assumed to be due me for the last forty-five years, I do not wish to be considered part of geezer power."

I like the word *geezer.* A century ago, this dialect form of *guiser,* or one dressed in the guise of a mummer, meant an old person, particularly a woman; over the years, it picked up and then partially dropped a connotation of eccentricity, but turned mainly masculine. It can now be used either in derision or with affection to refer to old people, particularly—to my ear—outspoken old people, usually men.

Old people did not like that description of themselves, and liked *aged* or *aging* not much more; soon they came to be called "the elderly." Even this euphemism seemed unduly doddering, so we were treated to *senior citizen* and *golden ager,* and old women keep their chins up by calling themselves *mature.* In satiric response, a cartoon in *Esquire* in the 1960's showed an old man shouting at a television set: "Call me Gramps, call me an old fogy—call me anything except a senior citizen!"

Anybody who is so sensitive about the word *old* that he insists on being called a "golden ager" or "senior citizen" is too old to cut the mustard of controversy. I am *middle-aged;* I wish I were young again, but I don't get any surge of youthful energy out of calling any crises in my middle-agedness "midlife." "Old" is something nobody likes to be (except considering the alternative), but if you are old, then old is what you are, and calling yourself "venerable" or "in the sunset years" isn't going to make you any younger.

Ah, but aren't euphemisms generally a way of making people feel better about what they are? Yes and no. *Cripple* is a word that hurts, and is limited to afflictions of the limbs, while *handicapped* has a connotation of built-in sympathy and dignity, and is a broader term covering any sort of disability. Certainly *handicapped* is a euphemism, but so what? Euphemism is not always bad, nor is a change in terminology always euphemistic: Yesterday's *insane asylum* is not today's *mental hospital.*

If a person is *deaf*—really stone deaf, cannot hear at all —then call him deaf; if he is partially deaf, then call him "hearing-impaired," or the older "hard of hearing." I would not use *hearing-impaired* on somebody who was quite deaf: it insults both speaker and subject. In a related case, *dumb* is a word to reject, because it has been stigmatized by its meaning as "stupid," which people who cannot speak are not necessarily; *mute* is the word for someone who speaks not at all, and I would reserve *speech-impaired* for someone who speaks with difficulty.

However, the euphemisms put forward by a federal agency in 1974 on specific speech problems should be rejected: a *lisp* is a lisp, not a "communication disorder," which could be a computer breakdown in a bureaucracy; nor is a *stutter* a "speech disfluency," and anyone who asks a stutterer to identify his trouble with that phrase is heartless.

But *special* is a gentle way of identifying children who are *retarded,* which was in its early days a euphemism for *slow* or *backward.* Perhaps *special* is on the saccharine side; certainly it is confusing when it is also applied to children who are *gifted,* a reverse euphemism for *talented* or "in the *genius* range"—still, if it comforts a parent to call a retarded child "special," only language purists will object.

Are these decisions all by-guess-and-by-God, or are some standards at work here? One criterion that emerges is the source of the pressure for change: If it is spontaneous, or fills a linguistic-psychological need, then it should be accepted, but if it comes in the form of fiat from government or demand by pressure group or propaganda for a movement, then it can rightly be resisted.

Without communication disorder or speech disfluency, I resist the word *gay* just because homosexual-rights groups insist upon it; I don't say *queer,* because that is a slur, but *homosexual* is neutral and accurate. If lesbians argue that *homosexual* should be limited to men, I would put up a feeble fight—arguing that the *homo* is the same as the *man* in *mankind* and covers women, too*— but I'd cave in; if many people used the separate terms, that differentiation would be in the direction of precision.

I reject *chair* and *chairperson* because they are propaganda words that convey less information than *chairman* and *chairwoman.* I would reject *Ms.* on the same basis, but resistance to pressure in that case is outweighed by a concern for privacy —if a woman wants to conceal her marital status, the way men do with *Mr.,* that's her business. *Black* was accepted readily because it was not imposed—black English generally is stolen by whites from blacks, and there was no official ukase to "stop using *Negro.* "

A second criterion about the use of euphemism is the nature of the condition being gentled or prettified. Physical or mental handicap has the most weight; minority status next; and the condition that still calls for respect, but permits flipness, is one from which we all come or are mostly going.

If my children organize to issue a complaint about being called *kids,* I will cut off their allowance until they bleat an apology. They can call themselves *youths;* I can call them *boys and girls,* or *kids.*

And so to *geezer.* Members of any group have a special dispensation to use what might be taken as derogations if spoken by outsiders, and if all goes well, I will be entering geezerhood myself one day. I like to think that in old age I will be blunter than I am today, and will rate the connotation of outspokenness that *geezer* carries.

Because it is a mark of good manners to respect one's elders, especially those who have gained a respect for directness, I am sorry for those who insist on being called *senior citizens,* because I will not speak as a junior citizen, or a silver ager. *Old* is not

*See "homogenized etymology."

an epithet, and *age* is not a word or condition to deny. If you don't like *geezer*, that's your privilege; holler about it and write letters about it. But you will not turn this geezer-to-be from a term that, in my lexicon, is no slur. *Geezer* is a word intentionally flip, but not profoundly disrespectful; "geezer power" is a force to be acknowledged and even admired, but not to knuckle under to.

"Being an old geezer endowed with a robust and irrepressible sense of humor," writes Leon Goldberg of New York City, "I can only tip my hat to you for your appropriate use of such a meaty epithet. But I am baffled by an apparent 'glitz' committed by you. . . . Your derogatory remark about the word *honest* as a sign of good quality in wine [in "Bloopie Awards"] is beyond my comprehension.

"Are you not aware that throughout La Belle France *'Ce vin est honnête'* signifies 'good' without being 'excellent'? Even a demanding nitpicker like you has to go along."

There's a geezer with a feel for the nuances in language.

I want to inform you that although I may fit your mental picture of a geezer, I don't fit mine, so please don't call me it.

A geezer, as I see him, is a not very well educated, sloppily dressed, not too clean old man with a couple of days' gray stubble showing in his face. And if you want to grow up to be a geezer that's your privilege, but keep me out of it.

I am an old man *(going on 70). I don't like that either, but there it is.*

Maturely yours,
Arthur J. Morgan
New York, New York

This old geezer thinks you are incorrect in your use of the words "stone deaf" in your euphemism samples. The correct descriptive is "tone" deaf.

There are several of these verbal distortions which I filed away over the years. "Squash" often is used instead of "quash" to denote legal suppression. Then there are "vicious circle" instead of "vicious cycle," "all told" rather than "all totaled" and, finally, "cold chisel" instead of the correct "coal chisel."

Maybe we geezers will help put the syntax in our language back where it belongs. Now, how about defending yourself against the word "punk"?

Jerome Meyer
Port Chester, New York

"Hearing-impaired" is not really a new euphemism for hard-of-hearing. Rather, it is a term which encompasses the whole gamut of hearing loss. Almost no one is as deaf as a stone. Most "deaf" people can hear something, although for some

people it might be sounds at the top of the scale and for others sounds at the bottom. What is significant is that they cannot hear and make sense of sounds within the range of human speech. Unlike blindness, which also covers a continuum of loss but often extends to a total loss, there is no designation of "legally deaf." When the term "deaf" is used it can mean a great variety of things depending on who is using it and in what context. In fact, within the deaf community it often denotes members of the deaf subculture regardless of their degree of hearing loss.

But back to the main point. Hard-of-hearing people generally have some usable hearing. Deaf people generally do not. However, some people who have usable hearing consider themselves deaf, while some people with little or no usable hearing consider themselves hard-of-hearing. And a great many people find themselves caught in the gray area. Are they deaf or only hard-of hearing? The term "hearing impaired" has come to the rescue. Everyone with a significant hearing loss is hearing impaired. Agencies no longer need to serve "the deaf and hard-of-hearing" in order not to slight some member of the group they are trying to serve. Now they can serve the hearing impaired.

In a related matter, "mute" is a term which seems to be on its way out among the hearing impaired and those who work in the field. I have never met a deaf person who could not speak and I have rarely met one who did not speak. I have, however, met many who do not speak in public or to strangers. Most people with a severe to profound hearing loss have spent years in school learning how to speak. For the pre-lingually deaf this is particularly difficult, and although some are able to master speech, most are very self-conscious about how they imagine themselves to sound. Therefore, they do not speak in front of people who may not understand. They do speak, however, to the hearing members of their families and to close hearing friends. As an interpreter for the deaf I have often asked, "Does she use her voice?" in order to find out whether I will be expected to voice interpret the person's sign language. The answer is often, "She prefers not to." But if communication is important and speech seems to be the most efficacious method, almost all deaf people will resort to it.

Thank you for your time. I do appreciate your efforts on behalf of my language. Without it I would remain dumb.

Casey Garhart
State College, Pennsylvania

When I was in Edinburgh some years ago, I was told that "geezers" or "guisers" were adherents of the French faction in the Scottish politics of the 16th century led by the Duke de Guise and his family. It was, I think, a term meant to be derogatory and sneering in tone.

Paul H. Silverstone
New York, New York

People over the age of sixty-five are older adults. Those under that age are simply younger adults. Why don't we all refer to all of them in this manner?

I think that you could say that Ronald Reagan is a hearing-impaired, older adult who is quite happy with his age, and enjoys life, and political power. That he is using it, to promote his ideas. He lives well, and neither his age, nor his disability, is easily detected. There are many older adults who share such feelings, and circumstances.

As a journalist, you could say that. Or, you might say that he is a deafened, old geezer, who flaunts his political power, but hates his age, and any labels, or names, that refer to it, for that reason. Some younger adults would share those feelings, too.

Imagine doing that, and having Ronald Reagan protest it. Would you consider it knuckling under to him, if you deferred to the offense to his sensibilities, and continue doing it, especially, because of his political power?

Is it any different, with anyone else? Of any age?

Nathalie Pitcher (Mrs. C.W.)
Rocky River, Ohio

I am like the cartoon character you wrote about, the man who said, "Call me anything except a senior citizen!" I love the term "geezer." "Golden ager"— phooey! I am seventy, and seldom think about age until someone coyly refers to my being a senior citizen.

I wish you had included in your article some mention of the silliness of avoiding the word "death." It is like the word "birth." Talking about it will not cause it to happen. "Passing away," "passing over" (over what?), "going to sleep"—what nonsense!

Rosemary G. Davis
Tucson, Arizona

You say: "I reject chair *and* chairperson *because they are propaganda words that convey less information than* chairman *and* chairwoman."

As a Leadership Trainor for Women's League for Conservative Judaism (Volunteer) I teach that the word chairman *has no gender. It is like the word* President. *You have often stated that we cannot just change words to suit our preference, but rather must use them correctly. In light of that don't you think we should continue using* chairman *and not resort to the cumbersome term* chairwoman?

Annette Blitzer
Plainview, New York

You reject "chair" and "chairperson" as "propaganda words that convey less information than chairman *and* chairwoman." *It strikes me that you are expecting a title to convey gender as well as position. So you therefore reject all position titles which do not specify gender? Consider the following list: president, vice-president, ambassador, justice, computer programmer, director, supervisor. Are these titles somehow inferior because they are applicable to both males and females?*

I agree that "chairperson" is a contrived word, but I consider the neuter term "chair" to be perfectly acceptable to refer to an individual who chairs a committee or similar group.

> Shawn A. Freeman
> Washington, D.C.

As a soon-to-be geezer, I agree with your attitude to the word. As a right-now disabled person who has to use a wheelchair, I strongly disagree that "handicapped" is a euphemism that makes me feel better. Mostly because it reverses concepts.

I am being *handicapped—by things outside myself. It is a penalty imposed as in the horse-racing sense (*Compact OED*—"To place at a disadvantage.")*

Disabled people (in wheelchairs at least) are certainly handicapped, but by stairs and doors and other people's attitudes, to say nothing of mass transit.

Unfortunately the so-called euphemism enforces the notion that the handicap is an irreversible condition. The disability may be; the handicap is not.

> Frances Barish
> New York, New York

In "Geezer Power," you wrote: ". . . there was no official ukase to . . ." As an highly irregular Irregular, I read your use of the word "ukase" not to mean a Russian emperor's proclamation, but rather an edict, which, according to my Webster, *is an official public proclamation. Is not "ukase" sufficiently official without the adjective "official"?*

> Harvey A. Eysman
> Great Neck, New York

Worse, even, than geezer—that emasculated goose—is the ubiquitous "dear," the current form of polite address to old ladies. A term properly used to children and dependents, it establishes a patronizing goodwill when directed to the elderly —the goodwill conditional on a suitable gratitude in the female so favored.

It seems not generally understood that while an elderly woman may have lost

*her youth, she has not necessarily lost her wits. And there's always the fair chance
she may be obtuse and difficult—not dear at all.*

Call me your cranky correspondent.

Shirley Carr
New York, New York

*As a deaf person and a member of the Board of Directors of the Alexander
Graham Bell Association for the Deaf (AGBAD), I would like to correct your
recent definition of "hearing-impaired." As explained by Dr. Winifred Northcutt,
an educator of the deaf and past president of AGBAD* (Volta Review *81:112,
1979), the term "hearing-impaired" is a generic term referring to any individual
with a hearing loss from mild to profound. It includes the subclassifications "deaf"
and "hard of hearing." It is extremely rare for a person to be unable to hear at all.
You would be correct, however, in calling a person "deaf" if he had a profound
(greater than 90 dB ISO) hearing loss. It would be equally correct, and certainly
not insulting, to call him "hearing-impaired."*

Nansie S. Sharpless, Ph.D.
Associate Professor,
Departments of Psychiatry and Neurology
Albert Einstein College of Medicine of Yeshiva University
Bronx, New York

A few observations relating to your article on euphemisms which I relished:
crippled *and* handicapped *(as well as* disabled*) are now démodé in social-worker
cant—there* mobility-impaired *is current. When I first heard the term here on the
University of Texas campus (where I'm a law student), I found myself wondering
whether someone's car had broken down. We might, by analogy, invent a euphemism for* illiterate: upward-mobility-impaired. *But perhaps that's not such a good
idea—some people might take it seriously.*

Bryan A. Garner
Austin, Texas

*Soon after we had bought our cottage in Kent, a dear old party from the
village knocked on the kitchen door and let herself in while my wife was cooking
and I was being idiotic in the corner with a* Times *crossword puzzle. "May I
come in? Oh, I see you've bought a new fridge and a new cooker and the old
geyser's (pr. geezer's) gone." (We had just installed central heating and refurbished
the kitchen.) "The old geezer's right here!" I protested. (I'm a short man, but not*

*that short.) It was all breathlessly and apologetically straightened out, with three
shiny new Briticisms in one sentence (*fridge, cooker *and* geyser *equal, respectively,*
icebox, stove *and* water heater *in the American terminology of that era;* fridge *has
now been naturalized here, somewhat,* cooker *remains strictly British, and wall-
hung water heaters are virtually unknown in centrally heated America).*

Norman W. Schur
Weston, Connecticut

Dear Bill:

*Around here, there's a simple definition of old. In our news columns, no one
can be called old, aged or elderly unless he is at least five years older than the oldest
executive in the place. By coincidence, the oldest executive around here is the
60-year-old publisher.*
Some rules are easier to make than others.

Best wishes,
Mike [Michael Gartner]
Editor and President, Des Moines Register and Tribune
Des Moines, Iowa

gender bender

State, the official publication of the Department of State, circulated around the
world to Foreign Service officers and State employees, has decided to adopt the
epicene, or bisexual, pronoun *s/he.*

Concerned about sexual stereotyping, some writers and editors have been
looking for ways to avoid sentences like "Everybody should watch his English."
One way to avert the suggestion that everybody is a he is to add the words *or
her,* which strikes me as awkwardly straining to be fair; a better way, if talking
to a horde of chairpersons, is to recast such sentences ("We should all watch our
English"). Some male supremacists take a fiendish delight in sticking *he* where
the pronoun refers primarily to women, while some ultrasensitive souls (the sort
who use *and/or* in everyday speech) have come up with *s/he.*

"The use of *s/he* is confined to this magazine," says Mr./Master/
Miss/Mrs./Ms. Sanford Watzman, the amiable editor of *State,* "and does not
represent official State Department policy."

What caused him to undertake this crusade? "Deciding which pronoun to use
in the nominative case always seemed like a pain-in-the-neck kind of thing, so

I decided to introduce *s/he,* which I came across in some newsletter from a diplomatic post. Seemed like a fun thing to do."

The department hastily passes the buck. Peter Knecht, a candid, forthcoming spokesman at Foggy Bottom, says, "The official State Department stance on nominative-case pronouns comes exclusively from the *Government Printing Office Stylebook,* available at the Superintendent of Documents. This is our bible. There are, however, heretics who might disregard the stylebook and use their own constructions."

This tolerance of diversity at State is as laudable as it is atypical. Where do I stand on the issue? For the average taxpayer, seeking guidance on the issue of sex in pronouns, here is my advice: When a noun excludes women in a blatant way, go along with the tide of change. The *workingman* is out, the *worker* is in; that is an improvement because it simplifies in a natural way. Similarly, though less enthusiastically, I would go for *firefighter* over *fireman,* looking toward that day when women bear as well as wear the hose. But then you start straining—with *waitron* instead of *waiter* and *waitress.* Such militant, manufactured nouns are to be avoided.

As for pronouns, when in doubt, let the man embrace the woman. Mankind does not need to be replaced by humankind. But don't knock sensibly nonsexist language. To say "According to Dr. Robert Baldinger, the average child loses his baby teeth at the age of six" is not as precise as " 'On the average,' says Dr. Baldinger, 'children start to lose their baby teeth at age six.' "

The use of *their* for *his,* when both *his* and *her* are meant, makes sense: "The tenant who loses his key" should be "tenants who lose their keys." But "anyone who loses his key" should not be stretched to "anyone who loses his or her key"—it imposes a point of view on grammar, which should have only the points of view of precision and naturalness. (Maybe I ought to go back to wearing a key chain.)

Let the editor have his fun; let editors generally have their fun, but do not let the editor have his or her fun. Avoid such artificial devices as "What did s/he say?" It's unspeakable.

You're right, we shouldn't strain to change to an "epicene" language as in the case of waiter/waitress *vs.* waitron *(a member of humanoidkind?)*

What's wrong with the word waiter *for both sexes? We do not speak of doctors and doctoresses, lawyers and lawyesses or Indian chiefs and chieftresses. Er is defined in the* Random House Dictionary *as a "suffix of nouns denoting persons or things concerned or connected with something: butter, grocer. . . ."*

A waiter waits tables. It is not as if we are served by waitmen as opposed to waitwomen. Can't we just call for the waiter, cancel the waitress and hold the dilemma?

> *Ellen Perlman (Perlperson?)*
> *Alexandria, Virginia*

Your discussion of gender-specific nouns and pronouns has prompted me to inquire about terms that imply leadership positions. It has always puzzled me why the suffix "-person" is so much more frequently used in the United States than "-member" when the latter more accurately describes the position.

To use examples, I find it curious that a U.S. Representative is called a Con-gressperson rather than a Congressmember since his official title is Member of Congress. Congressmember *can be made plural much more easily than* Con-gressperson; *neither* Congresspersons *nor* Congresspeople *seems at all appropri-ate, not to mention easy to pronounce.*

Along the same line I wonder why members of city councils are not more often referred to as councilors *or* councilmembers *rather than the more cumbersome* councilperson.

The use of chairwoman *pointed out the peculiarity of the word* chairman *as much as it pointed to the need for a neuter title. Here again I find* chairperson *to be cumbersome, especially when used in the plural. Does* chairman *always refer to a member of a body who leads and, if so, would it not then be appropriate to use* chairmember?

Though I strongly favor gender-neutral terms, I find many lose their effectiveness (as does the full context of what is being said) when they are used in excess.

Helene Sahadi York
Cambridge, Massachusetts

I propose, when in doubt, let the woman embrace the man. Women do outnum-ber men, and man *already is included in* woman, he *in* she. *Problems do remain with the use of* her/him *and* her/his, *but not so different from existing difficulties and perhaps of a lesser magnitude, since there are fewer of you.*

Let woman have her fun. She should do her work, put out her fires, and woe to woman if she should lose her key.

Now how do you feel? Left out? Shame on you for casting aside attempts to correct the sex bias of our language. When you can truly solve the pronoun problem, you'll have come a long way, baby.

Mary Riskind
Ridgewood, New Jersey

It struck me that we already have available an epicene personal pronoun for the third person singular. This word now serves as the neuter form "it." Why not begin using "it" in place of "he" or "she"? Why not "Let the editor have its fun"? After all, we do have a precedent for this shift. English has in time become decreasingly gender-specific. Old English had grammatical gender; its speakers referred to mountains, rivers, etc. as "he." However, somewhere in the course of our language's history it became preferable to refer to these as "it." Of course, one might argue, the actual mountain or river doesn't have a particular sex, so this change was logical. But what of animals? They do have natural gender, yet it is now perfectly acceptable to refer to them as "it": "The cow chewed its cud." We may even refer to human infants as "it." And further, in modern English, as a nominative of the verb "to be," "it" may refer to any person at all: "Who is it?"

English speakers have come this far down the road to "neuterization" apparently without balking. Why not ask them to take a step further? Since many of us feel the need to make some contrived change in the language to eliminate sexual discrimination in personal pronoun usage, perhaps "it" is the best solution. As unnatural as it might at first seem, it is certainly more fluent than "s/he." (How in the world is "s/he" pronounced?)

Vincent L. Rossano
Underhill, Vermont

"According to Dr. Robert Baldinger, the average child loses his baby teeth at the age of six" is not as precise as "On the average, children start to lose their baby teeth at age six" not only because of the pronoun but because of the statistic. "Average child" is ambiguous (really nonexistent!) whereas in the latter, "the average" clearly refers to average number of years it takes.

David Bernklau
Brooklyn, New York

genitives, *see* double genitives

getting personal

When *Washington Post* columnist Maxine Cheshire reported on Nancy Reagan's activities at the royal wedding, a reader protested about the use of the phrase *personal friend*. Wrote Sandra Gottlieb of Bethesda, Maryland: "Is Susan Meyer really a 'close personal friend' of Nancy Reagan's? Are you sure she isn't a 'close, impersonal friend' . . . or a 'distant, personal friend'?"

Personal is a word that has been snuggling up too close to *friend*. To have a friend goes beyond knowing somebody personally—that is, as between individuals, or, in sports lingo, "one on one." When a television performer says, "All my friends out there in televisionland," he does not mean friends, if the word *friend* has any meaning: A friend is someone with whom you have a personal relationship. "He's my personal friend" is, then, redundant and a fit object of scorn by the Squad Squad.

Personal is a word taking a beating in other respects. Advertisers have been using it to mean "not bath size"—that is, "personal-size Ivory." In that same small sense, a "personal car" is a small car, not a "family car." One traditional meaning of *personal* is "individual," and such usages are not mistaken, but they are being overused. What is a "personal computer"? Presumably it means that one person can work it, but can't one person work any computer?

Personal and confidential is a redundancy most of the time. *Personal* can mean "not official" or "not corporate," but the intended meaning is usually "This is between him and me, Nosy Parker, and keep your prying eyes off it" —that is, "private." When *personal* is used in that sense, *personal and confidential* is redundant. Letters addressed to me with that stuttering stricture are examined by hordes of secretaries and news clerks, while letters marked "private" *or* "personal" are opened by me, personally, after I soak them in a tub of water.

While I agree with you that PERSONAL and CONFIDENTIAL are mostly misused in today's business correspondence, I do not agree that they are always redundant. The proper use of PERSONAL, I believe, is for letters of a nonbusiness nature sent to a business address. CONFIDENTIAL would then be appropriate for a business letter sent to a business address which one intends to be seen by the addressee only. Either would indicate to a secretary that this should not be opened by anyone other than the addressee.

However, once sent a letter belongs to the person it is sent to, to do as he wishes with it. Someone can receive personally—but then decide to share it with others. Thus CONFIDENTIAL is a flag to the recipient of a letter that it is not only personal, but should be held in confidence also.

Mrs. Anne Kavanaugh
Crozet, Virginia

It seems to me that "personal" and "confidential" tap two different dimensions of privacy. A letter to my sister is personal, but she may share it with her family unless it is marked "Confidential: under fourteen or over forty not admitted." On the other hand, a letter of reference is confidential, but is personal only with regard to its subject.

A "confidential" letter imparts "confidences" or secrets about the subject, which may be personal or impersonal. A "personal" letter contains information about the author or recipient, which may or may not be sensitive. I agree that as commonly used, most letters marked "Personal and Confidential" are not per-sonal, but that makes the phrase inaccurate, not redundant.

Robert E. Davidson, Ph.D.
Assistant Professor, Sociology
University of Texas
San Antonio, Texas

I noticed that you'd overlooked one of the most appalling bastardizations of the word "personal," the "personalizing" of Christmas cards, birthday cards and all that junk—by the mere act of writing your name on them. (The more egregious perpetrators of this horror, if that phrase doesn't offend you, are likely in any case to have had their cards preprinted with their name and address; but that, of course, is too impersonal!)

JAC Mackie
Canberra, Australia

Call back the Squad Squad before it does in another innocent victim.

"Close personal friend," I submit, is not redundant, but is, rather, an appropriate expression of the intimacy of a relationship (friendship). Your mistake is in viewing "friend" as an absolute, when in fact it is something that can be measured by the depth/warmth/closeness/etc. of the relationship. Frequently, in expressing friend-ship, the feeling must be modified or enlarged.

Someone can be, simply, a friend. Or, you can refer to someone as "a dear friend" or "a very dear friend."

You can be a "good friend," or the closeness of the relationship can be under-stated, as in: "We're just friends." Or (and this is used particularly at times of great emotion), it can be said "He (or she) is a true friend."

Also, Sandra Gottlieb's comments on "close personal friend" were not well taken and completely missed the point—the issue is not one of extremes, but of degrees.

Just as a heat wave can be torrid, so friendship can be close and personal.

Louis J. Ganim
Clifton Park, New York

given, *see* the present absent

glitziana

In *Cursors!*, *The Washington Post*'s internal publication of language self-criticism, omwordsman Dan Griffin pointed out a couple of recent uses of *glitzy*, a recently coined adjective meaning "ostentatious" or "extravagantly showy." He speculated that the word might be the offspring of *glitter* and *ritzy*.

Not even close, but give him a cigar. Fred Mish, editorial director at Merriam-Webster, says that *glitzy* is not a portmanteau word at all, but from the Yiddish *glitz*, meaning "glitter," akin to the German *glitzernd*, or "glittering." Its first citation was in 1971, and the word has been gaudily gaining in use lately.

Having aptly identified *glitz* as "the noise a lightbulb makes when it burns out," editor Griffin adds fanciful etymological speculation: To him, *glitz* conjures up a blend of *glitch* and *klutz*.

Now he is heavily into Yiddish. A *glitch*, or niggling breakdown in technology, is from the Yiddish verb *glitschen*, "to slip"; a *klutz* is from the Yiddish and German "block of wood," and means "blockhead," with a recent connotation of clumsiness.

Dear Bill,

Fred Mish gave you a mish-mosh of an answer regarding the origin of glitzy. *There is no such word in Yiddish as* glitz; *the Yiddish word for* glitter *may be* finkel, glants, blank, fechl, *but not* glitz. *As we stated in the* Second Dictionary of New English, glitzy *probably came from German* glitz(ern) *"to glitter," but I wouldn't entirely rule out Dan Griffin's conjecture of an English blend. Mish was close, but no cigar for him.*

> *Shalom,*
> *Sol [Sol Steinmetz]*
> *Clarence L. Barnhart, Inc.*
> *Bronxville, New York*

I was zapped by the heading "Glitziana." Was the word Glitziana *your serendipity, new-word concoction, or atavistically your Jewish heritage? Since you failed to expatiate on it, I am compelled to.*

Glitziana is an old-fashioned, gutter-al Yiddish fighting word. When a Litwak Jew (Lithuanian-Russian, fast-talking) met a Glitziana Jew (Austro-German, gemütlichkeit, *slow-talking*), they harangued each other like *Irish Kilkenny cats,* always. The Glitziana belabored the Litwak about being a sneaky lowlife and a cheap chiseler. The Litwak hammered the Glitziana for being a stuttering blockhead and a klutz.

There is an old folks' tale about a Litwak-dog meeting on a bridge a Glitz-dog with a blood-dripping steak in his mouth. The wily Litwak-dog with a voracious hunger for meat, knowing the slow speech of the Glitz-dog, asked where he got the meat, and the reply came slowly with wide-open vowels, enabling the Litwak-dog to get the prize meat and dash away from slowpoke.

In concussion, you might gather from my mistreatment of the Litwaks that I'm a *Galiziana* . . . a gestrufter . . . a cursed one . . . an epithet that often shamed us into silence.

Ben Ganz
New York, New York

gnat swallowers

"The United States is straining at gnats and swallowing camels," wrote Hodding Carter 3d in *The Wall Street Journal.* When sculptor Elijah Pierce tried to depict that familiar figure of speech, *Time* magazine reviewer Robert Hughes wrote: "Pierce's carving of one person straining at a gnat while another literally swallows a camel, the beast halfway down his throat, comes out of the same impulses that drove the Romanesque carvers at Vézelay or Autun to their didactic grotesqueries."

"How did such an expression ever arise?" asks Eileen Evans of Chapel Hill, North Carolina, alarmed at the sudden rise of figurative straining and gulping.

The original spokesperson, lest we forget, was Jesus of Nazareth, who rebuked the hypocrites of his time in Matthew 23:24 with "Ye blind guides, which strain at a gnat, and swallow a camel." Writers who keep using it should remember that the original blast was directed at scribes.

go à go-go

Now that *bop* has been established as a merry slang synonym for an intransitive *go,* what has happened to *go?* It has become a synonym for *say.*

Dick Cavett, who brings a concern for language to the taxpayer-subsidized airwaves, was asking me, "Have you noticed the way *he says* is out and *he goes* is in?"

I have. So has Ronald Butters of Duke University, writing in *American Speech* magazine about what he terms "the narrative *go.*" Example of the new use of *go:* "So George comes at Louis with the knife, and Louis goes, 'Don't cut me.'" The same use can be in the past tense: "I looked George in the eye, and he went, 'I don't like nobody starin' at me.'"

When did people start talking that way, or going like that? Mr. Butters cites a couple of meanings of *go* that border on *say: go over* means "repeat" and *go through* means "discuss." But he believes that the origin of the narrative *go* so common in young people's slang today is in imitative interjections—"go bang!" —and in the introductory word to the imitation of an animal's sound: "The cow goes, 'Moo.' The duck goes, 'Quack.'"

He cites the nursery rhyme: "This little pig went to market / This little pig stayed home / This little pig had roast beef / And this little pig had none / And this little pig went, 'Wee-wee-wee,' all the way home."

"I do not mean to imply," writes Mr. Butters, "that Americans now under the age of thirty-five were so influenced by having their little piggies pulled that a semantic change resulted. My own little piggies were regularly and vigorously pulled in the early 1940's, but no such change took place. . . . At the same time, however, the imitative use of *go*—present in the language for centuries—would seem in a more general way the most likely candidate for the source of the semantic extension."

There's a careful linguist, couching his startling discovery in the craven conditional. Next time Cavett goes, "Howcum nobody says 'say' anymore?" I'll go, "Wee-wee-wee," all the way home.

The rhyme "This little piggie" may well have been one of the elements that encouraged the current usage of "go" and "went" for "say" and "said," but I thought your readers might like to know that authorities on children's rhymes report that in the original version of "This little piggie," the final piggie "went wee wee wee all over the barn door." And "went wee wee" signified not the piglet's oink, but another, nonverbal, animal function.

Carol McKee
Crafton, Pennsylvania

You speculate upon the ancestry and usage of the verb go as a synonym for say. May I point out the unique and hitherto-unperformed function of go as say? Go meets a need in spoken (but not written) English to clarify ambiguity in quoted speech.

The difference between "She says, 'You're crazy,'" and "She says you're crazy" is clear when written. In the former, we know that we are reading her actual words and that the crazed one was the listener. In the latter, her intent but not her words are reported; this is an indirect quotation.

If this utterance is reported in speech rather than in writing, the distinction between direct and indirect quotation disappears. Unless the speaker says, "Quote, unquote," or points at the listener as "you" or (God forbid!) makes four little jabs in the air with her index and middle fingers as though playing charades, the listener cannot be sure whether it is he or another who has been maligned.

The use of "She goes, 'You're crazy' " immediately informs the listener that a direct quotation has been made. Result: no ambiguity.

I must admit that I did not discover this explanation of the usefulness of go *myself; I must credit Professor Mary Ann Geissal of the Linguistics Department of Northeastern Illinois University.*

Kathryn Reyen Judd
Chicago, Illinois

goodbye, Mr. Justice

Until recently, the way to address Justices of the Supreme Court was "Mr. Justice So-and-so." Then, mysteriously, without explanation, the *Mr.* was dropped from the printed publication of opinions: The Justices were called, simply, "Justice So-and-so."

Court sources whispered to me that the change was in anticipation of the appointment of a woman as a Justice. The prime mover in this far-seeing linguistic judgment was then–Associate Justice Potter Stewart, whose resignation in 1981 made way for an appointment that turned out to be the first female Supreme Court Justice.

Without taking credit for originating the change, Potter Stewart confirms the reasoning: "I remember sitting with the first female circuit judge in history, Florence Allen. Lawyers who wanted to be correct used to say, 'May it please the Court and Miss Allen,' which burned her up. A judge is a judge, and a Justice a Justice—no need for anything additional." The former Justice added: "Who knew whether a woman Justice would want to be called 'Mrs. Justice,' or 'Madam Justice,' or 'Ms. Justice'?" In that swift and unanimous decision, the Court solved a problem that threatened to loom before protocol chiefs making out place cards and headline writers grappling with honorifics. Under the Stewart Doctrine, all male-female designations are dropped: The correct way to address Sandra Day O'Connor is "Justice O'Connor."

Meanwhile, the man we used to call "Mr. Justice Stewart" need not worry about being called plain "Mr. Stewart," since judges, like senators and Presidents, always are given their title as a mark of respect after leaving office. Potter Stewart is relaxed about the change: "Nervous lawyers used to call me 'Mr. Justice Potter,' anyway."

good courtesanship

The most stunning language mistake of the year appears on the cover of the *Harper's* February issue. The title of an excerpt from a book about Clare Boothe Luce is "From Courtesan to Career Woman."

The problem is with the word *courtesan*. Simply put, it means "prostitute." Put with a touch of class, it means "prostitute with a wealthy clientele," and put with as much elegance as the word can muster—going back to its derivation from *female courtier*—the word means "royal mistress."

That is not what Wilfrid Sheed, a gifted writer who turned out a generally laudatory book about Mrs. Luce, had in mind. In his book, titled *Clare Boothe Luce,* Mr. Sheed uses the word in passing: "As a bridge-figure between the courtesan and the career girl, Clare has sometimes seemed a funny kind of feminist, and the women's movement finds her a difficult patron saint."

In excerpting the work, *Harper's* ignored the subtle distinction that placed Mrs. Luce "between" the two categories, and chose a headline that identified her as having started as a courtesan.

What did the editor of one of our more literate publications think the word meant? "I had a nightmare last night that I was going to get a call from you on this," says Michael Kinsley, editor of *Harper's.* "I just heard from Reed Irvine, of Accuracy in Media, demanding to know why I called a member of his board of directors a prostitute. That's not my understanding of the current meaning of the word."

His definition? "I would say," said the editor with a profound sigh, "that a courtesan is a member of a court whose role is to serve a great or rich man. The sexual connotation is only one part of it." That explanation evidently did not ring too well in his own ear, and he added: "As Reed pointed out, courtesans were not married to the king, and Mrs. Luce was married. She was not in any literal sense a courtesan. I certainly did not mean to insult her. I guess I didn't realize the offensive nuance, but we're allowed a figurative ———."

Would he take offense, granting all the figurative leeway, if the word were applied to someone close to him—say, his mother?

"I don't think I'd mind," said the editor. "It would be highly inappropriate in the case of my mother, but I wouldn't take offense, I think. Hey, look, I wish I'd picked another word. A better title for that piece would be 'Woman of the American Century,' tied to Harry Luce's 'American Century' theme, but it's too late now."

The reason for belaboring this talented editor is to illustrate a point in English usage: Words not only mean what you want them to mean, words mean what they mean to most people who understand them. That was Lewis Carroll's satiric point, as Humpty Dumpty dismissed Alice's objection to stretching words until they lost their meaning and became sources of confusion.

A courtesan was and is a woman who sells sex to the high and mighty. That was true in 1565, when Bishop John Jewel wrote about "Open Stewes so deerely rented: so many thousand Cortegians so well regarded." What Bishop Jewel had against flight attendants I don't know, but the word's spelling and meaning are both apparent in a 1607 citation in the *Oxford English Dictionary:* "Your whore is for every rascall, but your Curtizan is for your Courtier." And it is true today.

"To a woman of her generation," writer Sheed says ruefully, "that word must pack a wallop." It does because the less specifically sexual meaning, evidently in the mind of Mr. Kinsley, has not replaced the meaning in the dictionaries and in most people's minds. What does *courtesan* mean to Wilfrid Sheed, in the sense he used it? "A courtesan is one who can get ahead only by using men," he reports, "as distinct from Mrs. Luce, who is one who knows how and when to use them but doesn't strictly need them."

Fair enough: That's an additional meaning, useful in discussing "mentor" relationships in business today, which will get into tomorrow's dictionaries because a respected author and editor used it, and because I have reported on it in this prestigious publication. But it is not the primary meaning, and the word should not be used when the primary meaning hurts or defames the individual described.

How is Mrs. Luce taking it? "I've had a lot of careers," says the former magazine editor, playwright, war correspondent, congresswoman, and ambassador and present adviser to the President on foreign intelligence, "but I don't know, at the age of seventy-eight, if I want to be provided with one I didn't have." She admires Mr. Sheed, and takes the error with good humor, but adds: "So I was a 'courtesan,' eh? Just don't let Harry Luce hear about that, wherever he may be."

I am not an airline steward. My wife is not an airline stewardess, nor are my daughters. Nonetheless, I take umbrage at [your comment on "Open Stewes."] While you correctly rail against Michael Kinsley for his misuse of the language, you indulge in comparable grossness yourself.

> Vincent Joyce
> Hong Kong

You used a quotation that had the phrase "open stewes" in it, and I believe that you professed puzzlement over the term and joked about a reference to airline stewardesses. A "stew" is an archaic word used as a pejorative for brothel or a bathhouse where naughty things go on—the "tubs" as Bette Midler, who used to sing in them, would say. I came across the usage in reference to Pope Paul IV, one of the most reactionary of the papal line, who called Michelangelo's Last Judgment *in the Sistine Chapel "a stew of nudes," the reason they all wear wispy chiffons today.*

> David L. Miles
> Charlevoix, Michigan

You say: "The reason for belaboring this talented editor is to illustrate a point in English usage. Words not only mean what you want them to mean, words mean what they mean to most people. . . ."

Wouldn't it be better to say: "Words mean not only what you want them to mean . . ." etc.? The misplacing of the word "only" is very common, but those of us who learned how to diagram a sentence in grade school English grammar know that the words "only" and "but" must be followed by equivalent phrases.

Herbert W. Osgood
Youngstown, Ohio

I was taught that Carroll's sympathies lay with Humpty Dumpty and not with Alice, that is, in the self-contained world of mathematics we may accept what axioms we like and in our own terms (this led Bertrand Russell to define mathematics as the subject in which we don't know what we are talking about nor whether what we say is true). As a mathematician, Carroll would no more object to Humpty Dumpty's specialized use of language than a chessplayer would object to the rules of chess on the grounds that in the real world peasants don't become queens after moving forward six paces.

I was taught this at Bronx Science, 1945–48; they may have changed the curriculum subsequently.

Morton D. Davis
Department of Mathematics, City College
City University of New York
New York, New York

You missed a great opportunity in Sunday's column headline—"Magazine reports Claire Booth loose."

Martin Verdrager
New York, New York

gorge rising

You know that inexplicable zigzag along the line of a lapel? What's it called? An indent? A cutout? In his "Notes on Fashion" in *The New York Times*, John Duka gives it both an insiders' and an outsiders' name: "For spring, Armani . . . has returned to his classic blazer, offering it in new overscaled proportions, with lapels with a very low gorge, or notch."

Though *overscaled* seems an odd cross between *upscaled* and *oversized*, the clear naming of the funny indentation in lapels is a contribution to my vocabulary. ("Can you narrow the lapels without cutting into the gorge?")

You get a good feeling when you learn the name of something that you once had to point at, or fumblingly describe. In the same way, you feel frustrated when there seems to be no name for a thing or a circumstance that needs a name.

"Two pedestrians come toward each other," writes Ernest Heyn, associate publisher of *Popular Science*, "one shifts to the right to miss the oncoming person, the other shifts to the left, then to the right as his 'opponent' moves to the left. Eventually, they stop and go their respective ways, blushing all the while. Is there an English word for this event?"

Of course—it's one of those whatchamacallit circumstances that make us all feel like idiots. To be more precise, I turned to Simon & Schuster's ace lexicographer, David Guralnik, who may be short of a precise answer but is never at a loss for words: "Not aware of any standard term for this contretemps, but I have heard it called a *pas de deux*—probably a nonce borrowing by a balletomane—and I seem to recall 'doing the (something) shuffle.'"

The wordsman allows that the circumstance described by Mr. Heyn is "a situation that calls for wit or creativity, but the wit usually stops at 'May I have the next dance?' or 'We've got to stop meeting this way' or 'Allemande left-right.'"

All of us in the word dodge obviously need help. Coinage immortality awaits.

I am appalled that you sought a name for the "inexplicable cutout or zigzag" in lapels, since the lapel begins below the cutout.

Think, fold over your lapels, turn your collar up and (if high fashion has not intervened) you have a chest warmer with a high collar to warm your neck. Think of Napoleon in his greatcoat, casually opened at the front. This later became the fashion. Hence something that had not existed came into existence, or more accurately apparel, and in need of a name.

Seek a name by all means but not at the expense of the definition of the poor lapel.

Max Lewis
Darien, Connecticut

The "inexplicable zigzag along the line of a lapel" has a very simple explanation that seems to have escaped your sartorial logic. The buttonhole on the left lapel was not designed to hold a white carnation, but to be combined with a button you will find under the right lapel in many a coat, to transform an open collar into a closed one that is snug around the neck. This would be impossible without the gorge or notch.

José de Vinck
Allendale, New Jersey

I dare say that the zigzag along the line of a lapel is far from inexplicable. A cursory glance at 17th and 18th Century jackets will readily disclose its function: the garment was capable of closing all the way up to the throat (hence, gorge). What we have today is the vestige of this once-indispensable feature of a man's jacket.

I say indispensable because, yesterday as today, it can get pretty chilly on a horse. It is interesting to note that only in the severest of climates did the military provide a great coat for its horsemen (Russia, Germany, and the Scandinavian countries). All others expected them to put up with the weather . . . reason enough to provide for a jacket capable of being buttoned all the way up. The reason is there if one cares to look: how can a mounted soldier be expected to wield a saber effectively if he has a great coat flapping about in the wind? The only way to keep the great coat from flapping is either to secure it under the rider's legs (then the rider loses contact with the horse and other problems ensue) or to so weigh it that the wind will not be able to make it flap about (extra weight for the horse to carry, though). But if the rider dons sturdy britches (two pair if necessary), and has a warm jacket that buttons all the way up, he is sufficiently protected to do his job. We do the same thing today when we ride to the hounds. As a matter of fact, when it rains, lucky is the rider who has had the foresight to train his horse to accept him on his back with a flapping poncho around him. Those who actually put on a poncho for the first time when it is raining do so at their own peril (there is nothing slimier than a wet saddle).

The gorge, then, is necessary to allow the jacket to close, which is then opened when the rider gets off the horse and adopts more civilized manners. Since riding a horse also moves the dust and/or mud about, this also kept his linen clean. The centuries pass and, to this day, the only vestige left of the gorge's true purpose is to be found in high-quality English tweed jackets: the buttonhole functions against a button which is hidden by the other lapel . . . furthermore, they usually have a tab folded back under the collar which can be unbuttoned from its hidden position and buttoned across to the other side of the collar, thereby making a high collar which completely hides the shirt. This old idea has been adopted by the U.S. Army in its new field jackets.

Arthur Woodgate
Rhinebeck, New York

It seemed odd to me that gorge is properly applicable to the notch on a lapel. Are you certain it isn't really a gouge, a noun for both the instrument and for the results (a gouge) achieved with its use? Since one can gouge out a sliver, or an eye, why not a lapel? This makes more sense to me (although I don't like the term).

Joseph B. Martin, M.D., Ph.D.
Boston, Massachusetts

There may be some confusion about "gorge" and "notch" at the junction of lapel and collar. The triangular notch is one thing; the line or seam extending to the neckline from the point of the notch is the gorge.

On a trench coat, the notch is usually deep, facilitating closing the lapels at the throat (gorge) against the weather.

Shawl collars lack the notch and the gorge.

Theodore M. McMillion
Beaver Falls, Pennsylvania

Miss Burger is mistaken.

The gorge, according to fashion curmudgeon Mortimer Levitt, who owns The Custom Shops, according to Dunhill Tailors, and according to The Dictionary of Fashion, is a "men's tailoring term [that] indicates seam where collar meets lapel, either high or low." Giorgio Armani astounded the fashion world (it does not take much) by lowering the gorge or notch from the shoulder area (where Ralph Lauren and Brooks Brothers place it) to an area two inches above the xiphoid process.

Best,
John Duka
The New York Times
New York, New York

Here's a quotidian crisis that fairly cries out for the invention of an appropriate word.

Entering a store, office or building, you notice someone a few yards behind you. So you hold the door open. No problem if the someone is just a few steps away.

But there has to be a distance beyond which such courtesy becomes downright silly. I've determined this distance to be a generous 30 feet.

But what do we call this line of demarcation? A delightful choice, I think, would be "the treinta" (TRAIN-TAH), which is, of course, the Spanish for 30.

Thus, I might say to an office colleague, "I wasn't being discourteous this morning. It's just that you were beyond the treinta." If he's still unforgiving, to hell with him. He's probably beyond the pale, as well.

Philip Minoff
Oceanside, New York

Much as I long for "coinage immortality" it must come on different wings. The term you seek exists as the definition of an old burlesque comic bit, good for a laugh in a thousand sketches.

In burlesque it was vital to the success of a sketch that each player understood clearly which bits were to be included, since much of the dialogue was determined by audience response rather than a script. These bits were given names which were actually cues. The one you describe is known as the dos-a-dos.

Donn Fahnestock
Tenafly, New Jersey

Perhaps the word you are looking for is one that the citizens of Tierra del Fuego find so useful: mamihlapinatapai, *which means, roughly, "two people looking at each other when both want a certain thing done but neither wants to be the first to do it."*

As you know, many "primitive" languages are more subtle and complex than our own.

Reuben Abel
New York, New York

Dear Bill,

You discuss pedestrian zigzag, saying: "coinage immortality waits." So like Claudius (when he ate poisoned mushrooms) I'm herewith a god: the phrase I coin is chiasmus shuffle. *Chiasmus, based on the Greek letter "chi" (= X: hence any shape looking zigzag-crisscross), is a poetry term for crisscross sound echoes, e.g., rhyming last word of one line with a first word of next line (I've writ poems in that form). If you resist Greek as affected, call it:* crisscross shuffle, *or* X-shape shuffle. *Even better:* X-rated shuffle, *as it results in porno encounters betw. members of opp. sex.*

warm regards as ever,

Peter Viereck
South Hadley, Massachusetts

greeting card

The New York Alumni Club of the University of Chicago sent a form letter to Dr. Leo Srole, professor emeritus of social sciences at the Columbia University Faculty of Medicine. It began with "Dear Alum."

Professor Srole, offended by the forced cheeriness and determined informality of the salutation, replied to his co-alumnus with a practically identical salutation: "Dear Co-$NH_4Al(SO_4)_2.12H_2O$."

He acidly added that the definition of *alum,* for which he supplied a chemical formula, included the words "used esp. as an emetic." One of America's foremost sociologists is not some geezer you can send form letters to.

What you and Dr. Srole did not appear to realize is that in writing "Dear Alum" the club was not trying to be excessively cute or cozy, but simply to avoid a gender suffix: Alumnus or Alumna.

Now that men attend women's colleges and vice versa, their respective graduates' associations have difficulty with the inflexible Latin. My college has a magazine for graduates called The Alumnus. *The question has arisen whether to change the name, and if so, to what. "Alum" sounds silly, and I can see why Dr. Srole disliked it.*

I suggested to the editor of our publication that it could be called The Alumniate, *which bypasses the Latin. It did not call forth any enthusiasm. But the problem remains.*

> Arthur J. Morgan
> New York, New York

Professor Srole may not be some old geezer, but he has a great deal to learn about chemistry. The correct formulae for alum are:

potassium aluminum sulfate	$KAl(SO_4)_2 \cdot 12H_2O$
ammonium aluminum sulfate	$NH_4Al(SO_4)_2 \cdot 12H_2O$

His formula, $Co\text{-}NH_4Al(SO_4)_2 \cdot 12H_2O$, adds cobalt to ammonium aluminum sulfate and he adds it in the wrong amount (I also believe the addition to be impossible!). Although I realize that he uses "Co-" to mean an association or fellowship, this meaning is obscured (?) by the chemical formula that follows.

> Stephen Arrants, jr.
> Associate Editor
> Creative Computing
> Morris Plains, New Jersey

It is unfortunate that a social scientist has misled you. The formula given by Prof. Srole for alum is incorrect. According to the Merck Index, *alum is aluminum* *potassium sulfate, AlK[SO$_4$]$_2$.12H$_2$O. A variation is ammonium alum, AlNH$_4$ [SO$_4$]$_2$.12H$_2$O. I have not been able to find a reference to a cobalt alum as depicted by Prof. Srole.*

Donald M. Kirschenbaum, Ph.D.
Brooklyn, New York

Come now! Surely you realize that "alum" was used in the Univ. of Chicago letter to cope with sexism in our language. Its author has recognized that the world is populated with great numbers of alumnae as well as alumni in these modern times. To address possible female readers of the letter as "alums" instead of the incorrect "alumni" is a linguistic victory for women right up there with letter carrier and fire fighter. In the same vein, I am hearing the noun "chair" used often these days to replace the cumbersome, if unisex, term "chairperson."

Karen Blair
Women Studies Program
University of Washington
Seattle, Washington

guerrilla wordfare

"With the continued fighting in Central America," writes Robert Glesner of Forest Hills, Long Island, "journalists are continually referring to antigovernment forces as 'leftist guerrillas.' My question is: 'What other kind of guerrillas are there?' "

His question—which might better have been "What other kind of guerrilla is there?"—is timely. As he notes, irregulars are rarely called *rightist guerrillas;* there are only *rightist extremists* (except in Lebanon, where there are *rightist Christians*). You don't find *leftist extremists* or *leftist Christians* in editorial lexicons.

Government forces label as *terrorists* those irregulars who prefer to be called *guerrillas* or *commandos;* the irregulars call the government the *hard right.* The use of *insurgent* is in sharp decline.

Groping for a neutral term to describe organized revolutionaries as well as government-sponsored militia, journalists have come up with *paramilitary,* an adjective that is now being used to cover any armed group not part of a uniformed, "official" army. *Para* is Greek for "alongside," and should properly be limited to a group serving as an adjunct to another group, but the need for the appearance of neutrality is breaking that down. Today, a *paramilitary force* can be a bunch of leftist guerrillas or rightist extremists, but never a bunch of leftist extremists or rightist guerrillas.

You gently rebuke a reader who wrote in a letter to you, "What other kind of guerrillas are there?" I suppose, if one's language is to be accepted as correct by present-day pundits, one might better say, "What other kind of guerrilla is there?" However, the word kind *as a plural noun is used persistently by native speakers of English—enough so that it has a pleasantly natural and unforced sound to it.*

Thomas Pyle, in The Origin and Development of the English Language *(1964, 1971, Harcourt Brace Jovanovich), makes the following explanation:*

> *Unchanged (or "zero") plurals survive from Old and Middle English times to the present in* deer, sheep, swine, folk, *and* kind. . . . *Despite the precedent of its use by many distinguished writers in "these (those, all) kind of," kind has acquired a new plural in -s because of the feeling that the older construction was "a grammatical error."*

Pyle notes that kind *was used as a plural word by Shakespeare, Sidney, Dryden, Swift, Goldsmith, and Jane Austen, so reader Glesner is in good—if not good contemporary—company.*

Marilynn Jewell
Erie, Pennsylvania

You referred to "revolutionaries" where I prefer the lesser used, but more precise "revolutionists." True, both words are nouns, but the former is also an adjective.

In both my teaching and writing I insist upon the use of "revolutionist," but I fear I am losing the battle. Still, wouldn't you wince, as I would, at the thought of Marx being characterized as a not particularly revolutionary revolutionary?

Robert Blackey
Professor of History
California State College
San Bernardino, California

I fear that you let your political feelings get in the way of your linguistic good sense (or good linguistic sense, if you prefer). You opined that all guerrillas are leftist guerrillas.

Historically there is no support for that assertion. The Basques in the Spanish Civil War, certain elements of the French Maquis and the forces of Miloradovitch in Yugoslavia are all mid-twentieth-century examples of guerrilla forces more of the right than the left. However, one need not rely only on historical allusions, for contemporary events have given rise to other partisan forces that cannot be identified with the left.

Robert Mugabe's guerrilla army, which played a major role in turning Rhodesia into Zimbabwe, was not leftist in any accepted sense, although it did accept aid from the Soviet bloc. (There is a tendency to call leftist any who accept such help. It is fallacious to do so, just as it would have been erroneous to call Stalin's government capitalist on the basis of Lend-Lease shipments.) At the present moment the forces captained by Jonas Savimbi occupy a significant portion of Angola—a case of guerrillas fighting a leftist government. Similar movements apparently exist in Laos and Cambodia, although very little is heard of such matters in the press.

I should like to take this chance to discuss another term you used: terrorist. It seems to me that that should be a neutral term. It describes those like the PLO that choose to attack civilian targets, and consciously eschew contact with the military or police forces of their enemy. Guerrillas, in contrast, focus their assaults on the security forces; civilian targets are secondary, and mainly of a distinctly political character.

Jonathan J. Margolis
Boston, Massachusetts

You speak of "irregulars who prefer to be called guerrillas or commandos." As I am sure you know, "commando" was at its outset not the person but the thing. In this respect our use of the word exactly parallels our use, or rather misuse, of "guerrilla" (of which more later). As for "commando," whenever the change in its meaning (in English at any rate) from thing to person came about, I'm pretty sure commando-persons were not yet irregulars: the commandos who raided Dieppe in 1942 were certainly official enough, as we know were later ones all through World War II. As the word itself (apparently adopted early by the Boers of the Transvaal from the Portuguese) suggests, the original commando was a regular formation, assembled for a particular purpose perhaps, but levied under the law of a government; one such was led in person by no less than the president of the South African Republic himself. Commandos, official all of them, fought against both blacks and British at least through the Boer War, and probably beyond. And they were still things. Any ideas, anyone, as to when commandos stopped being things and started being persons? Or when those persons started being irregulars? (Not all those persons, by the way. I refer you and others to the very busy and efficient Israeli commandos, who are certainly not irregulars. And it occurs to me they may be things: is something perhaps being lost in translation?)

I know what Spanish speakers think of our use of "guerrilla" to describe a person: they think very little of it. To them "guerrilla" is still what it always was: "little war," or perhaps more accurately these days, "undeclared war"—a great convenience to belligerent states with a feeling for the diplomatic niceties. And any Spanish-speaking participant in "guerrilla" (not "guerrilla war," please—for obvious reasons) is a "guerrillero" or "guerrillera": "guerrilla soldier," or "guerrilla fighter" if you wish—both terms gloriously unredundant.

Arnold H. Weiss
Department of Spanish and Portuguese
University of Kansas
Lawrence, Kansas

gypsy moths, *see* boll weevils whomp gypsy moths

hairy

"The market's been a little hairy the past few months," said stockbroker Arthur Gray Jr. A hairy stock market? Yes: Any situation that causes nervousness or fear is now said to be "hairy."

"My theory," writes Michael Johnson, director of McGraw-Hill World News, "is that it originally was someone's idea of a colorful way to modify *hair-raising.*"

Good theory, with which the *Oxford English Dictionary Supplement* appears to agree: "Frightening, hair-raising" is one slang meaning, following the older meaning of "out-of-date, passé," which I assume came from a combination of bewhiskered age and *hoary.*

But what is so scary about *hairy*? The hirsute state—"face lace," as it has been called—was never more desirable than in the 1960's, when this adjective first came into its latest vogue. *Psychology Today* reports on a study by psychologists Parley Newman and Darwin Gale of Brigham Young University: "Beards frighten children." When 250 boys and girls aged three to seven looked at four drawings of a man's face—from clean-shaven to fully bearded—the peach-fuzz-cheeked tots proclaimed the beardless face to be "the nice man" and the same fellow with a beard to be "the scary man."

The magazine's headline summation, based on a reduplicated sound conjuring the image of a frightened rabbit, was apt: "Hair 'Em, Scare 'Em."

Scary has risen along with *hairy,* and now has chased *frightening* to the edge of the vocabulary. *Scary* has been embraced by doves to describe hawks, as illustrated in a recent *New Yorker* cartoon that labels an old-style clubhouse "Institute of Scary Foreign Policy."

Not one ordinarily to engage in etymologic hair-splitting, I cannot resist the necessity of advising you of a more likely derivation of "hair-raising" to denote a state of fear. It is well known to anatomists that hairs grow out of follicles located within the dermis of the skin. Attached to each follicle is a tiny band of involuntary (smooth) muscle, which is in turn innervated by sympathetic nerve fibers. In times of sudden stress, along with other sympathetic "fight or flight" messages from the adrenal gland, are those to the body's hairs to stand on end. In aroused cats this can be a dramatic sight and a clear signal of preparedness to those inducing the response. The vestigial response in humans is "goose bumps," usually apparent only to ourselves.

Laurence I. Alpert, M.D.
Mount Kisco, New York

When Caucasians, many of whom were quite hirsute, including body hair, first came to the Far East, the Japanese (and other smooth-skinned Asians) called them "hairy barbarians," along with even less affectionate appellations. Nor can we forget the shaggy haired, mustached and bearded youngsters (hippies, flower children, et al.) of the '60s who were regarded by their elders with a curious mixture of fear and rage. And a fine expression of the times and the mood is the musical Hair (1968), "a staccato plotless gesture of youthful defiance," etc. It's no coincidence that the performance was so named.

David Gordon
Tokyo, Japan

I beg to differ, but not to disagree, with the etymology of the word "hairy" offered by Michael Johnson of McGraw-Hill. Perhaps the word's use did develop from "hair-raising" as Mr. Johnson suggested.

But I suggest the word stems from a popular slang among a small subculture, that of California surfers in the 1960s. I often heard surfers use the term with several variations.

To "show hair" still for bodysurfers and the like means to display courage. Courage is necessary when thrusting your unarmed body into tons of crashing water. I think the term came into being among beardless youths who attributed hair growth with being manly and courageous.

Mystically perhaps, the word came to be applied to "hairy" things and situa-

tions. Big waves and strong rip tides were called "hairy." At the same time a fellow who conquered these natural forces "had hair." A display of fear in the face of the ocean would be summed, "he haired out."

The word "hairy" could have found usage among the growing hippie countercul-ture of one coast and over the years passed to the established culture of the other coast—to Wall Street. I like to think so. By the way, the surfers are still making up their own language with new meanings for words like "hectic," "totally" and "tweaked." None of these terms has been applied to Wall Street conditions yet.

But the next time you're out body whompin' and you get caught in a totally hectic rip and there's a hairy ten-foot grinder coming at you, don't hair out. Be cool. When you get outside, GO FOR IT!

> *Douglas Green*
> *Editor,* The Saga Weekly Post
> *Stavanger, Norway*

heavy weather

Just about every newspaper in the country carried the etymology of *Weather Underground:* A line in a Bob Dylan song, "You don't need a weatherman to know which way the wind blows," became the basis for *Weatherman;* then some women members objected to the male-sounding ending, and the name was changed to *Weatherpeople;* when some members stormed about that, *Weather Underground* was adopted, with its immediate overtones of World War II resistance fighters and a deeper etymology from Dostoyevsky's *Notes from the Underground.*

Some reporters, however, were entrapped by the language of political activism and did not treat the holdup of a Brink's truck as a heist: "I say it's a bank job," writes Thomas Allen of Bethesda, Maryland. "I also say that newspapers and the police ('law-enforcement personnel') should stop elevating crime to political activity. . . . The C.I.A. may question agents in *safe houses,* but outlaws scram to *hideouts.* Politics is politics, and crime is crime. There are no political crimes in this country, but there are criminals who are adding to their crimes by robbing words of their meaning."

The Americanism *hideout* was first cited in 1885, derived from "hiding place." *Safe house* is a term which former Director of Central Intelligence Richard Helms tells me probably originated in World War II: an address to which agents being dropped into France were directed; its meaning has changed in C.I.A. parlance to "a place where defectors are kept." The elevation of *hideout* to *safe house* in the Weather Underground story was an unconscious acceptance of the inherently political, rather than primarily criminal, nature of the act.

I failed to observe the wipeout of *hideout* because my attention was fixed on *shot to death.* In most of the stories, the robber and guards who were slain were described as "shot to death," which may be acceptable to sloppy writers as an idiom, but is worth resisting. The *to death* construction implies the continuation of a process until it proves fatal: starved to death, beaten to death, burned to death, or hyperbolically nagged to death, tickled to death, bored to death.

But when it comes to killing by shooting, the correct expressions are *shot dead* and *shot and killed;* for cases in which the death occurs hours or days after the shooting, *shot fatally* or, if you prefer the archaic, *mortally wounded.*

"Taken literally," writes a Connecticut English professor who takes aim from the ambush of anonymity, "*shot to death* suggests hundreds of separately trivial wounds: like the Death of a Thousand Cuts."

Regarding your column in which you take potshots at "shot to death," I regret to say that you are off-target. There are several ways in which people can be done to death instantly; in fact, there are some cases in which instant death can be described only in terms of this idiom.

What, for example, would you say about a person who has been dispatched by a single knife thrust through the heart? That he has been "stabbed dead" or "stabbed and killed"? If so, you speak a peculiar brand of English; I would say "stabbed to death."

Similarly, the luckless soul who happens to be under a falling 50-ton concrete block will surely be crushed to death, not "crushed dead" or "crushed and killed."

A person who is beaten, or bludgeoned, to death need not succumb slowly under an accumulation of blows; he could just as well have his skull crushed immediately by a blunt instrument. Again, an English speaker would not normally say "beaten dead" or "beaten and killed."

Finally, it is perfectly possible to put people to death via guillotine, firing squad, or other methods that give instant results.

I therefore conclude that the phrase "——— to death" can be used to indicate both gradual and instantaneous ways of meeting one's maker. "Shot to death" is a perfectly good idiom of English, and not at all "sloppy." The only difference between it and the others mentioned above is that the synonymous phrases "shot dead" and "shot and killed" are also good, idiomatic English.

(Ms.) Penny Willis
Flushing, New York

The term "shot to death" also occurs in the U.S. Army's definition of capital punishment, i.e., "shot to death by musketry."

Euclid M. Hanbury, Jr., M.D.
Belfast, Maine

I don't usually check up on you, but when I read something as pedantic and trivial as your opinions on "shot to death" I jump for the OED and whatever else is at hand to defend against defense.

Please see OED, "shoot" v. IV 28. trans. b. "amplified with dead or to death added." You may find the citations of interest, for they inform us that people have been shooting others to death (tragic as that is) for at least seven centuries, with everything from javelins to bullets. My knowledge of Old English would lead me to believe that you might even find similar constructions in that language; keep an eye on the dictionary being compiled at Toronto for more on that. Come to think of it, I can cite enough modern authors who have used the form to make all that old stuff unnecessary. I think you are looking too hard for goblins in cupboards.

Keith Denning
Brooklyn, New York

P.S. This was only a "one shot" (i.e., not a process to continue until it proves fatal); hope I haven't shot you to pieces.

Dear Bill,

After some reflection, I've decided that it was quite reasonable to use safe house in the stories about the Weathermen. There's more of a difference between a hideout and a safe house than what you suggested. As I understand the terms, a hideout is any place where a fugitive hides (e.g. a previously uninhabited cave)

whereas a safe house is a place where someone provides hospitality to fugitives.
This difference is reflected in the interpretation of genitive modifiers:
  This building was John Dillinger's hideout for 2 weeks in 1931.
  This building was Agent 009's safe house for 2 weeks in 1943.
  The latter sentence could mean either that Agent 009 was the host who provided
hospitality to fugitives or that he was one of the fugitives who took refuge there.
What were called safe houses in the stories about the Weathermen were places
where fugitives were provided hospitality, weren't they?

> *With best wishes,*
> *Jim [James D. McCawley]*
> *Department of Linguistics*
> *University of Chicago*
> *Chicago, Illinois*

heirs, *see* splitting heirs

holding the fort

Time magazine was zapped in "Scaling the Depths" for using *fortuitously* ("by chance") when it meant *fortunately* ("luckily"). In a story about the Awacs aircraft, *Time* wrote that these had been ordered by the Shah of Iran and were "planes that fortuitously were never delivered."

Comes now George Church, senior writer at *Time:* "I wrote that story, the word I had in mind was *fortuitously,* and I defend its use." Asserting that the failure of delivery to Iran of aircraft that would have been grabbed by the Khomeini regime was "sheer dumb luck," and granting that the word *fortunately* also would have been appropriate, he opines: "But in my judgment *fortunately* emphasizes the happiness of the outcome, and since that was so obvious as to need no underscoring I chose *fortuitously* to stress (at least subliminally to those readers with some knowledge of Latin word roots) that this outcome came about by chance."

When masterly writers clash with masterful language shamans, where is Truth? For adjudication, let us turn to Jacques Barzun, author of *Simple and Direct* and the man to use for usage.

"I am sure Mr. Church's argument is sincere, not made up after the fact, and that his intention was as he says," writes Professor Barzun, in one of those sure-he-means-well sentences that usually precede a verdict of guilty. "But even though he is not patently wrong, his meaning is flawed by the placing of *fortuitously* and the use of that.

"The adverb should come after *delivered,* as a comment on the whole event. With a comment, the pronoun should be *which.* It is a matter of style, not grammar or diction as such. Compare: 'I regularly talked to him' and 'I talked to him severely.' It's clear that 'I severely talked to him' is impossible. In the same way as *regularly, fortunately* slips easily in front of the verb but *fortuitously* will not. Try: 'He fortuitously found her at home.'

"In any case," concludes Professor Barzun, "the frequent confusion between these two qualifiers makes a cautious writer avoid writing the one where the other might be expected. Had Mr. Church written 'which, by chance, were never delivered,' the sentence would have been above reproach."

I suppose *Time* can appeal, but I don't know who to. (To whom? Whom to?)

Tell Prof. Barzun that it would not be newsworthy to hear that the planes were not delivered fortuitously. One would hardly expect such expensive items to be delivered fortuitously. If he means that they were not delivered, fortuitously, he's imposing more commas on that poor sentence than it can bear.

> Steve Treat
> Chicago, Illinois

I vehemently protest (or protest vehemently) against the sage Mr. Barzun's placement of "fortuitously." The phrase which he suggests, "planes that were never delivered fortuitously," not only limps to a prosodically deplorable conclusion but also implies the corollary, "planes that were always delivered on purpose." It is thus both awkward and confusing, while Mr. Church's original "planes that fortuitously were never delivered" is merely awkward.

Instead, one should surely write (leave that "surely" where it is!), "planes that were, fortuitously, never delivered." The comment thus takes its place between appropriately parenthetical commas, we neatly avoid the vexed and vexing "that vs. which" question, and the rhythm of the sentence joins with its meaning in a happy accord.

This is obviously the solution . . . Obviously, this is the solution . . . This, obviously, is the solution . . . This is the solution—obviously!

> Allan J. Curran
> Boston, Massachusetts

I hesitated before taking on Jacques Barzun; after five minutes, temerity overcame timidity.

The placement of adverbs is a matter not merely of style, as Barzun says, but of emphasis and meaning.

In his example, "I regularly talked to him," the adverb is correctly placed if the speaker is just throwing it in as an added comment on the discourse. But if someone had accused the speaker of neglecting an old friend who had then died of loneliness, the reply might have been, "I talked to him regularly." At the end of a sentence, as all good writers know or sense, an adverb is more emphatic because it lingers in the reader's mind a split second longer before the next thought intrudes.

Barzun's second example, "I talked to him severely," underlines my point. No mysterious magnetism within the word "severely" prevents it from slipping in before a verb. "Severely" must go at the end of that sentence simply because it is so obviously the emphatic word, the important word. The sentence would be ungainly, anticlimactic, with the strong adverb "severely" placed before the weak and common verb "talked."

But try, "I severely reprimanded him." This is acceptable because "reprimand" is strong enough and unusual enough to follow a strong adverb. This one, of course, can go either way, depending on the precise shade of meaning intended. "I severely reprimanded him" emphasizes the fact of the reprimand; it might be used if the speaker is not a disciplinarian and may even be astonished at his own audacity— as in, "I severely reprimanded Professor Barzun." On the other hand, a Marine Corps drill instructor who wants to make clear to his commanding officer that this time he really chewed out the sonovabitch might say: "I reprimanded him severely."

As even "severely" can precede a verb if the weather is right, so with "fortuitously," which started this squabble. Mr. Church's explanation of his choice of the word makes sense to me and I see nothing wrong with his placement of it. Professor Barzun would put the adverb at the end of the sentence. Perhaps he means like this: "Planes that were never delivered fortuitously." Were they delivered some other way? the unwary reader might wonder.

Or perhaps Barzun would insert a comma: "Planes that were never delivered, fortuitously." That avoids the ambiguity, but it gives more emphasis to the luck of it all than the writer intended and might even lead the reader to expect to hear more about it. As a former Time writer myself, I know that the second quickest way to lose a reader is to confuse him with false signposts.

Rafael Steinberg
New York, New York

Dear Bill,

Barzun's remark about severely *is a red herring, since neither the use of* fortuitously *that he deplores nor the use of it that he would reserve for use by the super-virtuous behaves at all like* severely. *None of the three other points that he brings up constitutes a difference between the good* fortuitously *and its reprehensible homonym: no matter which one* Time's *Mr. Church intended, the word would have been "a comment on the whole event"; an adverb that is "a comment on the whole event" can be used in any of three positions that come into the picture (before the subject, after the subject, and at the very end, though with a twist that Mr. Barzun neglects to mention, namely that it must be preceded by a comma if it is in final position); and the status of the adverb has no bearing on the choice between* which *and* that. *Mr. Barzun is admonishing Mr. Church to avoid* fortuitously *except where syntactic and stylistic features of the context leave the reader no choice but to interpret it as "by chance." I know of only two ways that one can comply with that advice: by using* fortuitously *in direct contrast with* fortunately *("Fortuitously and fortunately, ...") and by avoiding the word entirely. Most of the time only the latter alternative is workable.* Fortuitously *(by chance) will live longer without friends like Jacques Barzun.*

Best wishes,
Jim [James D. McCawley]
Department of Linguistics
University of Chicago
Chicago, Illinois

homogenized etymology

"You are waxing prolix in your middle age!" observes John Simon, my severe brother in wordwatching, about a tiny, little mistake I made. (It's about time I waxed prolix; poor Roth has been suffering from waxy buildup.)

In a piece about "Geezer Power," designed to draw fire from golden oldies, I wrote: "If lesbians argue that *homosexual* should be limited to men, I would put up a feeble fight—arguing that the *homo* is the same as the *man* in *mankind* and covers women, too. . . ."

No letters from geezers. But 208 letters, six postcards, and a telex from people who know the difference between Latin and Greek derivations.

"Egad, sir, did you ever take Greek?" wires Christian P. Hansen, a word-processing supervisor from the Bronx. "The *homo* in *homosexual* comes not from the Latin word meaning 'man,' but from the Greek *homos*, meaning 'same.' The most that the Latin *homo* and the English prefix 'homo' have in common is that they are homonyms."

"I suppose that you are going to get a pedantic letter on this from every soul who ever suffered through *amo, amas, amat,*" wrote Robert A. Kaster of the University of Chicago classics department, "but what the hell, here goes. . . . As its antonym, *heterosexual,* shows, *homosexual* is one of those modern hybrids composed of a little Greek and a little Latin: Although the last three syllables are firmly rooted in the latter, the first two are derived from the former, specifically from the adjective meaning 'same' (versus *hetero,* 'other')." He cites the origin in an 1897 coinage by Havelock Ellis.

"Gotcha!" shouts Raymond Connolly of Harrington Park, New Jersey. "You would put up a far less feeble fight if you were to remind lesbians that the prefix *homo* is not the same as the *man* in *mankind* but rather the same as 'same' in *homonym* and *homogeneous.* . . . Now, don't I get a T-shirt or something?"

All you get is immortality in *The Times*'s Memory Bank, pal. More in the spirit of charity is this instruction from Friar Raphael Barousil, O.S.B., at the St. Joseph Abbey in St. Benedict, Louisiana: "It is the same *homo* that you find in *homophone* and *homogenize.* . . . With the understanding that *homosexual* means 'same-sex-preference,' there can be no reasonable linguistic motive for lesbians to object to the term as applied to themselves. Thus armed, you may take up the battle with more determination."

"Surely you must have written that as a provocation, or come-on," observes Taliaferro Boatwright Jr. of Stonington, Connecticut. Would that I had. "Can you hear me, buried under that mountain of horrified mail?" cries Barbara Holland of Philadelphia. "Boy, that was a beaut. What on earth did you think *homogenized* meant? Milk made into man?"

"I have resisted the urge to write you on previous occasions when you expressed opinions I found loathsome," snarls Barnett R. Rubin of Chicago. "Both you and the anonymous lesbians to whom you refer have been deceived by an orthographical homology. A homology, by the way, is a similarity of structure, not a word containing *homo* or *man,* where linguistic reformers would have us substitute *person.*"

How do you remember the difference between the Latin *homo,* meaning "man," and the Greek *homo-,* meaning "the same"? Eugene J. O'Sullivan of Tampa suggests the use of a mnemonic: Pronounce the Greek-rooted words to rhyme with "Tom": "The *o* in *homosexual* should be short, in fidelity to its Greek root, whereas the *o* in *Homo sapiens* should be long, in fidelity to its Latin root." He then goes off the deep end: "The *homo* (hommo) in *homonym* is not a homonym for the *homo* (hoh-mo) in *Homo sapiens; homo* (hommo, same) is, rather, a homograph for *homo* (hoh-mo, man)."

One reason for the space being given to this exercise in self-abasement is to demonstrate the frustration of thousands of classicists across this vast land (the Hong Kong mail hasn't come in yet). For years, they have found no outlet for their fury at the promiscuous mixture of Latin and Greek etymology by languaslobs. Now, at last, they have discovered the National Shame-on-You Center.

John F. Collins of Rockville Centre, Long Island, takes off this way:

"Dear Noah: Your column calls for this new entry: **Sa fire** (să' -fīr) *n.* One who leaps before he looks into his favorite dictionary, thus causing hundreds of classicists to write him a smug little note such as this one.

"*Homosexual* is a hybrid, coined in the 1890's by sociologists (itself a hybrid word!). *Homo-* (*pace* Safire) is a Greek element meaning 'one and the same.' Teamed with the Latin element *-sexual,* it makes for a cozy word which either sex should be able to cohabit with. Ironically, it is *lesbian* which is the slur: It prejudges the sexual orientation of all Greek citizens who happen to be Lesbians —i.e., inhabitants of Lesbos.

"(Extra fun: Short as it is, this note contains examples of antonomasia (3X), hyperbole, hysteron proteron, metaphor, prolepsis, paramoeon, anaphora (or epibole), prosopopoeia, asyndeton, not to mention paraleipsis. Can you spot them?)"

I can't spot a thing. Homoecious readers get me down.

In the midst of all the sound and fury about homo, homoi *and* homeo *(enough to provoke emotions not seen since the mid-fourth century when the semi-Arians proposed that the Son was of similar—*homoi*—substance, but not the same— *homo*—substance as the Father . . .), you called a Benedictine monk a friar. So you should be politely singed, if not roasted.*

Friars include Franciscans, Augustinians, Carmelites, Dominicans and Trinitarians—and perhaps a few others. But Benedictines are not friars. They are sometimes called "Father" or "Brother" or "Dom," depending on the customs of the particular house or monastery. I hope Father (Fr.?) Raphael Barousil, O.S.B. (Order of St. Benedict) does not find himself red-faced in Chapter over being turned into a religious mendicant against the traditions of his venerable Order. After all, Benedictines are 1,400 years old; the Franciscans are only now celebrating the 800th anniversary of the birth of their founder, after whom I an named. By the way, the Catholic Directory *lists Fr. Raphael as Barousse, not Barousil. Which just goes to show you how one has to research everything.*

Francis Tiso
Editor, Seabury Press
New York, New York

I am sure that many of your Catholic readers have called you on your use of "Friar" in connection with a Benedictine monk, possibly even Dom Raphael Barousil, O.S.B. himself.

The O.S.B. means Order of St. Benedict, the members of which are called monks. Their prefix is Dom. If Dom Raphael signed himself Fr. Raphael, which some monks do, it meant that, in addition to being a professed monk, he is also an ordained priest. It is true that Benedictine monasteries have Brothers as well as Fathers, depending on whether or not the particular monk is ordained, but these Brothers are not called "Friar"; that is reserved for the "Mendicant Orders," such as the Dominicans and Franciscans. There is a reason. I quote The Catholic Encyclopedia:

"The word 'friar' is to be carefully distinguished in its application from the word 'monk.' For the monk retirement and solitude are undisturbed by the public ministry, except under exceptional circumstances. His vow of poverty binds him strictly as an individual, but in no way affects the right of tenure of his order. In the life of the friar, on the contrary, the exercise of the sacred ministry is an essential feature, for which the life of the cloister is considered as but an immediate preparation. His vow of poverty, too, not only binds him as an individual to the exercise of that virtue, but originally at least, precluded also the right of tenure in common with his brethren. Thus originally the various orders of friars could possess no fixed revenues and lived upon the voluntary offerings of the faithful. Hence their name of mendicants. . . ." The Encyclopedia goes on to say the word "friar" occurs "at an early date in English literature with the significance of brother, and from the end of the thirteenth century it is in frequent use referring to the members of the mendicant orders. . . . "

> Bolling W. Haxall
> Riverdale, New York

Quoted in your article is a reader's suggestion that HOMO, the Latin for MAN, should "in fidelity to its Latin root" be pronounced HOHMO. That first "o" in HOMO was actually short in Latin, I believe. In the expression HOMO SAPIENS, both words have been anglicized for use in English; that is why HOHMO is given in standard dictionaries as the current pronunciation.

It is not so difficult to distinguish between the Greek and Latin HOMO. The Latin HOMO appears only in homicide *and* homiform, *in English words, and in* homunculus. *Perhaps* homage, *also derived from HOMO, should be added—the Greek HOMO, same, is much more common.*

I doubt if it is useful to talk about faithfulness to the quantity of vowels in their original Latin form. Time and chance have worked many changes; otherwise we should say fidEELITY not fiDELLITY, for instance.

> Mildred Williams
> Chicago, Illinois

Bill Safire:

I was enchanted by the way you fielded all the lemons showered on you for confusing Greek and Latin homos *and made a column of lemonade. It recalled one of my own ventures in learning Greek one word at a time.*

I was a sophomore at Rice when I put together the Greek-letter root words in Webster's Second International *and found that most diagnoses were merely repetitions by the doctor of what you have just told him: You say "sore throat" and he says "laryngitis."*

I worked in the biology lab, and the backs of my arms broke out in an itchy rash from handling some stuff we used to preserve dogfish. So I went to Oldoc Kyle —he must have been 25 years younger than I am now, but Oldoc he was.

He looked at my arms thoughtfully and finally said in a portentous tone: "We have a little dermatitis here." I was not as patient with other people's shtiks as I have since become, so I said:

"Doc, I realize that that impresses hell out of most of your patients. Does it ever occur to you that to some of them it is a pain in the ass?"

He looked at me dolefully and murmured: "Proctalgia."

So now you have a new word, but I must warn you it isn't easy to work it naturally into a conversation.

> *Love,*
> *Grandfather T. [Hal Taylor]*
> *Teaneck, New Jersey*

---

hooliganitis

The riots in Britain in 1981 revived a word that has become a favorite of government spokesmen: *hooligan.* Many reporters attribute the riots to a mixture of racial unrest, unemployment frustration, and "hooliganism."

The *Supplement to the Oxford English Dictionary* puts the word in the challenging category of "origin unascertained." Robert Burchfield and company have done a careful job: "The word first appears in print in daily newspaper police-court reports in the summer of 1898. Several accounts of the rise of the word . . . attribute it to a misunderstanding or perversion of *Hooley* or *Hooley's gang,* but no positive confirmation of this has been discovered." A rowdy Irish family called Hooligan was featured in a music-hall song of the day, and Navy snobs later derogated the United States Coast Guard as a "hooligan navy."

A hooligan is a young street tough, a member of a gang; the three essentials of the word are (1) young, (2) organized to do violence, (3) in cities. *Hoodlum* —from a German dialect *Hudilump,* or "wretch"—is the most frequently used synonym, but has no youthful connotation. *Thug*—from the Hindi name of a murderous religious organization in India—implies neither age nor urban activity. *Ruffian* seems as bookish as *blackguard,* which has been dropped because whites can be rowdy, too.

The Communists adopted the word *hooligan* in the Soviet Union, and you can hear the word pronounced as we do, in the midst of a streak of Russian, although often raised to the level of a way of life: *hooliganism.*

How do hooligans describe themselves? Never as hooligans; rather, as demonstrators, activists, militants, dissidents, or—if they want to add a connotation of thought—dissenters.

You remark that "the Communists adopted the word hooligan *in the Soviet Union. . . ."*

Actually the introduction of this word into Russian must predate the October Revolution, as I heard the word in my mother's Yiddish, where it formed part of the Russian vocabulary she brought with her. And she left Russia in 1907, so it must have been used in Czarist days. Its pronunciation was, of course, somewhat Russified: it could be phoneticized as "khuligan" with the accent on the last syllable. And I can assure you she wasn't in the least influenced by post-Revolutionary Russian, as she read no Russian once she left that country. The word was generally used by her to describe pogromists.

> Ben Kayfetz
> Toronto, Ontario

P.S.: While glancing through a volume of Sholom Aleichem (Oreme un Freilache) *I came across his use of* khuligan *in the identical use given it by my mother as referring to ruffians, perpetrators of pogroms. It was written in the year 1900. He gave it a Yiddish plural form* khuliganes *(in 4 syllables) but it's clearly via the Russian via the English.*

I was always under the impression that it came into English from Ireland. Am I wrong?

I write in regard to the origin of "hooligan" and "hooliganism."

Your source, the Oxford English Dictionary, *and my source, the* Random House Unabridged, *agree that the words are of Irish origin. (The* Random House Unabridged *states that they are a variety of the Irish surname, Houlihan, ". . . which came to be associated with rowdies.") Such explanations, even when as lucidly put as yours was, seem to me to be overly complicated. I'd like to take you on a brief trip to the wondrous world of Irish etymology and history.*

Several years ago, while on holiday in the wild west of Ireland, I heard the word "hooligan" used several times by native Irish speakers in regard to some activities that I was sharing with them. Cognizant of the differences of language in various parts of the English-speaking world and aware of the negative connotation of the word "hooligan" in American English, I asked about their meaning and received the following reply.

"Hooley," which has a variety of spellings, is Irish for "party." (The Irish no longer call their language "Gaelic," as they have given that term to the Scots along with tartans, whiskey, and the bagpipe.) E.g., "Let's have a hooley."

"Hooligan" is a party-goer. The "-igan" addition seems to be the equivalent of the "-er" suffix in English. E.g., "party" becomes "partier"; or, "help" becomes "helper."

English colonists in Ireland, shocked at the occasional lapses of decorum at hooleys by hooligans, added the suffix "-ism" to describe these alleged breaches of the King's peace or etiquette or their property. Thus, "Hooliganism."

Today's hooligan may be a young street tough but his remote ancestors were Irish party-goers (who probably held their party at the local "shebeen" or illegal pub which is and was often pronounced as a "shebang") and who probably were young, rural, festive, boisterous, loud, and prone to obnoxious behavior toward their English landlords. Nineteenth-century Irish migration probably took the intermediate ancestors of today's hooligan into the cities of the British Empire and North America and wherever else the Irish went. What is more certain is that the Irish seem to have gotten into trouble wherever they went and the stereotype of the loud, drunken, Irish tough certainly existed in those cities.

J. R. Williams
Department of History and Philosophy
Shippensburg State College
Shippensburg, Pennsylvania

Mr. Safire is in error when he states that the word "hooligan" is pronounced in the U.S.S.R. as it is in the United States. I know because, while sitting next to a woman on a bench in Moscow, I saw an irate seller of watermelons grab a young man who had apparently taken a melon without paying. I turned to the woman next to me and muttered sympathetically, "Bedny chelovek" ("Poor fellow"). Her response was a scornful "Hooli-GON," accent on the last syllable, pronounced as in "gone."

Stanley W. Page
Professor of History, City College
City University of New York
New York, New York

The Russians are indeed prone to use "hooligan," and have extended its meaning to cover any kind of antisocial activity, so one can read about "literary hooliganism," for example. But Russian does not have an initial "h," so the word is written "gooligan" in that language (just as the Führer was written "Gitler")—but the pronunciation, I believe, is the same as in English.

Robert Arndt
National Geographic Society
Saudi Arabia

Your article destroyed one of my favorite anecdotes. It concerned the derivation of the word "Hoodlum."

Many years ago I read somewhere that a reporter writing about corruption but fearful of a lawsuit identified a corrupt politician by writing his name backwards. The politician was named "Muldoon" but the typesetter is supposed to have misread the reporter's "Noodlum" as "Hoodlum" and so a new word was coined. It's a good story even if untrue.

Incidentally, the Random House College Dictionary *credits "Hoodlum" to the Bavarian "hodalum"—a ragged beggar or rogue.*

> Ramon F. Berger
> Providence, Rhode Island

Did you know that in the beginning of this century (I believe) a group of young conservative MPs led by Lord Hugh Cecil was called "hooligans" or "hugh ligans"? One of the members of the group was Winston Churchill. The group opposed inter alia the official conservative policy of imperial preferences.

> Guido Hofbauer
> Abconder, Holland

You failed to mention an early American Hooligan.

Happy Hooligan was the star of one of the first comic strips. The artist was Fred Opper. The strip started in the Hearst papers about 1905 and ran, I think, for more than 25 years.

Happy was hardly a revolutionary. He was a jovial, simple-minded bum, whose most distinguishing article of apparel was the tin can he wore as a hat.

> Vic Bloede
> New York, New York

hush-hush studies

Every administration likes to have its own hush-hush name for its hush-hush studies.

In the Nixon-Ford era, those ultrasecret, wide-ranging, argument-stimulating memorandums about national-security problems (rating only compound adjectives) were called "nissims." "Have you read the nissim on China?" was the first secret question I heard as a White House aide. When I asked, "What's a nissim?"

I was promptly dropped "out of the loop" for lack of clearance (or irreverence, which was worse), but I soon discovered that *nissim* was a nonce word for "N.S.S.M."—"National Security Study Memorandum."

When the Carter men replaced the Republicans in the basement of the White House, Zbigniew Brzezinski wanted a change of name for the top-secret reports that his men would soon be churning out. The order went out that the words *National Security* would be replaced by *Presidential*—thus, the new "Presidential Study Memorandum." Before this could be implemented, as they toolishly say, an astute member of the conceptual frameworkers' union realized what the resulting acronym would sound like, and the word *Study* was changed to *Review*. Through the Carter years, the P.R.M. was the target of all the tugging and hauling, and I found myself asking a source on a street corner, "Can you get me a copy of Prim-10?"

The first thing the Reagan men did upon taking office was to scrap the P.R.M. Their name for the same old stuff is not well known, because it defies pronunciation: "N.S.D.D." It stands for National Security Decision Directive, a candidate for obloquy by the Squad Squad. You don't hear pundits and malice-absent reporters on street corners asking, "Can you glom onto N.S.D.D.-1?" because (1) there have not been studies this time around and (2) nobody in the bureaucracy knows how to ask for one.

How unbelievably disillusioning to see the last of the remaining language diehards using the plural "memorandums." Back in the days when we were force-fed suffixes (ices) this would not have been tolerated. Should not this have been "memoranda"?

> Fred Hirshfeld
> Monroe, Connecticut

The item on "nissims" reminds me that the Council on International Economic Policy, a creation of the Nixon White House, had its own study memorandums, referred to in the early 1970s as C.I.E.P.S.M., or "sipsims" (I suppose that's how they would have been spelled). I recall reporting a story for National Journal that involved a successful effort by the staffs of the National Security Council and the Council on International Economic Policy to paper over some differences on U.S.-Soviet trade. The agreement between the two agencies was ratified in the form of a N.S.S.M.-C.I.E.P.S.M. or, as I was informed, a nissim-sipsim.

> Richard Frank
> Editor, National Journal
> Washington, D.C.

image maker

Republican pollsters fret about the President's image becoming too much the skinflint; Democratic pollsters complain about his "father image"; independent journalists worry about manipulation by image makers.

Psychologists in the 1920's began writing about "fantasy images"; that was stolen by admen in the 50's for use as "brand image," which was swiped in turn by public-relations men talking of "corporate image" and "public image." Etymologists have wondered: Where did it all begin? Where is a citation that shows early use of the ancient word *image* to mean the public's perception of a person?

The *Supplement to the Oxford English Dictionary* offers this use by G. K. Chesterton in his 1908 book *All Things Considered:* "Between the King and his public image there was really no relation."

Comes now Rachel Hermann of Chautauqua, New York, with this quotation from *The Life and Times of Frederick Douglass.* The Negro leader was speaking at the unveiling of the Freedmen's Monument in Washington on April 14, 1876, and had this to say about Abraham Lincoln:

"Even those who only knew him through his public utterances obtained a tolerably clear idea of his character and personality. The image of the man went out with his words, and those who read them, knew him."

Such a discovery contributes to the persona of the Lexicographic Irregulars as a philological resource. (I think *image* may be in eclipse; these days, *persona* is grata.)

Regarding your discussion of the use of "image" in a political context, surely one obvious source is Eikon Basilike, *or image of the king, supposed to have been written by Charles I of England before his execution. In response Milton wrote* Eikonoklastes, *or the image-breaker (1649). Milton writes:*

> *In one thing I must commend his openness who gave the title to this book,* Eikon Basilike, *that is to say, The King's Image; and by the shrine he dresses out for him, certainly would have the people come and worship him. For which reason this answer also is entitled* Eikonoklastes, *the famous surname of many Greek emperors, who in this zeal to the command of God, after long tradition of idolatry in the Church, took courage, and broke all superstitious images to pieces. . . .*
>
> *But now, with a besotted and degenerate baseness of spirit [the English] are ready to fall flat and give adoration to the Image and Memory of this Man. . . .*

I have modernized from the Columbia edition of Milton's works, V, 68–69. Eikon
Basilike *was an enormously popular book, one of the great successes in political
image-making, and it is clear that Milton understood the significance of such
activities.*

Anthony Low
Department of English, New York University
New York, New York

important(ly), *see* more important(ly)

innuendo

In comes an angry letter from a member of the White House "troika," irritated
with a political column of mine. Writes Michael Deaver of the trio with brio:
"You implied that I am using my White House position to obtain clients for the
future, or assisting former clients for personal gain. I resent the innuendo."

Innuendo is a word that looks and sounds as sneaky as its meaning. In previous
administrations, the favorite riposte to journalists was "scurrilous," but after a
brief flirtation with that word by Attorney General William French Smith, the
vogue counterattack has become a denunciation of "rumors, insinuations and
innuendo."

Learned counsel know that the word has a legal background: From the Latin
word for "give a nod to," *innuendo* came to mean "that is to say" and was used
to introduce explanatory material in a brief; its legal use has withered, although
arguendo, a related word, is now used in general discourse to mean "for argument's sake" and to show off.

From its start as "a nod," *innuendo* became "a hint" and, ultimately, "indirect
derogation," a type of action rather than a specific act. In the instance that Mr.
Deaver cited, I charged that his announcement of intended departure one year
ahead of time was either for getting future clients or for fear of being attacked
about assisting former clients. That was a direct blast, perhaps mistaken, perhaps
on the button, but hardly "innuendo." In his shoes, I would demand: "By what
right do you impugn my motives?"

President Reagan, whose favorite word threatened to become *disservice,* has
found a fine Americanism to use in denying stories: *made out of whole cloth.*

The original English phrase carried no connotation of trickery; *whole cloth,* or
broad cloth, connoted the entire object, similar to the sturdily honest *all wool
and a yard wide.* In 1840, Canadian author Thomas Chandler Halliburton,
writing about an unscrupulous Yankee in *The Clockmaker,* had a character say:

"All that talk about her temper was made out of whole cloth. . . . What a fib!" By ironic transference, the fabrication (cloth) was treated as a fabrication (lie). Beats *innuendo* any day.

Your remarks about innuendo *brought to mind one of the most awful of Groucho Marx's awful puns. As I recall it, he said with a leer that when a husband goes out the door, love may fly innuendo.*

> Stanley H. Brams
> West Bloomfield, Michigan

inoperative, *see* overload inoperative

intensive-related orientation

A new and virulent strain of compound adjectives is attacking the body of language.

Two decades ago, *-related* was the heavy-use compounder, a favorite of people who littered their sentences with *in terms of* and *vis-à-vis*. I still get complaints about this; R. R. Jeffels of Richmond, British Columbia, kicks about "the mania for compounding adjectival clusters using *related:* health-related problems, computer-related errors, family-related incest."

Then came *-oriented*. If you had a word-oriented mind, you could watch the jargon-oriented people take their action-oriented siestas. The assistant secretary of state assigned to Pacific-Related Affairs was called "Orient-oriented."

Today the hot new combining form for adjectives is *intensive*. Robert Sisco of Piscataway, New Jersey, sends in this clipping from the *Bridgewater Courier-News*: "The most effective way to overcome dryness is to install a humidifier in the home. Unfortunately, this method is cash-intensive. A cheaper but labor-intensive method is to place dampened cheesecloth over your radiators."

The temptation is to stuff dampened cheesecloth into the speaker's pretension-intensive mouth. This compound began, I think, with *labor-intensive,* soon followed by *capital-intensive*. Margaret Mead nominated both words for inclusion in the *American Heritage Dictionary* in 1975, but the lexicographers wanted to wait for more citational evidence.

Came the avalanche. Nobody now says requiring *heavy investment* when *capital-intensive* will do, and *labor-intensive* has been stretched to include "back-breaking." In an article by Steve Lohr in *The New York Times Magazine* about semiconductors and microprocessors, Robert Noyce of Intel Corporation was quoted as saying: "Unlike steel, autos and some others, this industry has never been an oligopoly. . . . It has always been a brain-intensive industry, rather than a capital-intensive one."

Disoriented economists tend to get pedantry-intensive; the solution-related answer is to laugh them out of it.

As a professor of the jargon-intensive subject of economics, I object to your equating "requiring heavy investment" with "capital-intensive." You are confusing amount with ratio. A capital-intensive method need not require heavy investment as long as the ratio of capital to labor is high. (Similarly, "jargon-intensive" means a high ratio of jargon to ordinary words.)

Jargon arises in part because specialists need terms with precise meanings. The terms may be badly chosen, as they often are in economics, but someone as concerned as you with using language precisely should recognize that jargon has a legitimate function. Besides, "capital-intensive" is shorter than "requiring heavy investment" and, mirabile dictu, well suited to the meaning.

All this does not exculpate the Bridgewater Courier-News, *which used "labor-intensive" ("A cheaper but labor-intensive method") where "laborious" would have been better.*

> *Rendigs Fels*
> *Graduate Program in Economic Development*
> *Vanderbilt University*
> *Nashville, Tennessee*

The USO lady who runs the Family Welcome Program for the U.S. Army in Korea got the job because she was Orient orientation oriented.

> *Sergeant Jayne Reed*
> *HHC 34th Sig. Bn.*

irregulars

"I'm just a regular woman who regularly reads your column," writes Patricia Oppenheim of New York City, who evidently considers herself a member of the Lexicographic Irregulars. "Why, then, do you call me (an) 'Irregular'? I have heard of garments which are irregulars; heartbeats which are irregular; even irregular verbs, but never people accused of irregularity (except in their behavior). Lexicographic Irregulars (along with Baker Street Irregulars) seem like dedicated people sworn to preserve the *consistency* of language. What, then, makes them irregular?"

As that nice reference to the determined readers of Arthur Conan Doyle suggests, the meaning is derived from "soldiers not of the regular army." No diplomas or commissions needed to serve. Clarity and color are our bywords, not consistency; with Whitman, the language asks: "Do I contradict myself? Very well then, I contradict myself. (I am large, I contain multitudes.)"

jazz, *see* all that jazz

last shall be best

Readers with annoying memories and a lust for a single standard have reminded me of a piece I wrote some time ago castigating Jimmy Carter's writers for changing Lincoln's line "the last best hope *of* earth" to "the last best hope *on* earth." The editing was done by a speechwriter who knew the correct quotation but who thought most people did not; in an attempt to seem correct, the writer deliberately erred.

Along comes Ronald Reagan in his budget message to a joint session of Congress with a new wrinkle on the old quote, hailing "the promise that is offered to every citizen by this, the last, best hope of man on earth."

This was no speechwriter's way of fudging the "of-on" issue; it was Reagan himself, quoting himself. In his national political debut, on October 27, 1964, making a televised pitch on behalf of candidate Barry Goldwater, Mr. Reagan said: "We'll preserve for our children this, the best hope of man on earth, or we'll sentence them to take the last step into a thousand years of darkness." In the sixteen years between lines, Mr. Reagan kept the last hope of man on earth, but has rejected as gloomy hyperbole the last step into a thousand years (250 presidential terms) of darkness.

Curiously, Mr. Reagan's editing of the Lincoln phrase probably states in explicit terms what Lincoln was getting at poetically: "The last best hope of earth" was not the hope of the planet, but the hope of mankind on earth. In getting back to the comfortable "on earth," Mr. Reagan scores a point in rhetoric —it now both seems correct and is not incorrect—but loses that handful of listeners willing to take Lincoln's poetic leap.

late, *see* better than never

lawyer, *see* we wuz robbed

lay on: Macduff strikes again

"The Sandinistas respected Pezzulo's performance," wrote Bill Roeder in *Newsweek* about a liberal United States ambassador in Nicaragua, "and liked him enough to lay on a farewell luncheon."

Victor Ockey of Brooklyn wants to know: "Since when do we 'lay on' a luncheon? All these years, I have been 'throwing' or 'giving' luncheons. I guess you only 'lay on' farewell luncheons."

Lexicographer Eric Partridge traced *lay on*, in its meaning of "arranged, assured," to British army use around 1930, speculating that it was taken from the plumbing trade. In 1590, Christopher Marlowe gave the phrase its current meaning "to pile on, be lavish," with: "Thou shalt have crowns . . . to outbid the Barons; and, Spenser, spare them not, lay it on." This was soon followed by Shakespeare's "Well said, that was laid on with a trowel."

"In British slang," reports Sol Steinmetz of Clarence Barnhart books, "*lay on* was extended to almost anything—one could lay on (i.e., prepare or arrange) a press conference, a campaign, a speech, a car, etc. And so Noël Coward wrote in 1944, 'I was unable to give a concert as the piano . . . had not been '*laid on.*' "

When the phrase traveled to the United States, suggests lexicographer Steinmetz, its use was confused with an American slang phrase meaning "to give" or "let have," as in "Lay it on me, ol' buddy," which means, "Give me the lowdown." Going further back, that idiom is rooted in the black English phrase for shaking hands, "Lay some skin on me," in which the meaning of *lay* is literally "to put down."

"The slangy sound of *lay on a luncheon*," advises Steinmetz, "is at least partly due to association with Black English and hippie usage."

Hold, enough!

lead-pipe cinch

Crime reporters are fond of writing about victims who have been beaten over the head with a "lead pipe." Many plumbers and pipefitters take umbrage at this anachronism.

"Nobody, but nobody, uses lead pipe in their business today," writes Gerry Houser of Tampa, Florida, who is a former plumbing contractor. "It is simply too expensive. For the past few decades, steel, copper, and PVC pipe have replaced lead pipe as the primary means of beating people, in addition to their use in conveying various liquids, such as water."

Since copper pipe is also on the expensive side and PVC (polyvinyl chloride) pipe is too light, Mr. Houser suggests that galvanized steel pipe is the under-world's preferred blunt instrument. "You might do our fellow countrymen a service in telling them which type of pipe is used in cracking their skulls," suggests the former plumber, not realizing that the Squad Squad will soon be after him for the redundant "fellow countrymen." He adds: "The lead-pipe manufacturers (are there any left?) have been taking it on the chin for a long time."

The pursuit of this inaccuracy led to the discovery of the origin of *lead-pipe cinch,* a slang term meaning "easy to do." I had assumed that the etymology was related to the slugging function of lead pipe, as described by generations of crime reporters: Someone clobbered by a lead pipe would be inclined to be cooperative, if still alive. That's wrong: Pipe made of lead, a soft metal, is more malleable than pipe of rigid cast iron. Plumbers (who must still undergo tests for soldering lead pipe to get their licenses) think of lead pipe as the easiest to work with—hence, the use of *lead-pipe* as a compound adjective meaning "easy as pie." (Easy as *eating* pie—*making* pie is no cinch.)

Your derivation of the phrase "lead-pipe cinch" from the plumbing trade is interesting but inexact. The word cinch *(from Spanish* cincha) *refers to the strap that holds a saddle in place. The rider of a well-cinched horse was a* cinch *to win over more poorly rigged opponents. A copper-riveted cinch was a secure harness, hence a safe bet, as in W.A. Fraser,* Bulldog Carney *(Toronto, 1919), p. 123: "Any kind of a talking bird can swing in on a winning if he's got a copper-riveted cinch bet."*

And Peter B. Kyne, Cappy Ricks Retires *(New York, 1922), p. 280: "Copper-riveted cinches sometimes aren't properly cinched and Fortune backs out of the packsaddle."*

To break or punish recalcitrant horses, a piece of lead pipe was sometimes substituted for the strap; cf. Laurie York Erskine, The Laughing Rider *(New York,*

1924), p. 129: "That saddle is light, and that horse is fixed to hit the ceiling. You want a tin saddle and a lead-pipe cinch, if you aim to ride that bronco."

Though Wentworth and Flexner's earliest dating is 1949, the phrase appears much earlier in the modern figurative sense: Charles Francis Coe, Swag *(New York, 1928), p. 190; Christopher Morley,* Thorofare *(New York, 1942), p. 403; Max Shulman,* The Feather Merchants *(New York, 1944), ch. 5: ". . . to borrow a plumber's term, a lead-pipe cinch," the first association, apparently, with plumbing.*

Mac E. Barrick
Prof. of Spanish
Shippensburg State College
Shippensburg, Pennsylvania

"Lead-Pipe Cinch"? This I know about! Your plumber Gerry Houser did his plumbing in Tampa, but in New York, Boston, Jersey City, Philadelphia, Chicago, Los Angeles, and in all the biggies, lead pipe is approved for connecting watermains to household lines, and there is a lead-bend wiped to a flange under every toilet bowl.

You are wrong! The required wiping tests applicants must take for their license is no cinch. Fifty percent fail this test.

Billies or cudgels, not to be confused with a policeman's club, are made of soft lead with a sheath of leather and a thong. Now to your "Lead-Pipe Cinch." When this is struck on head or buttocks, it actually conforms with the blow. It is a lead-pipe cinch that someone clobbered by such a pipe will be alive and cooperative.

Now for that pie! Making a pie is also a cinch. Buy two half-shells of unbaked piecrust, found frozen in all supermarkets. Thaw out, fill with fruit, place in oven, and you get a nice pie quickly.

Jack Gasnick
JAKE THE PLUMR
PLUMR SPECIALTIES
New York, New York

The "cinch," I would suggest, refers to the last twist of the pipe, the one that makes the joint snug. In this context, the etymology is to "cinching the saddle," the last application of force.

Richard B. Stockton
San Andreas, California

"Easy as pie" refers, I suspect, to the ease with which a (hand)set form of type can be "unset."

Pie (or py or pi) refers to the mess obtained by dropping a set form or to any other mixed-up type.

David N. Smith
Danbury, Connecticut

Had your construction man been a millwright rather than a plumber he could have told you this: Heavy equipment is attached to a masonry floor slab by means of anchor bolts. One means of securing these bolts to the floor is the cinch anchor. In particular, the anchor bolt with facing washer is inserted, head down, into a hole drilled in the slab, with threaded end extending above the surface. A lead sleeve is slipped over the bolt into the hole, then punched down, expanding the diameter to secure—to "cinch"—the anchor bolt in the hole. In former days (as pointed out by your contractor), what better source of these sleeves than a short section of lead pipe? Et voilà! The "lead pipe cinch."

While I'm certain of the foregoing, I can only guess at how the phrase came to mean "easy." The word "cinch" has the connotation of certainty, hence, "a sure thing." In turn this connotes "easy."

R. Richard Ritti
University Park, Pennsylvania

A cinch is a joint or attachment which holds by constriction. Thus, a cinch is the belt that goes around the belly of a horse to secure the saddle, or a ring which, being shrunk by heat, pounding, or other means, secures an outer sleeve to an inner pipe or rod. A belt on a well-rounded beer belly would be a good example of a cinch. Since lead is very malleable, a lead-pipe cinch would be a cinch that is very easy to make.

Richard A. Lockshin
Great Neck, New York

Back in the days when I was a working newspaperman on The Cleveland Press, *we had a managing editor who would dramatically descend with admirable wrath upon any of us who dared write of someone's having been beaten over the head with anything.*

In his view, when you beat someone over the head, you wave your cudgel—lead pipe, baseball bat, ball-peen hammer or whatever—about in the air above your victim's head, producing a menacing state of affairs but doing no actual damage because he is not being struck.

We were compelled to report that victims were beaten ON the head. Such a statement leaves no doubt as to the viciousness of the attack.

Perhaps what you meant to say was that crime reporters like to tell of people having been beaten ON the head with a lead pipe.

If and when the time for me to be set upon by an assailant with a heavy weapon arrives, I fervently hope I am beaten OVER the head instead of ON the head.

W. A. Rice
Cleveland, Ohio

I would like to add to your treatment of the phrase "lead-pipe cinch." John Ciardi does not agree with your plumber's origin. He states in his book A Browser's Dictionary *(p. 77) that it is a midwestern American term, the result of the use of a short length of galvanized iron (called commonly lead) in saddling a horse with what was known as a cinch.*

However, rather than accepting your or Ciardi's explanation, I prefer the origin presented by the Denver Times Almanac *for 1899 (p. 435) for two reasons. It is given almost at the time the term came into use—the first recorded citation is 1898, and being from Brooklyn myself and chauvinistic about that borough, the following origin I quote from that almanac claims it started in Brooklyn:*

> *The expression originated in Brooklyn. Though it is very frequently used by sporting people, it is not over 25 years old, and probably not that old. It indicates a sure thing . . . we are satisfied that Brooklyn was its home. It was coined in this way: Some years ago a fellow entered a plumbing shop and stole a piece of lead pipe. He wanted to take it over to New York, and to keep it from being seen he wrapped the pipe around his body and then put his clothes on over it. A cinch, in turf language, means a girth or saddle band, or anything that is used to keep a saddle on a horse or mule tight. "Cinching up" means, therefore, tightening up, and is of Spanish origin. As the fellow with the lead pipe around his body jumped to catch the ferry-boat he fell overboard, and, of course, the weight of the lead carried him down. A horseman, in explaining the occurrence, said the thief had a "lead pipe cinch" and he had, and it drowned him.*

Actually, it's no lead-pipe cinch to explain its origin. The thief could have done better stealing gold instead of lead. Also, the horseman seemed psychic in knowing that the thief had that piece of lead on him before he drowned.

David Shulman
New York, New York

leak age

The President is furious about leaks. The Secretary of State is incensed at all the leaking. Pentagon legend has it that Deputy Secretary of Defense Frank Carlucci sports a lie detector strapped to his arm at all times to demonstrate that he is not a leaker.

Over at the Cuban Interests Section of the Czechoslovak Embassy in Washington, Counselor Ramon Sanchez-Parodi took offense at a story I wrote about a secret meeting of United States and Cuban officials, not so much on the substance of the article as on the more sensitive issue of how the information passed: "If Mr. Saffire *[sic]* wants to imply that a Cuban source was responsible for any 'leak' on the meeting, he should be advised to look elsewhere." Since the word is an informal Americanism for "unauthorized disclosure," the Cuban correctly put the noun in quotes. (Unfortunately, he referred to the headline over the piece as "Sand on My Shores"; the title was "Sand in My Shoes," the name of an old song about Havana which is evidently no longer sung in those parts.)

The verb *to leak* has a fine pedigree in political slang: Noah Webster, in 1832, defined *to leak out* as "to escape privately from confinement or secrecy; as a fact or report." In that early use, and for more than a century afterward, the verb was intransitive—that is, it did not take an object. Things simply leaked; they did not leak as the result of a person's action (or, as a grammarian would have it, as the object of the subject's action).

That was then. Today, with *leak out* clipped to *leak,* the verb has shifted from the intransitive to the transitive: The verb now takes an object. Somebody leaks something. This simple shift in grammar illuminates a great change in the way we think about receiving news.

"Originally, when information 'leaked,' " observes Daniel Schorr, the Cable News Network senior correspondent who helped raise leak-inducing to a fine art in Washington, "it was thought of as an accidental seepage—a lost document, a chauffeur's unwary anecdote, loose lips in the Pentagon. Today, when information 'is leaked,' it is a witting (if sometimes witless) action. One leaks (active) to float or sink an idea, aggrandize self (the 'senior official on the secretary's plane') or derogate an opponent."

The change from the intransitive (something leaked) to the active transitive (somebody leaked something) implies a sinister hand causing a leak. No longer does a secret leak *out,* as if by its own accord, inadvertently, or by chance; when it is leaked, the action is guided by a subject. The predecessor verb was *to plant;* the manipulative politician planted a story he wanted to see in print. When the plant was rooted out, we were inundated with leaks.

In the process of changing from the intransitive to the transitive, *leaking* lost its original connotation of "the embarrassing revelation of truth." With a manipulator at the controls, truth has taken a beating. Formerly, only the truth could leak out; now, lies can be leaked. "In older times," recalls Mr. Schorr, "it was considered inconsistent for an official to complain of a leak and then deny the authenticity of its content. No longer. It has become commonplace to charge the leaking of falsehoods, for which *slander* would be a more accurate appellation. Perhaps we need a new term, like *disleak,* on the analogy of *disinformation.*"

Another change: *To leak out* was considered benign, but *to leak* is considered sneaky or disloyal. Nobody wants to be called a leaker these days; newsmen looking for leakers like to call them *whistleblowers,* which has the connotation of honesty in anonymity.

Curiously, some unwary reporters who successfully squeeze sources to get stories do not boast of *scoops* or *beats* or even *exclusives,* but have come to accept the noun *leak* to describe the result of their efforts. That is foolish: That accepts the nomenclature of the adversary, and weakens the desired connotation of enterprise. I refuse to admit to having been leaked to; on the contrary, I assert that I have unearthed some fascinating information, or claim to have discovered the truth.

The TV networks have caught on to the pejorative quality of *leak* and have adopted their own locution to signal exclusivity: "ABC has learned." That means "somebody leaked."

You describe some of the effects of deliberate "leaking," and refer to the relatively new phenomenon of "leaking" falsehoods. You also point out that, formerly, the truth would leak out, but you neglect to tell us what happens when a lie is leaked.

I would like to suggest that, in such a case, the unwitting reporter who prints the leak has been "leaked" on." The meaning is quite clear, and there is similar usage in the current expression "lean on," as in "He leaned on me to issue the permit." The phrase deserves to become part of the language at least as much as another expression invented in Washington, "normalcy."

Roger P. Griswold
Irvington, New York

In 1979, while researching my Bachelor's Paper ("The First Lady and the Symbolization of American Culture") at the University of Chicago, one of the first ladies I focused on was Lou Hoover. I came across a news item that might be of particular interest to you.

Lou Hoover was actually the first First Lady whose speeches (to 4-H and Girl Scout conventions) were recorded expressly for newsreels and radio. About a year after she first spoke over radio, a White House employee (whether a cook or a Cabinet member remains unknown) leaked to the press that "To improve her voice for appearances before sound picture cameras, Mrs. Herbert Hoover has been taking voice tests in a small improvised laboratory on the second floor of the White House." ("Mrs. Hoover Takes Voice Tests to Improve Talkie Technique," New York Times, November 6, 1931.) "Dissatisfied with her recent talking pictures," the story explained, "she is seeking a method of speech and intonation that would make her voice record better."

The next day, The Times headed a story " 'Leak' on Voice Tests Annoys Mrs. Hoover; White House Seeks Source of News Story." After several paragraphs describing Mrs. Hoover's "displeasure," the story concluded:

> Some weeks ago President Hoover called for an investigation both by and of members of the White House Secret Service detail to determine the nature of news "leaks" about happenings at his Rapidan fishing camp. He was reported particularly irked over published stories concerning his personal activities during the formative days of his moratorium proposal. At that time questions were asked of both newspaper and Secret Service men concerning the source of the reports. Later, Theodore Joslin, one of Mr. Hoover's secretaries, asked formally that reports touching upon White House activities come from "stated sources." There was objection to this policy, however, from some of the older correspondents.

So you see, neither "leaks" nor the battle between the First Lady and the press is anything new under the sun!

Claudia Keenan
New York, New York

leeching halt

"Bdellzphobe," suggests John Ciardi, author of A Browser's Dictionary.

"Dolephobe," writes Tom McClintock of Wyndmoor, Pennsylvania.

"Sanguisugent" is the entry of Natasha Konigsford and Harvey Sheirr of New York City.

These are thoughts stimulated by the need expressed in a piece called "Neologe Seats" for a word to describe a person who hates people who wheedle their way through life. In creating a word, the Greek *phobe* is a handy device; it means "fear," which often leads to hate, so the suffix is used to mean "one who fears or hates." *Bdellz* means "leech"; *dole* refers to "on the dole"; those coinages are self-explanatory. *Sanguisugent* can be found in *The Grandiloquent Dictionary*, by Russell Rocke, and means "bloodsucking."

"As a limnologist," writes Jay Bloomfield of Charlotte, Vermont, splashing around in his study of the waters in lakes and ponds, "I would like to define several words which describe symbiosis, the relationship between cohabiting dissimilar organisms." He compares *mutualism* or *commensalism*, which is an association that benefits both partners, with *parasitism*, in which one partner benefits at the expense of the other.

"As a centrist," Dr. Bloomfield writes—plunking himself right in the middle of the lake, as a centrist limnologist—"I opt for the term *synoecy*, as a root for your word to describe the dislike of freeloaders. The animal analogy that I like is the relationship between the shark and its symbiont, the remora. The remora is a fish with a sucker on top of its head, which allows it to cling to the shark's belly. The remora feeds on debris that the shark does not swallow, and is a true synoecist, as it does not harm the shark."

If sharks turn you off or if a fish with a sucker on its head seems silly, Dr. Bloomfield suggests an alternate animal pair to illustrate synoecy: the African rhinoceros and the cattle egret. "The egret walks in the wake of the rhino, feeding on insects stirred up by its massive tread, but renders no service in return. Ah, what potential for use in an article on the federal welfare system."

This understanding of the underlying motive of my query causes me to acknowledge Dr. Bloomfield's remonstrance about my original derogation of leeches, barnacles, and sponges. (See? I can write like Bill Buckley.) "Only some species of leeches are bloodsucking parasites," the man of the lake argues, "and barnacles are definitely not parasites, since they do not harm their host, whether oyster or jetty. Sponges have received much undue bad publicity because of the utility of their corpses in mopping and sopping. The living sponge is quite self-sufficient and is even a host to symbiotic algae, or zooanthellae."

This has gone far enough; rather than sponge off my readers further, let me declare the winners: Florie Scheintaub and Sylvia Gassel of New York, who combined Yiddish and Greek to come up with *schnorrerphobe*, and an anonymous reader from Hicksville, New York, who obviously thinks some of his in-laws are scroungers and deadbeats and who brilliantly lobs in *freeloather*.

I am 16 years old and I take Advanced Placement Biology for college credit while still in high school. You quoted Jay Bloomfield comparing mutualism and commensalism with parasitism. Mr. Bloomfield defined mutualism or commens-

alism as an association that benefits both parties. When our class studied ecology, we learned that mutualism and commensalism are not exactly alike. Mutualism is the association in which both parties benefit while commensalism is the association where one party is benefited and the other receives neither benefit nor harm.

> Debby Pollack
> Hartsdale, New York

Dr. Bloomfield is wrong when he says barnacles "do not harm their host, whether oyster or jetty."
*Goose barnacles (*Lepas *species), the so-called fouling barnacles, grow in tremendous numbers on the bottoms of ships and seriously impede the speed of the vessels, just as the human variety may impede the ship of state.*

> Bill Helfrich
> Portland, Maine

Horrors! With respect to "Dr. Bloomfield suggests an alternate animal pair . . ." I alternated *between elation and despair over the* alternatives: *question or keep quiet.*

> Selma Ziff
> Fairfax, Virginia

Please accept my apologies for not having been in on the matter to begin with. The word is misomendicant. *Greek: Hate. Latin: Beggar.*
The suffix phobe *worried me a bit. There are too many things I hate but don't fear. I am not, for example, afraid of sweet potatoes. (Sweet potatoes as we have come to know them, of course. Not a twenty-pound bag falling from a high place; a terrifying thought.)*
Misomendicant is the spelling of both noun and adjective, with also misomendicand *for adjective. With this in mind,* misomendicance *becomes almost irresistible.*

> Shelley Berman
> Beverly Hills, California

P.S. Besides, I tried schnorrerphobe *at a party recently and everybody kept asking me to spell it. After a while I tried* misomendicant *and everybody acted as if they'd heard it before.*

left field

Because baseball's third strike so impoverished the daily reading of the nation's national-pastime junkies, here is a survey from the Hot Stove League of the effect of baseball on the American language.

When a professor of atmospheric science predicted that recent changes in the sun's activity foretold a dry spell of several years in the Northeast, another expert —Robert Harnack, a meteorologist at Rutgers—called that forecast "completely out of left field."

Where in the heavens or on earth is left field? How did that area on the baseball field become the metaphoric epitome of far-outedness? To come *"from out of* left field" is to be rooted in the ridiculous, crackbrained, farfetched; to *"be* out *in* left field" is, according to *American Speech* magazine in 1961, to be "disoriented, out of contact with reality."

When asked for the derivation, members of the Abner Doubleday Lodge of the Lexicographic Irregulars lobbed in these ideas:

"In the older, less symmetrical baseball stadia," writes Robert J. Wilson Jr., of Riverside, Connecticut, "left field was usually 'deeper' than right, and thus coming from left field was coming in from a 'far-out' region."

Our ambassador to the European office of the United Nations, Gerald Helman, writes from Geneva: "Right field was thought of as the most difficult to play because it was the 'sun field,' and required the fielder to have a strong arm for the long throw to third. As a consequence, the good-hitting, poor-fielding players were put in left. . . . Because of the defensive inadequacies of left fielders, you could expect almost anything to happen when the ball was hit to them."

On the other hand: "The power of a batter in baseball or softball is to his/her 'pull,' or opposite field," posits Thomas Carter of Dayton. "Since some 90 percent of the population is right-handed, this means that many more long hits can be expected to left field. Therefore, the left fielder will usually play farther back than the other outfielders. This then leads to the linking of *left field* to a person, thing, or idea that is far-out." Could be.

"Left field is about as far as one can get from the desirable seats," suggests Morton Brodsky of Lancaster, Pennsylvania. "The home team's bench is generally, if not always, along the first-base line. This makes the preference for home-town fans (1) from home plate to first base, (2) from home plate to third base, (3) right field, (4) left field. Of course, modern stadia have seating all the way around, but I think that *out in left field* originated in the days when there was nothing out there but a fence."

"Imagine some right-hander of yesteryear (a preponderance of pioneer pitchers were right-handed)," says Jerry Oster of New York City, "with a big sidearm delivery such that the ball, especially to a right-handed batter, seemed to come out of left field."

Since the earliest citation of the phrase appeared in *American Speech,* I queried the editor of that publication, John Algeo, who is one of the heavy hitters in the big league of linguistics today. He assumed it had at least a pseudobaseball origin and appeared early in psychiatric slang; then he tossed himself a fat pitch:

"The explanation that the left field was far off from the home base overlooks the fact that the right field is equally far from the home base and the center field is even farther. Why then left field instead of right field or center field?"

Professor Algeo took a hefty cut: "My guess (and it is no more than a guess) is that the expression is a metaphor referring to a baseball field, but was never actually a baseball term. Probably it was coined by someone who watched baseball but was not a player or real aficionado.

"To be in the *outfield* is to be far out. However, the expression *out in the outfield* is uneuphonious, redundant, and too general; it doesn't make a snappy remark. *Center* and *right* both have highly positive connotations that conflict with the sense of isolation that the term was wanted for. . . . *Center* suggests all the virtues of moderation and the golden mean. *Right* suggests correctness, dexterity, and so on (we don't have to go into the political associations). *Left* is certainly the best word for associations—lefties are a minority, they are sinister (etymologically at least), and (at least by pun) they get left behind."

Mr. Algeo concurs with Irregular Carter's observation that balls hit to left field are usually hit harder, causing the fielder to play deeper: "Since the left fielder is farther removed from the center of action in the infield, his position becomes a metaphor for isolation."

In addition, consider the flakiness factor. "Center field would not be appropriate," agrees David Zinman, science writer for *Newsday,* after checking with Stan Isaacs, who used to write a sports column called "Out of Left Field," "because it is the mainstream of the outfield. 'Right' field denotes correctness. . . . On the other hand, 'left' field has overtones of radicalism in politics. Also, left-handers, particularly pitchers, are often thought of as slightly different, sometimes screwy or dizzy individuals."

Like Lucy in the comic strip "Peanuts," Mrs. Melvin Gollub of Dunkirk, Maryland, disagrees with everybody; it is her experience that "one rarely hits to left field. The outfielder has little to do; hence, he is lonely. . . . When our company plays softball, my son sends me out to play left field so I can't get into too much trouble." Such an iconoclastic view flies in the face of all statistics about where most hard-hit balls go, and is truly out of left field.

In the social revolution of the late 60s, it was common to hear black activists tell us that "it's a brand-new ball game." The activists were implying that the rules which dictated how social problems had been solved in the past were now (late 60s) obsolete. Therefore, new rules were being concocted—hence a "brand-new ball game."

(Ms) Mary Nicole Ferri
Trenton, New Jersey

Although I can't document the following baseball metaphors which have come into wide use, I am sure that others among your readers can.

(1) STRIKE OUT	*(TO FAIL)*
(2) GET TO FIRST BASE	*(BEGIN TO MAKE PROGRESS)*
(3) PINCH HIT	*(TO SUBSTITUTE FOR)*
(4) TOUCH ALL BASES	*(COVER ALL CONTINGENCIES)*
(5) BUSH LEAGUE	*(SECOND RATE)*
(6) HEAVY HITTER	*(VERY ABLE PERSON)*
(7) SWITCH HIT	*(SEXUAL CONNOTATION)*
(8) FOUL BALL	*(ONE WHO FOULS UP)*
(9) SOUTHPAW	*(LEFT-HANDER)*

Herbert L. Finkelstein
New York, New York

The original Cubs' ballpark was located at the corner of Wood and Polk Streets on Chicago's near West Side. In fact the ballpark was called West Side Ballpark. This site is now occupied by the University of Illinois College of Medicine, and has been since the 1920's. Home plate was located on the corner of Wood and Polk, and left field was located down Wood Street. Immediately behind the left field stands was located (and still is located) the Neuropsychiatric Institute, which is now part of the University.

In Chicago, when someone said that one was "out in left field," the implication was that one was behaving like the occupants of the Neuropsychiatric Institute, which was literally out in left field. After West Side Ballpark was torn down, it was a number of years before the remainder of the medical school was built, and ball games on the vacant land still took place. It didn't take long before the phrase "out in left field" became commonplace to describe someone who was acting like they were "nuts."

> Gerald M. Eisenberg, M.D.
> Chicago, Illinois

When I was in my teens, living in the Bronx, we kids were always most anxious to get our seats in the right field where we would be closest to Babe Ruth, so I suppose anybody in the left field was far out.

> David Shulman
> New York, New York

lesser-known

The phrase *lesser-known writers* bothers John Maass of Philadelphia: "There are 'little known writers,' there are 'less well known writers,' there are the 'Lesser Antilles,' but 'lesser-known writers' makes no sense at all."

That's because he's treating *lesser* as an adjective, modifying a noun like *Antilles*. In perfect logic, "lesser writers" would be best—using *lesser* to mean "smaller in critical stature." But you can treat *lesser* as an adverb, too, marrying it to an adjective to form a compound comparative—like *lesser-known*. That way, it makes sense.

Mr. Maass is also intrigued by the similarity of *valuable* and *invaluable*, words that, he says, "are opposites but have come to mean the same—namely, 'of great value.'" He's mistaken: *Invaluable* is so valuable that its value cannot be measured, which is different from merely valuable. Although the *in* means "not," *value* is treated as a verb to come up with "cannot be valued" and not "not of value."

I am sensitive to this because I recently wrote about "a shameful whitewash." Mr. Maass points out: *"Shameful* and *shameless* are opposites but they now have the same meaning—namely, 'odious' or 'despicable' or 'outrageous.' "

Shameful means "full of shame." *Shameless* means "without shame." Opposites, yes, but they have not come to mean the same at all: *Shameful* means "disgraceful," and is applied to an act; *shameless* means "brazen," and is usually applied to a person. Such are the delights of synonymy.

But what of *flammable* and *inflammable*—are they not seemingly opposite and yet the same? Yes. Forget the *in* in *inflammable;* it's confusing. Use *flammable,* or its opposite, *fireproof.*

Among words with opposite meanings consider "impregnable." Its common meaning is "resistant to assault, unassailable, unable to be broken into." But there is also a more biological usage, "able to be impregnated," as would be a female animal in estrus.

One must now wonder at the intent of the phrase "an impregnable mind." Is it a mind that is closed, fortified, unassailable, or on the contrary, one ready for the fertilization of ideas?

The twist of course is supplied by the two meanings of the prefix. One is "in, into, inward" (as "implode") and the other is "not" (as "immoral"). As you pointed out, that ambiguity may reach the flashpoint of hazard in "inflammable," but the choice of "flammable" is impeccable.

There already is a "pregnable" which seems to be a synonym of "impregnable" in its biological meaning and an antonym of the common meaning. Still, in this case I vote to retain "im-." It is the sort of disjunction which gives iridescence to our beautiful language. "Inflammable" is impermissible, but "impregnable" is just, well, impish.

Richard C. Pillard, M.D.
Boston, Massachusetts

It has been said that there is no greater thrill in American life than that of running to a fire.

Likewise, as a volunteer fireman of oh, these many years, I got a kick out of your column relative to "flammable" and "inflammable." Those seemingly opposite words have bothered us in their use. We would like "flammable" and "nonflammable." I am sure you will agree there would be no confusion in their use. But, I guess we will not be able to overcome Noah Webster.

Now, as to "fireproof." We shy away from the use of that word for, in the eyes of the fire service, there is nothing fireproof. Any material will eventually disin-

tegrate or buckle when a sufficient amount of heat is applied to it. That goes for steel, concrete, etc.

We like to use "fire-resistive." That covers it.

> Charles M. Fales
> Past President, Hudson Valley Volunteer Firemen's Association
> Stony Point, New York

I am pleased to correct a bit of bad advice you gave on in-'s. Fireproof is not the antonym of flammable. *Paper, which will burn, is flammable, but water, which will not burn, is hardly* fireproof. *Certain safes, many brick dwellings, and perhaps the National Archives are fireproof. Water is nonflammable rather than fireproof.*

While the OED *equates* flammable *with* inflammable, *much common technical usage considers* inflammable *to be an intensive construction of* flammable. *Thus wood and paper are flammable; gasoline, mineral spirits and similar hazardous substances are inflammable. They really go when you set a match to them. Currently, nonflammable is taken as an appropriate word for something you can't set fire to.*

> Carl H. Snyder
> Professor of Chemistry
> University of Miami
> Coral Gables, Florida

You are wrong about "flammable" and "inflammable." The words are neither opposite nor quite the same in meaning.

The prefix "in-" has more meanings than simply "not." It may also denote position as in "inter" and it may convey an intensive sense, a sense of "very" as it does in "inflammable" and "invaluable." Trucks carrying gasoline should be marked "inflammable," and the way that stuff is costing, "invaluable" could be appropriate too. When alcohol replaces gasoline, its carriers may be marked merely "flammable" and "valuable." In fever and passion, one is inflamed.

There is still more to the prefix "in-." In its several senses, it may appear euphoniously as "em-" (embalm), "en-" (entomb), "ig-" (ignoble), "il-" (illiterate), "im-" (imbecile) and "ir-" (irritate).

To advise against "inflammable" is flimflam.

> Morris Leider, M.D.
> Editor, Journal of Dermatological Surgery and Oncology
> New York, New York

I was shocked, if not inflamed, by your explanation of words which sound like opposites but are not. While I agree fully with the distinctions you made between such words as "valuable" and "invaluable," I fail to understand how you could be fooled by "flammable." Allow me to quote from the latest edition of William Strunk and E. B. White's The Elements of Style *(1979):* "Flammable. *An oddity, chiefly useful in saving lives. The common word meaning 'combustible' is* inflammable. *But some people are thrown off by the* in- *and think* inflammable *means 'not combustible.' For this reason, trucks carrying gasoline or explosives are now marked* FLAMMABLE. *Unless you are operating such a truck and hence are concerned with the safety of children and illiterates, use* inflammable."

"Inflammable" is just one of many English words having a built-in en-, or in- on the front. To ignore this fact is positively furiating.

> David A. Rabson
> Pittsford, New York

Your advocacy of "flammable" as against "inflammable" kindles a warm response. I hope you will pursue this to its logical conclusion and henceforward oppose flammatory rhetoric that does nothing but flame the public's passions.

All telligent readers will applaud you. And soon it will be the in thing to do to lop off that sipid little prefix that causes so much confusion.

> Piero Weiss
> New York, New York

---

liaison, *see* Reaganese, standing corrected

---

master charge

Under the headline of "The Luxury of Full Leather Bindings," a company reprinting a hundred classics in snazzy editions warns: "Do not confuse these masterful editions with other volumes which feature *partial leather* bindings on the spine only."

More important, do not confuse *masterful* with *masterly.* The words started out with the same meaning, and Language Slobs use them interchangeably today, but a distinction has developed that good writers like to preserve.

Masterful means "with the imperiousness of the master" in a kind of master-slave relationship; a masterful person is domineering, the sort of take-charge type who is revered in books about how to become a success by intimidating one's colleagues. The adjective verges on the insulting; it is used in admiration mainly by masochists.

Masterly means "with the skill of a master"; expertly. In "Light Metres," Felicia Lamport, the punning poet, describes Richard Nixon during Watergate as "grown skilled in arts of masterly escape; / I have measured out my life in reels of tape." One reason he did not escape was that he was too masterful and not masterly enough.

Since the words have distinct meanings, it makes sense to keep them apart, and makes no sense to go with the permissivists who begin their argument with "Ah, hell. . . ." "Everybody does it" is no excuse. (What reminded me of that?)

The only thing clumsy and amateurish about this ukase is that there is no easy way to turn the adjective *masterly* into an adverb. When you want to say, "He handled the Chinese with the skill of a master," you should not say, "He handled the Chinese masterly." It is awkward. You would more likely say, "He handled the Chinese masterfully," which means "in a domineering way" and not what you mean at all. In that instance, use another word: *skillfully, expertly, adeptly.* A masterly writer is masterful with his adverbs; get off my ukase.

Leather may be "real" or "imitation"; but "full" and "partial" leather? Does the latter derive from partial animals?

My opinion—impartial, of course—is that you are bound to venture a full opinion. However, it's possible that you feel I am being too thin-skinned and hidebound about this whole matter.

Peter Garnham
East Hampton, New York

---

meld, *see* pre-emptive correction

---

menu-ese, *see* carte before the horse

---

more important(ly)

"When I was in school," writes Betty Hoyt of Youngstown, Ohio, "the phrase used to be: *But more important . . .* When did the *ly* come into vogue, and since when is it correct? Shouldn't the ending *ly* be used only when modifying a verb, such as, 'He strutted importantly into the room'?"

A great many readers take umbrage—indeed, have become umbrage mainliners—at sentences that begin "More importantly . . ." They point out that the phrase is a shortening of *What is more important* and that the addition of the *ly* turns the adjective into an adverb and is incorrect; as several complainants put it, "Wrong wrong wrong!"

The issue was drawn in the late 1960's with the publication of the *American Heritage Dictionary,* which included this usage note: *"Important,* rather than the adverb *importantly,* is prescribed by most grammarians in the following typical construction: *His research has helped to verify several medical theories; more important, it suggests a whole new field of inquiry. More important* is thus construed as an elliptical rendering of *what is more important,* with *important* (adjective) modifying *is. "* The note went on to declare the adverb *importantly* an "acceptable alternative" in such a sentence, a tolerant attitude which surprised some hardliners who considered the usage prescriptions in *American Heritage* as antidotes to the roundheeled descriptiveness of Merriam-Webster's *Third New International Dictionary.*

A few years later, Randolph Quirk's *A Grammar of Contemporary English* showed how the mysterious *ly* popped up in other cases where an ellipsis was taking place: The first word in "Strange, it was she who initiated divorce proceedings" was the short form of *What is strange;* although you could not say "What is strangely," you could start the sentence with *Strangely,* with what Quirk called "little or no difference in effect."

The reason that the adverb with the *ly* on the end is acceptable—the reason it sounds right to so many native speakers—is, I think, that it is a sentence adverb. (Mail will arrive in bulk on this; there are those who become incensed at the very notion of sentence adverbs. Thankfully, I remain fearless; hopefully, so will you.)

Prof. John Algeo of the University of Georgia illustrates the function of the sentence adverb with this example: In "He died happily," the adverb *happily* modifies the verb, but in "Happily, he died," the adverb *happily* modifies the whole sentence and changes the meaning to something like "It's a lucky thing he died before he blew up the world in his pique at her strange initiation of divorce proceedings."

Here is Algeo on the Importance of *Important(ly):* "There's been a lot of pontificating on this question already, so I'll do a bit too: (1) Both *more important* and *more importantly* are correct because both are used by good speakers and writers. (2) Both can be described grammatically as modifiers of the whole sentence, though the adjective form can alternatively be described as what is left after an ellipsis of *(What is) more important* or of *(It is) more important (that).* (3) The adjective form *(important)* is doubtless the older and more conservative, so those who favor continuity may prefer it; however, the adverb form *(importantly)* is simpler to describe grammatically, so those who don't like to be confused, and have limited knowledge of grammar, may prefer it. (4) Anyone who thinks anything of importance depends on the choice is a fool."

He has tenure and can afford to offend the hordes of those who take their *importantly* hating seriously; since I am relatively new at this dodge, and tend to identify with masterly writers who preserve distinctions, I am inclined to wish the *importantly* haters well as they defend their burning, crumbling ramparts. Were it not for that sentence-adverb notion (and where else but in this space can you find a sentence adverb used as a compound adjective?), I would join them in denouncing *More importantly.*

Sadly, however, I am copping out. (I have heard that expressed as "outcopping," which I hope is not upcoming.) *More important* is my preference, but if *more importantly* turns you on, go ahead and use it. Now, at least, you know how to defend yourself.

"He died happily" is far from "Happily, he died," but does it express what some people mean when using it: "He was happy when he died." Is it proper to say "He died happy," which would express the thought? It doesn't quite ring proper to this ear, but it may be perfectly correct.

Guy Henle
Mount Vernon, New York

As a longtime admirer of and most-of-the-time agreer (is there such a word, or should it perhaps be "agree-er"?) with you—lexicographically, not politically—I am dismayed by your acceptance of what is, to me, an indefensibly incorrect usage: "importantly" for "important."

It was bad enough when you abandoned the bastions on "hopefully," but this is almost too much to bear. There is a subtle but distinct difference between the sentence-adverb use (and I'm still not sure what I think about that concept) of "thankfully" and the similar-but-not-matching use of "importantly," although I'm not sure that I can articulate the difference clearly. I think that the addition of the comparative or superlative "more" or "most" is what causes the distinction. You never see "importantly" used in this sense without the "more" or the "most," and you never see "thankfully" or others of its ilk used with "more" or "most." Also, I can't see the worth of lengthening a word unnecessarily; "more important" is a syllable shorter than "more importantly," and it says just what it means quite nicely.

As far as I'm concerned, "more importantly" will always be just as incorrect as "irregardless," regardless of how many people persist in using it and regardless of how many keepers of the language, no matter how much I admire them, give their blessing to the usage.

Ellen L. Kobrin
Massapequa, New York

Thank goodness for your reasonable discussion of most importantly *that deflated those commentators who so virulently protest its present-day use but who know so little about how the English language derives words. It may be that a few sentential adverbs in English derive from the ellipsis of such a clause as* What is more important, *but it is far more common for such adverbs to derive from such a clause as* It is more important that. *The latter process is the typical one:* It is evident that *=* Evidently; It is obvious that *=* Obviously; It is possible that *=* Possibly; *and so on. It is difficult to see how these sentential adverbs and most others ending in* ly *can derive from* What is . . . , *so it is quite easy to understand* *how speakers of English take* It is more important *and simply add* ly *to derive* most importantly *as the sentential adverb.*

Michael Montgomery
Director of Linguistics
University of South Carolina
Columbia, South Carolina

Plainly and simply—as opposed to *plain and simple*—*anyone who defends "more important" as a sentence modifier is wrong, wrong, wrong.*

First, "sentence modifier" is a perfectly sound grammatical concept. (See? I'm on your side.) But the only logical *sentence modifier*—*logical because only it, at the beginning of a sentence, unmistakably modifies what it's intended to modify* —*is the adverb; your seventh-grade English teacher, who said adverbs may modify only verbs, adjectives and other adverbs, was merely regurgitating what her own seventh-grade English teacher told her.*

(And in case anyone thinks he's caught me contradicting myself, let me point out that the first word in the preceding paragraph is an adverb, and is so listed in every dictionary I know.)

Second (another adverb), if you accept an adjective at the beginning of a sentence as a sentence modifier, you destroy its proper and universally accepted function, which is to modify the first following noun. Grammatically, therefore, "More important, his research has helped to verify . . ." is a correct—though terribly clumsy—way to say his research *is more important than something else. If you deny that, you can find nothing wrong with "Walking through the forest, the trees were green," or "Broiled, baked or fried, your family will love our chicken."*

The "ellipsis" argument just doesn't hold. If "more important" is elliptic for "what is more important," "walking through the forest" is for "as I was walking through the forest," and "broiled, baked or fried" for "whether it's broiled, baked or fried."

Anyway, who ever appointed American Heritage *the arbiter of English usage? Its panel of alleged authorities even includes schoolmarms (probably mostly male) who still think you mustn't split infinitives or end sentences with prepositions— people who apparently haven't the capacity to understand that grammar is basically just language logic, and are therefore (1) content to just regurgitate or (2) arrogant enough to regard their own whims and prejudices as "proper" for everyone.*

And Algeo's argument that either way is correct because "good speakers and writers use both" also doesn't hold. First, many good speakers and writers are ungrammatical; Shakespeare is just one example. Second, while usage must obviously be a factor in determining correctness, when usage contravenes logic, and begets ambiguities, usage must yield. I've known many good speakers and writers to misuse—for example—"literally," "anticipate," "anxious"; will Algeo defend those misuses too?

> *Robert S. Burger*
> *Glen Mills, Pennsylvania*

Dear Bill:

Your stance on "more importantly" is unforgivable. I always suspected you of being a soft liner—but your willingness to pursue detente with the adverbial aggressors makes you the Henry Kissinger of word watchers.

There is probably a law against this sort of thing. I am having Roy Cohn check on it.

In the meanwhile, I hereby cease all communication and you are declared persona non grata at the EOB.

> *Best regards,*
> *Tony [Anthony R. Dolan]*
> *Chief Speechwriter and Special Assistant to the President*
> *Washington, D.C.*

I was interested in your use of the word complainant. *Your usage of this word indicated that the definition would be "one who complains."*

Several years ago, I ran across the same usage in a practice published internally by our company. The continued use of the word throughout the practice was annoying to me, since I felt that the word means "one who brings a legal action." Out of curiosity I wrote to G.&C. Merriam Company and asked them for a clarification. Attached is their reply, which I thought might be of interest to you. They indicate the word complainant *should be used in a legal sense and the other usage is archaic.*

> *John W. Weaver*
> *Leawood, Kansas*

Dear Mr. Weaver:

Thank you for your letter regarding the word complainant *as it is defined in* Webster's New Collegiate Dictionary. *The legal sense of the word as given in the* Collegiate *is the one current today. The more general sense (i.e., "one that complains") is now archaic, and is so labeled in* Webster's Third New International Dictionary, *our unabridged book. An archaic word or sense of a word is one for which we have only a few citations showing its printed usage since 1755 and then chiefly in special contexts (as poetry or historical fiction). In view of this, I would suggest that you use the term* complainer *when referring to one that complains.*

Anne H. Soukhanov
Associate Editor, G.&C. Merriam Co.
Springfield, Massachusetts

Something that's been roiling about in my mind for years just broke surface: adverbs are really unpleasant little bastards. An adjective comes by its identity honestly, but most adverbs are illegitimate parasites with no moral integrity whatsoever. Equipped with their -ly blood-suckers, they fasten themselves to an adjective corpus and feed off its juices. If they aren't removed promptly, they take over the organism completely like those alien parasites in sci-fi movies. "Hopefully, it won't happen"—indeed! "More importantly"—phooey! It isn't ignorance or carelessness that produces such deformities; it's the nature of the killer adverb against which modern man has lost his defenses.

Lora S. L. Heller
Dayton, Ohio

I'll bet you get at least a dozen pieces (you should excuse the expression) of mail on your easy use of "roundheeled" in describing Merriam-Webster's TNID!

Although the general usage may currently suggest it means "permissive," the specific derivation proclaims "promiscuous." A roundheels in the old days was a maid of loose virtue who was inclined (as it were) to fall on her back at the slightest suggestion.

Conversely, a girl with squareheels was tougher to tilt. These days, you've got to keep on your toes if you don't want to be caught flatfooted!

Norman N. Gottlieb
Flint, Michigan

mustard cutters

"He's too old," sang Marlene Dietrich, "too old—too old to cut the mustard anymore."

Richard Hisgen of Vienna, Virginia, has sought this department's help in tracking down the origin of *cut the mustard.* He cited the *Webster's Third New*

International definition: "Cut the muster or cut the mustard. Slang: to achieve the standard of performance necessary for success." He flashed a letter he wrote to *The Times* of London, which had done a piece on Coleman's Mustard, asking if the expression started with the cutting of mustard plants (which grew to twelve feet and were cut gently at harvesting to avoid scattering the seeds). Polite responses, he reports, but no leads.

Here's what I have been able to unearth, thanks to Anne Soukhanov of Houghton Mifflin Company. "The first printed evidence for this idiom," she reports, "is the 1904 O. Henry citation ('Heart of West') 'I looked around and found a proposition that exactly cut the mustard.' . . . While we can pinpoint its earliest printed use, we can't definitely say exactly *how* it originated." (Come on now, Anne—take a speculative leap.)

"I personally believe," ventures the world's leading female lexicographer, "it comes from *cut* in a sense meaning to outdo; excel. The second element, *mustard,* comes, I believe, from *muster* (the sense meaning an act or process of critical examination). The *OED* tells us that the phrase *pass muster* (to come up to the required standard) was originally a military term meaning to undergo muster or review without censure or criticism."

"Perhaps," says Mrs. Soukhanov, taking the leap, "the term *mustard* evolved by means of dialect or speech alteration from the earlier *muster.*"

Good guesswork. Now where do you suppose the phrase *cut a deal* came from? That phrase was all over the airwaves during the Republican convention in 1980. From a combination of *cut the cards* and *make a deal*? I dunno. Maybe I'm too old to do the etymology anymore.

Come now. Why do you label Anne Soukhanov "the world's leading female lexicographer"? Do women lexicograph differently from the way men lexicograph? Or are you trying to grant Ms. Soukhanov a distinction even greater than if you had called her merely, for example, "one of the world's leading lexicographers"?

Surely you are aware that, while such groups as female jockeys may be a legitimate special category, certain functions such as thinking have been considered for some time to be equally practicable (or im-) by both sexes.

Caroline Hancock
Princeton, New Jersey

I believe the clue to the origin of the phrase "cutting the mustard" is in the preparation of mustard for eating. As you will gather, this was no easy task. From Webster's International we have:

MUSTARD—A yellow powder of mustard seed mixed with water for use as a condiment and as a rubefacient or counter irritant. It is called French

Mustard when prepared by the addition of salt, vinegar, *etc. and German Mustard when made with Rhine wine or tarragon* vinegar, *etc. Mustard is a stimulant and diuretic and in large doses an emetic.*

AND WE EAT THIS STUFF! Let me add a few more rash *eye-openers(?).*

Vinegar—a sour liquid used as a condiment or as a preservative and obtained by acetic fermentation of dilute alcoholic liquids. The sourness is due to acetic acid usually 3 to 9% strength.

How mustard and vinegar ever got to be considered food is the real mystery. However, I learned some time ago from someone who worked for a condiment company that vinegar was used to "cut" the mustard mixture to make it more palatable. Hence, the phrase "cutting the mustard" refers to reducing the harshness of the mustard powder.

Evidently the mustard is chemically a base. Adding the vinegar (acetic acid) neutralizes it sufficiently to reduce burning and blistering our insides. As Webster's noted, both the French and Germans were aware of the power of vinegar over mustard.

So . . . one who can "cut the mustard" is the vinegar who can stand up to mustard powder . . . a brave soul indeed.

> Joe Mislan
> Lawrenceville, New Jersey

My can of mustard powder is labeled Colman's, manufactured by J & J Colman of Norwich and distributed in the United States by the R. T. French Company of Rochester.

Back to the spice rack?

> Mark Spevack
> The New York Times, *Culture Desk*
> New York, New York

Dear Bill,

Recently you called Anne Soukhanov of Houghton Mifflin (i.e., American Heritage Dictionary) "the world's leading female lexicographer." Were you trying to start a debate or argument? I don't know her and she may be great, but you should know of Joyce Hawkins, who has worked with Burchfield on the OED and other Oxford dictionaries for many years and is the absolutely best definer I have ever met; or Professor Audrey Duckert of the Univ. of Mass., who is one of Fred Cassidy's great contributors on DARE and its editing; and Random House's own Leonore C. Hauck, who has been a key person on our dictionaries for many years —and I bet there are many, many more on various scholarly dictionary projects all

*around the country and in Britain. So I don't want to take anything away from Miss
Soukhanov—BUT LET'S HEAR IT FOR THE FEMALE LEXICOGRA-
PHERS!*

> Regards,
> Stuart [Stuart Berg Flexner]
> Editor in Chief, Reference Department
> Random House, Inc.
> New York, New York

*You refer to Anne Soukhanov as "the world's leading female lexicographer."
Why is the word "female" necessary in that sentence? You have already identified
her as a woman, and a "lexicographer" seems just as eminent as a "female
lexicographer."*

*It has been observed that when the word "female" is used in this way, as for
example, in "female doctor" or "female lawyer," it is meant to diminish, trivialize
or gratify.*

> Angela Danzi
> Massapequa Park, New York

N.C.A.A., *see* Double-A rating

near miss

On the morning after he was wounded, Ronald Reagan was quoted as having
quoted a line of Churchill's: "There is no more exhilarating feeling than being
shot without result."

Good memory, for a man in that condition: The line was from *The Story of
the Malakand Field Force,* Winston Churchill's first book, an 1898 effort sometimes called "A Subaltern's Advice to the Generals."

The exact quotation was: "Nothing in life is so exhilarating as to be shot at
without result." The line was popularized in America by Bernard Baruch, a friend
of Churchill's,* in a speech in the late 1940's written by Herbert Bayard Swope,
which included a suggestion by John R. (Tex) McCrary to quote the Churchill
line.

The quotation is usually misquoted as "shot at and missed." *The Malakand*

*See "double genetives."

Field Force, rarely consulted at the Library of Congress, was checked out to the White House a few hours after President Reagan used the quotation.

Could William Safire be guilty of grammatical gaucherie?

I read a reference to "Bernard Baruch, a friend of Churchill's." Period. End information. A friend of Churchill's what? His generals? His family? His wife, in which case I would like to know more?

Or was that a stumble into the language of the street? Was it a double possessive, which should be as abhorrent as a double negative?

Oh well, all of us are, I hope, entitled to an occasional slip.

> *Ronald F. Dixon*
> *Newark, New Jersey*

In regard to your recent note concerning Ronald Reagan's use of a line from Churchill's The Story of the Malakand Field Force, *it is probable that the President learned of this quote through watching the recent television special entitled "Churchill and the Generals." At one point in the dramatization, Churchill is regaling Alan Brooke, Anthony Eden, and others with stories of his early military career, and, if my memory serves correctly, he concludes the stories by saying that "nothing in life is so exhilarating as being shot at without result."*

> *(Mr.) Christinger Tomer*
> *Cleveland, Ohio*

negative reaction, *see* quantum leaping

neologe seats

"I have developed an overwhelming dislike for people whom I call 'sponges' or 'freeloaders,' " writes Perkins Bass of Peterborough, New Hampshire, "that is, people who habitually borrow or live at the expense of others. There must be some word which describes one who has an obsessive dislike for freeloaders . . . but perhaps there is no such word, simply because there are so few people who share this obsession with me. Am I wrong?"

Yes, Virginia, the spirit of freeloading is alive, but the language offers no suitable "phobe" to describe the haters of freeloading. A lexicographic regular suggests *hiruphobia*, from *Hirudinea*, the scientific class to which the leech belongs. Words like *barnacle, bloodsucker*, and *parasite* also offer possibilities.

S. J. Perelman once wrote of a man giving a long and sentimental toast to his beloved family, who, he said, had stuck to him faithfully through thick and thin, adding the zinger, "like leeches."*

neologism watch

New words are being coined all the time. Travelers in the nation's airports have learned of the dreaded *gatehold*, the delay at the gate to the aircraft, which is similar to *gridlock*, the "Little Scarlet" of traffic jams.

Advertising copywriters try coinage constantly: Searching for a translation for *décolletage* (literally, "low-cut top"), Henri Bendel's copy ran "perfect-for-right-now party dresses/ which means short, sensational and lots of skinshow." The neologism *skinshow*, like *gatehold*, marries a noun and a verb to make a new noun, and is as praiseworthy as the misplaced virgule is silly.

Publishers Weekly, in an article about book covers by Elene Kolb, featured this: "Lee Fishback, art director of Berkley-Jove, also speaks of this feminal, 'woman-to-woman' emotional approach, but chooses to employ a soft-edged realism on her books." I sneer at *soft-edged*, an offshoot of *hard-edged* that will never replace *fuzzy*, but am impressed by *feminal*, which is either an oxymoronic blend of *seminal* with *feminine* or a misprint.

It's never too early to begin planning a new word to denote an event that is rushing toward us. Did you enjoy the American Bicentennial? So did I; the nation's two hundredth birthday, tall ships and all, was a bash. But fifty years from now, what anniversary will we be celebrating?

"I have interrogated my colleagues and searched the standard sources," writes Prof. Stephen Stigler of the University of Chicago's department of statistics, "and it appears that no such word now exists. The 50th has *jubilee;* the 100th, *centennial;* the 150th, *sesquicentennial*, but then things start to thin out. We have *bicentennial, tercentennial, quatercentennial*, and *millenium*, but the 250th remains, apparently, unnamed."

Professor Stigler, one of America's great statisticians, even if he can't spell *millennium*, has had several suggestions from colleagues in his preparation for our 250th blowout. One is *dhaicentennial*, from the Hindi word for two and a half; another, *demisemimillennium*, from "half-of-half"; and *quartermillennium*, from me. He suggests *sestercentennial:* "*Sesterce* is an old and honorable word, of Latin origin, meaning a Roman coin worth two and a half asses or a

*See "leeching halt."

quarter of a denarius. It seems to come from 'half *(ses)* of a third one *(terce).*' "
I don't think it will fly. *Sestercentennial* sounds too feminal.

Although the coining of a neologism is abundantly appealing, I cannot claim the word "feminal" as a product of my own cerebrations. Neither "an oxymoronic blend of seminal with feminine [heaven forfend!] [n]or a misprint," the word "feminal" is a perfectly legitimate—albeit slightly obsolete—adjective which first appeared as a Middle English derivative of the Old French via Latin femina, *and means "of or pertaining to a woman"* (Oxford Universal Dictionary, *p. 687).*

My own use of "feminal" began in 1979 in my Ph.D. dissertation on the voice of the female persona *in medieval literature. I discovered a continual need for an adjective meaning "of or pertaining to a woman," but one that had not been charged with modern political significance by the women's movement. The word "feminine" has unfortunately taken on derogatory connotations—implying vast, vapid wastelands of "Total Women" flaunting pink powder puffs and lace-edged hankies—and the word "feminist" cannot be divested of its bluestockings. Therefore the only acceptable alternative I found was the resurrection of the untainted "feminal," which until your column went unsung and uncontested in various articles, papers, and a book I have written on women's literature.*

So thank you, thank you for being impressed. As for the "soft-edged" quagmire, you must have at the artists themselves, for "soft-edged" is their word, not mine.

Elene Margot Kolb
New York, New York

If you think "sestercentennial" sounds too feminal, how about "bi-sesqui-centennial," which will immediately become slanged (slung?) into the "bi-sexy." That should be neither too feminine nor too masculine!

Mary McNair
Grosse Pointe Woods, Michigan

Dear Bill:

It's not too early to think of the 250th. Since you're coining, what about semiquincentennial?

I think it has a nice, optimistic ring, that we'll be halfway to the 500th.

Sincerely,
George Kelley
Editorial writer, Youngstown Vindicator
Youngstown, Ohio

How about the use of Sesquibicentennial *for 250?*

> *Heskel M. Haddad, M.D.*
> *New York, New York*

Your use of "oxymoronic" to describe the word "feminal" is incorrect. "Feminal" is not an oxymoron, but a portmanteau word.

An oxymoron occurs when two contradictory words or ideas are combined to form a figure of speech, as in "bitter sweet," or "deafening silence." But, and here is where you err, the words themselves remain intact.

A portmanteau word is, on the other hand, the lexical and phonetic hybrid produced when two words are fused into one, as in the ill-conceived "feminal."

> *John G. Tucker*
> *New York, New York*

Your literal translation of décolletage *caught my eye because it literally lacked the word "neck." My trusty dictionary says it is from French* décolleter, *to bare the neck and shoulders, from* dé + collet, *from Latin* collum, *neck. I think you would agree that "low cut top" is not "literal."*

Do you need a dictionary?

> *Bertram Levinstone, M.D.*
> *West Orange, New Jersey*

Your article fascinated several people in Vincennes. More than a year ago a committee was formed to seek funds from the state legislature. In order to impress the legislature, it was felt that we should use the word Sestercentennial as a title for the group. With this idea the stationery was designed. The legislators were impressed by our actions and by our solid front . . . however, we were clipped in the economy move.

The word Sestercentennial was used several times by our local media so that it was not foreign to the intelligentsia. The committee felt that we had made our point and used the word enough. While our committee felt that the word Sestercentennial was not too "femiated" it lacked a traditional American familiarity. With the printing of our new stationery we emphasized the fact that '82 is our 250th birthday . . . "Celebrating 250 years on the Banks of the Wabash."

Up to this point there was agreement in our committee. We knew that a logo was needed. We were faced with choices. If we illustrate the literal meaning of the word the committee saw the problem of showing 2½ asses and who would pose as the half ass. This would be an injustice to one person. Confronted with such a prospect, the committee decided to have a logo contest. The winner shows our

*city's founder, Sieur de Vincennes. He established the French fort here in 1732.
He is not dressed as a rugged frontiersman because we know from inventories of
his estate and from the trousseau of his wife that they carried French culture and
dress into the interior.*

*It was flattering to know that we had used this word Sestercentennial before your
article in* The New York Times. *Generally, there is a slow process for new words
to filter from New York to Vincennes, as we know that we are dependent on eastern
culture.*

*This summer come join us for a piece of birthday cake on the Banks of the
Wabash.*

*August Schultheis
President, Spirit of Vincennes Inc.
Vincennes, Indiana*

newsletterer

In a piece called "Anti-Ethicist," I gave a hard time to Senator Patrick Moynihan
for what he called his "experiment in newslettering." Some of us felt that
newsletter was better left unverbified.

Several of his constituents in New York sent along copies of what he has
newslettered, in which the following appears as a matter of pride: "Cosponsored
an amendment that authorizes medical and legal services to rape victims." It's
as if the world of verbs got back at him.

However, the senator has his defenders: Bruno Stein, professor of economics
at New York University, writes that "the sacred text of *Merriam-Webster's
Second* edition shows that *letter* can be used as a verb, one of whose meanings,
albeit a rare one, is to 'make, write or carry letters.' This is precisely what the
senator did when he newslettered his constituents, except that he did not trouble
to carry the letter himself."

Professor Stein cheerfully accuses me of being a letter myself—that is, a
hinderer, using *letter* in the old sense of "without let or hindrance." Nice play.
"Keep that in your noodle (back of the head)," he advises, "before essaying
further attacks on the belles-lettrists among our statesmen."

Dear Bill:

*You take Sen. Moynihan to task for saying in his newsletter, "I would especially
welcome comment about this adventure into newslettering."*

The objection is to the word "newslettering." You contend that this is a new word and that the Senator coined it.

Such is not the case. In the book How to Make $25,000 a Year Writing Newsletters, *published in 1971, author Brian Sheehan quotes the pioneer newsletter editor Mrs. Denny Griswold: "Newslettering is basic free enterprise." Mrs. Griswold founded the* Public Relations News *newsletter in 1944, so we know the term goes back at least 38 years.*

"Newslettering" as well as "newsletterer" have been, up until your column, part of the private language of the few thousands of us who make a living publishing newsletters. These terms came about partly for convenience, partly because we have some problems in making precise identifications of ourselves.

While we are a branch of journalism, "journalist" is not specific enough when we want to make sure that we are talking about a newsletter journalist. In this context, then, I think the two words flowed naturally from the lips and typewriters of many of us. And this, I suggest, is what happened with Sen. Moynihan. In the phrase he used, "newsletter writing" doesn't seem complete because producing a newsletter is more than writing—"newsletter publishing" is not the precise meaning—"newsletter genre" is too cute. I think that Sen. Moynihan's fluency in the written and spoken language told him that it had to be "newslettering."

All good wishes.

> *Cordially,*
> *Howard [Howard Penn Hudson]*
> *Editor/Publisher,* The Newsletter on Newsletters
> *Rhinebeck, New York*

P.S. Please note that the descriptive tag on the front page of Editor & Publisher *is "The Only Independent Weekly Journal of Newspapering." How long they have been using this, I don't know, but I'm sure it's not a recent coinage.*

To Bill Safire:

Professor Bruno Stein's letter regarding use of "newslettering" as a verb concluded with "Keep that in your NODDLE . . ." (which means back of the head), not NOODLE.

You may rue the day you ever printed Professor Wilson's letter . . .

> *Helen [Helen Galen]*
> *Personal Secretary to Senator Moynihan*
> *Washington, D.C.*

Both Professor Stein and you erred in your fencing over Senator Moynihan's verbal gambol in the phrase "experiment in newslettering."

Point 1: *As used in the phrase quoted,* newslettering *has not been "verbified,"
but rather was used as a gerund functioning as the noun object of the preposition
in. Prepositions do not take verbs as objects.*

Point 2: *Professor Stein's use of* newslettered *as a verb is extremely awkward.
Following his line of thought, one could write "I lovelettered my girlfriend," or
"The postal clerk deadlettered the mail," or "I redlettered my calendar." A poet
or advertising copywriter might get away with this fanciful approach, but the
average writer would feel foolish in doing so.*

> Anne M. Lange
> Adjunct Instructor in Communications
> Pace University, Pleasantville
> Katonah, New York

Dear Bill:

*It is only to be expected that people who write dictionaries can have but little
time left over for consulting them. And for the purpose of restoring a measure of
balance to the spirits of Professor Wilson now that you have referred to him as
"the great political scientist," I enclose the appropriate excerpt from the* OED *in
which it will be learned that "lettering" is indeed a verb. The first and presumedly
preferred meaning is:* the action of writing letters; letter-writing. *As in Lord
Byron's quote, "I hate lettering." I beg to argue that "newslettering" is at least
defensible usage.*

*Lest you suppose I am merely disputatious in these matters, I enclose my most
recent newsletter in which I acknowledged Wilson's complaint. I would have let
it go at that save for my concern that having encountered your accolade, he might
get out of hand altogether.*

> *Best,*
> *Pat [Daniel P. Moynihan]*
> *Washington, D.C.*

no-no boo-boo

As a service to administration spokesmen, here is an up-wrap (an upcoming
wrap-up) of verbal boo-boos committed by President Reagan and his men in their
first hundred-and-whatever days.

Chewing-gum flavor. "When Jimmy Carter started pronouncing it 'guvamint,' " writes pet-peevish Pat Gallagher of Verona, New Jersey, "I attributed it to his southern background. Then everyone started pronouncing it that way. Wait, I thought, till Reagan starts talking—he'll say it right! Not so," she notes glumly, as Mr. Reagan inveighs against the swollen federal establishment. "It's still 'guvamint.' " This may be a carryover from Gerald Ford's "judg-a-ment," and is an improvement over the newly popular "gummint."

Instinct for the juggernaut. One problem with the guvamint, according to President Reagan, is that it has produced an "economic juggernaut," which he pledges to stop in its tracks. "A juggernaut cannot be stopped," Gordon Fels of Richmond, Virginia, argues. The word comes from the Hindi term for a principal god, based on the Sanskrit for "lord of the world"; it was believed that followers of Vishnu sometimes let themselves be crushed under the wheels of a cart bearing his name and statue, which moved forward inexorably. (The last time "Sanskrit" was cited here, it came out "Sanskirt," and has not been corrected until now for fear of stumbling into an ethnic slur.) Metaphorically, a juggernaut is a movement that can be slowed, but at considerable cost.

Zero mistakes. H. R. Haldeman used to set as his efficiency goal "zero mistakes"; the man who sits in a White House position akin to his these days has committed a zero mistake. "Reagan's man Ed Meese," writes David Sopher of Jamesville, New York, "indicating that one would probably not need to begin all over in negotiations with Iran, spoke of not having to 'go back to ground zero.' " In this, he confused *go back to square one,* from a dice-throwing game of the Monopoly type, with the phrase *time zero,* at which social scientists sometimes start their models of process. "Ground zero" is the epicenter of an atomic blast, and not even the most determined hawk wants to go back to that.

Private parts. Norman Ture, under secretary of the Treasury, deliberately launched a neologism at a seminar sponsored by Burson-Marsteller in Washington. The public-relations firm wisely set aside substance to lead its release with the coinage of *reprivatize,* which Mr. Ture prophesied "will be heard more and more in Washington." The word is neither a description of the action taken by a lieutenant busting a corporal for leading a platoon into the swamp nor a plan for a designer of swimwear (formerly bathing suits) to reintroduce modesty into the product. According to Mr. Ture, *reprivatize* means the systematic reduction of the government's intrusion into the private sector. (Federal intrusion into the private language has evidently been prioritized.)

Dictated but not read. In a memorandum to "All Senators," Senator Howard Baker (who occasionally speaks for the administration) wrote: "In the future, the entrance to the Republican Leader's Office will be in S-233 (the former Disbursing Office) instead of S-230 where it had been since time in memoriam." A Senate source passed this gem along to me with "in memoriam" underlined, and the notation "Senator Baker obviously enjoys 'killing time.' " "All Senators" now await an invitation from the Senator to visit the Lincoln Immemorial.

No-no boo-boo. It has been officially confirmed that President Reagan told his first Cabinet meeting: "The one no-no that I'll tell you for discussions is: I don't want anyone ever to bring up the political ramifications of an act." The reduplication* of *no* subsumes the influence of babytalk, and was thus particularly apt in the context of a warning to politicians never to think of politics. *No-no* is a noun meaning a prohibited act, and though citations can be found of its use as far back as 1942, most citations are in the late 1970's. Akin to *no-no* is *boo-boo,* a blunder, which Anne Soukhanov of Houghton Mifflin thinks may be an alteration of *boohoo,* imitative of the sound of crying, a noise heard during Mr. Ture's introduction of *reprivatize.*

"Boo boo" most probably remains from "buboe," as described in Barbara Tuchman's A Distant Mirror, *as the feared manifestation of the bubonic plague—"a black swelling about the size of an egg or an apple in the armpit and groin."*

This imperfection in the flesh was looked upon with dread as the precursor of the pestilence, and it so retains a mild onus to the present.

Janet Long
(English 11, Thousand Islands High School)
Watertown, New York

To family and old friends I am "Booboo." Because I cried a lot when I was little I was nicknamed "Boohoo." "Boohoo" soon became "Booboo." I feel that I am living proof of Ms. Soukhanov's theory.

Virginia Riley
Riverside, Connecticut

Your juxtaposition of the two phrases "No-no Boo-boo" leads me to wonder about the origin of "boo-boo" which Ms. Anne Soukhanov (rather desperately, I think) links to "boo-hoo," the sound of crying. I would be willing to bet a bottle of Tientsin (Tianjin) beer that the phrase goes back to the days of the China theater of World War II, and comes from the Chinese indicator of the negative, pu (bu). Although dictionaries sedulously avoid giving "no" as a meaning for pu, in fact Chinese often use the word—duplicated—to mean "no." "Is this the way to Chairman Mao's mausoleum?" you might ask on the streets of Peking (Beijing). "Bu, bu! (No, no!) That is the way!" would be the answer.

Nicholas R. Clifford
Middlebury College
Middlebury, Vermont

*See "one more time."

Pooh-pooh to Ms. Soukhanov on "boo-boo." At least as early as 1950, California high school students referred to a facial blemish-pimple, acne or whatever, as a "boo-boo." A boo-boo on one's face, on the day of the prom, was a disaster of intergalactic dimensions.

A small etymological step, from the literal to the figurative, transforms the blackhead to a black mark, from "I have a boo-boo on my chin" to "I made a boo-boo at the meeting."

Insofar as the teen-agers' cosmetic boo-boo made a mountain out of a mole, its popularity in the newer sense can be seen as a way of playing down the importance of one's own errors: I may have made a boo-boo, but the boss really screwed up.

> James J. Burke
> New York, New York

You used the word "reduplication." This registers a triple "no" in my mind— to duplicate once again. Would not "duplicate" suffice, and in fact, be more correct? Perhaps a "no-no-no" is a "no-no" only with emphasis.

This term occurs frequently in medical literature. A kidney having two collecting systems indicates the congenital anomaly of "duplication." However, I often see the word "reduplication" used in its stead. Triple renal collecting systems are very rare indeed.

> Marvin S. Podolnick, M.D.
> Northfield, New Jersey

Not so! I don't know Norman Ture, of course, but I do know that "reprivatization" is not his very own neologism.

Peter Drucker used it in 1969, writing about the "sickness of government" in The Age of Discontinuity. *(The idea, for Drucker, was that government was so big and clumsy that it tended to botch all its programs; business, being held accountable for performance, would do a much better job of it.)*

> Mary Duroche
> Minneapolis, Minnesota

Although strongly suspecting that the parenthetical reference to "Sanskirt" was inserted for the sole purpose of provoking comment from Lexicographic Irregulars, I shall rise to the bait. If "sanskirt" is not a word, it deserves to be. Obviously it derives from "sans-culotte" of the French Revolution and describes a modern revolutionary feminist who has passed beyond bra-burning; a "Jean d'Arc."

> William D. Jenkins
> New York, New York

Your passing comment on "government," either its spelling or its pronunciation, reminded me that I had been intending to write. It should be "guvimint." I don't have to tell you that I am considering working towards a Natural English Spelling Association. I've had years of work in the field of language disabilities, especially dyslexia.

Harold Blau
Hollis, New York

O.D. couple

Craig Claiborne, food editor of *The New York Times,* responds to my queries on estimable comestibles and occasionally passes along food for thought: "Have you ever heard of a Southern term, *pure O.D.,* as in 'To my mind that is pure O.D. nonsense'? My mother used it often in Mississippi and it is fairly current throughout the South."

At first, that assignment seemed like a piece of cake. In current slang use, *O.D.* means "overdose," derived from police and coroners' reports in the 1950's about people who died from an overdose of drugs. In the 60's (no, I don't use the apostrophe before the number and stop writing me about it because that's that), the drug culture turned it into a verb. As a noun, its meaning varied from the simple overdose to any sky-high behavior.

That drug meaning was used by writer Richard Corliss in *Time* magazine in reviewing *Buddy Buddy,* a movie with Jack Lemmon and Walter Matthau. Since that pair had starred in *The Odd Couple,* and Mr. Corliss had written that the two actors were "overdosing on the cruelest twists of the plot," the headline writer was inspired to title the piece "The O.D. Couple."

But that could not have been the expression Mr. Claiborne's mother had in mind long ago in Mississippi. For what else does *O.D.* stand?

"Officer of the day" does not fit, nor does "olive drab," the name of a color unique to the military which some fashion designers are now trying to fob off as "forest green," which it is not. The new Army color is a dark green, not olive drab, a color that has to be worn for a few years to cause the wearer to swear off the color for life.

"Out of date" is another, less common meaning of *O.D.,* and may have also been in the mind of the creative headline writer at *Time,* who would then have succeeded in a triple-meaning head. But that meaning is hardly the catfish's meow in Mississippi.

Stuart Berg Flexner, the king of slang, has come up with the answer: "Another use of *O.D.* is as an abbreviation for 'ox dung,' which has been a rural euphemism in parts of the South and Midwest since the early part of this century." Mr.

Flexner notes the slang derogation of brown gravy as "O.D. gravy," which Mr. Claiborne may recall from either his southern childhood or culinary background, and then the noted lexicographer proceeds to burden me with a detailed analysis of the referent for the euphemism, which he must know I cannot print even under the rubric of scholarly inquiry.

Thus, *pure O.D. nonsense* is a gentlewoman's euphemism for a succinct barnyard epithet that comes more frequently to the lips of modern mothers, and might well have been used in innocent ignorance of what the initials stood for. Might be a good idea to bring it back; we're overdosed on barnyard epithets, and their shock value is gone.

O.D. also stands for Doctor of Optometry of which I am an example.

> Dr. M. Klein
> Staten Island, New York

Opus Dei is an organization upon which the Society of Jesus looks with a less than enamored eye.
While this may have little to do with the origin of the expression, "pure O.D. nonsense" might be used by a Jesuit with a double meaning.

> Arthur J. Morgan
> New York, New York

In Texas and Louisiana the term was spoken the other way around, sounding like "D.O.," rather than "O.D." And a favorite expression in which it occurred was the same as Mr. Claiborne's example: "pure D.O. nonsense." But my recollection is of a slightly different sound: "pure-dee ol' nonsense." The "O" is really "old" and the "dee" seems to be a sort of intensifier, not unlike the "dee" in "Lordy, Lordy."
My wife's mother, a Southern lady who still uses the expression, agrees, and adds an additional thought. When pressed for her idea of what the "dee" means, she assumes that it stands for "darned." ("Damned" isn't in her vocabulary.)

> Robert T. Pando
> Houston, Texas

With all due respect to Mr. Flexner's suggestion that the abbreviation "O.D.," as used in the rural South, refers to "ox dung," much in the same manner as "B.S."

today serves as a tame substitute for "bullshit," we write to proffer some alternative explanations.

If one were familiar with that lovely, distinguished dialect found in the Hills and Delta of Mississippi, a brief effort at transcribing the written word into the way it is spoken there might prove illuminating.

"D." is a euphemism ubiquitous to this day throughout the Deep South; and, simply, stands in place of the word "damn." It is suggested that it may also serve instead of the words "damnation" and the "Devil," when such are uttered out of church.

The word "pure" is pronounced "pee-yew-OH-rr." Thus, "pure O.D. nonsense" would be spoken "pee-yew-OH-rr dee nonsense," referring of course to "pure damned nonsense."

Another interpretation, received telephonically this morning from Mrs. J. C. Dalton of Cleveland, Mississippi, who recalls hearing her father use the term frequently, is that "O.D." is itself a derivation of the explanation above. More likely, it is an earlier version of the same school of euphemism, referring to "Old Damn," "old Damnation," or to the "Old Devil" himself.

The above represents the consensus of three generations of native Delta Mississippians. We feel that any notion that "O.D." as used in Southern idioms as a euphemism for "ox dung" is simply pure D.B.S.

> John J. Dalton
> A. C. Dalton
> Mrs. J. C. Dalton
> Plandome, New York

The expression folks used to use when I was growing up in the South, North-Louisiana and East Texas, was PURE-D as in "that's PURE-D wonderful!" or "that's PURE-D disgusting!"

I have always thought PURE-D was a form of PUR-DY, a countrified rendering of "pretty." "That's a right PURDY lil chile you got there." The same word PURDY can be found in abbreviated form in the expression PURD-NEAR as in "Don't go way now—it's PURD-NEAR suppertime."

Of course, if you happen to drink your tea with your pinkie lifted, you are more apt to say, "Don't go way now—It's PRIT-NEAR supper time," but that's a whole 'nother can of worms.

> Martha Hudson Walsh
> Groton, Connecticut

It is not "pure O.D." at all, but "pure ol' D," which is obviously in lieu of damn, or damned. The use of either hell or damn was more than enough, in my childhood *in Alabama, to warrant a "switching." ("Go cut off a peach tree switch and bring it here right now!") Many more things down there are "old" than they are up here, and a true Southerner pronounces it "o' "—"o' man Bob Cox, o' lady Henderson, the o' bull down in the pasture."*

Thom Jonson
Bronx, New York

Back in Oklahoma, when I was a kid, people said "Pure D" to mean: pure, complete, excellent or unadulterated, as "That's Pure D lard" or "He told a Pure D lie" or "Man, that's Pure D whiskey."

Some other people said "Old" (pronounced O') to show affection or familiarity or something as in Old Bosco the horse or Old Bill the hired man or Old Yeller the dog.

Both these sets of people were liable to say, too, "That's Pure old D honey" or "Now that's what I call Pure old D good singin'." Where the "Pure D" originated I don't know, or the use of "Old" that way, either.

Lt. Col. Alden E. Clifford, R'T'D
Boulder, Colorado

Dear Bill:

I am much obliged to you for tracking down the origin of O.D. My mother would have been appalled to know that she was shoveling such words out of her mouth.

Incidentally, is it possible that I am food editor of The Times *and not food news editor? Since I went on a diet about three years ago I have been editing my food, start to finish, at every meal.*

Best,
Craig [Craig Claiborne]
East Hampton, New York

one more time

Recently, in a piece called "No-no Boo-boo," I dealt with the use of *no-no* by adults to mean "forbidden action," and *boo-boo* used by grown American Presidents to mean "egregious mistake." I wrote: "The reduplication of *no* subsumes the influence of babytalk. . . ."

Gastroenterologist Lawrence J. Brandt, M.D.—one of the more redundant members of the Squad Squad—could not quite stomach one of those words: "Since you were not referring to *no-no-no-no,* the reduplication or duplicate duplication, of *no,*" he writes, "but rather *no-no,* the duplication of *no,* I think you meant 'duplication,' not 'reduplication.'" He signed off, "Sincerely yours, Sincerely yours," which is enough to turn your tum-tum.

Since more than one yo-yo has been pooh-poohing my use of *reduplication,* it is time for me to point out that the word comes from the Latin *reduplicare* and has been adopted by real, honest-to-God linguistic heavyweights to mean "to duplicate again and again, if need be," as in the description of what I occasionally think of doing to physicians who should stick to finding a cure for heartburn: *rat-a-tat-tat!*

I turn for support to world-renowned grammarian Randolph Quirk—that's his real name, and not a comment on the irregularity of English—who defines reduplicatives as "compounds that have two or more elements which are either identical or . . . slightly different—e.g., *goody-goody.* . . . The difference between the two elements may be in the initial consonants, as in *walkie-talkie,* or in the medial vowels—e.g., *crisscross.*"

Anne Soukhanov, a lexicographer at Houghton Mifflin who thinks that quirkiness is next to godliness, has grouped reduplicatives into four categories so that we can examine them:

1. Redupes that imitate sounds: *boohoo, bowwow, ding-dong, ticktock, pitter-patter, clip-clop,* and other nursery *chitchat.*

2. Words intended to connote vacillation or repeated alteration of movement, as when some of us criticize the *wishy-washy shilly-shallying, seesaw flip-flops* of this or that *wiggle-waggle* administration.

3. Pejorative words, casting aspersions before swine: *dillydally, fiddle-faddle, higgledy-piggledy, hoity-toity, ticky tacky.*

4. Redupes that intensify: *teeny-weeny, itsy-bitsy, palsy-walsy, tiptop.*

You now know more than you need to know about redupes. Lexicographer Soukhanov insists: "You did not make a boo-boo; you did mean reduplication, not just duplication or even duplicationcation. Now I have to go bye-bye."

Don't you need a 5th category of redupes for place names?

> *Sing Sing*
> *Pago Pago*
> *Walla Walla*

You can say that again!

> Chuck Branch
> Memphis, Tennessee

"The reduplication of no subsumes the influence of babytalk. . . ."
Why "subsumes"? "Subsume" means in logic: to include one term in (or under) another, as in a classification or syllogism. It is almost always used in the passive voice (" 'Socrates' is subsumed under 'man' " not: " 'Man' subsumes 'Socrates.' ")
I don't know of any use of "subsume" except the one in logic, so I don't understand your sentence.

> Lewis W. Beck
> Rochester, New York

out, damned gnat

I was trying to be helpful. In tracking the derivation of "straining at a gnat and swallowing a camel" in "Gnat Swallowers," I pointed to the King James Version of the Bible, Matthew 23:24, and wrote: "The original spokesperson, lest we forget, was Jesus of Nazareth."

"That would have been appreciated by 'Ma' Ferguson, the Texas Governor," writes the Rev. J. Carter Swaim, pastor emeritus of the Church of the Covenant near the United Nations in New York, "who, when Spanish was proposed as a second language for schools in the Lone Star State, replied: 'Not while I am Governor! If English was good enough for Jesus Christ, it is good enough for Texas children.'"

The original words, which may have been spoken in Aramaic or Hebrew, have come down to us from the Greek New Testament, and it was my luck to have picked up one of the classic misprints in biblical history.

"The expression 'strain *at* a gnat,'" writes David N. Freedman, director of the University of Michigan's studies in religion, "in the King James Version is an error for the correct rendering of the Greek text of the Gospel, which would be 'strain *out* a gnat.'"

That changes the metaphor. The mental picture of scribes and Pharisees turning blue in the face trying to swallow a small bug (straining *at* it) is quite different from the same bunch carefully filtering out any little critters in their drinks (straining them *out*).

The mistake in the first edition of the King James Bible was not spotted and went through subsequent printings over the centuries. The erroneous translation put a new idiom in the English language, which sage commentators use to this day, despite the possibility of a saint in Heaven trying to explain that it was not his fault that Jesus was misquoted.

Because the wrong reading was plausible, the *at* stayed in until 1881; it takes at least a century to straighten people out. "Usage alone has guaranteed the permanence of the false image," says Mr. Freedman, general editor of the Anchor Bible, "while the correct reading has made very little progress in general usage, and is likely to remain a curio of interest only to scholars."

Not so; right here and now, generations yet unborn (is that redundant?) will be set straight. The Anchor Bible rendition is: "You blind guides! Straining a fly out of your drink, and then swallowing a camel!" Sooner or later, even the scribes get it right.

out, damned year

What did Howard Baker mean when he acquiesced in revenue enhancement "in outyears"?

"Think 'outyear,'" writes Senator Daniel P. Moynihan in his newsletter to

"Yorkers." "That is the term we use in the Senate Finance Committee for a tax provision that does not go into effect for one or two or three years after it is enacted."

Outyear—one word as used by insiders, two words as misused by outsiders—is a contribution of the budget arts to the language arts. " 'Outyear' refers to future spending estimates," explains Glen Goodnow of the Congressional Budget Office: "The *current year* is fiscal '82; next January—1982—the President will present the *budget year* for fiscal '83; beyond that, fiscal '84, '85, and so on are the *outyears.* "

Let's agree to write *outyear* as one word. That would end the confusion for those politicians who consider the Out Years as the parched period when they are not the Ins.

out there

In Vienna, Alan Levy has been clipping certain New York Times Service stories out of the *International Herald Tribune.* The common denominator is *out there.*

In one story about show business, Lila Wisdom, godmother of actress Brooke Shields, is quoted as warning: "Everybody has the million-dollar deal. There are a lot of phonies out there."

On the business page, Edward Telling, chairman of Sears, Roebuck, observes: "We can't forget those 40 million accounts out there. . . ."

On the news pages, Arlene Weidner, an organizer of the Save-Our-Shrine Committee in Chicago, commented on the charges aimed at John Cardinal

Cody: "There are two and a half million Catholics out there who must feel awfully bad. . . ."

Noting these usages, Mr. Levy observes: "When my family and I moved to Europe fourteen years ago, we thought we went Over There. Now I keep reading about somewhere called Out There. Since we're planning a return visit to the States next summer, I'd like to book a Super-Apex ticket to this newest In place, but we can't find it on the map.

"All I know about it from the enclosed clippings," continues the far-out would-be out-there traveler, "is that Out There has a population of two and a half million Catholics with forty million Sears charge accounts and a million-dollar deal in every pot. Sounds like a nice place to visit."

But you sure wouldn't want to live Out There. I, too, have been tracking printed references to this much-mentioned place, and have tucked in my wallet a passage from a satiric article in *The New Republic* in which Michael Kinsley parodies a Washington columnist on a television panel named "Haynes Underwear": "I'm just back from Out There, taking the pulse of the nation, speaking to millions of ordinary Americans, be they shopkeepers, or baseball fans, or Presbyterians, and all of them agree with remarkable unanimity that this is a very critical time for our nation. . . . Americans are nervous, yet they remain calm. They have lost faith, yet they retain, I think, an underlying confidence. They are certain, yet somehow unsure. . . . I know, because I've talked to every single one of them."

Out There is the insider's derogation of the vast wasteland outside. It is, as Pundit "Underwear" indicates, not so much a place as a collection of unsophisticated people—the amorphous audience, the mob upon which the opinion makers like to say they "impact."

The predecessor phrase was *the Great Unwashed,* said to have originated with Edmund Burke; in this sense, its faintly contemptuous adjective was first recorded in the United States in 1844: "The larger element of ignorance and 'unwashed' humanity, including our foreign-born population, gave victory to Mr. Polk."

For a time in the early 1970's, *the Silent Majority* was the operative phrase, spoken less in derogation than in defiance, but that phrase had ancient roots in a description of all the people who had ever died. It was quickly replaced with *Middle America,* a neutral-connotation coinage by columnist Joseph Kraft. While many of us were comparing *heartland* to *Sun Belt* (columnist Kevin Phillips) to *Frost Belt* (both belts were derived from H. L. Mencken's *Bible Belt*), an old show-biz phrase slipped in to take over the characterization of the masses by the elitists: *Out There.*

I think the phrase was popularized in the 1930's with "all you folks out there in radioland," though we must await citations from the Lexicographic Irregulars to be certain. Another source might be Australian, from the Outback, wilderness (now a wilderness area).

The central element of *Out There* is the conscious separation between a speaker and the group to which he scornfully, or fearfully, or even admiringly, refers. As in any lumping together of a proletariat, the phrase drips with condescension. The speaker is obviously happy to be In Here.

A note of dread sometimes combines with the patronization, probably rooted in the melodramatic cliché "But, Captain, we don't know what's out there." This, Dear Reader (note the unpatronizing singular), is only fitting: When a star begins to think his audience is Out There, he soon loses his stardom.

No, Mr. Levy in Vienna, the Super-Apex fares do not apply to the trip you seek; you're already Out There.

After reading your analysis of the phrase "out there," it occurred to me that you overlooked an important aspect of the phrase.

In the college community to be "out there" is not so much to be a member of the Great Unwashed, or a citizen of Peoria who lives on Main Street, as it is to be someone who tends to take great flights of fancy.

When, several years ago, the dorm's Space Cadet explained the process for making olive oil in the middle of a rather routine dinner, we agreed that L—— was "out there, and seems to be having trouble finding the way back."

But the Out There description of cognitive skills is being replaced by the term "to lose it." "He's really lost it this time." "Yeah, and he doesn't know where to start looking for it." I suppose that he has lost it somewhere out there.

> Suzanne Bremer
> Boston, Massachusetts

I think you may have been a little off in the "out there" department last week. Have you ever heard a woman say, "There just aren't any good men out there"? Or, "Look at what's out there to choose from"? "Out there" seems to be a cold place, the tundra of alienation and lost hopes that lies outside everyone's door. The elitist element creeps in perhaps for those who believe the problems of society are caused by the Great Unwashed. But for most people the phrase is not truly elitist so much as separatist. It reflects a me (or my little group)-against-the-world attitude. "Out there" is a message we are sending through our language about how we've come to feel about each other and our culture.

> Robert Karen
> New York, New York

Your column has put me in a particularly theologic frame of mind. Might I suggest to you that "the Great Unwashed" carries with it not only a derogatory reference to personal hygiene, but a reference to the gap between the saved and the damned, as well. I've always assumed that the washing implied in the phrase was the act of Baptism, which symbolically cleanses the individual of sin, and inducts him into the faith. This rite of passage separates the washed initiates in the "us" camp from the unwashed outsiders in the "them" camp.

Gary Clinton
Philadelphia, Pennsylvania

I envision John Wayne and Harry Carey, Jr., crouched and peering into the black of night, a campfire crackling behind them.

CAREY: *"I can't see anything."*
WAYNE *(confidently): "They're out there."*

Yes, those sneaky red devils were the first ones on this continent to be "out there."

Thomas E. Reid
Toronto, Ontario

---

overload inoperative

A press release floated in the other day announcing that Senator Paul Tsongas, Democrat of Massachusetts, had signed a contract to write a book about "the future direction of liberalism in America."

In time, the banshees toiling for Tsongas will probably issue a series of press releases: The senator has just hired a ghostwriter; the first chapter has been successfully completed; the publisher, Knopf, has coughed up the next payment on its advance; and, finally, the manuscript has been mailed. (The book itself would then get lost in the shuffle.)

What caught my eye in the exciting news about the agreement to begin this enterprise was the accompanying statement that among the "basic realities" on which the book will focus are "finite resources," "third-world strivings," and "biosphere overload."

Biosphere overload? That's frightening stuff, like a halitosis pandemic. The biosphere is that portion of the world that can sustain life: the earth's crust (lithosphere), the oceans (hydrosphere), and the air (atmosphere). By extension, *biosphere* has come to mean the environment capable of sustaining some form of life.

A "biosphere overload," presumably, is the state of Malthusian disaster known as overcrowding. The word *biosphere* was coined in Germany in 1875, and it took until 1962 for a group of astronautical seers to come up with the answer: "A mature civilization . . . would possibly create an artificial biosphere at a comfortable distance from its star to sustain a greatly expanded population." So much for the problem of biosphere overload.

"Liberals hold a number of assumptions," states Senator Tsongas, a thoughtful fellow although afflicted with book-contract overload, "that are simply inoperative." There's a term I thought had been fried to a frazzle in the firestorm of Watergate. *Inoperative* was once a respectable word, used four times in amendments to the United States Constitution, and at least once by Abraham Lincoln: "inoperative, like the Pope's bull against the comet." R. W. Apple, a reporter for *The New York Times,* placed the word in the mouth of White House Press Secretary Ron Ziegler; when that harried spokesman spoke it aloud, *inoperative* became tainted as an example of programmed deception.

Thank you, senator, for making *inoperative* operative again, and for alerting us to the reality of overloading our biosphere, while conservatives are foolishly worrying about lithosphere underload. Be sure to let us know how the book is coming along.

I was, for the briefest instant, delighted as I started to read your reaction to the press release about Senator Tsongas's book-to-be about "the future direction of liberalism in America." The term "future direction" ranks right up there with "general consensus" and "at that point in time" as something I tell my college composition students is almost always a tautology, in no way sanctioned by wide use, and almost always arousing in me a harsh, intolerant, and repressive response. "Think what the words you use mean," I keep saying, hopefully, since unwarranted hopefulness is an attitude teachers much cultivate. Therefore, "Oh, good!" said I to myself; "Safire is going to provide me with a paragraph I can read to my classes, and then put on my office bulletin board."

Alas, you went by "future direction" to respond to other things in the same press release which, while amusing, lack the oppressive ubiquity of "future direction" and its cousins. Have you given up? Or did you fail to notice it? Either thought is depressing to those of us still trying to fight the good fight.

> R. W. Tucker
> Philadelphia, Pennsylvania

penultimatum

"A Perceptive Professor," subheadlined the *Bergen Record*, "Perfects the Penultimate Presidential Poll." That was nice Peter-Piper alliteration, but the word *penultimate* was misused. In the same mistaken way, an Associated Press story last year told of "Walter Cronkite's penultimate presidential convention."

Ann Rubin, lately of Oakland, New Jersey, sent in these clips with the notation: "In each instance, the writers use *penultimate* to mean ultimate or final, and not next-to-last, which is what I understand it to mean." James Montgomery, M.D., from Mandarin, Florida, echoes the complaint: *"Penultimate* is used by television newscasters when they want to emphasize how terribly ultimate something is. It's an example of what my great-aunt Madna used to call 'puttin' on airs.' "

Penultimate does not mean "real-real ultimate" or "the absolute livin' end." From the Latin *paene ultima,* or "almost the last," the word is used in linguistics to denote the next-to-last syllable of a word, and is used more widely to mean "the one before the very end."

This confusion of "the last" with "the next to last" is caused by people who have an ultraurgent need for emphasis. Take *essential,* which used to be a fairly strong word: Nowadays, if something is not *quint*essential, it's hardly needed at all. In that case, the *quint* is a legitimate intensifier, meaning "the fifth essence," derived from the medieval belief that a mysterious fifth essence permeated the four elements of fire, water, earth, and air. If stressful emphasizers are going to add to *essential,* why not add to *ultimate?*

Because it's a quintessential mistake. At Random House, dictionary editor Keith Hollaman says, "If *penultimate* gets to sound too familiar, the next misuse would be *antepenultimate,* which traditionally has meant the third from the end, the one before the penultimate."

Lexicographer Stuart Flexner, a frustrated adman, adds: "I'm surprised a copywriter hasn't claimed that Mr. Cross's or Mr. Bic's product isn't the 'pen ultimate.' " That way lies Aunt Madna.

You claim the word "quintessential" comes from the medieval belief that "a mysterious fifth essence permeated the four elements of fire, water, earth, and air."
While the medievals did believe in a fifth essence, it was not supposed to permeate the others. Rather, the fifth essence, of which our knowledge was necessarily limited, was postulated in order to account for the eternal motion of the heavens.

The problem was that each of the four terrestrial elements was supposed to have a natural resting place, earth at the bottom, then water, air, and fire. Each element had a natural tendency to seek its resting place, and such striving was thought to be the cause of a great deal of terrestrial motion, including the dissolution of terrestrial bodies. But since the natural thing to do upon reaching one's natural resting place is to stop, it was taken for granted that all terrestrial motion was finite and of limited duration.

This accords perfectly well with the facts of terrestrial life, with one exception: the only seemingly unending motions we perceive are those of the heavenly bodies. But if those bodies were composed of the four terrestrial elements, they too would seek a natural resting place or would be subject to ultimate dissolution as their components sought their place in the order of nature.

Since celestial motion is not linear, goal-directed, and finite, but circular and eternal, it was thought celestial bodies must be composed of an entirely different substance and operate upon different principles than terrestrial things. It was not until Newton succeeded in uniting Galileo's laws of terrestrial motion with Kepler's laws of celestial motion in a common system that a convincing case against an ontological distinction between the heavens and the earth could be put forward.

Willem A. deVries
Assistant Professor, Department of Philosophy
Amherst College
Amherst, Massachusetts

I take umbrage with Random House's Keith Hollaman. He states that "antepenultimate" means "the third from the end." Now, it may be third word from the period. But it is only the second word from the last. The ultimate is the last, the penultimate is the first from the last, and thus the antepenultimate is the second from the last.

Carl Sandler Berkowitz
Chester, New York

personal, *see* getting personal

Pike's Plateau or bust

"Have you noticed how the misuse of the noun *plateau* has proliferated?" notes Melvin Fauer of New York. "Has everyone forgotten there's such a word as *peak*? Or *pinnacle*?"

Either something odd has been happening in geology or a metaphor is going through a metamorphosis. A plateau is an elevated tract of level land—flat, high ground, often jutting dramatically out of a low plain. From this topographical use, we draw the metaphoric sense: a stable period, a cessation of climbing. In psychology, a plateau is a period of no apparent progress in a person's learning. The essence of the metaphor has been flatness, stability, no growth, a leveling-off.

But consider these recent citations:

■ In a *New York Times* review of the Woody Allen play: "So it's only natural that one expects *The Floating Light Bulb* to take him to another plateau—if not in terms of achievement, at least in terms of daring."

■ In an advertisement for men's shoes: "The evolution of Roots reaches another plateau with our new spring collection."

■ In a statement by Secretary of State Alexander M. Haig Jr., who said his trip to Peking had taken Chinese-American friendship "to a new plateau."

What's happening up there? Is the reviewer hoping Woody Allen's daring will flatten out? Is the shoemaker bragging about a leveling-off in the evolution of his clodhoppers? Is the SecState touting a period of no progress in our relations with the Middle Kingdom?

Hardly. The *plateau* metaphor is changing from its accent on flatness to a new meaning of "step upward." Today, to reach a plateau—especially a "new" plateau—is no longer evidence of stagnation, but a hopeful sign that a "higher" plateau will soon be reached.

Here's the metaphoric problem: In nature, there is not necessarily a higher plateau—most of the time, you climb to a plateau, walk across the level, as on the Golan Heights, and go down the other side. But the language has made a leap from the source in nature to the referent on paper, from the high level ground to a level on a graph or chart.

The leap is good, for the figure of speech is useful: A *new peak,* or *new pinnacle,* implies a high to be followed by a drop, but a *new plateau* can be a place of momentary rest before another step upward. So, dictionaries, get with it: *To reach a plateau* may still mean to level off, but *to reach a new plateau* implies a step upward in a series of advances.

During the so-called golden age of television quiz shows, there was a weekly epic entitled "The $64,000 Question." In the game, every time a contestant answered a question correctly, he (no sexism intended) increased his winnings. Along the route to the ultimate title prize, the contestant arrived at a series of "plateaux" (I assume the word should be pluralized with an "x"), each of which, to quote your article, "is no longer evidence of stagnation, but a hopeful sign that a 'higher' plateau will soon be reached."

As I recall, the patter of the Master of Ceremonies, Hal March, went something along the following lines: "You have reached your first plateau. You can stop here and keep your $1,000, or continue on."

I am glad to see that with especially stimulating columns such as this you have reached a new plateau.

> Robert Bookman
> Century City, California

Podunk to the boonies

"Welcome," says the flight attendant in her soft-edged (formerly fuzzy) vernacular, "to the wherever-we-are *area.*" Not to a specific place, but to an amorphous environs fit more for denizens than citizens.

The lust for soft-edged areas led city planners to call the combination of city plus suburb a "greater wherever-we-are area," which in New York gulps down Newark, lets Chicago spread out over Evanston, and takes Los Angeles halfway out to Hawaii.

This urban encroachment led nineteenth-century vituperator William Cobbett to warn that all England would become "The Wen," a slopping-over of London, spoiling his rural rides; similarly, I feel an urge to castigate the Census Bureau for designating cities-plus-adjacencies "Standard Metropolitan Statistical Areas." (I'm from S.M.S.A. 8840—what S.M.S.A. are you from?)

Recently, the human bean counters have extended the designation of S.M.S.A. to thirty-six more locations, turning them overnight into big cities. There are now 323 such places where flight attendants can welcome you, and civic boosters can extol their Greater Squedunk Metropolitan Areas, including Glens Falls, New York, and Casper, Wyoming.

"Glens Falls and Casper are undoubtedly appealing towns," writes a big-city editorialist for *The New York Times.* "They might even be appealing cities. But it does neither the places nor the language any good to pronounce them *metropolitan.*"

Even as place-name sprawl has afflicted us, a related phenomenon can be observed: People who live within the 323 S.M.S.A.'s have begun to call all places not so blessed "the boonies."

"The boonies" is the land of the people Out There. This slang term of the 1960's is a shortening of *boondocks,* from the Tagalog *bundok,* the native Philippine Islanders' term for "mountain." (During World War II, United States Marines were equipped with "boondockers," heavy boots for plodding through rugged mountain terrain.) Any out-of-the-way place or remote village soon became known as "the boondocks."

Our language would suffer a great loss if all rural places were lumped together and derogated as "the boonies." To resist this homogenization—and to encourage the creative, colorful derogation of small towns that has always studded the American language—I turned to F. G. Cassidy, director-editor of *DARE,* the great research project under way in Wisconsin that will one day be published as the *Dictionary of American Regional English.*

To a question his interviewers posed to thousands of native speakers about "a small or unimportant place," these were the most frequent responses: *sticks, wide spot in the road, boondocks, burg, hick town, backwoods, one-horse town, podunk, four-corners, no-man's land, hideaway, whistle-stop,* and *jerkwater town.* The last two are from railroad lingo. *Jerkwater* comes from an operation of railroad crews when small boilers required frequent refilling, and water tanks were few: A leather bucket at the end of a long rope was used to jerk the water from nearby streams. (Railroad buffs will send in a hundred other derivations; no frantic flagging-down will stop them.)

Other delightful put-downs of small towns uncovered by the man from *DARE* include *dump, ghost town, hell's half-acre, dogtown, neck of the woods, timbuktu* (a real place, in West Africa's Mali), *tules, back 40, dogpatch, hicksville, last chance, plumb-nelly, baddy's cowpasture, tank town.* Not included is what Liz Carpenter, of the Johnson White House, calls her place of origin: *Resume Speed, Texas.*

Curiously, *God's country*—hardly a put-down, more of a boast, first recorded in the Civil War as a proud description of the North by Union soldiers—has been taking on a pejorative connotation, as in *the middle of nowhere.*

The alert reader (I wish my readers were merely alert—most are profoundly suspicious) will note unexplained references herein to Podunk and Squedunk. These are the quintessential hick towns, located on the outskirts of the middle of nowhere, way beyond the back 40.

The great etymologist of Americanisms, Allen Walker Read, who discovered the origin of *O.K. (oll korrect,* 1839), is the man to see about *podunk.* Forty years ago, he pointed to the 1911 book by the noted Algonquinist W. W. Tooker,

The Indian Place-Names on Long Island, in which the etymology of *podunk,* formerly *potunk,* is explained. The first syllable, *pot,* means "to sink," and the *unk* is locative; thus, *podunk* means "where there is a sinking."

But whence the figurative use of this boggy place, dreaded by Indians, to mean the hickiest of the hicks? In a return to Podunk for the Northeast Regional Names Institute, etymologist Read recently noted the discovery in the *Dictionary of Americanisms* of an 1841 use in the *New Orleans Picayune:* "My native place is down in Podunk." In that era, American humorists were using names like *Skunk's Misery, Weazletown,* and *Squashborough;* cartoonist Al Capp repeated the trend a century later with *Dogpatch.* This was the usage in New York's *The New Mirror* of 1843, unearthed by David Shulman: "the unsteady and frolicsome youth who ran away with the belle of Podunk." The same use is current; over an article about the backwardness of New York's teaching of geography, *The New York Times* headlined in 1973: "Among Geographers, New York Is Podunk."

Squedunk, sometimes spelled with two *e*'s , is a spin-off that illustrates the doctrine of the phonestheme, which maintains that some sounds have a meaning in themselves. "The 'ee' sound," writes Professor Read, "as in *teeny* for *tiny* or the Scottish *wee* ('fond of the wee drappie'), apparently carries the notion of smallness. Therefore, *Squedunk* is a variant shaped by its phonetic character." Perhaps that caused financier B. C. Forbes to expostulate in 1951: "The time is past when companies can get away with holding their meetings in damned inaccessible places like Squeedunkus or Ho-Ho-Kus."

Is there hope for Ho-Ho-Kus—that is, will the tradition of creating funny names for rustic places continue? Or will the imaginative sneering at small towns be overwhelmed by the blanketing of *the boondocks* and its shortened *boonies?*

One clue: Professor Cassidy picked up a hybrid form of *boondocks* that mates the old with the new: *Podock.* Such fresh scorn shows that there's life in the S.M.S.A.'s still.*

Dear Bill:

You went and touched me to the quick of my secret identity when you spoke of "noted Algonquinist W. W. Tooker." You see, in real life as a linguist, English is not my special field. Like you, I only speak it. I am, however, an Algonquianist.

Algonquin is a language, spoken by American Indians in Quebec (as German . . .). Algonquian is a family of a couple of dozen related languages (as Germanic . . .). The -(i)an suffix is commonly used to refer to a language family,

---

*See "sufferin' succotash."

as Malayo-Polynesian, Sino-Tibetan, Dravidian, Indo-European, and the like. Regards.

> Yours,
> Karl [Karl V. Teeter]
> Professor of Linguistics
> Harvard University
> Cambridge, Massachusetts

P.S. I'll stay out of the discussion of the etymology of Podunk *after I (1) express my skepticism; the word is more likely to be made-up mock Indian, (2) confirm that* -unk *is indeed a locative suffix such as commonly appears in Algonquian place names, and (3) point out what I figure you already know, that as an Algonquian place name the term would have been a fairly colorless objective description, not a pejorative, which shade comes from English usage, another reason to think it mock. By the way, my father's word (he lived 1902–69) for a jerkwater town was the generic* Horseneck Junction.

You may not hear from too many railroad buffs but I'm sure you'll hear from New Jersey residents, especially residents of Ho-Ho-Kus.

As you will undoubtedly learn, Ho-Ho-Kus was the name bestowed upon the community by the American Indians, not a funny name created for column fodder.

> Burns Copeland
> Waldwick (ha-ha), New Jersey
> (Times wire room, New York)

You mention Timbuktu and point out that it is a real place. No contest there —but you list Podunk, Ho-Ho-Kus and Hicksville—and fail to mention that these places also exist. I can't be sure whether you just decided to omit these facts for lack of space (understandable) or whether you knew not of them.

Podunk is a city in eastern Kentucky, I was there!

HoHoKus is in northern New Jersey, not far from the Nixons' new house at Saddle River.

And Hicksville is in Nassau County—on Long Island; my Aunt Alice lives there, so does my boss.

And "Squashborough" does remind me of another real place—South Succotash, Iowa, which is what I use for points west of the Hudson, north of 245th St. in the Bronx.

> James Hlavac
> New York, New York

My mother and friends in her Viennese-Jewish circle have a charming way of saying Podunk. To refer to the one-horse town my wife and I call home, they use a German phrase which translates as "where the devil says good night."

David Lehman
Lansing, New York

When all is "said and done," and everyone "sends you round the bend," just think that one day when you retire you can go and live "at the back of beyond" where nobody, but nobody will "get at you"!

J.P.H. Pietrolewicz
Brooklyn, New York

I was amazed that somewhere in that long list of out-of-the-way places there was not a reference to the "Toolies." I am not even sure how to spell "Toolies," as I have never seen it used in that sense in writing. However, this one is a pretty easy one to figure out. Thule was, of course, the ancient Greek description of an island far far far to the north probably in the Shetlands; in any case it defined a way-out place way up north, very cold, etc. The expression Ultima Thule expressed the ultimate in far-outness as far as I can ascertain.

In the last few weeks out here in the Thule of southern California I have heard the expression "Toolies" used more than once. I do not know how the expression started. I did not know that southern Californians were so deeply into Greek mythology. As a matter of fact that last statement is Ultima Thule; in a semislang expression as expressing the most far-out of situations.

Arthur L. Finn
Los Angeles, California

You referred to a word which you spelled "tules." May I suggest the spelling "Thule," which my Webster's *(Collegiate, 1937) defines as ". . . the northernmost part of the habitable world." This is certainly an appropriate metaphor (?) for a place in the middle of nowhere, and both Webster and the OED agree that the word is at least 1,000 years old.*

While Webster claims that Thule should be pronounced "thū'lē," I have learned it as tōō'lē. I have no knowledge of the pronunciation of your word. Thule may still be found on modern maps, and it is also used to describe a certain people, the Thule Eskimo.

Mike Schneider
Albuquerque, New Mexico

posh bosh

The ad in *The New Yorker* for the Portside Yacht Club, peddling "townhomes" for 350 G's and up, starts with a barefaced bit of misinformation: "For decades, the word POSH has epitomized the finest accommodations aboard the world's best cruise ships. 'Portside Out. Starboard Home.'"

This phony etymology was started in the mid-1930's and it drives wordsmen bats (from "Born After The Sixties"). In the *Merriam-Webster Book of Word Histories,* weary lexicographers traced and rejected the supposed derivation: "Favored passengers traveling from Britain to India in a P. & O. ship had tickets stamped P.O.S.H. and were given cabins on the port side on the outward voyage to India and on the starboard side on the homeward trip. These cabins, being on the north, away from the sun, were cooler and more comfortable than those opposite."

A happy whimsy, but without evidence to support it. In his slang dictionary, Eric Partridge identified the noun *posh* as "money, specifically a halfpenny," as used in 1839, and cites a P. G. Wodehouse line in 1903: "quite the most push thing at Cambridge," suggesting that *posh* was a later confusion of *push*. When a writer in *The Times* (of London) *Literary Supplement* came up with that speculation of acronymic origin in 1935, amateur etymologists seized upon it and now whenever anybody says he's in the word dodge, he gets asked, "Do you know where *posh* comes from?"

At Merriam-Webster, editorial director Fred Mish resolutely sticks to "origin unknown" on his *posh* file, and doesn't get taken in on acronymic origins of *tip, news, cop,* and *spiv,* either.

Acronyms are tricky. POSSLQ, pronounced "POS-ul-kyoo," was the designation by the Census Bureau of a live-in, or roommate, or co-habitee; it stood for "Persons of Opposite Sex Sharing Living Quarters," and for a time had a vogue among men who were reluctant to say, "Meet my mistress, paramour, or tootsy."

But not all acronyms are acronyms. Clarence Barnhart, the nabob of neologisms, who is issuing a new quarterly *Dictionary Companion* from his aerie in Cold Spring, New York, points out that Mossad, the Israeli intelligence agency of fact and fiction, should not be capitalized as it so often is. The word is not an acronym: It derives from the modern Hebrew word *mossad,* "agency," which is the first word in the full name of the Israeli Secret Service. But perhaps because of SAVAK in Iran and BOSS in South Africa, the word has been taken to be an acronym, which is bosh.

A reliable work, The Slang Dictionary, *John Camden Hotten (publisher and author), London, 1865, contains the entry: "POSH, a half penny, or trifling coin. Also a generic term for money."*

> Gerald Kelley,
> errant student of
> Professor F. G. Cassidy,
> the man from DARE,
> Ithaca, New York

A friend of mine told me she had read of POSSLQ in a Saturday Review, *with a poem from "some Harvard paper." She pronounced it POSS-LI-QUE as in the poem:*

> Come live with me and be my love
> And share the pain and pleasure of possliquity,
> And I will whisper in your ear
> The things you dearly love to hear
> And love will be forever new
> If you will be my posslique!

> Ruth Shipley Busch
> Bronx, New York

Regarding your speculation about the origins of the word "posh," I always thought it came from the Russian word "pyshnost," which means splendor or pomp. The root of the Russian word is "pysh-." Is it possible that the vowel could have broadened to become "posh"?

Even if there's no relationship etymologically, I think it's interesting that they are so close, and the softness of "sh" after the preciseness of "p" seems to suggest exactly the notion of luxurious elegance.

> Catherine B. Heimsath
> Austin, Texas

Maybe you denigrate too often.

When I lived in the Orient the P.&O. (Pacific & Orient) Line out of London did put beside the names of important people "POSH," so they would have the cooler side of the ship.

> Ellen Thackara
> Switzerland

I am an electrical engineer working in the computer field. A field, as you well know, that is notorious for its constant and usually unnecessary use of acronyms. Computer languages for instance seem to always be named with an acronym, e.g., the language called BASIC is an acronym for Beginner's All-purpose Symbolic Instruction Code, FORTRAN stands for FORmula TRANslation and COBOL for COmmon Business Oriented Language.

Dramatic change seems to be taking place in the naming of the newer computer languages. Two of the latest, "hot" languages are named Pascal and Ada. Pascal is indeed named after the 17th-century philosopher and mathematician Blaise Pascal. The other new language has a more romantic etymon being named after Ada Agusta Lovelace, the daughter of poet Lord Byron, and assistant to Charles Babbage, a computer pioneer. Ada Lovelace is reputed to be the world's first computer programmer because of her work with Babbage.

I can't help but wonder if we've reached a new era when the mania for acronyms in specialized fields and the resulting confusion to the layman is past. Let us hope that the computer industry which is in the forefront of so many technical innovations will be the leader in restoring some purity to our language.

Florian M. Ptak
Pittsfield, Massachusetts

Mr. Yehouda Mindel
Lower Galilee
Israel

Dear Mr. Mindel:

William Safire kindly forwarded to me your letter concerning the Hebrew word mōsād.

I have checked with my Hebrew expert and found that you are quite right. The word does mean establishment, institution, foundation, and the like (from the root yəsōd, *meaning base, basis, foundation) and cannot stand for "agency."*

I used "agency" as a gloss in my Dictionary Companion *partly because of the influence of Central Intelligence Agency (CIA), with which I contrasted the Mosad, and partly because it sounded more natural in the context than either "institution" or "establishment," which was indeed how the Hebrew dictionary glossed the word* mōsād. *But obviously I was taking liberties with the meaning and so I apologize to you, to the Hebrew language, and of course, the Mosad.*

Clarence L. Barnhart
Bronxville, New York

pre-emptive correction

The word *meld,* used in the piece entitled "Boniprops," triggered torrents of abuse. (How can you trigger a torrent? You trigger a fusilade; torrents happen by themselves.) The word originally meant "proclamation": In card playing, when you had a few cards that fitted together into a trick, you proclaimed, or melded, "Gin!"

But that is obviously not what I meant. I meant "blend, merge, unite," and I used a new word that is probably a combination of *melt* and *weld.* People whose marbles are all puries will object: If I mean "blend," why not say "blend"? Is my expensive new blender to be called a melder? They have a point, and they are free to resist the new word for a generation or so. I shall use it, however, because it is a nice coinage and I never win at gin rummy. But I promise the Squad Squad not to say "meld together."

I am a stage manager and have heard the word "meld" used frequently in the context of shifting from one scene to the next, or one lighting cue to the next. It implies, in these contexts, that the scenes or lighting cues blend one into another so that it is impossible to tell exactly where one ends and another begins. This may also be called a "cross-fade." For this usage, clearly, "blend" or "melt" would not suffice.

Bruce Conner
New York, New York

While you are correct in stating that "meld" is card terminology, I do not believe that "Gin" is its basic card game use. In pinochle the cards which are laid down for point count at the beginning of the game are called "the meld." In other rummy games such as "500" or "Rummy" the runs are also called melds. In this I quote The Pocket Book of Games *printed in 1944: "Laying down is often called showing, or—a pinochle influence—melding," on page 61 in a discussion of* Rummy.

But you are correct in your other usage of "meld"—to blend. In Webster's New World Dictionary *under MELD we have, "v.t. & v.i. (merging of melt and weld) to blend; merge; unite." And in the* Random House *unabridged there is almost the identical wording.*

In tobacco, pipe tobacco especially, they are always discussing how the various tobaccos are melded or blended together for a pleasant smoke.

So you are now in the same position as the man who said, "I once thought I made a mistake, but I was wrong."

Al Horowitz
Torrance, California

Say it ain't so, Bill. You didn't really use "meld" as a synonym for melt or blend. Editor and writer, man and boy, I've been fighting this one for ten years—and now you go over to the enemy.

My Webster's *continues to insist that "meld" is from the German "melden" —"to announce," and that it's a card-playing term. In pinochle you meld cards from your hand, or even lay out your meld.*

The misuse of "meld" seems to me to have begun with music reviewers in the early '70s. I was one then, and saw it coming pretty early. It is likely the wordsmiths wanted another—maybe more "sophisticated"—way of saying "blend." "Meld" became an immediate hit.

Lately this egregious error is creeping into mainstream journalism—into The Times, The Washington Post, The Christian Science Monitor, *the wire services and even magazines.*

It's still utterly wrong. If writers mean "melt" they should say "melt"; if they mean "blend" they should say "blend."

David W. Chandler
Editor and Publisher, City Lights
Madison, Wisconsin

the present absent

"Absent some international crisis," said Dan Lundberg, noted oil-glut watcher, "I would foresee a continuing decline in price."

I clipped that quotation not because of its use of the craven conditional—the unneeded "would" burns me—but for its use of *absent* as a preppy preposition. It's all over the public prints (good name for a newspaper): Former Ambassador Seymour Weiss warned of "supplying this high-technology item to the Saudis, absent adequate conditions on its use. . . ."

"The use of *absent* in this form really bugs me," observes a comrade who desires anonymity. "Needless to say, don't print this letter," she writes, adding, "*Needless to say,* needless to say, is another of my pet peeves."

My heart does not grow fonder at the vogue use of *absent* as a preposition, because vogue usages—especially elitist ones—are to be eschewed by speakers who like freshness in their discourse. But let us set aside that prejudice and confront the issue: Is *absent* in this use legit?

Of course it's legit. (Even *legit* is legitimate in colloquial circumstances.) The word is a shortening of *in the absence of* and can sometimes be substituted for *unless there is.*

Without *absent,* we would be obliged to use the longer phrase; on the other hand, absent *without,* we would be in bigger linguistic trouble. *Without* is a broader term, covering both "lacking" and "the absence of," and also means "outside." (This double meaning led to the Marx Brothers routine: "There's a girl waiting without." "Without what?" "Without food or clothing." "Well, feed her and send her in.")

Go ahead and use *absent,* but never more than once in a single foreign-affairs lecture; there's a jargon-hater waiting without.

A similar preposition is *given,* as in "Given the presence of *without,* why use *absent?*" This stems, I think, from the first word in a mathematical problem listing elements that are to be accepted without question by the problem solver. That word has come to appear in noun form as *givens.* When you hear, "That's a given," the speaker means, "That is understood" or, if he is a lawyer, "That is stipulated."

Granted, *given* as a preposition is sometimes used for *granted,* but the words have different shades of meaning. *Granted* means "stipulated" or "I'll accept that as a fact"; *given* means "because we have" or "specified." *Granted* is a shortening of *if it be granted,* and *given* is a shortening of *if we are given.* Needless to say, *granted* is the one that takes a comma afterward.

I have titled this item "The Present Absent" to denote the current use of the word; it is an obscure turnaround of the phrase once applied to the representative from the United Nations who did not show up where a "U.N. presence" was required, and who was promptly dubbed "the absent presence."

I suggest that a lawyer would not stipulate a "given," but might enter a stipulation, i.e., agreement with his adversary, over a fact or issue which may be in dispute or open to question. The non-lawyer often stipulates basic propositions, but the lawyer usually advances them as such or as "incontroverted," or, cast in a pseudo-scholarly turn, as "assuming arguendo. . . ."

Joseph J. MacDonald
Ridgewood, New Jersey

You refer to absent *in the phrase "absent some international crisis," and* given *in the phrase "given the presence," as prepositions. They do not function as prepositions; they function as participles.*

It seems to me that your discussion misses the point because you did not have the advantage of studying Latin as a boy. The kind of construction which you are citing is known in Latin as the ablative absolute. When you have a clause which does not modify the principle clause directly but is "cut off = absolute" you put the subject in the ablative case and for the verb you use the ablative case of the participle. Thus, "after his father had died" becomes "patre mortuo" "his father having died." We do not use the absolute construction much in English because it is clumsy, although in Latin it is very elegant and economical. "Mutatis mutandis" is a very good example of the ablative absolute which we do not translate because it is so economical a phrase.

You say go ahead and use absent, *but I wouldn't. It is awkward. Absolute constructions do not adapt themselves well to English idiom.*

Robert F. McNeil
Toronto, Ontario

"Absent some international crisis . . ." uses "absent" as a . . . preposition???!!?

Do you really believe that? Or did you write it to test readers' interest, to see how many of us would scream in anguish at your English?

"Absent," dear Mr. Safire, is used here as an adjective—which it has always been —in an elliptical construction, the original wording of which is "some international crisis (being) absent," and in no *other way.*

Putting the "absent" first in its clause is indeed very voguish, and is a bit of contemporary sententiousness, the perfect example of an unoriginal speaker trying to pass himself off as a "with-it" stylist. And yes, "absent" could be replaced by "without" but that would change the designations of the grammatical parts of the clause:

1) "Absent" (adjective modifying "crisis") + "being" (copulative verb, elliptically omitted) + "some international crisis" (subject of verb); or

2) "Without" (preposition) + "some international crisis" (object of preposition)

Such a substitution, however, cannot turn an adjective into a preposition.

As for your contention, farther on in the column, that "a similar preposition is given" (but you never proved "absent" was a preposition, you merely called it one): "given" is also an adjective, never a preposition; it happens, as well, to have the same form as the past participle of the verb "to give."

Lastly, using "given" as a noun is not new, although it has become part of our modern gabble. Webster's Second Edition, *unabridged, of 1934, defines "given" not only as an adjective, but also as a noun meaning "that which is given; a datum" —a word we use all the time, generally in its plural form, "data."*

You have been carried away by your own trendiness, Safire; shame on you. Back to Grammar I!

Alice R. Golden
New York, New York

You really blew it on "given." (Blew it? When did "to blow" come to mean "to botch" or "to ruin"?) You composed the sentence: "Given the presence of without, *why use* absent?*" Then you claimed that in that sentence, "given" was a preposition. Preposition? Preposterous.*

"Given" is a past participle of the verb "to give." It may function with auxiliary verbs ("He was given his choice." "Is your love given freely?"). Or it can function within a participial phrase, as it does in the sentence you used in your column. Since "to give" is a transitive verb, "given" may take a direct object, which is what "presence" is in your sentence. Functioning with auxiliary verbs, "given" may even take an indirect object, as in the following sentence: "Having given Mr. Safire a severe scolding, I feel quite smug."

So you blew it. Cheer up. ("To blow" something connotes that repairs are possible and that one may atone and receive forgiveness, doesn't it?) Whenever I blow it, I cheer myself by recalling the words I discovered on a student's exam several months ago, in response to a question concerning the importance of writing: "Writing is important in getting the message across when words cannot."

Barbara J. Keiler
Branford, Connecticut

pretty

"What does *pretty smart* mean?" writes Barbara J. Voglewede, ten, of St. Mary's Star of the Sea School, Hampton, Virginia. "You would say: 'You are *pretty* smart.' But why do we say *pretty* smart instead of *very* smart? Love, Barbara."

I started to give that my standard response—a picture postcard of W.C. Fields saying, "Get away from me, kid, you bother me"—but Miss Voglewede's question threw me. As an adjective, *pretty* has a fairly straightforward couple of meanings: "attractive," in a delicate rather than striking way, or when used ironically, "tricky"—as in "a pretty fix"—which harks back to the Old English *praettig,* meaning "crafty."

But as an adverb, modifying adjectives, the word can get ugly. It seems to pick up meaning from the word it modifies, or depends on intonation for its meaning. "Considerably" is one meaning: "He's pretty smart," with the emphasis on the "smart," tells you he has the smarts to a considerable degree. But when the accent is on the adverb—"He's *pretty* smart"—the meaning changes to "He ain't all that smart." When the accent is on neither the adverb nor the adjective, "He's pretty smart" means he is somewhat smarter than the average—fairly smart, rather smart, but hardly "pretty *smart.*"

The craftiest use of *pretty* is to express *quite* or *very* in an understated way. When he is smarter than all get-out, and you want to describe him as awfully smart but you know how to emphasize by meiosis, you say in a low and even tone, "He's pretty smart." That is stronger than a matter-of-fact "He's very smart."

That is why, Miss Voglewede, we say *pretty* smart rather than *very* smart. Now I have one for you: How come we don't spell it *pritty*? Nobody, but nobody, pronounces it the way it looks.

I think you managed to give your ten-year-old correspondent the back of your hand, after all. In your comments on "pretty," she asks why "pretty" can be substituted for "very." You tell her and us lots of things about the use of pretty, but not why a word with the primary meaning "attractive" can correctly be used in place of "very" (or, for that matter, "quite," "terribly," "extremely") to modify "smart."

Praettig, *according to my* Webster's New Collegiate Dictionary *and* OED, *also means crafty though not tricky—having craft; artful. ("Cunning" has this meaning as well.) Could it be, then, that "pretty smart" is like "prettily done" or "nicely (another word with a similar meaning and origin, according to the* OED*) done," meaning done with art or craft or skill? "Very smart" appears to have been modified in form in the same way, from "verily," in truth.*

Joel Latner
Rochester, New York

Hou kum wee doughn't spel it "pritty"?
Pardon me while I cough. *I'm willing to bet a lot of* dough *that it would be* rough *to get* through *any paragraph without finding some non-phonetic stuff (stough?). William, methinks you're out on a* bough.

Jacques Penn
New York, New York

You are, of course, 100% right that no one pronounces "pretty" as it is spelled. But does anyone today pronounce it "pritty" as you suggested? I only hear "pritty" once a year, when they revive The Wizard of Oz *on* TV, *and the Wicked Witch keeps calling Dorothy "My Pritty." But outside of that talented actress, whom I believe is the sole survivor of that great movie, who else articulates the "t" sound like that today? At best, people pronounce it "priddy" in normal, everyday speech, but more often it comes out as "perdy." Even* Webster's Third International *indicates the common use of the "d" sound replacing the "t" in many words, such as city, scooter and critic, and in names as Carter, Connecticut and Patty.*

John Tenca
Stamford, Connecticut

It would have been inappropriate to send Miss Voglewede a picture of W. C. Fields saying "Get away from me, kid, you bother me" because he didn't say that. He said "Get away from me, boys, you bother me."

Francis C. Jameson
Washington, D. C.

You got me. Why do we write "pretty" but say "pritty"? And for that matter, why do we write "of" and say "ov," or write "knee" and say "nee"?

The reason is that at one time these words were probably said in a way suggested by the spelling—in German and Scandinavian, "knee" still has a k-sound (Knee, kne). But I don't see why present speakers of English should be overwhelmed with orthographic trivia.

Something else I don't see is why language monitors such as you may inveigh against imprecision in idiom or even punctuation, but seldom against the massive madness of official spelling (your acceptance of "sluff" as opposed to "slough" was a notable exception). There aren't even enough symbols to represent standard pronunciation. For example, the spelling cannot differentiate between "mouth" (noun) and "mouth" (verb)—though "moudh" for the second makes perfect sense. Or between the sounds written "ng" in "singer" and "finger"—"fingger" is probably the most practical solution.

It's one thing to inherit an inadequate, inaccurate, and hard-to-learn system. But to keep on using it is "pritty" crasy.

Spelling reformers of the world unite! You have nothing to lose but silent k's and e's pronounced like i's. (Or, in the version suggested by the Simpler Spelling Society: Speling reformerz ov dhe wurld ueniet! U hav nuthing to luuz but sielent k'z and e'z pronounst liek i'z.)

Edgar A. Gregersen
Professor of Anthropology
Queens College
Flushing, New York

You discussed the word pretty *and this conversation which took place many, many years ago came into my mind. It took place during my early school days in a small country town. We had all written compositions, and some members of the class were copying their masterpieces on the blackboards at the front and side of the room. I sat in an aisle seat (an attempt to isolate me because I was a "talker"), and the girl who was writing on the board next to me turned and asked, "How do you spell* pritnear?*" That's all I remember. Did I spell it or did I tell her there was no such word? Perhaps a frown from the teacher cut further conversation short. Can you guess in what part of the country this took place? It was northwest New Jersey, now rapidly turning into a bedroom of New York but then a lovely farm and forested area. However, the dialect can still be heard.*

Ethel G. Lewis
Brunswick, Maine

The phrase "emphasize by meiosis" is pretty unusual. As a biologist familiar with the process of meiosis it surprised me that meiosis could also be a means of emphasis. I am puzzled by the phrase and puzzled by your use of such an uncommon expression to explain the meaning of a very common expression. That's like the worst tendency of bad dictionaries.

From the context, your meaning seemed clear. The word "pretty" in "pretty smart," you observed, may be a form of understatement, meaning very smart indeed. "When he is smarter than all get-out, and you want to describe him as awfully smart but you know how to emphasize by meiosis, you say in a low and even tone, 'He's pretty smart.' " So, to emphasize by meiosis is to underscore by understatement. But what is the connection between the biological process of meiosis and your etymological usage as understatement?

Meiosis of course is a form of cell division in which chromosome pairs are separated, one member of each homologue pair going to a different daughter cell. The products of meiosis are haploid germ cells, sperm and eggs. When egg cells are fertilized by sperm cells, the normal diploid chromosome number is restored; both members of each homologous pair of chromosomes are present again. The fertilized egg and all diploid somatic cells divide by mitosis, a process which faithfully distributes one copy of each chromosome to each daughter cell. By mitosis diploid cells beget diploid cells. By meiosis diploid cells beget haploid cells. Since the total number of chromosomes is halved by meiosis, the latter is also referred to as a reduction division.

It seems then that you might be using meiosis as reduction. In that way to emphasize by meiosis comes to mean emphasize by reduction, which I suppose might mean to underscore by understatement. But this is only a guess, and to my mind not a very satisfactory one.

No doubt you'll want to explain your own imaginatively fertile use of the biological term "meiosis." It occurs to me that you purposely seeded your benign explanation with a germinal idea (pun fully intended) for a future column.

Pretty smart, Safire.

> *Jason Wolfe*
> *Associate Professor*
> *Wesleyan University*
> *Middletown, Connecticut*

You use "meiosis" in the rhetorical context to illustrate emphasis by diminution, and I found myself wondering if you were doing this deliberately to draw letters like mine, or whether it was really an example of the scientifically illiterate.

"Meiosis" is a familiar word to literally millions of Americans, indeed everyone who has taken high school biology. It specifies that form of cell division which produces ovum and sperm, and is characterized by halving of the number of chromosomes. (Fertilization restores the full number and starts a new individual on its way.) Since this is the established common usage, could you tell us whether

*you meant your reference as a deliberately provocative ejaculation, or whether you
in fact laid a literary egg—and a sterile one at that?*

C. Loring Brace
Ann Arbor, Michigan

prose and cons

Here's a trend in the right direction: News organizations have taken to issuing
periodic newsletters about their language blunders, with an occasional pat on the
back for a well-turned phrase or glue-fingered lead.

The granddaddy is *Winners & Sinners* at *The New York Times,* which was
begun in 1951 by the late Ted Bernstein, but other self-criticisms have been
sprouting as well. *The Washington Post* now has *Cursors!* (from the you-are-here
sign on a video-display terminal), edited by Daniel Griffin; the *Louisville Courier-
Journal* has *Crumpets,* created by Robert Crumpler.

For the past six months, the Associated Press has been distributing *Prose and
Cons,* which it terms "Notes, Nuances and Nits from the A.P. News Report."
Louis Boccardi's baby has comments like this:

" 'A half-hour later, a solemn-faced Reagan walked to the front door of the
White House and, standing with his wife, Nancy, at the North Portico, expressed
his remorse.' Remorse," the A.P. newsletter pointed out, "is a sense of guilt or
sorrow for one's own misdeeds. He was talking about Sadat's murder. We meant
sadness or anger, not remorse. While we're at it, a 30-word sentence with five
commas *is* something to be remorseful about."

*One thing I am sure the Associated Press' newsletter does not mention is AP's
asinine policy of not capitalizing titles taking the place of proper nouns (e.g., "the
president," "the pope," et al., ad nauseam).*

David Bernklau
Brooklyn, New York

*P.S. If you are of the belief that most people write the way they speak, then "a
30-word sentence with five commas" is not that unusual!*

P.P.S. I hated to write the P.S.

psyche delly

A delicatessen in my neighborhood calls itself the "Psyche Delly"; such parody is proof that the word *psychedelic* has earned its place in dictionaries. People who get spaced out on hot pastrami may be interested in the coinage of the word.

In his book *Predicting the Past,* Dr. Humphrey Osmond, a British-born scientist now working at Bryce Hospital, Tuscaloosa, Alabama, recounts his creation of the word in the spring of 1956. In a paper for the New York Academy of Medicine on mescaline and LSD, he first thought of *psychotomimetic, psychotogen,* and *deleriant,* but they suggested mimicry of psychoses, and that was not precisely what he had in mind.

He sent a draft of the paper to his friend Aldous Huxley, the author and psychic experimenter, and asked for a suitable word. "By return post came a beautiful word," recalls Dr. Osmond, ". . . 'phanerothyme.' Its roots are *phaneroin,* a Greek word meaning 'to reveal,' and *thumos,* 'the soul.' " Huxley included a little rhyme: "To make this mundane world sublime/Take half a gram of phanerothyme."

The suggested word did not transport Dr. Osmond. "I had at hand a little Latin dictionary for medical use that had some Greek words in it. It seemed to me that 'psyche' should be part of the word. The 'thumos' may not be revealed, but the psyche is certainly altered. I wanted a neutral word that would suggest transcendence in some splendid way. I found *'delis'*—'to reveal.' I put the pair together and came up with 'psychedelic.' "

He then wrote back to Huxley with his concoction and included an answering rhyme: "To fall in Hell or soar angelic/You'll need a pinch of psychedelic."

In his book, Dr. Osmond tut-tuts at the misuse of his word by Timothy Leary, and cautions that psychedelic drugs are "mysterious, dangerous substances and must be treated respectfully."

A year after Osmond coined the word, Huxley used it; a decade later, as the bad trips on LSD became widely known, Huxley was assumed to be the originator. His worldwide reputation as the popularizer of the magic mushroom and other hallucinogens caused him to be credited with the creation of the word that described the dangerous delights.

Is Osmond's counterpoint true? Sol Steinmetz, one of the authors of the *Second Barnhart Dictionary of New English*, is inclined to believe him. First, he finds a Huxley coinage unlikely: "Words compounded from *psyche* normally appear as *psycho-*, as in *psychoanalysis, psychopathic*, etc. . . . It seems very unlikely that a linguistic sophisticate like Aldous Huxley would have coined a word as deviant in form as *psychedelic;* he would have instinctively opted for the traditional *psycho-* form.

"On the other hand," ruminates the lexicographer, "there is an unflattering reason for taking Dr. Osmond at his word. Dr. Osmond is much less of a stickler about his forms: In his own story of the coinage he refers to *delis* as a Greek verb meaning 'to reveal,' whereas the actual form of the verb is *deloun,* unless what he meant was the adjective *delos,* meaning 'visible or manifest.' "

From such clues are great cases decided. Because Dr. Osmond's Greek usage is a bummer, he is adjudged to be the coiner of a significant addition to the vocabulary of weird trips. I'm ready to celebrate with a turkey-tongue-corned beef on seeded pumpernickel, which is pretty far out.

publish or perish

"Best seller before publication," trumpets Harper & Row, in an advertisement for the new Saul Bellow novel; "100,000 copies in print before publication."

"But how can this be?" asks Vivian Lee Nyitray of Stanford, California. "Can you clear up the mystery of printing before publication?"

At Harper & Row, Dan Harvey says: "The pub date is set so that book reviewers can review the book when it is in the store. It is based on the shipping date of the book."

Over at Doubleday, a distinction is made between distribution date and publication date. "Publication date is an official, arbitrary date set by the publisher to indicate when the book will be ready for sale," says Sam Vaughan. "The book is physically ready weeks in advance of that date. The distribution date is usually three to five weeks before the publication date, in order to get an even and simultaneous distribution of books across the country."

Harvey Shapiro, the *New York Times Book Review* editor, to whom I owe a review and am using this as a delaying device, is skeptical: "Publication date is the date the publisher *assumes* the book will be ready. It is kind of a fictitious

event. Often books are distributed before the publication date, and sometimes they are not. We run a review only if the book has been distributed."

Publication, then—to people in the book business—is that moment when a book is sitting on shelves in bookstores around the country and is reviewed and advertised simultaneously. Good luck; it doesn't always happen.

The semanticist must turn to the law for a specific answer. When is a book "published"? "A book is considered published," says Anthony Bogucki of the United States Copyright Office, "under the copyright laws, when it has been publicly distributed. That means that as soon as one copy is available for sale on the shelf of one bookstore, that book is published." But what if the book's distribution date is in March, with a publication date of April 30? "The copyright office considers that book to have been published in March."

Ah, certitude is sweet. This column was published on the date at the bottom of the page, unless you bought an advance copy of the paper from some unscrupulous newsie, in which case that was when it was published.

You probably remember what Dick Simon of Simon and Schuster said was his definition of the deadline for delivery of a manuscript—"the day the publisher drops dead if the manuscript actually comes in."

Bob Crowell
(formerly of Thomas Y. Crowell Co.)
Newfane, Vermont

push comes not to shove

Lexicographic Irregulars were asked recently for the origin of *when push comes to shove,* which means "when the chips are down," or "when things get serious."

A. J. Gracia of Southbury, Connecticut, holds that it comes from the English game of rugby: "In a rugby 'scrum,' the opposing forwards huddle closely together over the ball, meanwhile trying to *push* each other off the ball so that they might kick it to their own team. When push comes to *shove,* the game is on."

To validate his somewhat offbeat etymology, he points out that "pushing is defined as the application of a steady force against an object, while shoving involves a violent thrust through space directed against the object."

Student unrest in the 1960's was often pointed to as the root of the expression, perhaps responsible for the title of a 1970 book by Harvard student Steven Kelman, *Push Comes to Shove.* On the book's cover, the five spread fingers of a hand, pushing, evolve into an obscene hand gesture (made famous later by Nelson Rockefeller) suggesting the escalation from push to shove.

Most Irregulars, however, ascribe the phrase to street argot. "All disagreements between boys follow a predictable pattern," observes Thomas Connelly of Fairfield, Connecticut. "First come the angry words, then the testing push, and finally, assuming the other pushes back, the more forceful shove. At this point, there is no turning back; one has committed himself to a fist fight."

"The push is a demand for surrender," agrees James Ehmann of Syracuse. "The shove is 'Nuts!' to capitulation. The point is that when push comes to shove both parties are committed and neither can withdraw without losing face."

Donne Florence of New York joins those who believe the expression has a black origin: "I first heard it when I was a freshman at U.C.L.A. My dormitory roommate, a sophomore from nearby Culver City, who taught all of us on Sproul Hall's fifth floor the latest dances and street talk, used that phrase to mean 'worst comes to worst.' 'The dry cleaner doesn't know if he can have my blue dress ready by Friday. If push comes to shove, I'll wear the green one to Eddie's party.'

"When I credited her with having invented the phrase, Andriette assured me it had been around (at least in Southern California's black community) for several years."

A scientific examination of the submitted data (I flipped through the letters that came in on this) prods me toward acceptance of a black-English origin. The most fanciful etymology, however, came from Lynn Kurtz, an assistant principal of a school in Manhattan: "My grandfather left Poland when the *Putsch* came to Tzcew."

I would like to prod you away from accepting black English as an origin for "push comes to shove."

The expression (never used with qualifying "if" or "when" but an implied "if") was in general usage in the north of England where I grew up (Nottingham c. 1935). At that time the only blacks ever seen there were likely to be sons of "chiefs" sent to England for a university education, hardly a seminal influence.

If its usage in the States lies predominantly with black Americans, then it is more likely that its transference to America had to do with English settlers in the Southern States.

> Peter Wingate
> New York, New York

For the origin of "when push comes to shove": I would treat as suspect the black-English hypothesis. People who went to college in the sixties thought every new catch-phrase they picked up had a black-English origin. A good example is the approving exclamation "Out of sight!" (more often, "Outa sight!"). Black-English? Not originally. Theodore Dreiser put it in the mouth of the drummer Drouet in Sister Carrie, *which was published in 1900: "You don't think I could [act], do you?" "Sure. Out o' sight. I bet you make a hit." (Ch. 16)*

"When push comes to shove" might be at least that old, older, perhaps, than the English game of rugby. I would swear myself that I once came across it in an eighteenth-century author; if I ever find it again, I will let you know.

> Fred Louder
> Montreal, Quebec

quantum leaping

My colleague in columny, Russell Baker, referred to me in one of his recent harangues as one "before whom every grifter in the writing game now quakes while wondering whether he dares write about the quantum leaping of parameters."

How come every leap these days is a quantum leap? "As a physicist," writes Dr. Joseph Keane of St. Thomas Aquinas College in Sparkill, New York, "I am constantly surprised at the regular misuse of the word *quantum*. A quantum (in my limited experience) is a discrete natural unit or packet of energy associated with submicroscopic vibrations in atoms—or a very small increment or parcels in which many forms of energy are subdivided. A 'quantum leap' is an abrupt transition from one energy state to another in a submicroscopic atom."

If a quantum is such an itsy-bitsy thing, wonders the professor, and its leap smaller than that of a flea abandoning a dog before a bath, what's the big deal about a little "quantum leap"? "A quantum leap in the number of traffic fatalities," he says, "if true, would not be an item of much concern."

Here's a case of the language glomming onto a technical phrase and stretching its meaning. To a scientist, the essential element to the leap is *suddenness*—the abrupt change of the amount of energy. To a layman, the essential element of the phrase came to mean *size*—as if a change that is sudden must also be a whopping change.

According to the *Barnhart Dictionary of New English, quantum jump* appeared in 1955 and *quantum leap* came loping along in 1970. Scientists should stop reacting negatively to the way the general public has snatched their baby and given it a new face; plain speakers subsidize a great deal of their research.

Did I just write "react negatively"? "In the minutes of a meeting held recently," writes Ellen Norbom in Switzerland, "the secretary wrote that the treasurer 'reacted negatively' to a proposition. The treasurer, when reading the draft minutes, objected to this phrase, pointing out that to have a negative reaction means to have no reaction at all. . . . Was our treasurer just being a nitpicker?"

Yes. In a patch test for tuberculosis, for example, a "negative reaction" is good news—it means no reaction, no disease. But the phrase long ago took its quantum leap from medical terminology; in business jargon and in general use, it now means "Ixnay" or "Take this suggestion out and deep-six it." Tell that to your Uriah Heep in the back office, Miss Norbom.

Give up your language gracefully, scientists. Never fret about losing a favored term—consider that you have gained the gratitude of the phrase-hungry public.

When an electron leaps from one quantum level to another in an atom it undergoes a relatively great change in energy. Therefore when a person makes a quantum leap in income, his income, by analogy, increases greatly. You, having read this letter, have now experienced a quantum leap in your knowledge of quantum leaps.

> *John M. McCauley*
> *Owings Mills, Maryland*

A quantum leap in the number of traffic fatalities is exactly one fatality, even as a quantum leap in the number of continents is one continent; in the number of planets of the solar system is one planet; in the number of known galaxies is one galaxy; in the number of germs in a culture is one germ.

To have a quantum, you must be dealing with a denumerable quantity (a "digital" quantity).

> *Dan Sheingold*
> *Waban, Massachusetts*

P.S. I wonder if people mean an exponential *leap when they say "quantum leap." Quanta jump from 1 to 2 to 3 to 4, but exponentials leap from 1 to 2 to 4 to 8, or from 1 to 10 to 100 to 1000, etc.*

There is no time element involved in the scientific use of quantum. *Discontinuity is the word you want, and that is a very different matter.*

Your taxi meter starts at 50¢, then jumps to 75¢—it does not stop at 62¢ or move continuously like the odometer reading of your car. It has made a quantum jump of 25¢.

David Todd
Shrewsbury, Massachusetts

Your explanation of the term "negative reaction" is totally wrong!

To be negative is to be opposed to something. A negative vote is a vote against a motion, not the absence of a vote (abstention). A photographic negative is an opposite image, not the absence of any image. A negative stance can be a strongly held position of opposition; it need not be the absence of any opinion.

You compound your error when you bring in the phrase "negative reaction" as a medical term meaning the absence of any reaction. You should have upbraided the doctors for a misuse of the term "negative," rather than the public for failing to use the term analogously to the doctor's collective error.

Dr. Frank Rubin
Wappingers Falls, New York

The significance of quantum, as in quantum leap, is in its discrete (as opposed to continuous) nature. This discreteness implies a separation of events, rather than an evolution or progression of events. Therefore, a quantum leap implies a change so radical that the natural progression of events has been stopped and a totally new line of events has begun . . . at least this is the imagery I see when I use the word.

Nidia Stone
Union City, New Jersey

The essence of the phrase "take a quantum leap" or "jump" is not the magnitude of the step, but the fact that the change was a discontinuous one, that is, it took place from state A to state B without going through any intermediate states.

This vernacular meaning is in keeping with the technical origin of the phrase in modern physics. The energy of subatomic particles is "quantized," that is, it exists *in only certain discrete values. Moving one of these particles from one such state to another is accompanied by a change in its energy; this change is both small (by macroscopic standards) and sudden. Its essence, however, is the discreteness of the states between which the "jump" occurs—no intermediate states are moved through in going from the initial to the final state.*

Michael Kaplan
Princeton, New Jersey

On the subject of quantum jumps I am the professional writer (I have taught quantum mechanics for many years and written a textbook) and you are the amateur. You have been badly misled by your friend Dr. Joseph Keane. A quantum is not an itsy bitsy thing at all. It is enormous, if you look at it the right way. It was the size of the quantum that created the revolution in physics that led to our understanding of the atom.

An electron moves in its orbit in an atom at the dizzying speed of a million miles per hour. But it cannot lose its energy gradually, like a car on a race track coasting slowly to a halt. And it cannot speed up gradually like a car accelerating on a race track. It can only gain or lose speed by quantum jumps. The jump means a sudden change in speed, either faster or slower by a few hundred thousand miles per hour. This is not an itsy bitsy jump at all. And the poor electron must gain these hundreds of thousands of miles an hour all in one jump, not in stages.

Before Niels Bohr invented the quantum jump, physicists were perplexed by the motion of electrons in atoms. Why didn't these electrons gradually slow down and give off energy continuously, like a rotating flywheel with its motor turned off slowly decelerating and finally coming to rest? The idea that they couldn't just slow down but had to jump to a slower speed in a step of a few hundred thousand miles an hour seemed incredible, and was not fully understood and accepted until many years after Bohr's brilliant idea.

So a quantum jump is really a very big thing. It is a whopping change. And the size of the jump is crucial. A laser beam of light is produced by a bunch of electrons all making quantum jumps as they emit light. And the key to laser operation is that all these zillions of quantum jumps are exactly the same size. So laymen do not have to apologize for using quantum jumps as something big.

Harry J. Lipkin
Argonne, Illinois

I too read the Russell Baker piece in which your colleague in columny referred to you as one "before whom every grifter in the writing game quakes while wondering whether he dares write about the quantum leaping of parameters." I know even less than you do about quantums—or whatever more than one of these critters is called. But my eye and ear stopped at the verb "dares." As my old Latin teacher used to ask, "What mood?" Quicker than The Funster Punster can reply, "The cow," I thought you could cry out, "Subjunctive!" Yes? No? Do you dare say "dare"?

Edward S. Dermon
Roslyn Heights, New York

What the dickens has Uriah Heep to do with the treasurer of Miss Norbom's acquaintance? In a word association game, "Uriah Heep" would doubtless evoke "humble," not, say, "fastidious." Pray explain what connection you find between Heep and the treasurer. I would wager there is none.

M.B. Richlovsky
Cleveland, Ohio

You advised scientists not to worry about losing favored terms, and to give up "gracefully." Didn't you really mean to say "graciously"?

If your opponents, with effortless skill, turned in a triple play against your team, it could be said that they had performed "gracefully," while you were supposed to congratulate the bastards "graciously."

Or is there really no difference between the two words?

Roderick Auyang
San Francisco, California

queuing for the net

The central metaphors of the first months of the Reagan administration have been the "ladder of opportunity" and the "social safety net." Initial etymological exploration in "Safety Nets" unearthed those phrases in a book written in 1979 by Representative Jack Kemp, which has served as a political primer for supply-side enthusiasts.

"I can trace *social safety net* back to the spring of 1975," one-ups Thomas B. Allen of the National Geographic Society's Book Service. He was editor of *We Americans,* published in 1975, and recalled that the book's summary chapter, by Ben Wattenberg, included this passage: "We learned hard lessons from the Depression and have made many changes . . . in ways of helping victims of economic storms. We have created a kind of social safety net."

Wattenberg, the author and television commentator who coined *social issue* and helped popularize *psephology* (the study of elections), declined coinage of *social safety net:* Cautiously, he says only, "It was in the air," an apt description of a safety net.

The caution is well placed. Chancellor Helmut Schmidt has been using *net of social security* for many years, perhaps after it was popularized in Germany in the late 1950's during a metalworkers' strike. Schmidt said in the late 1970's: "We must be careful not to take measures which will make this net too widemeshed so that people fall through."

Antedating Reagan, Kemp, Schmidt, and others, however, is a speaker with a special flair for metaphors (iron curtains, necks of chicken, etc.).

Leslie Lenkowsky, director of research of the Smith Richardson Foundation (which, coincidently, helped finance a book by Jude Wanniski, who slipped the safety-net metaphor into Kemp's book), passes along this selection from a speech made by Winston Churchill on October 8, 1951:

"The difference between our outlook and the Socialist outlook on life is the difference between the ladder and the queue. . . . We ask: 'What happens if anyone slips out of his place in the queue?' 'Ah!' say the Socialists. 'Our officials —and we have plenty of them—come and put him back in it. . . .' And then they come back at us and say: '. . . What is your answer to what happens if anyone slips off the ladder?' Our reply is: 'We shall have a good net. . . .' "

In regard to "Queuing for the Net":

1. Was the title influenced by the sub-discipline of applied mathematics and computer science, the study of queueing nets, i.e., queueing network theory? (Queueing networks are used as models of the performance of many systems involving contention for resources, including telecommunication systems, computer systems and assembly lines.)

2. Though "queueing" may be a second spelling in the dictionaries that list it at all, it seems to be the dominant spelling in the literature of queueing theory (including queueing network theory). This literature dates back to the work of Erlang at the turn of the century.

3. Besides noting the five consecutive vowels, one might say that "queueing" has four consecutive silent letters, "ueue."

Charles H. Sauer
Thomas J. Watson Research Center
Yorktown Heights, New York

Reaganese

Considering the enormity of the President's
error when he says, quote-unquote, "layizon"—
is that cause to be hung in effigy?

The preceding sentence contains two mistakes in word usage, one pronunciation stumble,
and a curious form of oral punctuation. All can
be tracked to Ronald Reagan.

"I can assure you," he told reporters about his
budget-cutting plan, "by morning I'll be hung
in effigy." No. A person cannot be hung in effigy
or any other way: A person is hanged. "Only
pictures are hung," protests Bruce Felton of
New York, "or was Mr. Reagan implying he felt
he'd been framed?" The difference in the past

tense of *hang* is useful to keep: *Hanged* now means "killed by hanging," while
hung is the past tense of *hang* in all its other meanings.

Common usage was killing the distinction between *hanged* and *hung*—even
the usage books were beginning to waver—but the slang uses of *hung* came to
the rescue of *hanged.* When most people say "He was hung" today, they probably
mean "He was hung over" (suffering on the morning after inebriation) or "He
was zonked or wrecked" (droopy from the effect of drugs), unless they are making
a taboo reference to physical endowment. To avoid confusion, it is useful to hang
tough and cling to the specific meaning of *hanged;* let us urge the President to
predict that he will be hanged in effigy.

On the challenge of the presidency, Mr. Reagan said: "I have always been well
aware of the enormity of it, the difficulties. . . ." A subsequent *Washington Star*
story used the key word in the headline: "Reagan Says He's Ready to Deal With
'Enormity' of Presidency."

Enormous is an adjective meaning "of great size" (rooted in "beyond the
normal"), but the noun *enormity* does not follow logically to mean "something
huge"; instead, *enormity* means "extraordinarily wicked," as in "the enormity of
the crime." Some of us have been taking care not to use *enormity* when we mean
"immensity," because *enormity* connotes the outrageous or monstrous.

A *Washington Star* reader, Richard Augenblick of Arlington, Virginia, argued
that the President's looser usage was becoming correct: "The word *enormity*
employed to mean something very big, not necessarily heinous, seems prospec-
tively acceptable in common speech. The correct word, *enormousness,* is somewhat awkward."

Awkward or not, he's right: I think the time has come to abandon the ramparts
on *enormity*'s connotation of wickedness. The noun has adopted the meaning of

the adjective, and only Thistlebottoms will continue to be very big on *enormity*'s meaning very bad.

Linking this piece together is *liaison,* the original French "connection." (See *ligature,* as the lexicographers say.) *Liaison,* with its two *i*'s, peers out over these interrelated times, covering everything from cooperation in a military operation to involvement in an illicit love affair.

Pronounce it "LEE-a-zon" and you're in the majority; pronounce it "lee-A-zon" and you're in a respectable minority; pronounce it "lee-ay-ZONH" and you're speaking French—but pronounce it "LAY-i-zon" and I'd say you're wrong. I realize President Reagan pronounces it "LAY-i-zon," but when President Eisenhower pronounced *nuclear* "NUKE-u-lar," that didn't make "nuku-lar" right.

Mr. Reagan has not yet committed the sin of verbifying his "layizon." Some bureaucrats talk of arranging for their agencies to "liaise with" others: Gordon W. Smith of Maine sends in a headline from the *Waterville Morning Sentinel* about a state official named Pease planning to cooperate with the University of Maine: "Pease to Liaise with UM." In Reaganese, that would be pronounced "laze with," and such a charge of mutual lollygagging is uncalled for.

Finally, in his budget message to a joint session of Congress, President Reagan gave the imprimatur of a state paper to a relatively new way to sneer at a word.

Up to now, the most favored way of kicking a word in the head has been to precede it with *so-called,* a verbal snicker that says, "Get a load of this." In print, quotation marks can serve that purpose of indicating "They use this, not me," but in the spoken word, the preferred derogation is *so-called.*

However, Mr. Reagan said: "Unlike some past quote-unquote reforms . . ." The presidential sneer was expressed as "quote-unquote" before the word, rather than around the word.

Unquote, cablese for "end quote," was created to make one word out of two (similarly, in sending this sentence by telephone, I will close the parenthesis with the cablese *unparens*). David Guralnik, editor of *Webster's New World Dictionary,* details the development of the spoken quotation:

"In the 1940's, the words *quote* and *unquote* were used frequently on the radio," recalls the lexicographer. "People couldn't see the words, and there had to be some method of separating the words of the announcer and the person quoted.

"The problem came with short quotations: 'The President said, *quote,* Nuts, *unquote.*' It worked much better to say, 'The President said, *quote unquote,* Nuts.' "

Thus, the phrase pointing to a forthcoming quotation began as an interjection before the words to be quoted. "Then in the late 1940's or 50's," adds Mr. Guralnik, long attuned to sign language as a medium of communication, "as people began to use the phrase *quote-unquote* to precede a comment, they added the two-hand, two-finger signal for quotation marks."

Fortunately for President Reagan, he did not use the little gesture of raising his arms and wiggling the fingers to accompany his locution. It would have invited comparison with a similar gesture used by another President to acknowledge the cheers of the throng.

You state, ". . . quotation marks can serve that purpose of indicating 'They use this, not me' . . . " Methinks we do not see I-to-I on this matter of grammar. And you call yourself a "lexicographer"!

> Jerome Touval
> Springfield, Virginia

One of the points in your column was our President's use, really pronunciation, of the word liaison. *I recalled that some years ago I had written him about the same deficiency. I am enclosing a copy of his reply.*

> Aldon M. Hoffman
> Walnut Creek, California

Dear Mr. Hoffman:

First of all, thank you for your note and your kind words; secondly, you are absolutely correct about my mispronunciation of the word liaison. I can only plead old military habit as an excuse. For some reason, in the old Army in which I served, liaison was always pronounced "lé-a-zon." In fact, my first service was as a liaison officer. I'll confess I have one other word from my cavalry days. I've managed to break the habit better on it but still not completely. The word is oblique. All too often it comes out Army-style o-blike.

Again, thanks and best regards.

> Sincerely,
> Ronald Reagan
> Governor

You got into the question of the pronunciation of "liaison." During the Second World War, I was a "Liaison pilot," meaning I flew spotter planes for an artillery battalion, and we always pronounced the word "lee-ay-izon," not only when referring to ourselves, but whenever liaison with adjoining bodies of soldiers was involved. Never, as I recall, did anybody I knew in the army try to make a verb out of the word, as in "to liase" with somebody. I think I first heard that usage from politicians back here in the states after the war was long over.

Now, I'd be the first to admit the army didn't always pronounce things correctly: in the Old Army, "longevity" was pronounced "long-divity," for some reason, and did not refer to life expectancy but to the number of years of service a man had completed. I also had a sergeant during basic training at Ft. Sill, Okla., who used to tell us, while giving instructions on how to maintain a VE-hicle, "We will now PRO-ceed to inflirtate *the tahrs," but that was probably because he was a Southerner, as were most members of the Old Army.*

Hughes Rudd
New York, New York

I question whether you are correct on the issue of hanged vs. hung in effigy. To hang in effigy is to hang an image or statue of an individual and not the individual himself, and therefore the past tense, I surmise, should be hung in effigy.

Bill Zinn
Cambridge, Massachusetts

Did you ever hear the one about the plastic surgeon who became a big hit with the ladies after he hung himself?

Don Bishoff
Associate Editor, Eugene Register-Guard
Eugene, Oregon

redundit again

Some wise-guy wiseacre is plungingly dipping his writing pen in acerbic vitriol to whiningly complain that my use of *together* in the phrase "linking this piece together" is redundant. Yes, *link* means "to bring together," and *link together* can be redundant, but not when used to differentiate internal from external linkage.

The reason for this surliness is a note from Adam Sachs of Waltham, Massachusetts: "You referred to a 'large dollop' of ice cream. A dollop is a large scoop, which would render your 'large' redundant." Yeah, yeah. And my colleague Frank Prial, of the Paris bureau of *The New York Times,* caught me at *old geezer:* "Has there ever been a young geezer or a middle-aged geezer? According to our old geezer of a *Webster's* here, a geezer is a 'queer old fellow.' " He concludes by offering "a gold doubloon for anyone who has used *geezer* unadorned," and then feels the urge to ask himself—as all redundancy spotters do—"Is there such a thing as a nongold doubloon?"

I am in full and complete agreement with the negative strictures against spotters of superfluous redundancy which you clearly enunciated in your column, but, with your permission, may I be allowed to complain whiningly of your failure to observe the established rule that one ought to not split infinitives.

David W. Miller
Full Professor
Carnegie-Mellon University
Pittsburgh, Pennsylvania

Don't allow readers of Webster *to push you around.* Geezer, *as I suspected and as the* Oxford English Dictionary *confirms, is a dialectal pronunciation of* guiser, *as in disguise. The* OED *cites the* Northumberland Glossary, *1893: "Geezer, a mummer; and hence any grotesque or queer character." To be sure, as it says, the word is now "a term of derision applied to elderly persons" (adding "especially women"), but this does not prevent most of the citations from employing "old geezer," and usage, if continued long enough, confers its own rights. So if it be redundant, soit.*

Karen Hess
New York, New York

Speaking of redundancy. Do you remember the story about the oral-visual redundancy of the man who owned the fish store in Borough Park, Brooklyn? He hired a window painter to do a gilt sign for him: FRESH FISH SOLD HERE. *When the artisan told him the sign would cost him a dollar a word (it was in 1911, of course), he said: "I'll tell you. You can leave out the word 'fresh.' Would I sell stale fish? Come to think of it, you can leave out 'here.' Obviously I'm selling it here. And wait a minute, this is a fish store. What else would I do in a fish store except sell fish. So cut out 'sold.' And what else would I sell in a fish store but fish. So leave out the word 'fish.' I'm sorry I bothered you."*

Martin Panzer
New York, New York

reduplication, *see* one more time

regime: ancient advice

"The substitution of the word *regime* for *regimen* is driving me crazy," fumes Heidi Jon Schmidt of Iowa City. "A television commercial shows a woman 'following her beauty regime' (perhaps *Evita* has had some effect here?) and a public-radio broadcast a while ago went into great detail on the 'regime' the ex-hostages followed in Weisbaden."

Calm down, Miss Schmidt. "Although *regimen* is the preferred term when the meaning is 'a systematic procedure' or 'a system of therapy,' " reports lexicographer Anne Soukhanov of Houghton Mifflin, "*regime* is nevertheless a legitimate synonym for *regimen* and has been so used at least since 1776." That was in a letter from Earl Carlisle: "Regime is better than physic," meaning, "Exercise beats medicine."

Stylistically, however, I align myself with the daughters of the regimen. People who use *regime* are usually being affected, trying to Frenchify their cosmetics copy; I would leave that word alone, using it only to derogate a government, as in "during Evita Peron's regime . . . "

Heidi Smith of Iowa City complains that "regime" for "regimen" drives her crazy, but proceeds to drive others crazy by spelling Wiesbaden "Weisbaden," albeit in conformance with frequent New York Times practice.

Observation leads me to conclude that if one changed "ei" to "ie" and vice versa in any German name or word printed in the American press, one would attain the correct spelling four times out of five. Why this should be so is baffling. Perhaps it is a phenomenon akin to a sandwich usually landing with the buttered side down.

Alvin Skipsna
Saratoga Springs, New York

reticent

"I hope you will draw attention to the increasingly frequent use of *reticent,*" writes Michael Novak, the columnist who was not at all shy about defending United States interests as representative to the United Nations Human Rights Conference, "by people who clearly mean 'hesitant.' The mental connection is probably through the image of shyness."

Reticent was a Jimmy Carter favorite. When the President said, "I won't be reticent," meaning "reserved, close-mouthed," he was correct; when he used the same word in a different way—"I won't be reticent to say . . ."—Mr. Carter was mistaken.

One who is reticent is inclined to shut up. The Latin root means "to remain silent," and the reticent person is not the least reluctant to issue a laconic "No comment," nor is he hesitant about turning down interviews. He is one lip-button short of "secretive."

But you cannot be reticent to do or say anything; that's when to use *reluctant* or *hesitant.* No usage roundheels have yet asserted that the frequency of its mistaken usage has made *reticent to* right. It is a solecism, a mistake, a demonstration of fuzzy thinking.

When somebody else uses *reticent* wrongly, and you know that misuser well enough to set him straight, you know what not to be.

robbery, *see* we wuz robbed

roll out the bbl.

In any free-association word test, say the word *oil* and you'll get back the word *glut.* Start to write a piece on the oil glut, and you will soon hit the button for the cliché *awash in oil.*

One day, awashing away on my favorite glut, I found myself writing, "We are importing some two billion bbls. a year at $34 per bbl." That looked silly: Children blow bbls. Grown men import barrels. Why does the abbreviation for barrels call up visions of kids playing with soapsuds?

Big mystery. Sol Steinmetz at Barnhart Books takes a shot at it:

"In the nineteenth century, the abbreviation for barrel was *bl.* and *bbl.* But *bl.* also stood for 'bale' and 'bill of lading.' To avoid confusion, the abbreviation with the extra *b* won out."

Over at Merriam-Webster, one of the editors was willing to speculate: "In the mid-nineteenth century, one abbreviation for barrel was *bar.*, and *bbls.* was the plural. The extra *b* was a plural marker, similar to *pp.* for pages and *mss.* for manuscripts. Eventually, *bbl.* became the abbreviation for the singular." He adds cautiously: "Don't ask me for backup on this. I'm only guessing."

Seems to me the much more sensible abbreviation for barrel is *brl.*, and the plural *brls.* Go tell that to an oilman. He's forever blowing bbls.

You say, "We are importing two billion bbls. a year at $34 per bbl." Fowler says, "It is affected to use Latin when English will serve as well" and continues by particularly excoriating the mixture. "$34 a bbl." seems fine to me. "Per annum" is OK, if affected; "per year" is not.

Francis C. Jameson
Washington, D. C.

I may have the solution to the puzzle of bbls.

In the British beer business there are many sizes of cask including firkins which contain 8 Imperial gallons, kilderkins which hold 16 Imperial gallons, barrels whose capacity is 32 Imperial gallons and Logsheads which accommodate 52 Imperial gallons. Brewers therefore measure their sales in "bulk barrels" or bbls. Which for calculating purposes contain 36 Imperial gallons.

Una Costello
Old Saybrook, Connecticut

safe house, *see* heavy weather

safety nets

Phrase detectives the world over are searching for the origins of the *social safety net*, a locution that seems to be slung under the Reagan administration.

The President has used it in formal speeches and in informal briefings; administration spokesmen carry the safety net around as a kind of security blanket.

What is it? The "official" definition—prepared by David A. Stockman, director of the Office of Management and Budget, a blow-dried Grim Reaper—goes this way:

"A social safety net encompasses the long-range programs of basic income

security, most of which were established
in the New Deal fifty years ago and are
now widely accepted."

"This includes," reports Stockman,
"basic Social Security and Medicare,
unemployment compensation, the two
components of what we call welfare (Aid
for Families with Dependent Children,
and Supplemental Security Income), and
basic veterans' benefits."

Using the circus metaphor of a "safety net," the budget cutters seek to allay
fears of many of the "truly needy" (but not, one assumes, of the "falsely needy")
that society is not about to shove them off the high wire onto the sawdust below.

Dictionaries have slighted *safety net;* many will list *safety match, safety pin,
safety valve,* but the net has slipped through undenoted. My hunch is that the
phrase originated in circus terminology, which often contributes to political and
media language: At *Newsweek,* the executive suite is called the "Wallen-
datorium," after the Flying Wallendas, a high-wire act that has operated without
a net and suffered casualties.

Who first applied the safety-net metaphor to social welfare? It may have begun
with Jude Wanniski, an editorial writer for *The Wall Street Journal* in the 1970's.
"The safety-net idea that I used," he recalls, "applied to the international banking system—that is, there would be an international lender of last resort that
would serve as a safety net for third-world loans in the event of international
turmoil. I always liked the idea of a safety net. When I got to that chapter in
the Kemp book, I held on to that metaphor."

The "Kemp book" is *An American Renaissance: A Strategy for the 1980's* by
Jack Kemp, the Republican representative from Buffalo who was the elected
official most closely identified with "supply-side" economics before that view
became popular. (*Supply side* was identified in this space as having been coined
by the economist Herbert Stein in derision; he advises me his coinage was "not
an act of derision but of taxonomy." That word denotes a neutral form of
classification and is a neat play on the name of a tax idea.) Kemp worked with
Wanniski on the book, which if not seminal was certainly of conceptual importance to the supply-siders who now people the Reagan administration.

"Americans have two complementary desires," asserted Kemp, on page 78 of
the book, published early in 1980 and written in 1979. "They want an open,
promising ladder of opportunity. And they want a safety net of social services to
catch and comfort those less fortunate
than themselves: . . . Yet because people
want this safety net in place, it doesn't
follow that they therefore want it filled up
with sufferers. Least of all do they want
their assistance to seduce others into habits of dependency."

Until an earlier citation of *social safety net* is found,* that coinage belongs to Representative Kemp, assisted by the not-so-obscure Mr. Wanniski. It's a vivid use of language to reassure, recalling F.D.R.'s fondness for *nest egg,* and is far better than the simple wordplay of *workfare.*

Since *welfare* had become a dirty word (farewell, Welfare Island) by 1969, some of the White House staffers at the time looked for a way around it during the attempt at Nixonian welfare reform. I piped up with "How about *workfare?*" Ed Morgan, the lawyer who did more than anyone else to shape the pattern of programs that became known as "Nixon's Good Deed," replied, "Isn't that kind of Madison Avenue?" In a fit of pique, I slipped the word into a presidential speech; the work-requirement label was bruited about briefly, and died with welfare reform.

Now, however, as part of the social-safety network, the word *workfare* has been resuscitated. Nothing is wasted.

Dear Bill:

Gotcha! . . . .

It's one of the commonest journalistic solecisms. . . . But, as a former (part-time) toiler for Ringling Bros.–Barnum & Bailey, I can attest that it is not *(and never has been) "The Flying Wallendas."*

"Flying" in circus parlance refers to trapeze performance, and the Wallendas have never been into this. They are a high-wire act, entitled "The Great *Wallendas."*

> *Best,*
> *Glad Hill*
> The New York Times, *Los Angeles Bureau*
> *Los Angeles, California*

The term "blow-dried" does not sit well with me. I think it's sloppy Madison Avenue newspeak, and may also contain an error of syntax.

One issue is whether you want the participle "dried" to be taken as verb or adjective. If as a verb, "blow-dried" makes a kind of sense as shorthand for the cumbersome constructions "blow-drier-dried" or "blower-dried." But as an adjective in "blow-dried hair" it works less well; it seems to me that "blown-dry" would be better usage for this situation.

If Mr. Stockman ever used a towel to dry his hair, you could choose between using "towel-dried" and "toweled-dry." The first emphasizes the means by which the dryness was achieved, in the same way as "kiln-dried" or "hand-sorted."

*See "queuing for the net."

*"Toweled-dry" treats the means and the result more even-handedly, and empha-
sizes the process of toweling. In Mr. Stockman's case, the switch to using a towel
would be the noteworthy item, and you'd probably go with "towel-dried." "Blow-
dried," though, doesn't permit such a choice of emphasis.*

*"Freeze-dried" is a poor parallel, because the process involves two separate
actions: freezing and then drying. Nor do phrases such as "blown up," "bowled
over" or "handed down" provide much guidance, because they use prepositions
rather than participles.*

*"Blow-dried" does possess the virtues of clarity, force and economy, and imparts
a mildly pejorative flavor of plasticity and image triumphant over substance. It is
probably too useful a term to be kept out of the American language altogether, but
perhaps we can agree that it makes lousy English.*

Trevor O'Neill
New Haven, Connecticut

salami tactics

When opponents of the sales of Awacs to Saudi Arabia spotted a future issue in
the potential sale of multiple-ejection bomb racks, an unnamed senator was
quoted in *The New York Times* as asking: "What will be the next slice of salami?"

This locution has its origin not in Hebrew National salami, as might be
assumed, but in Hungarian salami. In 1945, Hungarian Communist Party leader
Matyas Rakosi vividly described how he came to power: by getting his opposition
to slice off its right wing, then its centrists, until only those collaborating with
Communists were left.

This image was picked up by Joseph and Stewart Alsop, the columnists, as in
the 1969 use: ". . . salami tactics will do the trick. Alexander Dubcek will certainly
not be the last of the liberals to fall victim to the salami knife."

Thanks to the Alsops, the phrase *salami tactics* has entered the diplomatic
vocabulary. It is far better than the sleep-inducing *gradualism;* its emergence
during the current debate illustrates its longevity, which is also a quality of hard
Hungarian salami.

*Referring to your explanation about the origin of "salami tactics": "In 1945,
Hungarian Communist Party leader Matyas Rakosi vividly described how he came
to power . . .":*

*Rakosi did not say this in 1945 because this expression refers to the destruction
of the opposition (including the independent-minded parts of the coalition part-*

ners) in 1946 and, mainly, in 1947. If I recall correctly, Rakosi used this expression
sometime in 1947–49 in a speech to the Party cadres.

Dr. L. S. Ettre
Norwalk, Connecticut

I come to your delicatessen analysis of the word salami *in political references.
I am troubled not by your brand of wurst but by your use of the adjective* unnamed,
in describing the senator who is quoted.

*In the AP, we have a rule of referring to people who either don't want their
names used or whose names we don't know as* unidentified. *Although this does
not appear in our general stylebook, it is noted in the AP broadcast stylebook.*

*The reason, according to the manual, is that people all have names, and there-
fore cannot be unnamed. Ha ha!, I laugh upon seeing your column, the poor
senator has gone through life without a name and will never be able to seek the
presidency because who would vote for ——?*

However, if one looks at the rule closely, it appears that unidentified *must mean
one without an identity, which this senator surely must have after attaining high
public office.*

*So I am sandwiched now between following what appears to be an authoritative
rule and my own deduction based upon that rule. I wonder whether you think an
unnamed person should really be unidentified, or vice versa or neither or either.*

Lise Stone
The Associated Press
Hartford, Connecticut

scaling the depths

When two newsmagazines covered the demise of a newspaper's afternoon edition, both used a word favored by mediamen, *upscale:* "The *News*'s upscale
'Manhattan' section will be eliminated," wrote *Newsweek,* using the word later
in the same story in hyphenated form: ". . . he could still work the up-scale
magic. . . . " *Time* magazine quoted an unnamed source as saying, "They are
trying to go back downscale now, but they forget the reason we went upscale
is that downscale wasn't working."

Jean Brandes of Whitehouse Station, New Jersey, asks, "Isn't it too pricey for
words?" Since newsmagazine editors are busy running up the down scale, I turned
to Fred Mish, editorial director of G. & C. Merriam Company, for the usage
pattern. He found a glossary of media terms published by Batten, Barton, Dur-

stine & Osborn, the ad agency, in 1966, which described both *upscale* and *downscale,* with the main entry for *downscale:* "a market or audience with above-average representation at the lower end of the socioeconomic scale."

"The flood of citations marking the present vogue began in 1979 and continues unabated," Mish reports, pointing to the extension of its meaning to include things as well as people: "To combinations like 'upscale audience,' 'upscale market,' and 'upscale consumers' are now added 'an upscale south of France treat' (of a recipe for bouillabaisse) and the designation of a fashionable men's jacket based on the old Air Force flight jacket as 'upscale fatigues.' "

One early example of *upscale* in its current nontechnical meaning is in Merriam-Webster's possession, and might mark the coinage of the word. Its gerund form is close to today's adjectival meaning, and is in an April 2, 1945, *Newsweek* piece about a seller of prefabricated houses near Cincinnati: "The Mullikin selling method, which he called 'upscaling,' aimed to build up the idea that prefabricated houses were rich-looking, comfortable and permanent."

How heartwarming to see what may be the first use of a trendy newsmagazine term appear in an old newsmagazine. Pundits (a *Time* term applying the Hindi word for "learned man" to longheaded columnists) applaud.

However, in a recent *Time* magazine account of the sale of Awacs aircraft, the editors permitted this reference to an order made by the Shah of Iran: "planes that fortuitously were never delivered." *Fortuitously* means "by chance, by accident, through a stroke of good or bad fortune"; the word *Time* had in mind was *fortunately,* which means "luckily, through good fortune." The distinction between the two words should be maintained. The acceptance of the blurring of this distinction is an example of downscaling.*

Concerning "downscale" and "upscale," when I was in Camp Croft during World War II, learning how to be an infantry soldier, our sergeant would use these terms instead of "descend" and "ascend" when we were climbing walls, ladders and ropes.

After the War, attending Cooper Institute, the phrases "upscale" and "downscale" were used by our "rendering" instructor in teaching us how to draw to scale.

My trump card as to its early usage, however, goes back to my first boss, Edward B. Marks, song publisher (from Tony Pastor to Rudy Vallee), who always said there was no surer way of starting a ragtime song off to popularity than to get it sung downscale (not fast). Music must have played a part in their coinage, because when a feller played a fiddle, a banjo or even a piccolo, it was always "upscale" and "downscale."

Jack Gasnick
New York, New York

*See "holding the fort."

scruff, *see* sluff it all off

sculpted, *see* exculpation

see you later, allegator

Part of the gruntwork of people in the language dodge is to keep track of neologisms (accent on the *ol*), or newly minted words. Most are nonce words—clever coinages that die aborning—but all the coins are worth biting:

In the media world, *infotainment* is being bruited about; the combination of *information* and *entertainment* was possibly coined by Ron Eisenberg in the February 1980 *Phone Call* magazine. This follows closely on *docudrama,* a melding of *documentary* and *melodrama,* and *faction;* all three words illustrate the trend toward the fuzzing of lines between fact and fiction, truth and fantasy. (Watch out for *factoids.*) Mediamen also like *narrowcasting,* derived from *broadcasting,* to mean rifleshot approaches to specific audiences, and *brandstanding,* which Art Stevens coined in the May 1981 *Harvard Business Review* to mean "long-lived product promotion," a meld of *brand name* and *grandstanding.*

In law, attorney Mark Lane was described in *The New York Times* as "the well-known conspiracy allegator." This word bids fair to replace *alleger* for "one who alleges," and can be used by lawyers with symbols on their tennis shirts. (See you later, alleger.)

In the death industry, *cremains* is the pasted-together version of *cremated remains* to stuff into your portmanteau. Liturgy would have to be altered to provide for "cremains to cremains, dust to dust," but whether the new word will catch on remains to be viewed. (Meanwhile, what's a body to do?)

In sports, tennis players are now being called *tennists,* according to Horace Sutton in *The New York Post.* The *ist* construction is evidently an upgrading, as in *piano player* and *pianist, publicity man* and *publicist, raper* and *rapist.*

In making new anatomical references, keep your eye on your mouth. *Poor-mouthing* (pretending to be penniless) has been with us for some time, and spawned *bad-mouthing* (to speak ill of someone). Reporter Curt Suplee used *big-mouthing* in *The Washington Post* last month to mean "to promote loudly." Other possibilities include *stretch-mouthing* (to smile); *small-mouthing* (to deprecate); *rich-mouthing* (to ostentate); *horse's-mouthing* (to write an insider's newsletter), and *mouth-mouthing* (to coin words using the *mouth* combining form).

My favorite recent coinages are *laser-sharp,* sent in by Philip Persinger, found in the *Syracuse Herald-American,* which brings the dull old *razor-sharp* up to a fine cutting edge. The other is from Angelo Gionis of Valley Stream, New York, who writes: "My friend made up a new word. It's called ziggly. Put it in the dictionary. It means wiggly lines going like Z's." Generations hence, lexicographers will say, *"Ziggly,* adj.—angular lines, probably combined from *zigzag* and *wiggly."*

The word *gruntwork* was used at the beginning of this item without explanation to show how a neologism can slip into the language with the greatest of ease. *Grunt* was a Vietnam-era noun for a soldier or servant who did menial tasks, taken from the sound one makes from heavy lifting. It was a quick step from that to *gruntwork,* on the analogy of *paperwork,* meaning the kind of job nobody likes to do. There's a neologism I bet will make it.

If you have occasion to again cite "docudrama," please note that I assembled this verbal concoction in 1964.

There was no word around at the time to describe the work I was staging, so I guess I just neologized. . . .

> *Charles Preston*
> The Wall Street Journal
> *New York, New York*

equity library theatre

226 West 47th Street • New York 36, N.Y.

PLAZA 7-1710

May		Master Theatre
18		(Riverside
1964	We are pleased to present	Dr & 103 St)

the final program in the current series of
Monday Night Informals

THE FORTIES

a docudrama of a decade

by

Charles Preston

Regarding the use of the word "allegator" to mean "one who alleges":

The word was used in this sense by James Joyce in Ulysses, *first published in book form in 1922. On page 337 in the 1961 Random House edition (p. 331 in the original 1934 American edition) the following passage occurs:*

> *—That's so, says Martin. Or so they allege.*
> *—Who made those allegations? says Alf.*
> *—I, says Joe. I'm the alligator.*

As the spelling would indicate, the pun is clearly intended.

*Joyce's method of composition—*Ulysses *is, among many other things, a record of Dublin speech and vernacular in the first decade of century—would suggest that this was a fairly common (and intentionally humorous) usage among the barflies, spongers and newspapermen who inhabit the novel.*

> *Mark Mosca*
> *Stamford, Connecticut*

Your very amusing column reminded me that as an employee of a greasy fingernail book publisher, I was privileged to be present at the birth of many new uses for English words and phrases and of neologisms.

My favorites were the persistent use of the term "added plus" and the word "incentivate" for motivate. The latter form was so pervasive in conversation and memo that my secretary, a bright young woman eager to advance, when asked if copies of a memo from me had gone out replied, "Don't worry, they've all been carbonated."

Have you stopped to consider that you may be dealing with a permutacious language?

> *Lucille Gordon*
> *New York, New York*

"Allegator" brings to mind a story my grandfather used to tell: Around 1900 when he was a Justice of the Peace in Lyndon, Kans., a suit was being brought against a farmer. After a long fiery harangue by his antagonist, the farmer rose and spit out only 8 words: "I deny the allegation and defy the alligator!"

> *Mrs. Ruth N. Schultz*
> *Fredericksburg, Virginia*

For your list of neologisms:
"Televangelist," for TV preachers.

Try putting your hand (or any other part of your anatomy) to the TV set when they are dispensing their "telecures."

Maria Bianco
New York, New York

You speak of "bad-mouthing" as a new anatomical reference "spawned" by "poor-mouthing." Not quite.

"Bad-mouth" is an old Gullah expression—generally used as a noun, not a verb —in the phrase "to put the bad-mouth on . . ." It means approximately to jinx.

> *"You're gonna fall off that ladder."*
> *"Don't put the bad-mouth on me."*

The new usage you refer to still manages to confuse some Southerners when they hear it.

Your acceptance of the shift certainly absolves you of any oral fixation.

Beverly Colman
Charleston, South Carolina

To your list of neologisms ending in -mouthing I'd like to add one routinely used by black Americans: white-mouthing. How old it is I cannot say, but since early childhood I have heard it applied to self-serving blacks who publicly curry favor with the white establishment at the expense of our interests.

Bernadette Soter
Los Angeles, California

You ascribed the word "grunt" to the Vietnam era. When I was employed by a public (N.J.) utility in the late 1930s, the term "grunt" was used to refer to an electric lineman's helper or a mechanic's helper. Your definition "one performing menial tasks" was right on the mark.

John Alden Keyser
Dunedin, Florida

You suggested that the origin of the use of the word "grunt" as a noun came from the Vietnam war where the infantryman or footsoldier was called a grunt.

I beg to differ with this suggestion as to the origin of this word as a noun. In 1937, to earn college money, I was hired by the Western Colorado Power Co. as a "grunt." This meant that I would be an assistant to a journeyman lineman to do the menial work associated with the maintenance and construction of electrical power lines in western Colorado. In sum there was no question that I was at the bottom of the electrical power industry hierarchy.

In 1945 I was discussing this experience with a high official of the Bell Telephone Company in Atlanta. He told me that he was quite pleased to say that he had started his career at the end of World War I as a "grunt." He, too, had had the experience of being at the bottom of the communications business as an assistant to a telephone company lineman.

Unfortunately, I do not have the resources to document the use of this word prior to 1918. Despite this, I would wager a small sum that its usage to describe someone at the bottom of a hierarchy began at least a generation before the year 1918.

Robert C.F. Gordon
American Ambassador
Port Louis, Mauritius

I can't believe it. Did I finally catch you? The seventh paragraph begins "My favorite recent coinages are . . . The other is . . . " Laser-sharp *may be a recent coinage, but I don't see how it could be more than one coinage.*

Sherry Kronhaus
Alexandria, Virginia

You mentioned the word brandstanding, *which was coined by Art Stevens in a recent* HBR *article. Though I do not wish to flout your authority or flaunt ours, I'd like to point out that the meaning of* brandstanding *is to use publicity to attract attention to a product. Such publicity, as in tennis tournaments (Volvo) and marathons (Bonne Belle), is especially suited for, but certainly not limited to, long-term promotion. I think you'll agree that the melding of "brand name" and "grandstanding" makes more sense in that context and also makes a worthier new word for your column.*

May I say I feel bad about this misunderstanding, as a way of asking you, incidentally, to attack, sometime in your column, the rampant misuse "I feel badly," a mistaken adverbial punctiliousness that is often evidenced even at Harvard.

Lynn M. Salerno
Associate Editor, Harvard Business Review
Boston, Massachusetts

You warn us to "watch out for factoids." You may be amused to know that a number of your readers have been watching out for factoids as part of their professional obligations for some years. When my colleague Professor Frank Stafford returned to the University of Michigan from a year on leave at the Department of Labor during the mid-1970's, he reported to us that there are three kinds of facts used in Washington: (1) True Facts, that is, facts that are true; (2) False Facts, i.e., things that everyone knows are true, but that are in fact false; (3) Factoids, which are created when either True Facts or False Facts are bombarded by a Memo. (Note that Factoids may themselves attain the status of True Facts or False Facts when they are themselves subjected to Memos.)

Paul N. Courant
Associate Professor of Economics and Public Policy
University of Michigan
Ann Arbor, Michigan

I am prompted by your bit on neologisms to contribute a few of my own manufacture:

apathete noun, an apathetic person. By obvious analogy with athlete and aesthete. I have taught many an apathete in my day.

numerate adjective, involved or obsessed with numbers, expert at manipulating them. By obvious analogy with literate (and the final syllable pronounced the same way to distinguish the adjective from the verb). Junior did well in math but flunked English; he is obviously more numerate than literate. Stockman is a highly numerate cabinet member. In these days of computers, calculators, cost-accountancy, and rampant statisticitis, the nation will soon be far more numerate than literate.

numeracy noun (probably more useful than the adjective), the condition or quality of being numerate. Numeracy is busting out all over. Excessive numeracy can result in idiocy. By obvious analogy with literacy.

Peterpantheism a faith in or worship of everlasting youth. Common among health nuts and in Florida.

tollster a toll collector or toll gatherer. By obvious analogy with the ubiquitous pollster, which has all but replaced poll taker. Not to be misapplied to a bell ringer. Incidentally toller (= toll collector) is, according to the OED, "now rare." Toller (= bell ringer) is still current.

William W. Watt
Professor Emeritus of English
Lafayette College
Easton, Pennsylvania

*Just thought you might want to know the weather has me confined to the house
on what I consider a very "drizmal" day today!*

Bernice Lasberg
Chappaqua, New York

send in the colognes

While at the cosmetics counter, try to make sense of the nomenclature for the
liquids used to slap on one's face after shaving.

Some of us still call it *after-shave.* That's the stuff that tingles and smells good
but doesn't make you worry about being called a sissy. It is made with varying
percentages of alcohol and contains a nice smell that disappears on the way to
work. Its name connotes manliness because shaving is an activity to which every
male adolescent aspires.

But strange things have been happening to after-shave. It is now differentiated:
Astringent after-shave, the tingly stuff, is a far cry from *after-shave balm,* or
soothing after-shave, which caresses the skin, gentles and soothes the face after
it has been through that ordeal of scraping, and makes your skin feel as if you
have just been embalmed and prepared for viewing by the bereaved family and
friends.

The product manager of Old Spice After Shave Lotion, Tom Kuhn, at first
provided me with this definition of his product: "After-shave is an alcohol-based
product which contains a fragrance used after shaving to provide a refreshing and
invigorating feeling to the skin." However, when scientists at Shulton Industries
looked that over, they said that Mr. Kuhn's description might as well be a
definition of cologne, and suggested instead: "After-shave lotions are functioning
products designed to provide soothing relief after the function of shaving. Consequently, they contain higher levels of water than cologne to minimize the sting,
and an emollient to provide a smooth afterfeeling." (I think they're mistaken, not
to say periphrastic: I want to be tingled, not soothed. The Mitchum company
used to call its after-shave a *refreshant,* which is closer to what I have in mind.)

The big thing happening to after-shave is its "upscaling" to cologne. Cologne
was once *eau de Cologne,* a diluted toilet water produced in the German city of
Köln, or Cologne, which has recently lost its *eau de.* As the most diluted fragrance
form, *cologne* is often used interchangeably with *after-shave,* but usually costs
more. No law stipulates the amount of essential oils in a cologne—caveat sniftor.
The choice of the name is made by the producer targeting men afraid to be sissies
(after-shave users) or men willing to pay more (cologne users).

A stronger fragrance is *eau de toilette,* a French term rooted in *toile,* cloth, from the cloth that hairdressers spread around their clients' shoulders while making up the head. Until recently, *eau de toilette* was a term limited to products aimed at women, but Chanel has come out with a toilet water for men.

But it is not called *toilet water*. Although the pronunciation "oh-de-twalette" evidently retains its sales appeal, the English term—*toilet water*—is going down the drain. That is because the word *toilet* is becoming a no-no, a trend begun generations ago when the British began calling the flushing facility a *water closet*. ("Why are Winston Churchill's initials on the toilet, Harry?")

In America, the toilet has become the bathroom. Go try to find toilet paper on the supermarket shelf—after a brief fling as *toilet tissue*, that product has become *bathroom tissue*. (Something must be offensively unsoft about *paper*.) Perhaps the "oy" sound strikes some advertisers as inelegant—hoity-toity—but the child who says "I wanna go tuduh toilet" will be shown to the *john* or *loo* by her well-dressed mother. (Why is it, in drugstores, where contraceptives are now hawked out front in brazen display, the word *toilet* is never whispered? Ask for "toiletries" and you get sent to "bathroom supplies." Pharmaceutical Hamlets must be asking, "Taboo or not taboo?")

Finally, you get to "perfume," sometimes called by its French name, *parfum* (from the Latin "to smoke intensely"), which contains the most essential oils. *Perfume* is pronounced with the accent on the first syllable by most men and on the second by most women. Perfume will never be worn by the truly manly. The man's man will wear "fragrance."

There's one smell manlier than "fragrance," I hear. My manly friend, a Paris resident by way of New Jersey birth, wears "SCENT." Smells good, too.

Eau revoir,
Lisa Schwarzbaum
New York, New York

Upon finishing your sweet-smelling article, I was wafted back to my childhood, when my mother sang me to sleep with a song in which the stress was on the first syllable of "perfume." It went:

> *"It was one day in June,*
> *When the bees hummed a tune,*
> *And the perfume of the rose filled the air . . . "*

Clearly the rhythm calls for perfume. *So it wasn't my mother's choice, but the songwriter's, to put the accent on the first syllable.*

Anyway I looked it up in my fat Webster, *and found that the distinction between*

per*fume* and *perfume is not by sex, but by part of speech. The former pronunciation is proper for the noun, the latter for the verb.*
    *It per*fumed *my day.*

Arthur J. Morgan
New York, New York

*After Shave and Cologne are not really interchangeable. After Shave, whatever
the form—tingly or soothing—is meant to be used on the face. Cologne, which
contains a greater concentration of scent, is meant to be splashed lavishly over the
body.*

Evelyn H. Lauder
Corporate Vice President, Estée Lauder Inc.
New York, New York

*Probably the reason that the British began calling the flushing toilet a "water
closet" generations ago is that they had called its predecessor an "earth closet."
So did we, according to posters at the entrances to "Women" and "Men" at the
Smithsonian Institution's Museum of American History (née Museum of History
and Technology).*
    *According to the posters, the earth closet was an indoor contraption, and earth
or ashes were spread over its contents from time to time to counteract odors. I
believe that the British may also have called outdoor privies earth closets. George
Washington called them "necessaries" on his plans for Mt. Vernon.*

Susan J. Finke
Washington, D. C.

sentence fragments, *see* fragging the fragments

s/he, *see* gender bender

shlepper and bungie

I have a favorite old suitcase covered with stickers from faraway places and tags from forgotten presidential summits ("Formal Wear—Offload Iran Only"). But carrying the big bag around gives me a backache, and I look with envy at people who breeze through airports with designer luggage (when did a suitcase stop being called a *grip*?) that rolls on built-in wheels.

Long hours of staring at flight attendants marching to and fro suggested a good way of eating my cake and having it too (not *having my cake and eating it,* which means nothing). At a luggage counter, I asked: "Do you have one of those metal things with wheels and a telescoping handle that I can put my valise on and drag behind me?"

"You want a shlepper and a bungie," said the clerk promptly. I immediately guessed the derivation of *shlepper*—from the German *schleppen,* to drag. In *The Joys of Yiddish,* Leo Rosten told the old joke about the formally dressed clerk in London's Fortnum & Mason department store who asked an American customer: "Shall I have these jars of marmalade shipped air express?" When the customer said, "I don't mind carrying them; I'm from the Bronx," the clerk replied, "I understand, madam, but still—why shlep?"

But *bungie* was a mystery. Recently, Lisbeth Mark of New York sent me this query: "I have been stumped by a word that I cannot find in my dictionaries.

It is an elastic cord with hooks on either end, wrapped by brightly colored threads and usually sold in hardware stores and bike shops. . . . I've heard them called 'stretchies,' 'shock cords,' and 'those rubbery things with the hooks.' I've always called them 'bungee cords.' I've never had occasion to spell the word *bungee* until now." She asked for aid in the spelling and derivation of the word.

As a traveler new to *shlepper,* I was not familiar with *bungee.* Whenever I tried to hook one around my suitcase, valise, grip, satchel, carry-on or designer luggage, the cord would lash back at me, and I never knew exactly at what I should curse. (A "carry-on" is a fat attaché case or small valise that fits under an airline seat, and thus need not be checked. I would have called it an "underfit," but I only report on words; I don't coin them.)

In the *Supplement to the Oxford English Dictionary, bungie,* or *bungy,* is defined as slang for "India rubber."

"I have checked in Madison, Wisconsin," reports F. G. Cassidy, director-editor of the *Dictionary of American Regional English,* who has shlepped millions of citations to the University of Wisconsin for his monumental enterprise. "Lisbeth Mark's spelling, *bungee,* is not given. . . . *Bungie cord* is the prevailing term, though *stretch cord* was given once as an alternative."

The man from *DARE* advises that the British term *India rubber* first came into American schoolroom use as a synonym for *eraser,* and during World War II developed new applications: He cites the *United States Air Force Dictionary* (1956) for *"bungee,* n. Any of certain tension devices, as a set of springs, a rubber cord used by itself, or a cable attached to springs. . . . A bungee is used . . . in certain aircraft to assist in retracting landing gear." Huge bungies were used on aircraft carriers to brake planes returning to the flight deck.

"Nobody seems to know the origin," says Professor Cassidy. "It ought to have an original connection with someplace where rubber was grown, which suggests Malaysia, but that is only surmise."

With a great lexicographer shrugging his shoulders that way, the help of the Lexicographic Irregulars is requested. In the meantime, never get into an argument with a bungie, unless you're ready to be shlepped to a hospital.

Dear Bill—

I was born and brought up in a rubber-growing area in Malaysia and have never heard the word "bungie" used there in connection with rubber or otherwise.

Could the Hindi word "bangy" have been adapted (adopted) to apply to a new appliance? I enclose a photocopy from a reprint of Hobson-Jobson, *"A Glossary of Colloquial Anglo-Indian Words etc" originally published in 1903. There are cords but the "yoke" straddles the carrier, not the load.*

BANGY, BANGHY, &c. s. H. *bahangī,* Mahr. *bangī;* Skt. *vihangamā,* and *vihangikā.*
a. A shoulder-yoke for carrying loads, the yoke or bangy resting on the shoulder, while the

load is apportioned at either end in two equal weights, and generally hung by cords. The milkmaid's yoke is the nearest approach to a survival of the bangy-staff in England. Also such a yoke with its pair of baskets or boxes.—(See **PITARRAH**).

b. Hence a parcel post, carried originally in this way, was called **bangy** or dawk-**bangy**, even when the primitive mode of transport had long become obsolete. "A **bangy** parcel" is a parcel received or sent by such post.

Yours sincerely
Punch Coomaraswamy
Ambassador of the Republic of Singapore
Washington, D. C.

Fifteen years ago when I was an avid bicyclist, "bungies" were well established as devices for attaching saddlebags to a "rattrap" carrier. However, anyone associated with the New York City Chapter of American Youth Hostels at the time would have told you that those stretchy things are called "Sandows." An AYH catalogue of bicycle accessories from that time would have confirmed this in print.

Curious of the origin of the name, I was told back then that Sandow was a French strongman. Come to think of it, sandows were also known as "French elastic straps," in keeping with an American tradition of terming anything odd or difficult to classify "French" (French toast, fries, kiss and "Frenched bed" from summer camp days).

Anyway, I'd rather ask the salesman for a "sandow" than a "bungie."

Steven Lewent
New York, New York

You will probably get a spate of letters regarding the following, but let me throw in my two cents (origin?). You noted that "shlepper" comes from the German schleppen, *which you follow up with a Rosten joke. Isn't it more likely that "shlepper" entered the English language from the Yiddish* shlepn *than from some ancient Teutonic strain? The Yiddish more nearly conveys the nuance of the English expression than does the German. I'm no Yiddishist, but there are many of them out there and you may hear from no small number of them.*

Joshua A. Fogel
Asst. Professor, Chinese History
Harvard University
Cambridge, Massachusetts

Yachtsmen/yachtspeople have used bungee cord for years; 20 that I can vouch for, anyway. It has dozens of uses aboard a boat—securing sails furled on a boom; tying halyards to the shrouds so they don't clang against the mast.

*In the Pacific Northwest, where I learned to sail in the '50s, the preferred usage
was:*

   1. shock cord
   2. bungee cord

Derivation of the latter? I haven't a clue.

Eugene Carlson
The Wall Street Journal
New York, New York

*The term "Rubber" for the widely used elastic substance is specific to the
English language. Other languages derive their term for the substance from either
"Gum" or "Resin" denoting its origin as a sap of a tree, or from the South
American Indians' name of the tree itself: "Caouchouc." (Gummi, Goma, Rezina,
Kautschuk, etc.)*

The elastomer's ability to act as an eraser was recognized very early. Priestley's
Familiar Introduction to the Theory and Practice of Perspective, *published in
London in 1770, has a reference to a London mechanic, E. Nairne, who kept in
his workshop pieces of raw Para Rubber which were excellent for erasing pencil
or charcoal. It is apparently from this that the English term India Rubber, later
shortened to Rubber, is derived.*

Anselm Talalay
Cleveland, Ohio

*Re "Shleppers and bungies," as a former motorcyclist, I know the latter as
"banjo strings." As for "shleppers," why is the "c" dropped? Does the rule apply
to all yiddishisms used widely in English—"schmuck," "schlemiel," etc.?*

Stephen Banker
Washington, D.C.

*Thank God that the aircraft carriers I landed on did not have "huge bungies
. . . to brake planes returning to the flight deck."*

*Actually, the arresting cables on a carrier were, and for all I know still are, woven
steel wires attached, not "to springs," but to hydraulic devices that absorbed the
momentum of a landing aircraft. Had bungies been used, the hapless plane would
have been snapped back off the fantail like a paper wad shot from a rubber band.
But what would the air force know about carrier landings?*

*The bungies I remember best were those on our parachute seat packs. They were
designed to peel back the canvas cover when the ripcord was pulled, thus allow-*

ing the chute's nylon canopy to billow out in the air. When we drew our chutes from the parachute loft, we always snapped those bungies to make sure they still had their elasticity. Otherwise the chute would not open properly, if at all.

In the navy we pronounced the word with a soft g, but I don't remember ever seeing it written down. I always thought it was an odd word, and now I wonder if it originated from "spongy cord." (We always said "bungie cord," not "bungie" alone.) "Spongy" is a synonym for "elastic," and it seems to me that the shift to "bungie" would be quite possible in oral transmission.

Ned Haines
Professor of English
Hillsborough Community College
Tampa, Florida

T.H. White, in Mistress Masham's Repose *(G.P. Putnam's Sons, 1946), describes a toy airplane:*

> *. . . she borrowed twopence from Cook and persuaded the Professor to buy a model for her in Northampton, with a propellor worked by elastic. It was a cheap and nasty one, having cost only 3/11½/. . . .*

Later Maria told the Professor her story

> *carefully from the beginning, how she probably killed the fisherman in her wretched bungee airplane.*

It is of no great consequence that I've never seen the word before your column. And it is coincidence that I picked the book up only a few days after. But without your definitions, I would have thought the word a British Military Expletive from Kipling's Time. You're more fun.

Gerry Gould
Fort Lee, New Jersey

Dear Bill—

To the column on bungie. *In American schoolrooms, so far as I know,* eraser *is the only word used for the rubber device on the end of a pencil, or as a separate piece, used to clean pencil marks from papers. It is in Britain that this is called a* rubber. *(And this is abbreviated from earlier* India rubber, *where "India" was vaguely oriental—the Far East.)*

Picture the Man from DARE not as merely shrugging his shoulders about the etymology. It's on my mind, and if and when I track bungee *to its origin I'll triumphantly let you know. (How does one unshrug shoulders?)*

> *Cheers—*
> *Fred Cassidy*
> *Madison, Wisconsin*

About your odd word "bungie":
There is a Bengali word bhuj, *which looks like this* 𑆃𑆯 *and means "arm, hand."*
There is another, related Bengali word bhujong, *which looks like this* 𑆃𑆯𑆁 *and means "snake, serpent."*
The British did terrible things to words from the Indian vernaculars in the process of transliteration. Many of those warped forms have passed into ordinary as well as Imperial usage. Perhaps "bungie" is one of those. (A Bengali would pronounce the bh *as an aspirated* b; *an Englishman would have been more likely to pronounce it as an unaspirated* b *sound, which produces another and quite different Bengali consonant.)*

> *(Dr.) Mary Lago*
> *Professor, Department of English*
> *University of Missouri–Columbia*
> *Columbia, Missouri*

You might be interested in my recollection of "bungee." This word appeared in the pilots' operating manual for the B-25 aircraft. This word was used as a description of control balance and I think the spelling was with the double "e" ending. The producers, North American Aviation, must have had this word in their vocabulary about 1940 or 1941. This reference predates the Air Force Dictionary *by many years.*

> *Jack C. Brier*
> *Colonel USAFR (Ret)*
> *Sacramento, California*

Dear Bill—

In ski country where they are in constant use—these bungees *(that was new to me) are called* spiders.

> *Best,*
> *Liz Smith*
> *The New York Daily News*
> *New York, New York*

I was interested to learn that the name of bungie cords has an origin in an Indian word for rubber. But I still prefer my son Allen's explanation, offered when I commented on the oddity of the name the first time he bought one.

He held it by both ends, stretched it out and said, "Listen." Then he brought his hands close together suddenly. The cord made a sound something like this: bun-nnn-nge!

Susan L. Blair
Copy Chief, Time
New York, New York

For your Incidental Intelligence Department (if you don't have one, create one), shlepper *is also the German word for tractor.*

Lena Meyers Klein
Fair Lawn, New Jersey

No. In The Joys of Yiddish *Leo Rosten* tells *the old joke about the formally dressed clerk. . . .*

At least so I have been telling my students for years: whatever is said in a book is said to be said in the present tense. Macbeth kills *Duncan; Jimmy Porter attacks the establishment; Uncle Duke shoots up; even Safire makes a mistake when he says that Leo Rosten* told*. . . .*

Christopher Rawson
Pittsburgh, Pennsylvania

shot to death, *see* heavy weather

shriftnin' bread

When a colleague of mine wrote that Ronald Reagan had "made the necessary bows to those of differing views—particularly to minorities who fear short shrift from his administration," Jim Perry of the University of Pennsylvania wanted to know: "Do minorities who fear 'short shrift' fear being shafted by the new administration? What is the derivation of this 'short shrift' anyway?"

To shrive (akin to the verb *to inscribe,* to write) is a religious term meaning "to listen to confession, to impose penance, to give absolution." Anthony Burgess uses it in that sense in his recent novel *Earthly Powers:* "I joined the seated bourgeoisie . . . awaiting shrift from Father H. Chabrier. . . . I was to go south unshriven."

In medieval times, a criminal was given a brief period of time to make his confession before execution. The shrift was short, and was so recorded by Shakespeare in *Richard III:* "Make a short shrift, he longs to see your head." In *Quentin Durward,* Sir Walter Scott kept to the gallows image: "They are like to meet short shrift and a tight cord." In the nineteenth century, the secondary meaning of "brief respite" gave way to "make quick work of," as it is used today.

Shaft, as used by Mr. Perry in his query, was taboo as a verb until a generation ago, when Richard Nixon used it in his "last press conference." The odious term has become a synonym for *double-cross* or *harm* that is now printable in a family newspaper, and has—in this item—been given short shrift.

---

shrinkmanship

One way to alienate an alienist is to call him a *shrink*. Taken from the tribal practice of head-shrinking, *shrink* is a breezy derogation, like *cop* for police officer or *pol* for servant of the public. Not many psychiatrists like *alienist* anymore, either, because it sounds foreign; the root—*alienatio*—means "separation, as from the normal." Nowadays *alienist* is used mainly by shrinks who testify in legal cases; most others prefer the term coined in 1890, *psychiatrist,* which triumphed over *psychiater* as the definition of "mad-doctor."

One way to alienate nonshrinks is to use psychiatric jargon in off-the-couch discourse. "Nobody is sad anymore," writes Barbara van Achterberg of Easton, Connecticut, "but *depressed.* Act suspicious and someone will call you *paranoid.* Grade-school children accuse their livelier playmates of being *hyper.* A person who acts indolent or merely relaxed is now likely to be called *catatonic.* " Roy Endersby of the University of Pittsburgh adds *support system*—"Smith isn't a mere friend anymore; he's part of my support system."

The general language gleefully snatches useful words from the specialized languages, and only hidebound mathematicians are totaled by the perversion of their parameters. However, what R. D. Rosen called "psychobabble" has been used all too often to lend a scientific aura to ideas better expressed in plain words.

Fantasize, for example. Nobody stares out the window and dreams about anything since this old word gained its Freudian meaning. The advertising slogan "I dreamed I went to the [whatever] in my Maidenform Bra" was dropped after hip copywriters realized the young woman was not merely dreaming, but fantasizing. Before 1960, the verb form was *to fantasy,* but that was swept into the *ization* craze with the help of alienist beings.

An old trick played with bureaucratic jargon was to set up three columns of words—two of adjectives, one of nouns—which could be used to create sensible-sounding but meaningless combinations. Karl P. Koenig of Albuquerque, New Mexico, has devised such a list for shringo.

In Column I, he includes words like *introjected, defensive, cathected, impulsive, incestuous, latent,* and *fixated;* in II, *phallic, oedipal, infantile, oral, narcissistic, neurotic;* in III, *gratification, anxiety, fantasies, ambivalence, guilt,* and *tendencies.* "I showed undergraduates the path to a thousand Freudian idioms," the psychologist recalls. "My own favorite is the rather elegantly abstruse *incestuous phallic ambivalence.* "

Does shringo—used to impress or confuse—make you angry? Don't get mad —get hostile.

You note that most shrinks "prefer the term . . . psychiatrist. . . ."
Not true: while all psychiatrists are shrinks, not all shrinks are psychiatrists. Many are certified social workers and clinical psychologists who in fact would shrink from the designation, which applies only to M.D.'s.

> Bruce Felton
> New York, New York

Your column contained another snide remark about those who prefer to use "parameter" correctly. Perhaps it is time you listened to the other side.

The Oxford English Dictionary defines "parameter" in a manner perfectly acceptable to mathematicians: "A quantity which is constant (as distinct from the ordinary variable) in a particular case considered, but which varies in different cases." For example Newton's laws enable one to determine (in principle, at least) the orbit of a satellite once one is told its position and velocity at some instant. The formula giving the later positions of the satellite at different times uses this initial information, of course, but for a given satellite the original data are fixed. Thus they are parameters, constant for a given satellite but capable of being varied if one is interested in examining what satellite orbits generally look like.

Politicos, flacks, and the like have recently taken to giving a new meaning to "parameters": the bounds on the values some variable can have, or more generally, the constraints imposed by a situation. Mathematicians need these notions, too, and use terms for them, such as "bounds" and "constraints." One reason that they don't use "parameter" to mean "bounds" is that they need a word to mean what "parameter" means and see no reason to make "parameter" do double duty. If the usual meaning is esoteric, so be it.

Why do I (and other mathematicians) care about this matter? I think it is because we object to having our subject and our language debased. As people in politics and advertising too often forget, an important function of language for many of us is to make our meaning clear, and this new use of "parameter" tends to do the opposite. Why, for that matter, does someone say, "Within the parameters of the situation" instead of "Considering our limitations" or the like? Probably because "parameter" sounds scientific and precise, and he hopes that his audience will therefore assume that he has given the subject profound thought. Some scientists object to having their credit squandered in this way. Perhaps speakers would use the word less if they realized their pompous phrases actually display their ignorance.

Lawrence Corwin
Professor of Mathematics
Rutgers University
New Brunswick, New Jersey

sleazy does it

Inveighing against the influence-peddling of a few of President Carter's friends and relatives, I searched for a noun that would encapsulate shoddiness, cheapness, trickiness, and generally off-putting behavior. The noun that presented itself was *sleaziness,* but I had heard a variant of that word, a shorter and punchier back-formation from *sleazy:* the unctuous *sleaze,* oozing meretriciously from every pore. My chosen headline: "The Politics of Sleaze."

In Joe Scott's newsletter, *The Political Animal,* the noun appears again, to excoriate one of Mr. Reagan's aides, derogating Richard Allen as "a veteran of close encounters with sleaze in the past." And in *Newsweek* recently, Meg Greenfield recommended the formation of a Sleaze and Embarrassment Bank: "You would be allowed so many improper interventions on behalf of a former client, so many envelopes, so many depredations by Presidential relatives and so on. . . . When they were gone that would be it—out!"

Since *sleaze* is rapidly becoming the preferred noun form of *sleazy,* giving that adjective a new life in political descriptions, it behooves us to unearth the derivation.

Most dictionaries say "origin unknown," but in *Webster's New World Dictionary,* etymologist William Umbach makes an informed speculation: Silesia is an area of Eastern Europe now a part of Poland and Czechoslovakia. Its German name is Schlesien. A cloth was produced there called "Sleasie-holland" (*holland* is also a name for a linen or cotton cloth), used for linings of garments because it was so fine.

However, the delicate cloth tore easily; hence (I like *hence* almost as much as *thus*), *sleasie* came to denote the cheap or ill-made. *Shoddy*—the word used most often as a synonym for *sleazy*—has a similar background: The term was popularized in the Civil War to describe material of reprocessed wool sold to the Union Army by unscrupulous contractors.

Hail to thee, big new noun! You can almost feel *sleaze* in the hand, like that green plastic putty that kids like to squeeze through their fingers. When thrown at a public figure, it is hard to get off, recalling the unprincipled advice of a politician: "Calumniate! Calumniate! Some of it will always stick."

You speak of sleaze oozing "meretriciously" from every pore. That would seem to suggest that the sleaze was either alluring in a gaudy sort of way, or that said sleaze was derived from a lady of the night. Neither sounds very likely.

Clifford D. May
Story Editor, The New York Times Magazine
New York, New York

During the early 1950's, in the rarified atmosphere surrounding the bar at the Sigma Nu fraternity house at Alabama, where the intellectual circle of the day met most of the day and night, the preferred noun form of "sleazy" was "sleazoid." I still like the ring of that one, particularly when speaking of politicians of another persuasion.

Louis E. Rice
Bay Head, New Jersey

I would like to offer an alternative etymology for the word "sleazy."
There is a German word "verschlissen," which Langenscheidt's German Dictionary *translates into English as "thin (fabric)." It is the past participle of "verschleissen," which means "to wear out, to use up." The technological term "der Verschleiss" means "wear and tear." Checking up in a German etymological dictionary* (Der Grosse Duden, *Vol. 9,* Etymologie, Bibliographisches Institut Mannheim, *1963, p.740) I found some justification for my surmise. "Verschleissen" is a strengthening of "schleissen" (which nowadays is only used for stripping feathers) which in Middle High German is "slizen" and Old English is "slitan," meaning "to split, tear or peel off."*

If such a long survival cannot be substantiated, I would rather suspect introduction by German-speaking immigrants than believing William Umbach's "threadbare" (another meaning for our word) speculation.

Gottfried W. R. Luderer
Brookside, New Jersey

You claimed to have observed a rapid rise in the use of the word sleaze. *I submit that you have been deceived, and have contributed unwittingly to creation of a geometrical illusion. The mechanics of this creation may be envisioned as follows: (1) Brainstorming columnist mumbles to himself, "Somewhere I saw* sleaze *used as a noun; should be good in a political article." (2) Newsletter author says, "I saw* sleaze *in one of Safire's columns; any meretricious dysphemism of his is good enough for me." (3) Groping* Newsweek *writer exclaims, "I saw* sleaze *used by both Scott and Safire; maybe it's a real word!" (4) Columnist surveys selected literature, finds* sleaze *in two publications (besides his own), and hails a big new noun.*

Unfortunately, you have only drawn the final line of that rare, two-dimensional figure, the "I saw sleaze" triangle, the one in which one side is never the same as the other two, and which is even more rarely a right triangle.

Roger C. Hahn
Dewitt, New York

If "sleaze" has so quickly supplanted "sleaziness," can the verb form be far behind? I can see it now—dozens of frantic Brooklyn mobsters, recalling the Abscam types, reflecting gloomily on their new D.A.: "What can we give her? She's so damned hard to sleaze!"

Leslie McAneny
Princeton, New Jersey

You wrote: ". . . recalling the unprincipled advice of a politician: Calumniate! Calumniate! Some of it will always stick." Knowing that this did not really do justice to the correct quotation, I became curious about its origin.

Plutarch (who lived A.D. 46–120 approximately), historian, philosopher and biographer, wrote Opera Moralia, *a voluminous work, containing some 60 essays. One of them was entitled: "How a flatterer may be distinguished from a friend." A certain Medius appears as the leader of the chorus of the flatterers in the retinue of Alexander the Great and Medius admonishes and encourages his followers "to grab and to bite their adversaries with calumnies audaciously, for even though the bite heals, the scar of the wound would remain!"*

As this has been a favorite mode of defamation, particularly in politics, through the centuries, Sir Francis Bacon, some 1500 years later (1561–1626), in his work: De Dignitate et augmentis scientiarum (an analysis of the faculties and objects of human knowledge) harked back to the quoted saying of Plutarch, which by then had become a proverb: "Calumniare audacter, semper aliquid haerit."

This is the true form in which it has come down to us.

Julius H. Manes, M.D.
Bennington, Vermont

Some of the "things" I collected in my school days were Polish proverbs of Latin origin. Maybe that is why I have a remark about the Latin adage you quoted.

"Audacter caluminare, semper aliquid haeret" seems to me more a sad cry from the heart than an "unprincipled advice." It was revived by Emile Zola in his efforts in the defense of Dreyfus. Surely rather a bitter irony, than advice ("Calomniez, calomniez; il en reste toujours quelque chose").

But—in context with "sleaze"—your interpretation could be as good.

Maria J. Hurwic
New York, New York

sluff it all off

Estée Lauder, the cosmetics firm, advertises its "Almond Clay Pack" with this copy: "The clarifying facial that facilitates sluffing from within." Another mask, it is claimed, "sluffs, softens, smooths. . . ."

A registered nurse, Frances Ewen of New York, wants to know what's with this sluff stuff: "The correct word is *slough*, pronounced 'sluf,' " writes Mrs. Ewen. She takes her definition—"to separate from the living tissue"—from *Stedman's Medical Dictionary*, and adds masterfully: "There is no such word as *sluff*."

June Leaman, senior vice-president of creative marketing at Estée Lauder—a title presumably chosen to avoid confusion with the senior vice-president of uncreative marketing—responds by pointing to the two spellings, *slough* and *sluff*, given in *Webster's New Collegiate Dictionary*. "Since *slough* has two meanings and pronunciations as well as two spellings, we chose *sluff*. It telegraphs phonetically the word we wanted as it relates to skin: to separate dead tissue from living tissue, to become shed or cast off."

Interesting word, *slough*. Spelled that way and rhyming with *cow*, it means a swamp or bog; in *Pilgrim's Progress*, Christian fell into the Slough of Despond, which undoubtedly caused little worry lines to form on his face. Spelled that way and pronounced "sluff," it is the skin a snake sheds each year; by metaphoric extension, *to sluff off* means to shake off or shed any unwanted covering or work.

For many years, the language has been trying to separate the snakeskin meaning from the bog meaning by means of a spelling change: from *slough* to *sluff* when it is pronounced "sluf" and has to do with the shedding of dead skin.

Since I roughed up Mrs. Lauder's company in a piece called "Beauty Part" for her unctuous treatment of *cream*—ritzily spelled *creme*—let me toss a smooth, soft salute to her copywriters for their intelligent use of *sluff*. The word and its spelling are correct; I just wish I could get rid of the word-picture of all those women snaking out of their skins.

The same creamy kudos cannot be directed at Clinique, another cosmetics firm owned by the Lauder family. "To look healthy and trim over its bones," says a recent ad, "skin needs a step beyond cleansing. It needs exfoliation." Nothing wrong with that word; *to exfoliate* means to strip, as leaves from a branch, and is accurately applied to the stripping of dead skin cells from the skin. (Do not confuse this with *defoliate,* the chemical stripping of leaves from foliage, a process which caused some controversy when tried in Vietnam.)

The product promising to exfoliate your skin is called "Scruffing Lotion." *Scruff* is an English dialect form of the noun *scurf,* which *Webster's Third* defines as "material like bran that becomes detached from the epidermis in thin dry scales. . . ." The verb *to scurf* means "to remove (as scurf) by scraping, rubbing or wiping." "The doctors who formulated Clinique Skin Care," says Carol Phillips, president of Clinique Laboratories, "have frequently used the term 'skin-scurfing' to describe the process of selective exfoliation which removes dead·flakes from the skin's surface. We fooled with that word a bit, transposed the letters, and came up with 'Scruffing Lotion.' "

No complaint there, either; there is a basis in dialect for switching *scurf* to *scruff.*

My only problem is that I now look *scruffy,* which the same dictionary defines as "of a worthless or slovenly character: shabby, miserable." During the 1960's, the word most often applied to hirsute protestors by self-righteous citizens was "scruffy," perhaps because dandruff is scruff. The adjective has always been used to deride and demean; by adopting it as a verb, the marketing people now have the task of scraping off the centuries-old connotation of scruffiness and replacing it with "that well-scruffed look." More power to them, but it seems a little flaky to me.

> *Slough rhymes with cow*
> *Slough rhymes with stuff*
> *Slough rhymes with slew*
> *That's more than enuf!*
>
> *Barbara G. Kendall*
> *Short Hills, New Jersey*

More on "slough":
When used to mean a swamp or bog, I have always heard it pronounced to rhyme with "stew," not "cow." I note that Webster's New Collegiate, *1979, allows both pronunciations but records that the first is more common when the word is used in the sense of a topographical feature, the second when used figuratively, as "a state of moral degradation." I don't recall such distinctions of pronunciation for different senses of* the same word and the same meaning *in English; are there others?*

Incidentally, the slough that I grew up with is the one that Webster calls "a *creek in a marsh or tide flat." In tidewater South Carolina, we used the word more or less interchangeably with "creek" or "gutter," though I may have forgotten some fine distinctions of size, length, or other characteristics.*

Charles S. Spencer Jr.
Arlington, Virginia

You suggest that dandruff *"is scruff." Having been "taken by the scruff of the neck" as a child, I suspected another origin. C.T. Onions' ODEE gives only the nape of the neck as scruff's meaning. It is said to come from the ON skoft, hair of the head.*

William J. McKeough
Greenvale, New York

Snakes do not shed their skins once a year. They shed them periodically as their bodies grow. You see, the snake's body grows, but alas the skin does not. Therefore the skin must be sluffed off and a new one grown to accommodate the growing body. This does not happen on "shed"-ule, as snakes come in all different sizes and grow at different rates.

Sylvia M. Friedlander
Bronx, New York

I enjoyed your article on slough *and* sluff, *and believe you will be interested in some further examples of the versatility of that fine word,* slough.
Consider the following, as used in the Pacific Northwest, and perhaps elsewhere:
A slough (pronounced slew) is a small waterway, much like a canal, only probably not man-made. I have wondered if the famous race horse, Seattle Slew, might have been so spelled to avoid mispronunciation.
To slough ahead (pronounced like plow) is to slog onward, usually in bad weather or on difficult terrain, or both.
Hence, one could slough (sluff) off from work, travel in a canoe down Sammamish Slough (slew), slough (like plow) through the woods, in order to visit Seattle Slough (Slew).
To slew around, however (i.e., to move erratically on an icy road, or out of control in a sailboat), cannot be spelled slough (slew).

R. W. Hubner
Darien, Connecticut

British bogs may rhyme with cow, *but the North American variety rhymes with the second word in "you blew it, Bill." One citation in* Oxford *seems to suggest a connection with* sluice, *but those are man-made while sloughs (also spelled* slew *and* slou) *were gouged by glacier. What we called sloughs during my youth in Illinois were idyllic ponds surrounded by lush growth, but the ones I saw on a recent visit to Saskatchewan were simply soggy, round depressions dotting the otherwise flat wheatland.*

Daniel Ruby
Assoc. Editor, Popular Science
New York, New York

Seems like Nurse Ewen is too involved hustling BPs (Blood Pressures) to scan the daily BPs (Bridge Pages). Then she'd have known that sluffing is not only acceptable usage, but a strategic ploy: casting off a losing card on a winner.

Jesse Levine
San Jose, California

The comments on slough *prompt me to share my longtime interest in collecting examples of this genre. These are words spelled alike but pronounced differently with different meanings. Some examples are* bass, ally, desert, dove, console, row, does, wound, wind *and* project.

Webster's New Collegiate *waffles when differentiating* homograph, homophone *and* homonym. *It says a homograph is one of two or more words spelled alike but different in meaning OR pronunciation, while a homophone is one of two or more words pronounced alike but different in meaning OR spelling.*

It would be more precise to label words spelled alike with similar meaning but varying pronunciation as examples of dialect, confining homograph *to words spelled alike with different meaning AND different sound. Similarly, words pronounced alike with the same meaning but different spelling are merely variant spellings of the same word while true homophones are words pronounced alike with different meaning AND different spelling.*

George Chapman Singer
Burlington, Vermont

social safety net, *see* queuing for the net, safety nets

socks-knocking discovery

Meg Greenfield, the *News-week* columnist who single-handedly torpedoed "water-shed" as a Washington cliché, has been off on an etymological dig. Her find has been startling enough to knock one's socks off.

"Have you noticed how often people have been using *knock your socks off?*" she inquired innocently one day. Not wanting to be the last on Pundit Row to notice a vogue term, I muttered that I had been tracking the phrase for months and was convinced it was a recent knock-off of *knock your block off,* which in turn was rooted in *knock off one's feet,* or *bowl over.*

Miss Greenfield then flashed her find: In *The Beechers, An American Family in the 19th Century,* by Milton Rugoff, a letter is quoted—written about 1844 —from Charles Beecher, pastor of the Fort Wayne, Indiana, Second Presbyterian Church, which includes this line: " 'Beecher, you must *put in your best licks today!* You must *knock the socks off* those Old School folks!' And so they stood by to see me fight."

The use of *lick* to mean "smart blow" has been traced by the *Oxford English Dictionary* to the fifteenth century, and is probably of a Scottish origin, rooted in "to lick on the whip." But nobody, to my knowledge, has previously unearthed socks that were knocked off as far back as the 1840's. In awe of this find, etymologists are standing around barefoot.

Your pretty conceit of etymologists standing around barefoot leads me to call your attention to a sign that is often found at the entrance to stores and restaurants —"No Barefeet Allowed." Here we have a simple, homespun adjective that has somehow become plural and turned into a noun. Evidently it fills a need; "Barefoot Persons" is pompous, and "No Bare Feet" seems to suggest "Unless Accompanied by Owner." I wonder why the need wasn't felt until fairly recently, and can only conclude that a general relaxation of social standards has caused a different class of people to start going barefoot.

Stuart R. Sheedy
Syosset, New York

I was delighted when Meg Greenfield called your attention to a letter in my book, The Beechers: An American Family in the Nineteenth Century, *in which a parishioner irreverently exhorted the Rev. Charles Beecher to "put in your best licks today" and "knock their socks off."*

As a longtime editor at Chanticleer Press and, before that, at Knopf and other houses, I have watched with a kind of proprietary interest how certain words have been slanted away from their traditional meaning or simply misused.

I gave up some time ago on the use of "finalize" (but not "concretize"), on "contact" as a verb, and on "host" as a verb, but I still reach for my blue pencil when "masterful" (domineering) is used for "masterly" (with surpassing skill), or "real" for "true" (as in "He's a real friend"), or "enormity" (an outrageous event) as though it meant "enormous," or "most unique" as though there are degrees of uniqueness, or "famed" when we can say "famous," or "intrigue" (a secret scheme) in such expressions as "It intrigues me," or as one reviewer, that role model of literacy, said of a book, "It's intriguingly informative."

Milton Rugoff
Elmsford, New York

Speakerspeak

"A folk hero," grumbled Tip O'Neill, Speaker of the House, about Ronald Reagan. "He can dialogue with the American people. He comes on the tube so beautiful. He could sell anything."

Ordinarily, I would castigate the Speaker for his participation in Linguagate: To change *engage in dialogue* to *dialogue with* is as bad as to subvert *give priority to* with *prioritize*, a favorite locution of Mayor Ed Koch. (In an abbey, the person below the abbot in rank is the prior; to appoint somebody to that position is "to prioritize." Mayor Koch has appointed hundreds of priors.)

On top of that, Tip tripped over an adverb: "He comes on the tube so beautiful." If *beautiful* is intended to modify *comes,* or *comes on,* or *comes over* (the verb phrase he meant to say), it should be *beautifully.*

But this week the Speaker has a free pass to mangle the language in any way he wishes. ("Free pass"? Redundancy spotters, who call themselves the Squad Squad, will ask, "When is a pass not free?" O.K.; the Speaker has a pass.)

That dispensation is given because he was mistakenly derided for his use of *I hate to think in my heart that.* In a recent political harangue, I quoted the Speaker's use of *think in my heart,* and added that he was "using that organ in an unfamiliar way."

However, Tip's phrase has an impeccable pedigree: "As a man thinketh in his heart, so is he" (Proverbs 23:7), and Matthew 9:4 quotes Jesus as asking, "Wherefore think ye evil in your hearts?" When sending those citations of previous usage, Bruce Dahlberg of Northampton, Massachusetts, suggested: "Safire, applying his mind, could do worse than to learn these time-honored texts—by heart."

That is why the Speaker can dialogue as beautiful as he wants this week. I feel in my head it is only fair.

Your definition of the word "prior" did not accord with my prior conceptions so I made it a matter of priority to check my references.

If one allows priority of authority in these matters to the Catholic Encyclopedia, *one finds that neither* Webster *nor the* Shorter OED *offers a fully satisfactory explication of this term.*

Omitting the cathedral prior, extinct since the time of Henry VIII, the Roman Catholic coenobitic establishment confers priority on several religious officials. A comprehensive Prior Analytics calls for a taxonomy which erects four species of the genus prior.

The Prior conventualis *is the independently elected, nonremovable head of a monastic community not large enough to be designated an abbey or, when the prior's a friar, the chief executive officer of a community of mendicants.*

The Prior obedientiarius *is the appointed, removable head of a small, geographically separated band of monks who are organized as a dependency of an abbey.*

The Prior claustralis *is a senior monk exercising such functions as the abbot may assign. There is no a priori implication that the Prior claustralis act as deputy abbot and a large community may have several monks bearing the title "prior."*

The Prior provincialis *is a religious exercising supervisory authority over a number of houses of the same order located in a given geographic area.*

One might summarize the priorities of priors with a naval analogy. The Prior conventualis *is a commanding officer, the* Prior obedientiarius *is an officer-in-charge and the* Prior claustralis *may be an executive officer or a department head. The* Prior provincialis *is, of course, the commodore.*

In sum, I find your definition of "prior" more conventional than conventual and wish to suggest that The New York Times *get its priorities straight!*

John R. Dooley, M.D. DTM&H
Chicago, Illinois

You express deep remorse for having unjustifiably derided Speaker Tip O'Neill's recent use of the phrase "think in my heart" in one of his speeches. One of the clinching pieces of evidence in his favor seems to be a verse from Proverbs 23:7 in which the phrase appears, hence legitimizing its use elsewhere.

You may be interested to learn that this particular quote bears false witness to your avowed transgression. In the original Hebrew text there is no reference to either the Hebraic verb for "think" or to the noun for "heart." The proper transla-

tion of this verse reads as follows: "For as one who hath reckoned within himself, so is he."

I do not know from which English edition of the Bible your correspondent Bruce Dahlberg was quoting but I believe you know that numerous translations of the Hebrew Bible, including the King James Version, contain many departures from the original Hebrew text. These alterations resulted from either sheer ignorance of the language or from intentional distortion in order to conform to a particular theological doctrine.

In the Hebrew Bible the heart is more often associated with attributes of deep yearning or conviction, rather than thought. This is clearly evident in Proverbs 19:21, where the verse is interpreted as: "There are many devices in a man's heart," not thoughts, as would appear from the literal text.

Of course, I would concur in the occasional use of this phrase as a figure of speech to indicate an impassioned concern. In Psalms 33:11 we do find: "The counsel of the Lord standeth forever, the thoughts of his heart to all generations." I can also envisage the following usage: "Think with your heart, not with your mind." In such usage, the image is clear and the figure of speech is in good form.

This does not seem to be the case with Tip O'Neill's application of the phrase. I heartily agree with your original evaluation that this is just another example of careless usage, a practice in which we are all sinners from time to time.

> Murray Povzea
> Valley Stream, New York

As to Speaker O'Neill's "thinking in his heart," surely Mr. Safire can inform him, and us, of the source, correct statement, and translation of: "Le coeur a ses raisons que l'esprit ne connait pas."

> Raymond S. Rubinow
> New York, New York

Quick! Take back the free pass "to mangle the language" which you awarded the Speaker of the House. You were correct, in my view, in your criticism of his "I hate to think in my heart that," notwithstanding Bruce Dahlberg's citations from Proverbs and Matthew.

In the biblical period in Israel, as well as in Egypt and many other places, the heart was considered to be the seat of mental processes, not the mass of gray matter in the skull. As a matter of fact, the Egyptians, while carefully preserving all the organs of the dead, most particularly the heart, threw away the brain, considering it as useless after death as before.

Thus, in light of their understanding of the heart's functions, it was quite logical for the authors of Proverbs and Matthew to write as they did. Unless Tip O'Neill's and Dahlberg's understanding of anatomical function is several thousand years behind the times, it is incorrect for them to think with their hearts.

Nisson A. Finkelstein
Wilmington, Delaware

Tip O'Neill was right in using a predicate adjective to complete the sentence "He comes on the tube so . . ."

Comes on in this context means the same as appears, becomes, grows, seems.

I remind you that those verbs, as well as look, feel, taste, smell, and sound, take predicate adjectives.

You would say, "He became pale at the thought."

To say "He comes on beautifully" puts the speaker in a class with those who "feel badly" when they mean "feel ill" or "feel sorry." A person who genuinely feels badly has a defective sense of touch.

Marjorie Crowley
Flushing, New York

Dear Bill,

I think you're still giving Tip O'Neill a bum rap. Dialogue as a verb is well-established—Shakespeare, Coleridge, Richardson, Carlyle, among others. Also, "he comes on so beautiful" is correct slang. Come on, originally jazz slang, is a linking verb (like appear, seem) and so is followed by an adjective, not an adverb (you don't want to make Tip feel badly, do you?). The mistake O'Neill made was in leaving out a preposition. Come on is a verb set of which on is actually an adverb. He should have written: "He comes on so beautiful on (or over) the tube."

And a pass (as for unlimited rides on a public conveyance) is not free when you have to pay for it. OK?

Peace,
David [David B. Guralnik]
Vice President and Editor in Chief
Simon & Schuster New World Dictionaries
Cleveland, Ohio

spearing the mint

"The Bureau of the Mint apparently has struck a new word," writes Robert Shilkret, associate professor at Mount Holyoke College in Massachusetts. "Enclosed with its material to order uncirculated coins this year, the bureau includes a card with instructions on how to 'expeed' one's order."

Slow to comprehend, I wrote away (why "away"?) for my uncirculated set of 1981 coins, which costs eleven dollars. I demanded the skinny on "expeed," which appears on their hup-two-three-four order form. A great many orders can be found on the Mint's form: "Do Not Fold," "Place in Return Envelope," "Detach and Discard All Coupons Below," "If Address Remains the Same Do Not Detach This Portion," and finally, "Expeed Order." I think *expeed* is a noun lying gently in a field of angry verbs.

Pressed for the word's coinage, Mrs. Michael Burke, assistant director of the Bureau of the Mint, directed me to the U.S. Envelope Company, a subsidiary of Westvaco, a name born in the hills of West Virginia (now the State of Westva).

Fred Russell, account executive at Westvaco's U.S. Envelope (why not "Westvalope"?), freely asserts his authorship: "I created the word *expeed* in 1971," he says briskly. "It relates to a printed form with a series of magnetic bars that are read by a magnetic reading head for sorting. This tripled the sorting capacity of the older binary code system."

How did his brain throw off the word *expeed*? "I wanted to convey the ideas that *speed, express,* and *expedite* represent in a single word." Mr. Russell had hoped his word would be copyrighted, and is sad that such was not to be.

For expeedy relief, go to the United States Mint; they're not only coining coins.

There are many gray areas in the copyright law. But if nothing else is clear, it is certainly settled beyond any doubt that a word or even a short phrase cannot be copyrighted, and the Copyright Office's Rules so provide. Section 202.1 of Volume 37 of the Code of Federal Regulations provides as follows:

The following are examples of works not subject to copyright, and applications for registration of such works cannot be entertained:
(a) Words and short phrases such as names, titles and slogans; . . .

Public policy could hardly be otherwise. If a person were able to copyright a word, no one other than that person could ever use the word, which would make little sense.

Now, if the word were attached to a particular product, such as Xerox or Coca-Cola, it might be possible to register the word under the federal trademark laws. Similarly, if the word denoted a service, such as TWA or Citicorp, it might be possible to obtain a servicemark. I gather from your discussion that the word expeed was not so employed.

So the next time you are tempted to write about someone's copyrighting a word, I hope you will remember that such has never been permitted under the copyright law, and for very good public policy reasons.

Lawrence P. Katzenstein
St. Louis, Missouri

spinach

When my brother in columny William F. Buckley took exception to a suggestion of mine that people in public life disclose their sources of income, he concluded his excoriation of my rodomontade with a scrumptious: "I say it's spinach."

That gave me pause: Why *spinach*? For years, the term for such rejection was *applesauce,* or the thinly disguised euphemism *Horsefeathers!*

Then, in *The New York Times,* a headline over an architectural review by Ada Louise Huxtable included the word again: "It's Stylish, But Is It Art—Or Spinach?" This was taken from Mrs. Huxtable's criticism of fashion-following architecture: "Fashion is spinach, and so, alas, is a lot of construction. . . . [Victor Bisharat's] buildings were, and are, inescapable. This observer, writing of an early, energetic crop in 1966, thought they were spinach." (Mrs. Huxtable's phrase comes from the title of Elizabeth Hawes's 1938 book about the garment trade which was titled *Fashion Is Spinach.*)

Despite the return of Popeye the Sailor to the silver screen, the word *spinach* is becoming a prime derogation. Mr. Buckley's use probably came from the caption of a 1928 cartoon by Carl Rose of a modern mother saying to her sour-faced child, "It's broccoli, dear," to which the tot replies, "I say it's spinach, and I say the hell with it." The cartoonist credited E. B. White with the caption.

Before the leaves of the nation's spinach growers turn limp from the unexpected heat, let me report that etymology gives the vegetable a clean bill of health. The word that was originally the basis of the present vogue term is not spinach but *spinnage*. The original phrase was *gammon and spinnage*, which meant "nonsense, humbug." Eric Partridge cited a Charles Dickens use in 1850: "What a world of gammon and spinnage it is, though, ain't it?" The lexicographer speculated that *gammon* came from the deceit at gaming, and listed the origin of *spinnage* as obscure.

So go on eating spinach, from the Persian *aspanakh*. In slang, its green color gave rise to its use as a word for money, and its bushiness is at the root of the metaphor for beards. I say its new use as a term of disapprobation is applesauce.

The origin of the phrase "gammon and spinnage" cited in your column is nautical, referring to the "gammoning" or turns of cordage used to secure the bowsprit on sailing ships and to spun cordage used for odd mending of rigging. I suspect the phrase refers to something hastily and ineffectually repaired by lashing with cord. Hence, the patchwork nature of the world, as used by Dickens in your citation, is indicated.

> *Ralph E. Heimlich*
> *Ithaca, New York*

More Spinach. For the 1932 musical Face the Music, *Irving Berlin wrote a shrug-your-way-through-the-Depression ballad, titled "I Say It's Spinach."*
My recording of it includes:

> *As long as there's you,*
> *As long as there's me,*
> *As long as the best things*
> *   in life are free,*
> *I say it's spinach, so*
> *   the hell with it!*
> *Oh, the hell with it,*
> *   that's all!*

> *Frank Jacobs*
> *New York, New York*

I was delighted to hear about gammon and spinnage, as in "Rowley, Powley, gammon and spinach," in my memory a nursery rhyme descended from 17th century British politics.
My memory also tells me that "spinach" was once a commercial artists' term for a doodle, as in the original front page of Time *magazine. I recall that the leafy*

*sketches that ran up each side of the cover illustration were described as "spinach,"
and were used because pressure of time prevented more* Time*ly artwork.*

Snowden T. Herrick
New York, New York

*God save us not only from the prose of Alexander Haig but from the scholar-
ship of would-be etymologists who go around conferring "clean bills of health"
on vegetables that they don't know anything about. In the phrase "gammon and
spinnage" you apparently take "spinnage" to be something unfathomed by the
mind of man. It is nothing but the old spelling of "spinach," and I am appalled
at you and Eric Partridge for not knowing that "gammon" means "bacon"!
Well, actually it means something a little different; we make bacon and ham
from cuts of pork that don't have precise British counterparts, and I'm not sure
that "gammon" corresponds to anything used for bacon in this country. You will
have to ask a Britisher about that. Anyhow, "spinach" was regularly spelled
"spinnage" or "spynage" in sixteenth- and seventeenth-century cookbooks. In
putting the word in the mouth of Miss Mowcher (in* David Copperfield*), Dickens was having her revert to a countrified old form. "Gammon and spinnage"
means a dish of spinach cooked with bacon—a perfectly delightful combination,
as all spinach-lovers should know. Perhaps the figurative meaning of "nonsense"
predates Dickens and has something to do with the use of "gammon" in gamesters'
cant. However, be advised that spinnage is spinach and you are back to Square
One.*

Anne Mendelson
New York, New York

*The derivation of "spinach" from the older phrase "gammon and spinnage"
brought to mind an interesting though expectedly ambiguous form of the latter in
James Joyce's masterpiece,* Finnegans Wake. *It occurs in his fable of "The Mookse
and the Gripes" found on page 152 of the Viking Press edition. The fable,
fashioned after Aesop's "Fox and the Grapes" and* Alice in Wonderland, *is an
allegoric parody on the conquest of Ireland, c. 1171, by Henry II at the instigation
of Pope Adrian IV.*
*The referenced passage describes the Mookse (Henry and Adrian) as partaking
". . . his good supper of gammon and spittish . . . " before sallying forth to
encounter the Gripes (i.e. Lawrence O'Toole, the then Bishop of Dublin).*
*The phrase, despite its derogatorily broadened implications in the cited passage,
suggests Joyce's familiarity with its straight connotation of nonsense and humbug.*

John Moriarty
Pompton Plains, New Jersey

Somehow, your columns inspire me to epistolary effort. "Gammon and Spin-nage": OK, I'm glad to have the Dickensian reference, but what about the entree I have seen on menus in the United Kingdom offering Gammon and Spinach to the diner, i.e. and to wit, ham and spinach (usually accompanied with boiled potatoes, as is every other entree in most of the UK including spaghetti and meatballs). I'm sure you are correct, but I find it interesting that the term has slipped over into the language of food.

> *Jean Davidson*
> *Hillburn, New York*

I should, perhaps, not cross words with you or Eric Partridge, but I am all safired up by your comments on gammon and spinnage; indeed, some of your ideas may be applesauce.

As a child growing up in England in the nineteen thirties, the phrase "gammon and spinach" was familiar to me as part of the refrain to a Nursery Rhyme. It is the tale of the frog and mouse, and I quote the first of many verses. In the USA it is known as "A frog went a-courting" and was collected in the Appalachians.

> *A frog he would a-wooing go,*
> * Heigh ho! says Rowley,*
> *A frog he would a-wooing go,*
> *Whether his mother would let him or no,*
> * With a rowley, powley, gammon, and spinach,*
> * Heigh ho! says Anthony Rowley.*

I think a case can be made that the "rowley, powley, gammon, and spinach" words all refer to items of food. As a child, the only meaning I attached to gammon was that of ham or bacon (I was unfamiliar with backgammon since my family played solo or crib). Gammon was either a particular cut of ham or a very lean bacon, and to the best of my knowledge, the word is still in common use in England. I can cite a reference to the 1967 book Traditional British Cooking for Pleasure *(by G. Mann), which contains a recipe for "Grilled Gammon Rashers." Parenthetically, why is the word "rasher" uncommon in the USA?*

As for spinnage, this appears to be one of many variants for spinach (others include spinage, spynnage, spenege, spynache, spinech, and spinache). There is a quotation in the OED *from 1530—"spynnage an herbe"—and another from 1586 —"spinage or spinech is an herbe lately found and not long in use." Gammon, deriving from "gambe" (leg) is even older, being quoted by the* OED *for 1486.*

Rowley-powley is one form of roly-poly, a word with several meanings. A roly-poly is a kind of (British) pudding—indeed, in a recent NY Times, *Susan Heller Anderson discussed a number of such puddings, including Jam Roly Poly. Another food meaning of roly-poly given by the* OED *is "a jocular name for a pea"; there is a citation to a London Cry of 1784—"Here's your large Rowley-Powlies, no* more than sixpence a peck." Thus, the Nursery Rhyme could be referring to "pudding, ham, and spinach" or "peas, ham, and spinach."

In the Oxford Dictionary of Nursery Rhymes, the editors (I. and P. Opie) state that the rowley-powley refrain is not found before the nineteenth century, although the song itself is much older. They also quote a correspondent as remembering rowley-powley as a name for a plump fowl, with the remark "both gammon and spinach are posthumous connexions." I am not sure what is meant by this quotation; however, if correct, the three terms boil down to chicken, ham and spinach.

While gammon has other meanings, the addition of spinach may have followed rather naturally in the development of slang, giving rise eventually to the "nonsense, humbug" meaning. Partridge relates "gammon and spinach" to "gammon and patter"—the language of the underworld. I suggest there is, in fact, a natural affinity between gammon (ham) and spinach. My wife's spinach salad is always liberally laced with bacon (and will henceforth be known as gammon and spinach salad); in addition, there is a fine recipe for Soufflé d'Epinards et Jambon in The Gourmet Cookbook.

In summary, it appears that the origin of spinnage is not obscure and its association with ham and bacon seems a natural one. I trust that these culinary conjectures have not led me to proceed from the safire to the frying pan.

Ronald Bentley
Professor of Biochemistry
University of Pittsburgh
Pittsburgh, Pennsylvania

splitting heirs

"The Pregnant Princess," headlined *People* magazine.

The Washington Post subheaded: "The Heir Will Be Apparent in June." I am already knitting my linguistic booties.

An *heir apparent* means more than "next in line"; it means one whose right to title or property cannot be denied, if the heir outlives the ancestor. An *heir presumptive* is one who would inherit if the ancestor died, but whose claim would be defeated by someone else born in more direct descent.

"The line of succession in Great Britain operates on the law of primogeniture," explains Prof. Terence Murphy of American University, "which means that the eldest male heir in the direct line succeeds. Prince Charles as the heir apparent succeeds his mother. Charles establishes a new line so that on his death, his children succeed to the throne."

As a child, Queen Elizabeth was heir presumptive, not heir apparent—her place at the head of the line could have been taken by a baby brother.

Splitting heirs further, there is also an *heir at law,* or *legal heir,* who should by rights receive an inheritance, and an *heir expectant,* who is somebody rubbing his hands in anticipation and not a pregnant heir at law.

It's good to see *pregnant* in headlines. For many years, that was a word seldom used in genteel company: *Expecting* was preferred, or the even more la-di-da French term *enceinte.* In a happy triumph over euphemism, *pregnant* is now showing itself to be viable.

A final clearing of the heir: The phrase *heir apparent* has a masculine connotation, from *son and heir* and the laws of primogeniture. This is changing. *Newsweek* wrote of the Joffrey Ballet's Denise Jackson as "the company's uncrowned prima ballerina; Cynthia Anderson, her heir apparent. . . ." The use of *heir* to mean "female successor" still jars, but why should it? The word comes from the Latin for "who takes what is left," and women have an etymological right to the grab bag.

I apologize for splitting hairs further, but you are incorrect in agreeing that Prince Charles' firstborn son would be heir apparent. He would be heir presumptive until Charles became King, because if Charles were to die before attaining the throne, Queen Elizabeth would be succeeded by her next son (Andrew, I believe) and Andrew's male progeny would supplant Charles' in line of succession. There can only be one heir apparent at a time and since Charles is heir apparent right now, Charles' son can't be heir apparent as well.

Jack B. Weissman
New York, New York

Your language column prompts me to ask what is the difference between the Prince of Wales, an orphan baby, a bald-headed man and a gorilla? The answer, of course, the Prince is an heir apparent, the orphan baby has ne'er a parent, the bald-headed gent has no hair apparent, and the gorilla has a hairy parent. This conundrum (a riddle involving puns) does not arrive on the current wave of P. of W. stories but is found in Mary Chestnut's Civil War, *C. Van Woodward, Ed., Yale Univ. Press, 1981.*

James F. Kelley
Myrtle Beach, South Carolina

standing corrected

What do you do when some wise guy corrects your English? I say, "Gee, thanks," and write a column about it, profiting handsomely thereby, while muttering, "Miserable nitpicker," under my breath.

Other language authorities react differently. In a column titled "Quotation Demolishers Inc.," I presented the saga of Hamilton Long, a determined fellow from Philadelphia whose lifelong aim it has been to correct a phony quotation: "The only thing necessary for the triumph of evil," goes the supposed Edmund Burke remark, "is for good men to do nothing."

Burke never wrote it, as Mr. Long told *Bartlett's Familiar Quotations* and everyone else who would listen. Now, at last, in the new, fifteenth edition of *Bartlett's,* the editor, Emily Morison Beck, gives in:

"It has been ascribed to Edmund Burke," writes Mrs. Beck, a bit grudgingly, in her introduction, "yet has not been found—so far—in his writings. Is it possible that it is a 20th-century paraphrase of Burke's view that 'when bad men combine, the good must associate; else they will fall one by one, an unpitied sacrifice in a contemptible struggle' (from 'Thoughts on the Cause of the Present Discontents')?" That seems like a pretty long stretch to me; perhaps a sixteenth edition of *Bartlett's* will say, "Falsely ascribed to Edmund Burke."

Another authority—in Washington parlance, the Highest Authority—is disarmingly open and carefree about acknowledging error. The Nitpickers League will recall a gibe in "Reaganese" about President Reagan's pronunciation of *liaison* as "LAY-i-zon," rather than the correct "LEE-a-zon" or "lee-A-zon."

A few days after that appeared, the President was talking to a group of congresswomen. "Someone told me the other day," he recalled, "by actual count, that I have met with, in these couple of months, more than 350 of the members of Congress in an effort to have a liaison, and—" He stopped himself. "You notice I said 'liaison,' " he said, pronouncing it "LEE-a-zon." "I was taken to task in the press the other day for calling it 'Lay-i-zon.' " He confessed his guilt, and explained the source of his mispronunciation: "The Army has some words of its own. And when I was a reserve cavalry officer, the Army called it 'LAY-i-zon,' just like they call 'oblique' 'oblike.' So now I'm a civilian, so I'll call it "LEE-a-zon."

Thank you, Mr. President—not merely for straightening out one word, but for displaying an attitude that sets an example for American Youth. If pop grammarians can gleefully turn solecisms into simoleons; if *Bartlett's Quotations* can bow to the pressure of one lone man clothed in accuracy, and note his revision of attribution of a memorable quotation; and if the President of the United States can not only admit but assert he was mispronouncing a word, and then fix it publicly—then who are you, stubborn Leetle Nudnik, to refuse to stand corrected?

If you can correct the misquoters of Edmund Burke, perhaps you can do something about the misguided quoters of Neil Armstrong as well. Now that the U.S. space program is getting back into high gear we are hearing once again the rather trite so-called first words spoken from the moon: "That's one small step for (a) man, one giant leap for mankind." In truth the dramatic first words from the moon to the earth were spoken by Armstrong hours earlier, and could not have been more thrilling: "Tranquillity base here—the Eagle has landed." Those electrifying words, not the later carefully rehearsed banalities, are the ones which deserve immortality.

Paul R. Chernoff
Berkeley, California

subhead

Subheads—those junior headlines over short pieces, or headlines over subdivisions of a story—are becoming a punster's paradise. Moreover, these two- or three-word phrases are the last refuge of the inside joke; writers who enjoy smearing caviar on crackers for generals have taken to writing for themselves or the cognoscenti, often leaving the ordinary reader behind.

Example: In a recent "Chatter" column in *People* magazine, an anecdote is taken from a new book on dressing for a successful career, *Working Wardrobe* by Janet Wallach. Representative Millicent Fenwick, the cigar-chomping Republican from New Jersey, told Mrs. Wallach that she carries a box of spaghetti in her red leather briefcase to prepare for each night's dinner. Does Mrs. Fenwick ever reach for a state paper and come up with a handful of pasta? "No," replied the congresswoman, "the bag is lumpy, so I know which side to go for."

The subhead over this mild thigh-slapper was "Lumpen Proletariat." Most readers know that *proletariat* is Communist jargon for lowest class, or working class, but not one in a thousand would know that *lumpen* is the German word Communists have used to denote the lowest of the low: "dressed in rags." The sophisticated subhead writer was playing on Representative Fenwick's lumpy bag and the rags worn by working women—a neat, bilingual pun.

Did anybody get the inside joke, besides lexicographers perusing *People* for clues to the lingo of Ryan O'Neal and his twisting Fawcett? Probably not, but I like the idea of occasionally slipping an elitist touch into a popular medium. We should read subheads as little mysteries, the way we look at crossword puzzles; there is a thrill to the discovery of an inside joke that makes us glad to be outsiders.

When I took a sneak peek at your subhead "subhead," my adrenaline shot way up: I took it to mean you were about to expose and excoriate that pun-icious clique at a certain magazine in New York, who each week in their eclectic selection of goods, inflict upon us the most wicked of word twists. Some of their contorted offerings are more precocious (and so "insy" and precious at that it is difficult not to physically shudder) than is tolerable. You, I thought, were about to put an end to this pun-ishment.

Yet as I read your piece sobriety came by degrees. It was not these cliché for pay and suit-o intellectual punned-its you had in the crosshairs of your usually laser-sharp sights; it was some innocent and well-meaning People *columnist who obviously had wandered unintentionally into a lumpen pun (might I be the first to title it a lump-pun?) which upon closer evaluation might be a lumpun. In any event I was not so much disappointed in your reaching an evaluation of this subhead much more negative than my own (for we do have to face the reality of those infernal shades of meaning); what really left me hanging was that you left the true and aforementioned verbal villains to go scot-free; and you'd best bet that until they are stopped in their tracts it is we "ordinary readers" who will pay the pun-alty.*

Lest you think I exaggerate their extremity in the art of pun-tification, here are random selections from their columns years past and to this date:

"Tanks for the Memory" (June, 1979)
"Floral and Hardy" (June, 1979)

"Where the Art Is" (June, 1979)
"From Here to Maternity" (June, 1979)
"Shoe Me" (May, 1981)
"Truffles and Flourishes" (May, 1981)

By comparison, Mr. Safire, I think you will agree that "Lumpen Proletariat" is a far superior example of pun and ink. It causes you to think. Your interpretation of it shows it got you thinking in a direction generations removed from the associations it conjured up in me. Having encountered the word lumpenprole *in my past readings (Dreiser in* American Tragedy, *I think), I got the connection with the ragtag working class. But the "bottom line" for me was not the "rags worn by working women" as you deduced, but rather in Mrs. Fenwick's "Like it or Lump it" affectations, including cigar and lumpy bag. (Truly an inde-pun-dent breed of woman.) Admittedly, this is one of life's impunderables but to me the line had a certain* punache. *You should thank your lucky stars that the* People *writer had not gone for a more im-pun-etrable contraction, e.g., "Lumpin' Proletariat."*

> Richard A. DeLia
> New York, New York

My thought was that the subhead "Lumpenproletariat" regarding a description of Millicent Fenwick was ironic, since everyone knows she cannot be so poor as to have to cook spaghetti every night. The word Lumpenproletariat *describes persons who are poor, but do* not *work for wages. A hobo, a vagrant, a lazy bum; but never a self-respecting worker.*

> Elizabeth Lunau
> New York, New York

Your etymology of Lumpenproletariat *was correct up to a point:* Lumpen *means rags, or tatters.* Lumpensammler *is a rag picker.*
But Lump, *as a singular masculine noun, means a scoundrel; hence the* Lumpenproletariat *is both that segment of the proletariat which dresses in rags (due to its poverty) and that segment which consists of, or turns into, scoundrels. When Engels and Marx used the term, they clearly wished to convey both meanings.*

> Alfred G. Meyer
> Mount Desert, Maine

You wrote: "Most readers know that proletariat *is Communist jargon for lowest class, or working class. . . ." Those misguided readers and you are mistaken.*
"Proletariat" derives from the Latin, proletarius, *and was used mostly pejora-*

tively to identify the urban masses in Rome. If one follows the spirit of the original Latin, the word should be rendered as "mob," "rabble," or "vile multitude." No less a worthy republican than M. Tullius Cicero used proletarii *in that sense in his orations against Catiline.*

The word came into common usage in France in the early nineteenth century; it was used by laissez-faire economists and socialists alike; and it was admitted officially into the French language by that hotbed of radicalism, the Académie française, in 1835. The OED *notes its first appearance in England in the columns of that notorious red rag,* The Times, *in 1853.*

Sanford Elwitt
Professor of History
University of Rochester
Rochester, New York

Was it a joke that failed to come off, at least for me, or the common error regarding "caviare to the general"? Hamlet was referring to the delicateness of the play, suited to the elite crowd rather than to the "general" population, hence the play was "caviare" (sic) to the general population, and had nothing to do with being caviar to the army officer corps.

Do I simply not appreciate your humor about smearing caviar on crackers for generals, or are you in error—or heaven forfend, has the military-industrial complex now become so all-powerful and pervasive that they must now be referred to as the general population?

James Nesi
Editor-in-Chief, National Press Service
New York, New York

---

subhead: superhead

I was impelled to entitle a recent political column about the Saudi oil minister, Sheik Ahmed Yamani, "Yamani or Ya Life."

At a party given in honor of America's new ambassador to Saudi Arabia by John Mitchell (so many of my former colleagues have sand in their shoes), an astute Arab diplomat came over to me and confessed he had spent half an hour trying to grasp the meaning of the headline. Fortunately for international understanding, an American lobbyist had explained to him that the pun came from a classic radio show episode where a thief snarls, "Your money or your life!" to Jack Benny, whose skinflinty answer was a long pause.

I told the Arab diplomat that the result of Sheik Yamani's harsh speech in New York was better for the Israeli than the Arab cause. "There is an old Bedouin saying," he replied mysteriously, "that sometimes we are better off with the neck of an ostrich."

The rest of my time at the party was spent buttonholing Arabs to ask, "Have you ever heard the old Bedouin saying—?" but nobody was an old Bedouin, and I had to go back to the original source to confess my ignorance. Then it was revealed: An ostrich, with its long neck, has an advantage over other speakers. Since the sounds that form in its chest take a long time to reach its mouth, the ostrich has a moment to think twice and to bite off his words before they get out.

That is an excellent proverb for anybody in the word business. It has become my favorite Bedouin saying, vouchsafed in return for the price of a pun, and points this moral: When you spot a rare ostrich metaphor, never stick your head in the sand.

Who entitled you to "entitle" your column with that title when all my stylebooks (titles provided on request) indicate "title" as the correct verb?

> Cheryl Solimini
> Hearst Special Publications
> New York, New York

Poem Poem

I suggest you measure your every word
and bite off extras like the wise Arab's bird.
For though you're surely a grammatical pundit,
Last Sunday's piece was twice redundant.

The first occasion was, of course,
Misuse of the phrase "original source."
Your only source was one diplomat;
There were no Bedouins with whom to chat.

"In return for the price," is the second example
'cause "for the price" is surely ample.
So the subhead you missed, at least in my view
Is "Do as I say, and not as I do."

> Martin L. Singer
> Englewood, New Jersey

Benny's response was something more than the long pause you mention. As I recall it, he ultimately said, "I'm thinking, I'm thinking"; however, it is sometimes cited as "I'm thinking it over." (This, of course, after a second demand by the hold-up man.)

Grant Sharman
Hollywood, California

sufferin' succotash

President Reagan has done for *succotash* what President Truman did for *snollygoster:* put the spotlight of pitiless publicity on an obscure Americanism.

"Is it news," asked Mr. Reagan, who likes to enliven his speeches with little stories about individuals, "that some fellow in South Succotash someplace has just been laid off—that he should be interviewed nationwide?"

As readers of this space are aware, a put-down of rural areas goes by many names: *podunk, Resume Speed, East Jesus, back o' beyond, plumb-nelly, baddy's cowpasture,* and the ever-popular borrowing from the Philippines, *boondocks.* *
The President's choice was new to me: *South Succotash* has the advantage of alliteration, and the use of a direction before the main body of the name adds to the remoteness of the place. (It's not even in downtown Succotash.)

The word is from the Narragansett language: *misickquatash,* an ear of corn. The dish originally consisted of corn and beans, with or without meat, and now is most often presented as corn (off the cob) with lima beans. A stretch of road in Rhode Island leads to Succotash Point.

If the President's opponents make a fuss—"South Succotash for Whomever" placards will surely be waved at conventions—the word will join those other Indian contributions to American politics: *sachem, mugwump,* and the more recent lobbying term *rainmaker.* Curiously, the Algonquian word for "sunken place" is *podunk*—which brings the red man full circle to South Succotash.

You sparked more than usual interest when you took note of "the ever-popular borrowing from the Philippines, boondocks."

Since several dictionaries, including the OED, *attributed the word's derivation to bundok, or mountain in Tagalog, I am willing to concede that this is at least one root of the word.*

However, my days as a writer and editor for the Old West *series of Time-Life*

*See "Podunk to the boonies."

Books offered the possibility of a wholly different derivation which I suppose I had formulated for myself. In a chapter of "The Frontiersmen" volume which dealt with the journeys of Daniel Boone, I kept coming across backwoods towns and settlements named by and after this famous scout: "Boonsboro," et cetera. Thenceforth, I naturally assumed that the expressions "the boonies" and "down in the boondocks" referred to places such as those explored by Boone.

If I am wrong, is Webster's at least postdating the word when it ascribes the Tagalog derivation to "WWII"-era? It seems to me that "boondocks" goes back farther—perhaps to our earlier involvement with the Philippines.

> Dalton Delan
> Associate Producer, ABC News Closeup
> New York, New York

You include the Great White Father's reference to South Succotash and etymology on other Indian words in popular political use. But wampum, perhaps the most popular, is omitted perhaps as a direct result of Reaganomic scalpings in South Succotash and other paleface tepees.

> Alfred Stern
> New York, New York

I thought you might enjoy this variation on the rural place names that has gained some local fame here in New Paltz, New York.

On Springtown Road, a major backroad connecting New Paltz and Rosendale, the highway department has been working on resurfacing sections of the road for some time now, and has placed diamond-shaped signs warning drivers of road conditions. One sign which was placed along the road simply read "loose gravel." To this mild warning, a graffiti artist added only "N.Y." below the original message, thus establishing a new community, where before there was only an empty stretch of road. Many people around here now talk of having been through Loose Gravel, N.Y., in their travels.

> Jack Murphy
> New Paltz, New York

---

summary executioner

"Could you explain the difference," asks Andrew Doty of Stanford University, "between a *summary* and an *executive summary*? The latter is gaining enormous momentum and threatens to overwhelm us all."

A plain, no-frills summary is a brief description of a work's contents; an executive summary, on the other hand, is a brief description of a work's contents designed for use by big shots who would not be caught dead without a frilled casket.

Similarly, a jet is an aircraft, and an executive jet is an aircraft intended for passengers who read only executive summaries and eat in executive dining rooms and practice sexual harassment on executive sweeties.

Years ago, a copy editor told me how to get rid of the weak modifier *very*. His advice was to change all my *verys* to *damns;* subsequently, a copy editor would cut out the *damns.* Here is a new application of that plan: Change all adjectival uses of *executive* to *big-shot,* and let the executive-inclined label their boilings-down "big-shot summaries."

Was the copy editor who gave you the damn-very *advice William Allen White? It appeared in his* Emporia Gazette *and was reprinted in edition after edition of* Index to English *by Porter G. Perrin. Wilma R. Ebbitt and I are now preparing the seventh edition of that textbook.*

> *David R. Ebbitt*
> *Newport, Rhode Island*

---

supersede, *see* top seeded

---

surrogate scandal

"I think it is time you dealt with the surfeit of *surrogates,*" writes David Broder, whose column is a pillar of *The Washington Post.* "I believe the word entered the language in the 1968 or 1972 Nixon campaign, and its growth is flourishing, if not healthy."

Mr. Broder encloses a release from the Republican National Committee which announces the appointment of one Mark Tapscott as public-affairs director, and reads: "Tapscott, 30, served as surrogate press director for the Reagan-Bush campaign. . . ."

That's confusing: "I suspect this means he was the flack for the 1980 surrogate speakers," speculates Broder, "but Lou Cannon says he thinks he was the fellow that Nofziger pushed on stage in the briefing room when Nofziger himself did not choose to appear."

A call to the R.N.C. confirms the suspicion that Mr. Tapscott handled the "surrogate speakers' " publicity, and was not the surrogate for Mr. Nofziger, a heavy fellow to work under.

But whence *surrogate* as substitute for *substitute*? Broder's recollection is accurate: It was in a Nixon campaign that the word was chosen to denote speakers who would appear on behalf of the candidate (not *in* behalf of—*on* is a physical substitute; *in* is a championing of a cause). In those halcyon days of 1968 ("halcyon" is from the legendary bird that calms the seas—and why am I stalling?) the campaign needed substitutes for Mr. Nixon at local rallies. *Substitute* was considered, but it had a built-in let-down; *pinch hitter* sounded too old-fashioned; *alternate* was presumptuous.

Someone familiar with the jargon of psychiatry put forward *surrogate*, which was used by native alienists to mean "an authority figure substituting for a father." Political figures who would scorn *stand-ins* took delight in being called *surrogates*—it sounded vaguely legal, and caught on. Oh, did it catch on. After Watergate, Koreagate, Billygate comes surrogate—there's no substitute for it.

I do not know how far back "surrogate" goes in English literature, but my first meeting with it was in The White Goddess *by Robert Graves (First American Edition, 1948) where, among other places, it occurs in the last paragraph, page 261: "Gwydion is a surrogate for Gronw. . . . " Graves uses it in many places in his* Greek Mythology *and, while I could not find it in a somewhat cursory search of Frazer's* Adonis, Attis, Osiris, *I believe it is used, there, before psychiatry; at least before Freud. In all these places it is used to designate the substitution of a SURROGATE sacred king for the real sacred king in some (usually unpleasant) rite such as human sacrifice. This, if you will consult your unabridged Webster (mine is the 1953 Second Edition), is an accurate use for the word; and so is its use in the case of the SURROGATE speakers; more accurate than the common, everyday SUBSTITUTE.*

Webster's Dictionary of Synonyms (a badly neglected source) makes the distinction clearer: "SURROGATE is a somewhat learned word for a substitute, often, but far from always, for a synthetic or artificial product designed to replace a natural product that is scarce or comparatively expensive." Example: "slang is . . . a facile SURROGATE for thought . . ." (Lowes).

Further: The SURROGATE of our courts that handle probate in New York comes from the fact that he (the SURROGATE) is a SURROGATE for the

Bishop, under whose jurisdiction this function was placed before the power was usurped by civil authority.

A reasonably good reference library is a fair substitute for erudition (Ungar).

Stanley Ungar
Valley Stream, New York

The word "surrogate" in the meaning of "substitute" may well be a good deal older than psychiatric jargon. The great Russian novelist Ivan Turgenev (1818–1883) used it in his letter of July 25 (O.S.), 1855, to V. P. Botkin and N. A. Nekrasov. In discussing N. G. Chernyshevskii's bigoted but influential work The Aesthetic Relationship of Art to Reality, *Turgenev wrote: "As for Chernyshevsky's book, my chief objection is this: in his eyes, art is (as he himself expresses it) only a surrogate for reality, for life, and is essentially fit only for immature people. But, in my opinion, this idea is nonsense. There is no Shakespearean Hamlet in life, or, if you like, there is one, but Shakespeare discovered him and made his accomplishment public." The Russian word Turgenev used is the cognate* surrogate.

Edgar H. Lehrman
Chairman and Professor, Department of Russian
Washington University
St. Louis, Missouri

Dear Bill:

I believe you could have gone a bit further in identifying the origin of "surrogate."

As you know, in New York and some other states, the judge who probates wills is the "Surrogate."

According to the 2nd Edition of the Webster's New International Dictionary *that usage occurred when ecclesiastical officials had authority over estates and the substitutes or surrogates of the Bishops handled the cases.*

Sincerely,
Bill [Bill Green, M.C., New York]
Washington, D.C.

syncopation

Everybody knows what syncopation in music is—the shifting of the regular accent to add distinctiveness, typically by stressing the weak beat. We sometimes do the same with words and use the same word to describe it.

Syncopation in grammar is the dropping of sounds or letters from the middle of a word, as in calling Cholmondeley "Chumley"; or Worcestershire sauce "Wooster-sheer sauce." This has taken place on a huge, languagewide scale with the past-participle ending of adjectives—that is, in the fifteenth century, we pronounced *pronounced* as "pro-noun-sed," and now we pronounce *pronounced* "pro-nounct." In most cases, the *ed* ending has turned into a *t.*

But when we want to sneer at a lawyer, as we so often do, we call him "learned counsel," pronouncing the adjective as "learn-ed," as in "he claims to be learn-ed in the law." Since we found it easy to have learned to say "learned" as the past tense of the verb *to learn,* why do we persist in using two syllables for the same word as adjective?

To put the question another way (since the question is more fun than the answer): "There is a dispute in my office over the pronunciation of *alleged* (verb) and *alleged* (adjective)," writes Penny Rogg of New York. "So far, we're divided between the bright young things and the old salts; the problem may be purely generational. We all agree on *alleged*'s pronunciation as a verb: 'ah-lejd.'

"But when it is used as an adjective, as in 'The alleged journalist couldn't pronounce his own words correctly,' my colleagues and I all say 'ah-lej-ed,' three syllables instead of two." Their bosses, the aged salts, stick to the two syllables. "Who's right?" she asks.

Dearly beloved, we are gathered here for the answer. Do not look to Shakespeare for help, because he and other Elizabethan poets treated that *ed* as an option, making the ending silent or not, to suit the needs of iambic pentameter.

Both the two- and three-syllable forms are acceptable today; but for those lovers of the native tongue who want to be correcter than correct, here is the way to decide when to pronounce the *ed:* If the word is a participle in function (as in *aged whiskey*), do not pronounce the *ed,* but if the word is an adjective in function (as in *aged salts*), you are permitted—nay, urged—to pronounce the *ed* loud and clear.

"We can say 'a very ag-ed man' but not 'very ag-ed whiskey,' " reports John Algeo, professor of English and linguistics at the University of Georgia, "because in the former *ag-ed* is an adjective, like *happy,* whereas in the latter *aged* is a participle."

An exception: When verbs end in *d* or *t,* they also get the favored sing-out-ed treatment—I have *prided* myself on *heated* discussions about this—but generally speaking, use the pronounced *ed* on adjectives only, and on them every blessed time.

What about nouns? Trouble: "Forms made by adding *ed* to nouns," says Professor Algeo, "are *crooked* (having a crook), *four-legged* (having four legs)— but note *one-armed*, with the vowel silent. So much for consistency in language."

Getting to the point, the well-taught counsel will say "learn-ed," since it is an adjective. The bright young things are correct: When *alleged* is used to modify a noun, as in "alleged journalist," you can go with "alleg-ed" and not only be right but stylishly archaic. Let the old salts syncopate.

Oh, come now! Where do you get that idea that "we persist in using two syllables for [learned] *as adjective"? Have you no ears?*
Read the following sentences aloud:

(1)   Learned counsel is a fool.
(2)   Saluting the flag is a learned response.

In the first example, learned *(meaning* having acquired learning*) has two syllables; in the second (where the word means* having been learned*), it has one.*
Generalizing, I'd say we use different pronunciations to convey different meanings. What would you say?

> *Christian S. Ward*
> *Brooklyn, New York*

I doubt you ever pronounkt "pronounced" "pronounct."

> *Helen Friedland*
> *Editor,* Poetry/LA
> *Los Angeles, California*

The word "alleged" in the expression "the alleged journalist" must be categorized as a participle rather than an adjective, according to the test which you cite, as one would not refer to "the very alleged journalist." As a participle, it would then merit a two-syllable rather than a three-syllable pronunciation; thus, your conclusion that "the bright young things are correct" is wrong.

> *Juliana K. Dulmage*
> *English as a Second Language Program*
> *Northfield Mount Hermon School*
> *Northfield, Massachusetts*

Dear Bill,

I take leave to doubt the verb-vs.-adjective explanation for learn'd-learned, and the like. To begin with, I have never in a long career of keeping my ears open heard "alleged." It's always: alleg'd crime, etc. If the ed has been heard in front of "journalist," it's because of the difficulty in saying two dj's close together.

But what seems obvious and was not said by your witnesses is that the difference in pronunciation marks a difference in meaning. The ag'd whiskey has been consciously made so—age is here a transitive verb. The aged have become so, quite unconsciously as we all know, intransitively. True, we say "he has ag'd much in the last year," but there the auxiliary has prevents the ambiguity. And if we wanted to be sarcastic about some article of food, we would say: "these look to me like aged vegetables."

Similarly with the learned, whom nobody has learn'd, and about whom you will note that they are a noun, not an adjective. If the verb-adjective difference were right, wouldn't it extend farther—to wash, trip, confess? With bless'd, both the short and long forms can be adjectives: "I am bless'd with good health"; "she is blessed among women (divine grace)." "Oh cursed spite!" cried the poets who called themselves accurs'd.

I could go on, but I am hard-presséd for time.

> *Yours,*
> *Jacques [Jacques Barzun]*
> *Charles Scribner's Sons*
> *New York, New York*

A longtime favorite of mine is the story of the hesitant diner in the fancy restaurant. After the snooty waiter had described all the day's specials, including the stripe-ed bass, our hero resolutely stated, "I believe I'll have the bake-ed chicken!"

> *A. H. Vito, Jr.*
> *Huntington, New York*

Native English speakers know how to pronounce the -ed of the regular past tense of verbs. We who teach English to speakers of other languages follow these pronunciation rules:

1. If the last sound of the verb root is voiced, as in dub or fizz, pronounce the -ed as -d.

2. If the last sound in the verb root is unvoiced, as in top or knife, pronounce the -ed as -t.

3. If the last sound of the verb root is -d or -t, as in sound *or* paint, *pronounce the -ed with the indeterminate vowel sound schwa— -id or -ud.*

Barbara G. Michaels
English Specialist
F. A. Day Junior High School
Newtonville, Massachusetts

The alleged rule on syncopation is causing me pronounced linguistic confusion. After a week's determined attempt to make sense of the damned thing, I must ask the distinguished Prof. Algeo what criterion one should use to pick out purely adjectival uses of a participle.

Patricia Greenspan
Associate Professor, Department of Philosophy
University of Maryland
College Park, Maryland

Dear Professor Greenspan:

Mr. Safire has asked me to answer your query about the difference between adjectives and participles in -ed.

The difference is not as clear-cut as one would like, but that is the case with most things in language.

Randolph Quirk and his colleagues, in A Grammar of Contemporary English, *point out the following differences (pp. 242–6):*

1. There is often a difference of meaning. For example, in an agëd man, *agëd means approximately "old." In* a man aged by vicissitude, *however,* aged *means something like "made old." Thus* agëd *whiskey would not be particularly desirable, whereas* aged *whiskey is generally thought to be so, since the latter means not just "old" but "made old (by a particular process)."*

2. With the participle, one can use the sort of adverb that goes with verbs: a rapidly aged man *like* a man who aged rapidly. *With the adjective, one can use the sort of adverb that goes with "gradable" adjectives: a* very agëd man *like* a very old man. *This is a bit tricky, of course, because not all adjectives can take modifiers like* very; *thus, the possibility of the use of* very *marks the work as an adjective, but the impossibility of its use is not a sure sign that it is a participle.*

3. When they occur in predicative use (the man was agëd, the man was aged), only the adjective can follow the linking verb seem *(the man seemed agëd, not* the man seemed /rapidly/ aged by vicissitude—*for the latter, idiom would require* . . . seemed to be . . .)

Of course, I am here using agëd *for the adjective and* aged *for the participle only for convenience. Many people use a monosyllabic* aged *for both functions.*

There are other differences too, but you don't need me to tell you what they are. You can read Quirk's Grammar of Contemporary English *as well as I. And, if you are not familiar with it, I recommend it highly as the most complete and accurate reference grammar of present-day English. A second edition of the work is now in preparation, but even the first edition is excellent.*

John Algeo
Professor of English and Linguistics
University of Georgia
Athens, Georgia

Prof. Algeo has kindly provided a criterion. It seems that the syncopation rule does not work in general, though I do agree about learned, blessed, aged, *and* beloved—*also* alleged, *at least where it's meant to express doubt about a reported allegation, rather than simply reporting it without commitment. As far as I can tell, it does function as a participle on some uses:* alleged murderer, *meaning "one [who has been] alleged [to be] a murderer," seems to allow for the syncopated pronunciation. I don't syncopate myself; but both* American Heritage *and the* OED *suggest that I should. They say the same for* supposed, *though; and this sounds wrong—to my ear, at any rate.*

Pat Greenspan

You say pronunciation of Worcestershire *sauce should be "Woos-ter-sheer." Having lived in Westchester County for over 23 years I know that that is the way it is said in America, but the English call it "Woos-ter-sher." As a matter of fact most English people ask for "Woos-ter sauce" and leave it at that. A* shire (shy-er) *when attached to its county name is always pronounced "sher."*

F. Eunice Born
Switzerland

You stated ". . . pronounce the ed *loud and clear." Would I be stirring things up if I asked why you didn't say "loudly and clearly"?*

Harry C. Wiersdorfer
Hamburg, New York

taking it neat

I am having a hard time getting
what I want to drink in a bar. (That
sentence originally had an *increasingly* in it, but *increasingly* is being
used more and more.) Aging bartenders and barmaids usually understand my order, but the cocktail
waitress who calls herself a "beverage attendant" around the corner
from my office operates in a new
linguistic world.

"Bourbon, neat, soda on the side."
That's my order.

"Neat?"

"Yeah, neat—straight."

"You mean straight up?"

(The phrase *straight up* was coined in opposition to *on the rocks;* a martini,
straight up, is one that stands, iced but iceless, in a glass with a stem. Since most
martinis are now served in a short tumbler on ice, or "on the rocks," the noun
has now acquired a modifier it never needed before, on the analogy of *day baseball*
and *natural turf.*)

"No, I don't want it straight up, in a glass with a stem—I want it *straight,* in
a shot glass."

"Shot glass?"

(A *shot* is the amount of liquor that shoots out of the bottle at a single twist
of the wrist, measuring about one and a half ounces, if poured by an experienced
bartender. The small glass containing that amount—often used as a measuring
glass by inexperienced bartenders, or those who wanted to show their patrons
they were not being shortshotted—became known soon after the turn of the
century as the *shot glass.*)

"Any kind of little glass will do. You know the kind you use for orange juice
in the morning? Put a shot of bourbon in that. No ice—neat."

"Neat?" she asked.

(Because *neat* and its intensified form, *neat-o,* have become such universal
forms of approbation in current slang, an earlier bartender's meaning—undiluted,
or without either a mixer or chaser—has fallen into disuse. In current usage, a
neat drink is any beverage that is real-real good.)

"Straight up," I said, caving in, "if you like, but in a little glass without a stem.
Soda on the side."

"You mean soda back?"

(*On the side* originated in food ordering about a century ago. *Potatoes on the side,* says Stuart Berg Flexner, coauthor of the *Dictionary of American Slang,* was first recorded in 1884, and *soda on the side*—originally *soda water on the side* —flowed from that. *Soda water* differed from *branch water,* a southernism for water from a stream, or branch of a stream, which was first used in the 1850's. *Soda back* is, I think, a western expression to describe a chaser of soda that stands behind, rather than alongside, the whiskey. Neither Flexner nor Dr. Frederic Cassidy, editor of the *Dictionary of American Regional English,* has heard of *soda back* and both suspect I may be hearing pink elephants. Those eminent lexicographers should get out of their offices and onto barstools, where the action is.)

"Yes, bourbon straight," I said straight out, "with soda back, with ice, in a highball glass."

"Highball glass?" asked the beverage attendant.

(A *highball,* which replaced *long drink,* was coined in 1898; *ball* was bartender slang for *glass.* The reason for this ball-glass connection is obscure: Perhaps *ball* was the glass manufacturer's name, or bartenders would toss glasses from hand to hand like a ball. *Highball* is now rarely used, having been replaced by *mixed drink* a generation ago.)

"A tall glass, I mean, with ice in it, and soda. Back. It helps a little snort go down."

"Snort?" She sounded as if she were speaking to Rip Van Winkle.

(*Snort*—one shot without a chaser—was first cited in 1889. It was superceded* by *belt,* as in "a belt of gin," about 1906; that noun might have seemed to come from "punch" or "blow," but actually had to do with putting a drink under your belt. Just as the vogue use of *neat* has obscured its "unmixed" meaning, a *snort* now means only a sniff of cocaine. The familiar *to go on a toot,* or to drink heavily and thereby lose a weekend, has been replaced by *to blow a toot,* or to inhale a "line" of cocaine.)

"Most people say," said the waitress sternly, " 'Bourbon,' or 'Scotch,' or whatever, 'with a splash.' "

That's what I'll do. For all I know, she'll hand me a bottle and push me into the swimming pool, but at least I'll stop getting funny looks in cocktail lounges.

Eighty-six on etymologies for *cocktail.* Along with Flexner, I prefer the Peychaud explanation: Antoine Peychaud of New Orleans created Peychaud bitters, which flavored the drink he called a *coquetel,* a cocktail. Originally, a cocktail —to be a genuine cocktail—had to contain bitters. Now, with the resolution in liquor linguistics, it could be whiskey with a splash and a cherry on top, soda front.

*See "top seeded."
See "behind the stick," "booze talk," "chasers," "cocktail talk," and "taking it straight."

taking it straight

I have written about the difficulty of ordering a straight serving of liquor. *Neat* used to be the operative term, followed by *straight*—now the preferred locution is *straight up,* the opposite of *on the rocks.* (An old-fashioned has become so old-fashioned that an old-fashioned glass is now called a *rocks glass.*)

"Some other locutions on straight shots are as follows," reports John Kearney of New York: *"a little rub of the relic, a touch of evil, a mite, a drop, a swap of the mop. . . ."* Measurements, he adds, go from *a li'l dab* (half a shot) to *king and queen* (double shot) to the term for a triple shot, or four and a half ounces, *a sewer full of booze.*

A bartender from Campbell River, British Columbia, A. Murphy, adds, "The development of drinking establishments with dim lighting has forced experienced topers into demanding their drinks *pure, solo, barefoot, unpolluted, without the trimmings,* and *a singleton."* Other words he has noted to denote straight whiskey include a *nip, wee droppee, noggin, taste,* and *smidgen,* but those "are generally derisive and used in watering holes known for tight measures. In the case of a more generous host, one would call for a *stiff belt,* an *eye-opener,* a *lid-lifter,* or a *dollop."*

The word coming up fast for a *straight shot* is a *shooter.* "A shooter is a shot of liquor swallowed in one quick gulp," says Jeff Dee in Sarasota, Florida. "For some reason, they are also called *hooters."*

The swallow-grimace-and-wheeze crowd also refers to what used to be known as a *snort* as a *jolt,* a *kicker,* and *three-fingers.* The word *snort* is receding from booze lingo, having been stolen by drug lingo to mean a dose of cocaine. Similarly, a *toot*—formerly a period of inebriation—now means a snort, or line, of the white powder, and is leaving bar talk. (A toot was never a serious bout of drinking, and never lost a weekend: "A *toot* can be a day or two," writes J. Fialla Gamsu of Saranac Lake, New York, "but the true nature of a *bender* is never revealed before the third day.") A *pop,* on the other hand, is moving from drug lingo into booze lingo to describe a series of drinks—"a few pops" can be either straight or mixed. The most popular current description of a drink, straight or mixed, is a *blast.*

I disagree with your instructions for ordering a straight serving of liquor.

"Neat," contrary to the dictionary definition, has not to do with the content of the drink but rather indicates no ice is desired; the drink is mixed as it normally would be. A European friend of mine orders "gin and tonic, neat," and gets what she wants every time: a gin and tonic served at room temperature, without ice.

See "behind the stick," "booze talk," "chasers," "cocktail talk," and "taking it neat."

"Straight" does mean without mixer, but "straight up" dictates the glass to be used: a stemmed glass appropriate for the cocktail ordered. It is often abbreviated by ordering the drink "up," as, "a perfect Manhattan, up." Drinks served straight up are usually chilled, and without ice, unless otherwise specified. Contrary to your advice, they are almost always mixed drinks: martinis, Manhattans, old-fashioneds, etc.

"On-the-rocks" is the antonym of "neat" and became necessary when people started ordering drinks, like martinis, in other than the traditional, and, some would say, correct format. As an inveterate martini drinker, it is my feeling that if one orders a martini, one should be served a gin and vermouth mixture, with an olive, in a stemmed cocktail glass. Any variation thereof should require additional information to the bartender; i.e., "a vodka martini on the rocks," "a very dry martini with a twist," etc.

"Perfect," in case you were intrigued by the above order for a Manhattan, is used in ordering a drink which can be either "sweet" or "dry," such as Rob-Roys or Manhattans, and tells the bartender to use equal quantities of sweet and dry vermouth. It is then neither sweet nor dry, but perfect.

A last note: a barperson is someone, like me, who spends a great deal of time in front of the stick.

Sincerely,
William Grenewald
Summit, New Jersey

think in my heart, *see* Speakerspeak

thin read I

"This book is a good read."

While other vogue terms in the literary dodge have faded—no longer do we hear of *books with legs*, and *page-turner* has curled up its toes—the barbarism *a good read* seems to be hanging on.

What can be done about it? Ridicule is the answer. Martin Willsted of New York has submitted these ultimate lunacies if the transformation of verb to noun gets out of hand: A restaurant can be *a good eat;* a plane can be *a good fly;* a play *a good sit,* and a funeral *a good bury.* This item has been a good short write.

thin read II

Publishers who called their books "a good read" received my nomination for the recent verb-into-noun awards. Alexander V. Areno of New York springs to the voguish nouns' defense:

"Are we not dealing here with gerunds minus the *ing* suffix?" he says, coming up with a good ask. "Do not archeologists say that they are going on a *dig*? When athletes get together to compete with each other, is not the event called a *meet*? On a hot summer afternoon at the beach, would one not be tempted to go for a *swim*? In slang, an elaborate social event can be referred to as a *do*. And, to slip into the vulgar . . ."

Let's stop there. I am aware of the *good buy* and its successor, the *real steal,* and of Rudyard Kipling's "And a woman is only a woman, but a good cigar is a smoke," after a *quick study* over which many feminists had a *good cry.*

The use of verbs as nouns, and vice versa, is as hilled as the old; it can make lively speech and writing, used in moderation or with originality, but becomes objectionable when used to excess.

To those who, like me, reject *a good read,* let me commend the ridicule implicit in Chicagoan Jim O'Leary's observation that "an Irish wake could be considered a *good grief,* " and Great Necker Frederic A. Wool's television criticism: *"Big Valley* was a bad view, while *60 Minutes* is usually a fine watch."

"Just the other Sunday morning after my wake," writes novelist Ira Avery of Stamford, Connecticut, "I had an inspire to indulge in an hour's plant in the garden. Unfortunately, however, it was a slight overexert and, really needing a sit, I made the discovery that I had a small bleed. Well, the family doctor has a live just a few doors away, so I gave him a consult."

Beware of too much of a good thing.

to demeanor born

A curious quirk in pronunciation is caused by television lights shining on a print journalist. The "ee" sound is changed to "eh."

"Whatever happened to the verb *wreak*?" writes Mrs. John Harrison of East Lansing, Michigan. She reports that on a television program, Karen Elliot House —the incisive, sophisticated diplomatic correspondent of *The Wall Street Journal,* who retains traces of her Matador, Texas, accent—said that someone was *wrecking* havoc in the Middle East. "I cringed," says the impressionable Mrs. Harrison.

Wreak—from the Old English *wrecan*, to revenge—is pronounced "reek." It's not that "reek" is preferred over "wreck"; it is that "reek" is the only correct pronunciation. One errs with "wreck," but one wreaks with chic.

I discovered that "ee-eh" phenomenon when correcting the world's English on *The Dick Cavett Show*. "I saw and heard his interview with you," writes Mildred Schroth of Trenton. "Did I hear you pronounce *demeanor* as 'de-MEN-or'?"

She did. The word should be pronounced "de-MEEN-or" and no other pronunciation is acceptable. It was as if the pronouncer of "LAY-i-zon" had wrecked vengeance on me.

to whom the credit goes

"No man is an island, entire of itself; every man is a piece of the continent," wrote John Donne in 1623, in his immortal "for whom the bell tolls" passage.

However, A. Larsen-Bookseller (I think that's his name, unless his last name is Larsen and he sells books) of Galena, Illinois, has come across a strikingly similar quotation in the works of Francis Bacon: "If a man be gracious and courteous to strangers, it shows he is a citizen of the world, and that his heart is no island cut off from other lands, but a continent that joins to them."

That was from "Of Goodness and Goodness of Nature," one of a collection of essays that was prepared between 1607 and 1612, and published in 1612. *Bartlett's Quotations* includes this line, but dates Bacon's work from 1625, when an enlarged edition was published, and includes a footnote directing the reader to the Donne quotation, as if Bacon had brought it home from Donne, or at least followed Donne.

But, in fact, Bacon came up with the image of a man not being an island, but being a part of a continent of men, some ten years before Donne. Therefore, Sir Francis, never send to know from whom the credit was stolen, it was stolen from thee.

As regards the Bacon quotation, at last I have tracked down a copy of the 1612 edition of the essays (in the Houghton Library, Harvard, which I should have gone to first).

You'll be interested to know that the quote in question, "If a man be gracious . . . his heart is no island, etc." does not appear in the much shorter and different version of the essay, "Of Goodness . . .," in the 1612 edition. As Mr. A. Wigfall Green states, practically all the essays for the 1625 edition were "altered and enlarged." This is borne out in examining the 1612 edition, which is about the size of a postcard and less than an inch thick. So, the Bartlett editors have been correct in using the larger, final edition of 1625. Still, we'll never know whether or not Bacon came independently to the metaphor, or perhaps was unconsciously influenced by the resounding Donne passage. . . .

Emily Morison Beck
Editor, Bartlett's Quotations
Canton, Massachusetts

top seeded

With the "Shame on you!" file overflowing and the "You, of all people!" folder crammed, I have just begun a new file for letters that begin: *"Et tu, Safire?"*

"Snort," I wrote recently in a paean to bibulation, *"—one shot without a chaser—was superceded by belt,* as in 'a belt of gin.' "

The most frequent comment was "Has *superseded* been superseded by *superceded?"* The word is properly spelled with an *s,* not a *c:* The Latin *supersedere* means "to sit over," presumably squashing the object underneath and thus causing its replacement, and has come to mean "supplant" or "succeed"; the Latin *cedere* means "to yield," from which comes our *cede.* I cede the point that *supersede* is spelled with an *s.*

"The only words I can think of that might be more often misspelled," notes William Lang of Southbury, Connecticut, with some sympathy, "are *impostor, liquefy,* and *sacrilegious."*

traffic talk

The message from Metro Traffic Control is ominous: "A traveler's advisory is in effect." To every commuting driver who hears that on his radio, the words mean: "The police say driving in this weather is dangerous."

So why does the snowbound announcer not intone: "The police say driving in this weather is dangerous"? Because that is not the new lingo of Trafficsnarl, which has transformed news about jams on the way to work into a kind of space

odyssey. "I love the morning radio traffic reports," writes Judy Katz of New York City. " 'The approach to the bridge is crawling,' they say. 'The Brooklyn-Queens Expressway is creeping.' 'The Bronx-Whitestone Bridge is heavy.' "

Years ago, Ed Bleier of Warner Communications had a great idea about a radio station programmed exclusively for people in automobiles, playing music for driving, featuring news about traffic, and editorializing about potholes, sponsored by auto companies and local carwashes. He was prophetic; today, many radio stations concentrate on drivers tuned to car radios during rush hours, and with this new concern for the driving listener has come the voice of gloomy Gus Gridlock, the anchorman of the freeways.

Gus is no longer shouting over the noise of a helicopter hovering over some accident which is backing up cars clear out past the beltway; high-flying reporters discovered that planes could not fly over many metropolitan locations or structures such as bridges. Today, traffic-caster Gridlock is pretending to sit in a Situation Room of the driver's mind, with videoscreens surrounding him, surveying every potential traffic bottleneck for miles around; in twelve cities, from Boston and Baltimore to Denver and L.A., this service is called "Metro Traffic Control," evoking Houston's "Mission Control," as if traffic jams could be aborted with the touch of a button.

This service, now carried by 126 radio stations, is the three-year-old brainchild of David Saperstein of Baltimore. Metro Traffic Control is the only network to sell information to any station in the local area, and is the only news organization in the media-saturated nation's capital with a man stationed in the Washington Monument.

"We train our reporters to deliver a traffic-cast," says Mr. Saperstein, who is my kind of entrepreneur. "Some expressions work only in certain areas of the country. For example, *rolling backup* works only in the D.C.-Baltimore area— it's not generally known elsewhere." Don't confuse that with *residual backup*, which means that the problem has been cleared, but because the jam was so long it will take time for traffic to return to normal speed.

Glen Ivey, a computer programmer and analyst for Metro Traffic Control, explains that *rolling backup* means that traffic is moving, but so slowly that the end of the backup continues to grow. In Denver, this condition is called *slow and go*, and in Los Angeles, it has been labeled a *sigalert*, after Lloyd Sigmund, a traffic alerter of a generation ago.

A person whose curiosity causes him to slow traffic is called a *rubbernecker* in Texas, a *gonker* in Detroit, and a *lookie-Lou* in L.A. Such obstructive gaping is called *gaper's block* in Denver.

How do traffic-casters refer to stalled cars? By converting adjectives to nouns: A disabled vehicle is called a *disable* in Texas and a *stall* in Baltimore. In Minneapolis, stalls and disables along the icy roadways are called *snowbirds*.

At interchanges, where freeways merge, the traffic-casters have a field day reporting trouble. In Dallas, beware *the Mixmaster;* in Denver, motorists dread *the Mousetrap;* in Detroit, the most jammable interchange is called *the Malfunction Junction.*

Rhyme and alliteration attract the troubadors of traffic trouble. In Detroit on days when roadways are icy, listeners are warned of *bunch and crunch;* after dry spells in Texas, when oil on the road is suddenly mixed with rain, the danger spoken of is *slip and slide.*

As a linguistic looky-Lou, I welcome much of the argot of Trafficsnarl; because the reporting is inherently local, there is a happy diversity of descriptions of similar situations in different places. However, a danger of semantic backup comes from patches of foggy locutions. Mission chief Saperstein of Metro Traffic Control is aware of this.

"Traveler's advisory is a phrase our people don't use," he says, veering off. "That's a Weather Service term. Those advisories usually encompass a monstrous area, while we are primarily concerned with metropolitan areas. Besides, it refers not only to roads, but to all modes of transportation—and we're more specific." Straphangers on subways are not the targets of Trafficsnarl.

Here, then, is a listener's advisory, straight from Gus Gridlock: Resist all "advisories," just as sensible people hoot at memos that begin "Please be advised"; it's foggy talk, not legitimate Trafficsnarl. When the traffic-casters come up with happy coinages like *Malfunction Junction,* wake up and applaud; if they adopt bureaucratic pomposities like *traveler's advisory,* roll over and go back to sleep. Wait for a simple declarative sentence from Central Vocabulary Control.

A person whose curiosity causes him to slow traffic is not a lookie Lou in Los Angeles. In this very real-estate-conscious city, the term lookie Lou *is used to describe one who looks at numerous houses which are for sale, yet never finds one to his liking.*

> *Ann C. Gold*
> *Los Angeles, California*

The word in Detroit for a person whose curiosity causes him to slow traffic is not "gonker," but "gawker"; "gawk," meaning to stare stupidly, comes from the Old English for a fool.

I know, because for ten years, I was ad director for the sponsor of newscasts on both radio and television in Detroit. Now, I've retired to New Bern, N.C., where traffic jams are unheard of.

> *John Eckels*
> *New Bern, North Carolina*

For your catalog of Trafficsnarlspeak, I submit the following, which I hear several times each rush hour: ". . . traffic headed westbound" and ". . . traffic headed eastbound."

Should we sic the Squad Squad on that trafficaster?

Ms. Jane T. Larsen
McLean, Virginia

You suggest traveler's advisories are written by the police but actually the National Weather Service is the culprit.

A traveler's advisory is a catch-all bulletin designed to describe a variety of weather problems such as high winds in mountain passes, dense fog or icy roads. Ninety-five percent apply to motorists but occasionally fog will also interrupt airline schedules. Ideally traveler's advisories should be issued before ice or fog get hazardous, but often the commuter is well aware of the phenomenon before the advisory is out. I write traveler's advisories for Southeast Texas and feel they only keep the timid, insecure driver off the streets. I would like to know precisely what is occurring over my area and be able to write declarative statements with useful information. Unfortunately the advisories cover hundreds of square miles affected by intermittent and nonuniform weather, so "bureaucratic pomposities" or general statements are about all we are able to provide.

D.J. Kava
Steward, NWS Employee Organization
WSO Port Arthur, Texas

Dear Bill:

Here in Boston we have an individual who has created his own often notable vocabulary items for "Traffic Talk," worth adding to your list. This is the redoubtable Kevin O'Keefe, recently grounded from helicoptering for economy reasons, but still on daily on WEEI-AM to report local traffic.

Among his phrases my wife and I can remember are one group of adjective phrases of the form "A and B," where A and B rhyme. So the traffic flow may be described as "beep and creep," "bump and grump," or "stall and crawl." Another group of nouns give Mr. O'Keefe poetic openings, based on such as the general item "fender bender." The best in my mind is another word involving "a person *whose curiosity causes him to slow traffic." An accident which brings such persons to the fore is described by Mr. O'Keefe as a "gawker blocker."* He has many other such, of which "stuck truck" or "snail trail" for a highway with slow traffic come readily to mind.*

Yours,
Karl [Karl V. Teeter]
Professor of Linguistics
Harvard University
Cambridge, Massachusetts

*To violate my injunction against subjective fiddle-faddle, this sounds particularly graphic, it seems to me, when done as Mr. O'Keefe does it, in r-less New England speech. KVT

trendy cushy

"About a year ago," notes Robert Davis of Utica, New York, "I noticed that a certain liquid detergent was making another claim, in addition to getting my clothes deep-down clean. The product began threatening to make my clothes 'cushy.' Now I see there is also a 'cushy' tissue on the market."

"This advertising usage is a heavy-handed theft from the world of lingo," observes Richard Schneider of Cambridge, Massachusetts, who noticed the same thing. "A job or a person's upbringing can be 'cushy.' To reduce the word to a merely literal reference—cushion—and to rob it of its strongly satirical connotation would do a great injustice to a nice little neologism."

A cushy job is nice work, if you can get it. The term may have been influenced by *cushion* (which is rooted in the Latin for "hip"), but Mr. Schneider's etymological objection is sustained: *Cushy* is derived from the Hindi word *khush,* which originated from the Persian *khūsh,* meaning "pleasant." British soldiers picked it up while a-servin' of the Queen in India; around the turn of the century, a *cushy wound* was an injury that was not serious.

In America, another reinforcement appeared: *Cush* is a Gullah word for a form of gruel or mush, taught to southern whites by slaves, coming later to mean "soft" or "sexy."

The adjective is now achieving vogue status in the United States, along with other Britishisms like *trendy* and *dicey.* If advertisers want to use it to attribute softness to toilet paper or newly washed clothes, that's their business, but the Hindi derivation is spot-on.

Dear Bill,

I have no comment on Latin *and* cushion, *but question that the British use of* cushy *in India came from the Persian word for "pleasant." I suggest that it comes from old Turki and Central Asia. In the 14th and 15th centuries the descendants of Timur (better known as Tamerlane) ruled in what is now eastern Iran and Afghanistan and conquered northern India. Annals of the time refer to a corps of their army as a koshun. The Timurids were succeeded in India by the East India Co. which basically adopted much of the existing civil and military administration the Moghuls had established. In the 1753* Journal of his Travels, *Jonas Hanaway wrote that the kushuns were foot soldiers and "the name is Turkish." By 1810 it appears in Col. Mark Wilks' history as "a division of five regular cushoons." (In the transliteration of area languages, spelling is very inconsistent—*koshun *sometimes appears as* qushin.*)*

Further confusion: As with most things touching on the subcontinent, there is a link to the Mahabharata, *which uses the Sanskrit word* ksuni *for a force of the empire.*

It might interest you to note that the most common use of the word kush *is hardly pleasant—I refer to the Hindu Kush. The source of the authentic name of the mountains is disputed but the accepted spelling is commonly held to mean "Hindu killer" because of the number of captured Hindus who died there.*

> *Best,*
> *Liz Moynihan*
> *Washington, D.C.*

trickle-down carrotsticks

Two intrepid phrase detectives have tracked down a couple of the most-wanted phrase origins of the year.

On *a carrot and a stick,** David Harris, M.D., of Huntington, Long Island, points to this press conference of May 25, 1943, held by Winston Churchill in the company of Franklin Roosevelt in Washington:

"All we can do," said the British leader about the Italian leaders, "is to apply the physical stimuli which we have at our disposal to bring about a change of mind in these recalcitrant persons. Of this you can be sure: We shall continue to operate on the Italian donkey at both ends with a carrot and with a stick."

The *Morris Dictionary of Word and Phrase Origins* cites that press conference and adds that the phrase could have been used earlier in a Humphrey Bogart movie of 1941 or 1942. If anybody finds that, just pucker up your lips and blow.

*See "carrotsticks."

On *trickle-down economics,** which budgeteer David Stockman reluctantly agreed to use, leading to a session in the Reagan woodshed, we have this find from David Ranson, an economist with H.C. Wainwright & Company in Boston. On page 946 of Samuel Eliot Morison's *Oxford History of the American People,* this 1932 attack on Herbert Hoover's Reconstruction Finance Corporation appears: "The money was all appropriated for the top, in the hopes it would trickle down to the needy."

The speaker was humorist Will Rogers, and if he had said "truly needy," he would have had a double. I never met a carrot and a stick I didn't like.

You attributed the expression "trickle-down economy" to Will Rogers in 1932. I myself heard that expression used in 1928 by Professor "Beppo" Hall in reference to what would now be called "McKinleynomics." (There were two Halls in the Princeton History Department at that time: "Beppo" taught American History, "Buzzer" taught European.) As it is highly unlikely that Will Rogers ever heard Professor Hall lecture, we must look for a common source. Could it have been Theodore Roosevelt or Woodrow Wilson?

> (Rev.) Nelson W. MacKie
> Greenville, Rhode Island

Regarding your discussion of the expression "trickle down," I have heard and read an expression with the same meaning, but put in a more earthy way. It is "feeding the sparrows by feeding the horses," or "feeding the sparrows by feeding the mules first."

I don't know where it comes from—could it be kin to V.O. Key's big mules in his book on Southern politics? Key described or quoted someone as describing the big businesses (in Alabama, I think) as "big mules."

> Ivan Swift
> Washington, D.C.

trying too hard

"I'll try and do that." That means: "I'll try to do that." So why not say "I'll try to do that"?

*See "woodshed blues."

Ah, but *try and* has become an idiom, say the roundheels of rhetoric. Never mind that *try and do* can be glossed, as David Jenness of Palo Alto suggests, as in: "I'll try, and by virtue of trying am likely to be able to do that."

I think the *try and* construction is sloppy English and stands correction. The trying is not usually a separate deed from the doing. If *try to* is what you mean, say what you mean.

Whenever anyone uses the pressure of usage to force you to accept the nonsensical and swallow the solecism, here's what to tell them: "Try and make me." (That is a time *try and* is acceptable, because it mocks tough-guy slang.)

Sorry, I think you've missed the nuances in "try and do it" and "try to do it." "Try and do it" means that the act will be attempted and accomplished! "Try to do it" means "I'll make the attempt but nothing is sure about the result." (Also "try to do it" has the fine feel of "okay I'll try it your way, you clod.") "Try and do it" means I will do it with a whole heart and true effort. "Try to do it" has the halfhearted sound of "maybe it'll work and then again . . ."

Eleanor A. Jones
Plainfield, New Jersey

In your article paragraph four contains a sentence beginning "Whenever anyone uses the pressure of usage . . ." and ending with ". . . here's what to tell them." Please—don't you, of all people, succumb to this lamentable tendency.

David Randolph
New York, New York

You and I are in agreement that try and *is a sloppy vulgarism for* try to. *Permit me, however, to take issue with one thing that you said in your article: "The trying is not usually a separate deed from the doing." I submit to you that the trying and the doing are indeed and necessarily separate.*

The to *in* try to *may be viewed as a synonym for* toward. *Thus "I will try to do it" may be restated as "I will make an effort toward doing it." Try to implies uncertainty. One may or may not be successful at what one tries to do. If one is certain of being successful,* try *is redundant: "I will do it," not "I will try to do it." Whatever may be the intention of the speaker, the words* try and *mean the successful performance of two separate actions: trying and doing. There is no logical possibility of an unsuccessful attempt.* Try and, *therefore, is a redundancy.*

Robert A. Barrett
Professor of Languages
Suffolk County Community College
Selden, New York

tsk force

"How do you pronounce *tsk, tsk,* the reproving noise of old novels?" asks James MacGregor of New York. "Is it a clenched-teeth, open-lipped cluck, or a spoken 'tisk, tisk'?"

This is not an advice-to-the-wordworn column, but I'll address that question. (I often write my address across questions, and when nobody is listening, I "speak to" questions; they never talk back.)

When you hear a story that makes you want to cluck sympathetically, the way to do it properly is to go "tsk, tsk"—thereby making a reduplicated clucking sound. A cluck is the drawing of air through the teeth, and it seems to make people who hear it feel better.

When referring to that clucking sound, however, or when mocking such an expression of sympathy, you turn the "tsk" sound into a word: *tisk.* The expression *tisk, tisk,* with the audible comma, is a sarcastic slap at the clucking sound and means "I'm not sorry at all."

While isking around, we should take care to preserve the vanishing *s* in *asterisk.* The little typographical flower that sends you down to the footnote is not, as some say, an "asterick." People who say that also say "ek cetera," as they bunk into each other.

Other pronunciation queries and ukases:

"On the spoken word—when did 'shake' replace 'sheek' for pronouncing the oily one: shiek?" asks Vi Hyland of Nassau County, New York. In American use, "sheek" was the standard pronunciation, as any singer of "The Sheik of Araby" will tell you. That explains the misspelling in Mrs. Hyland's note—if it were supposed to be pronounced "sheek," it would be spelled *shiek,* like *shriek.* But it is spelled *sheik,* from the Arabic *shaikh,* pronounced "shake," which the British have been doing all along. (The Arabic word has a scraping sound at the end, called a voiceless velar fricative, which we can safely ignore.)

In recent years, Americans have been adopting the British pronunciation, which is closer to the Arabic (though the Brits don't go for that little "kh" fricassee at the end). As a result, pun-loving headline writers have given up on *radical sheik* and turned instead to *fair sheik.*

In another development, the "see-for-she" substitution is rampant on television. Phil Donahue, the Moral Majority's least favored sex therapist, pronounces *controversial* as "contro-ver-seeul," rather than "controvershul," which Mrs. L. Neumetzger of Newburgh, New York, finds abrasive. In the same way, elitist newscasters knock the "she" out of *negotiate* in their chi-chi pronunciation, "nego-see-ations." "She" is right; "see" is incorrect and an affectation.

Like "processees." The plural of *process,* a vogue word in diplomacy, ought to be *processes,* pronounced "PRAH-cessuz." (British is "PRO-cessuz," but the first syllable is not what's bugging me.) For no good reason, language snobs have been pronouncing the last syllable "ease," as if on the analogy of *crisis* and its plural, *crises.* "The same is true for *emphasis, diagnosis, prosthesis* and many other words ending in *is,*" writes Dene Walters, M.D., in the *Journal of the American Medical Association,* "but not for *process,* or for *abscess* either; two of them are *abscesses,* not 'absces-sees.' " Although some laid-back lexicographers may accept anything, I stand with this Wilmington, Delaware, physician, who correctly points out that while the plural of *basis* is "base-eez," the plural of *base* remains "base-uz."

Which brings us to the Great Chemotherapy Debate. Is it "kem-o," as in *chemist,* or "kee-mo," as in the endearment that Tonto used to direct at the Lone Ranger? Logic suggests "kem-o"; dictionaries prefer it; it is "correct." Yet most people I know, including doctors, pronounce the word coined by Paul Ehrlich in 1907 as "kee-mo"; curious. Why?

Frank Turaj, dean of arts and sciences at American University, holds that "the preceding consonant alters the vowel that follows in favor of the sound that is most natural to pronounce." He says that "kee-mo" is easier to pronounce than "kem-o".* You must set the back of your throat to make the "k" and then open your jaw a bit more to make the "eh" sound than to make the "ee" sound. (It is impossible for a man wearing a tie to try this experiment.) Professor Turaj's view of vowels snuggling up to preceding consonants is illustrated by *woman:* The original "woe-man" changed to "wuman" because it is easier to pronounce, as did the plural "woe-men" to "wimen." So that's why it will be "kee-mo-therapy," Keemosabe. The current dictionary preference will be short-lived.

"In *short-lived,* the second word should rhyme with *dived,*" reports Frederic Cassidy, director-editor of the *Dictionary of American Regional English,* "though a great many people rhyme it with *sieved,* as if it were the past tense of the verb *live.* But that makes bad syntax, since *short* is an adjective, not an adverb, as it would have to be to modify a verb."

The man from *DARE* points out that *-lived* goes back to the noun *life,* which is modified by the adjective *short.* The suffix *-ed* is not the verbal suffix (as in "You haven't lived until you get this right") but a second suffix which means "having" (as in "Reader interest in extended explanations is having a short life"). The *f* becomes *v* by normal phonetic process, as more than one *wife* becomes *wives,* and more than one *life* becomes *lives.*

Therefore, we should use the long "eye" in *short-lived.* Mnemonic: If you spend every night jiving in dives, you'll be short-lived. Or: A man who keeps marrying tiny women will be known as "short-wived." (Tisk, tisk.)

*See "vehement objection."

I am perplexed by the statement about short-lived. *If I understand correctly, Mr. Cassidy is saying that* short-lived *may be divided into two words in order to determine its correct pronunciation.*

According to the Merriam-Webster Dictionary, short-lived *is an adjective meaning "of short life or duration." It is an adjective compound and cannot be divided into separate words, or parts of speech, as Mr. Cassidy suggests. Although the* -lived *of* short-lived *may be derived from the noun* life, -lived *is not a noun.* Short- *is not modifying* -lived. *Rather,* short-lived *is one word and it can be either an adjective or a predicate adjective.*

Okay, then, maybe I am missing the point. Perhaps what Mr. Cassidy really means is that -lived *should be pronounced with a long* i *because the adjective* live *is pronounced with a long* i. *If that's the case, why isn't the adjective* live-long *pronounced with a long* i? *Can this compound adjective be separated into two words to explain the reason? Is* live- *somehow a masquerading verb? Or is* livelong *merely an adjective compound that happens to be pronounced with a short* i?

As to the pronunciation of short-lived, *the* Merriam-Webster Dictionary *gives either long or short* i *as acceptable, although the long* i *is preferred. In the (ahem) long run, I think Mr. Cassidy insinuates that the long* i *is the only acceptable pronunciation, and that an adjective compound can be divided into separate parts of speech to explain its pronunciation.* DARE *I complain?*

Virginia Bready
Spencerport, New York

About long- and short-lived: Tell me, how do they hire dictionary editors these days? Can there exist a regional English in which "short" is denied adverbial status? Indeed, that editor's astonishing statement brought me up short!

As you probably realize, many common monosyllabic adjectives can correctly be used adverbially, "slow-moving" is an example.

Still, I grant you, "long-lived" does seem to stem from "long-lifed," and in the US the "eye" vowel is overwhelmingly predominant. In Britain however the "lived" is apprehended as past participle of "live," and the word is—I should say— invariably pronounced accordingly. Can 50 million Britons be wrong, any more than 200-odd million Americans? I say then that both pronunciations are acceptable. This transatlantic discrepancy no doubt will be pointed out in some "primmer" or "preyemer."

Bravo for "processēs," an old bugbear of mine. And likewise down with "chēmotherapy," and nuts to Mr Turaj for his unconvincing dēmo.

Ian Graham
Cambridge, Massachusetts

PS. Were you trained in law? If so you may know the old term "longest liver," meaning survivor (in wills etc.). The term may argue against the "long-lifed" origin.

On pronunciation, let me draw your attention to my favorite entry in Webster's

2nd ed. Orthoepy is, as we all know, the "art of uttering words correctly; correct or accepted pronunciation of words." But note: "The dictionaries from Walker (c. 1800) have nearly all preferred or ´tho-e-py, *but the accentuation* or-tho ´e-py *is perhaps more usual in actual present good usage."*

When doctors disagree, they can at least all pronounce the name of their profession. But wait; is it med-sin, or med-i-sin?

So, if sheik were supposed to be pronounced "sheek," it would be spelled "shiek," huh? How then do you account for the "ee" pronunciation of leisure, seize, and weird? And Keith and Leigh? Are they to be pronounced "Kayth" and "Lay"? Why not just admit that there is no rhyme or reason to the spelling or pronunciation of some English words?

> Mrs. R.W. Dixon
> Weston, Connecticut

"Tsk" or "tisk" is neither a word nor a cluck. I remember when we read comics aloud in the '40s how funny it was when someone pronounced "tsk, tsk" phonetically, because I knew very well that the word was merely an attempt to duplicate a sound my grandmother used to make when she might otherwise have said "land sakes" or "dear me" or "tut tut." She did it by pressing her tongue against the gum just behind her top front teeth and drawing it quickly back, just as you might do to get rid of something stuck between your teeth. Try it; it's more of a rapid hiss in reverse than a cluck. I always thought a cluck was the popping sound you make when you make a vacuum between your tongue and the roof of your mouth and then force them apart.

> Walter Darby Bannard
> Princeton, New Jersey

Your recent piece on the word "asterisk," which is mispronounced "asterik" by those who (unlike you and me) are ill-informed on such matters, reminded me of a little poem familiar to all boys of my era. (Present Age 76 plus.) It runs:

> *Mary had a pair of skates*
> *Upon the ice to frisk.*
> *Wasn't she a foolish girl*
> *Her little *?*

> Richard R. Levie
> New York, New York

In dealing with the Great Chemotherapy Debate, it seems to me that you put the emphasis on the wrong syl-la´-ble.

My Random House *dictionary lists the preferred pronunciation of the word* chemotherapy *with the first syllable as /kĕm/, but the second syllable is listed phonetically as /ə/,—schwa, not /ō/. The first syllable /kĕm/ gets secondary stress, and since /ĕ/ is a stressed form of /ə/, it blends with the /ə/ of the second syllable, posing no problem, (/kĕm'ə·ther´ə·pe/).*

Your pronunciation, /kē'mō·ther´ə·pē/, uses /ō/ in the second syllable. In this case, the first syllable /kē/, which also has secondary stress, seems to me to be more comfortable and easier to say with the /ō/.

(Mrs.) Clare Vann
Commack, New York

As far as those plurals in -es are concerned, why not point out the very simple rule that should do away with most of the confusion on the part of half-literate language snobs and non-snobs alike?: It all depends on how far Anglicized the usually Greek word had become before it entered our language via Latin and perhaps, as in the case of "base," via French or something else. Add the English -s or -es, pronounce "-uz"; substitute -es for Latin third-declension -is, pronounce "-eez."

Ursula Schoenheim
Chairman and Professor, Department of
Classical and Oriental Languages
Queens College
Flushing, New York

The sound represented by "Tsk, tsk" in the old novels is made by pushing the tip of the tongue against the base of the front teeth of the lower jaw in a bed of saliva then snapping the tongue tip upward, thus bursting a partial vacuum and making the sound.

It's impossible to transliterate such a sound. "Tsk" merely gives readers a clue as to what kind of mouth sound is intended.

To actually say "tisk, tisk" is an affectation of the semiliterate who obviously never heard the sound that the old novels try to represent as "tsk, tsk." It's easier to make the sound itself.

Human communication includes many mouth sounds that defy transliteration. These include giggles, moans, screams and varieties of the flatulent Bronx cheer, including the Archie Bunker type.

Edward A. Morse
Port Washington, New York

You are quite wrong in assuming, in spite of the spelling, that the original sound in the first syllable of woman *and* women *was "woe."*

The original forms of these words in Old English were wīfman *and* wīfmen. *They were pronounced "weefman" and "weefmen." Wifman means "female human."*

In the course of the Middle Ages, the "f" sound was lost and the long "ee" sound became the short "ih" sound. In the singular this "ih" was reduced to "uh," but the sound remained in the plural.

There were many ways to spell these two forms of the word in Middle English. In the singular it was spelled wifman, wymmon, wummon, wyman, wiman, *and* woman. *In the plural it was spelled* wifmen, wimmen, wymmen, wummen, *and* women.

The forms with wo *have survived. Under Norman French influence, the letter* o *was often used to represent the "uh" sound, especially next to a* w.

I think that wimmen *is a better phonetic spelling in the plural than is your* wimen, *but you are in good company. Queen Elizabeth I spelled it* wimen.

Connor P. Hartnett
Department of English
Saint Peter's College
Jersey City, New Jersey

Hartnett is essentially correct in his description of the development of the word woman, *although he necessarily oversimplifies. Clearly, though, the first syllable was never pronounced (w ō), except in jocular allusion to a fancied derivation from* woe man *(and* wee men *for the plural).*

As for the change of spelling from u *to* o, *John W. Clark, in his study* Early English *(Andre Deutsch, 1957), suggests that it was probably a graphic device. In the writing of that period, certain characters (i, u, n, m, w) were made simply by one, two, or three upright strokes (called* minims*), with no connecting strokes between them and no dot over the* i. *And so a cluster such as* wu *(five consecutive minims) could be variously misread as* mu, um, imi, *etc. Because* o *did, in fact, have the sound of* u *in some French dialects at that time, French scribes tended, in the interest of clarity, to substitute* o *for* u *when it was accompanied by other minims, and English scribes began to imitate that practice. That is how Old English* sune *became Middle English* sone *(both pronounced* soon'ə*), which became Modern English* son. *Incidentally, a pronunciation for* woman *in which the* o *rhymes with that of* son *was one of the variants in the 16th and 17th centuries, but it now survives only as a rare dialectal variant.*

Sincerely,
David B. Guralnik
Vice President and Editor in Chief
Simon & Schuster New World Dictionaries
Cleveland, Ohio

twenty hundred

In an economic address, President Reagan pointed to Social Security funding as being endangered in the year 2030. He pronounced the number as "two-thou-sand-thirty."

Similarly, most moviegoers pronounced Stanley Kubrick's film *2001: A Space Odyssey* as "two-thousand-and-one."

Dan Woog of Westport, Connecticut, asked why: "Using past practice as our guide, one hundred years after 'nineteen-thirty' should be 'twenty-thirty.' And one hundred years after 'nineteen-oh-one' should be the year 'twenty-oh-one.' "

The man who thinks twenty is grand is willing to grant that the year 2000 need not be called "twenty hundred," but argues that usagists should prepare now for the language of future dates—just as check printers will have to, if checks remain in use.

My preference in dating, come the millennium, is "two thousand" for the year beginning after midnight, December 31, 1999, and "twenty-oh-one" for the following year. "Two thousand and one" may sound mysterious and futuristic today, but by the time we get there, it will be a laborious mouth-filler. So it will be twenty-oh, Daddy-o, no matter what Presidents in one thousand, nine hundred and eighty-one say.

I like Mr. Woog's conclusion: "Thanks for your prompt attention to this matter."

You stumbled badly in stating that the next millennium will begin at the onset of the year 2000. Since there was no year Zero A.D., centuries and millennia end rather than start with the even hundreds. Just as you don't have a dollar without the hundredth penny, you don't have a century without the hundredth year. Thus the next millennium will commence in the year 2001 (however you choose to pronounce it). I suspect, however, that most people, abetted by the inveterately gun-jumping media, will indulge in all manner of millennial hoopla on 1 Jan. 2000 —and they will all be wrong. But at least you spelled millennium *with two n's, for which two cheers.*

Caldwell Titcomb
Auburndale, Massachusetts

Dear Bill:

Gotcha. You wrote: "My preference in dating, come the millennium, is 'two thousand' for the year beginning after midnight, Dec. 31, 1999. . . ."

Unfortunately, the millennium will not begin for another 366 days, on January 1, 2001. Figure it out: The first day of the first century was January 1, 1; the last day, December 31, 100; the first day of the second century was January 1, 101, etc.

A further analogy to your point: The Battle of Hastings was fought in "ten-sixty-six," not "one-thousand-sixty-six."

> Yours,
> Paul [Paul Hoffman]
> New York, New York

The truth is—if the 20th century is a trustworthy guide—nobody'll say "two-thousand-oh-one" OR "twenty-oh-one" past the month of January, 2001. From February on, it'll be "oh one" and it'll keep up the shorthand till December, '09. Yes?

> Helene Hanff
> New York, New York

Oh, no! No oh in twenty-oh-one, twenty-oh-two through twenty-oh-nine.

Here is the way we did it in the first decade of the present century. My father was graduated from Harvard in nineteen-two (not nineteen-oh-two); my parents to be were married in nineteen-eight (not nineteen-oh-eight); I arrived in nineteen-nine (not nineteen-oh-nine). Nineteen-ten follows a natural progression.

The omission of the awkward oh made the year easier to say; it never caused misunderstandings as far as I can recall.

Often my father's class of '02 was vocalized aught-two. For the coming century I prefer oh-two.

> Clarence A. McCarthy
> Center Sandwich, New Hampshire

The year 2000 is the last year of the 20th Century. The year 2001 is the first year of the first decade of the 21st Century, and the first year of the second millennium.

> Thomas A. Lesser
> American Museum–Hayden Planetarium
> New York, New York

I rarely agree with Mr. Reagan, but 2030 is "two thousand thirty" and 2001 is "two thousand and one" (or two thousand one). As zero is naught a letter, O is not a number. Mr. Reagan won't have to worry much about it, and maybe neither you nor I, but the first decade of the next century may all go for naught if people insist on calling the noble zero O.

Start your crusade now to return zero to its rightful place as the foundation of our numbering system. O is naught but the 15th letter of our alphabet.

> *Allen Amsbaugh*
> *Menlo Park, California*

When you state your preference for what to call "the year beginning after midnight, December 31, 1999" to be "twenty-oh-one," it seems to me a needless overlooking of the word "zero." It seems important that we should keep alive the numerical concept that "zero" represents.

A more proper choice on how to pronounce the years of the next century would be: Two thousand, two thousand one, two thousand two, two thousand three, etc. Or: Twenty hundred, twenty one, twenty two, twenty three, etc.

If we have to manually indicate the years, there should be no problem to indicate: 2000, 2001, 2002, 2003, etc.

In our increasingly alpha-numeric society, to confuse the letter "o" with the numeral "zero" does both a disservice. We must try to remember that "zero" really does stand for something, even if it's nothing.

> *Kevan L. Brown*
> *Des Moines, Iowa*

upscale, *see* scaling the depths

v-hicks

The airport in Atlanta is a wondrous place where you can pull your bungie-wrapped shlepper* onto lower-level shuttle transports and be whisked to the far reaches of the terminal. Aboard the train, the recorded voice telling you where to get off has a distinct southern accent, which is enjoyable. It refers to the train as a "vehicle," pronouncing it not "VEE-uh-cul," as most people do, but "vee-HICK-el."

In the Army, "vee-HICK-el" was used, I was told, because the word came across more clearly over a field radio; perhaps because of this military dissemination, the southern pronunciation is growing.

*See "shlepper and bungie."

"Atlanta's location on the southernmost edge of the South Midland dialect area," reports Joan Hall, associate editor of the *Dictionary of American Regional English*, "makes this an expectable pronunciation there."

The word is rooted in the Latin *vehere,* to carry, just as is *vehement,* meaning "carried away with emotion," although nobody says "ve-HEEM-ent." I suspect the usage of "vee-HICK-el" will grow, because the word sounds punchier and more authoritative than vowel-joined "VEE-uh-cul."*

The goochie-goochie-goo construction (rhymes with "TICK-el") is not limited to subterranean transports, but is sometimes applied to magazine pieces: "The same kind of variation is found in the word *article,"* writes the woman from *DARE.* When I write about Bert Lance's campaign for the governorship of Georgia, I hope he enjoys the ar-TICK-el.

On the pronunciation of vehicle, *as frequently heard in the South: My company uses the word* vehicle *interchangeably with* unit *and* truck, *to describe all of our rented and leased equipment. Many of our employees pronounce it "vee-HICK-el" and after reading your explanation I realized that by and large, these individuals are Southerners or had spent years there before moving to our Parsippany, N. J., offices.*

> *Rayna E. Becker*
> *Director of Fleet Assets, Hertz Truck Division*
> *Parsippany, New Jersey*

"Vehicle, article . . ." etc. I wonder whether it is of any linguistic significance that these words derive from Latin roots with stronger suffixes which accordingly have the emphasis on the second rather than the first syllable? Moreover, whereas romance languages have retained four syllables (sp. vehiculo, artículo, fr. véhicúle but article), German knows both "Vehikel" and "Artikel" and accents the second syllable in both cases. Of all the languages that have adopted these words, English is the only one, to my knowledge, that places the accent on the first syllable and this, apparently, is shifting in the south.

Of course, accents shift according to the region in England and in America, with American generally preferring the first (e.g., laboratory and others).

> *(Mrs.) Lu Fenton*
> *New York, New York*

*See "vehement objection."

As a native East Tennesseean and South Midlander, I am quite familiar with the typical pronunciation of vehicle *and other words such as* police, motel, *and* insurance *that are frequently cited as having first-syllable stress in South Midland speech. While this is true, it is not the case that the stress shifts from the second syllable to the first. Rather, the first syllable receives primary stress as well as the second syllable. I am quite sure that the pronunciation "vee-HICK-el" is an impossible one. On the other hand, "VEE-HICK-el" is our typical pronunciation of the word, with each of the first two syllables receiving primary stress. Likewise, our pronunciations are "PO-LICE," "MO-TEL," and "IN-SUR-ance." I am quite sure too that Joan Hall will agree with me on this.*

Michael Montgomery
Assistant Professor, Department of English
University of South Carolina
Columbia, South Carolina

vehement objection

Sometimes I get the creepy sensation that this column is being graded. When a Miss Thistlebottom writes in to give the lie to *lay,* or when a sharp-eyed copy editor (never met a blunt-eyed copy editor) fulminates about the *which* which should have been a *that* (as that *which* should have been), my reaction is serene: They are playing into my hands. Fiorello La Guardia used to say, "When I make a mistake, it's a beaut"; when I make a mistake, it's another column.

Of late, however (which has a more scholarly feel than *but lately* and avoids opening a paragraph with *but*), I have been receiving mail from some of the giants in the field of linguistics, guys who could chew up Chomsky on the archaeology of underlying structures.

One such is Karl V. Teeter, professor of linguistics at Harvard. When it comes to pronunciation, nobody tangles with Teeter. He is a thundering curmudgeon: irascible, opinionated, brilliant, intimidating, and I wish I had taken his class. When a news clerk comes in holding a letter with tongs, it is likely that Teeter is tottering at full tilt.

When I commented on the pronunciation of *chemotherapy* in the piece called "Tsk Force," quoting a less linguistically prestigious source who speculated that "ee-mo" was easier to say than "e-mo"—something about the sound going across the oral cavity more easily—Professor Teeter blazed away with a denunciation of "subjective fiddle-faddle." He wrote that ease of pronunciation is neither quantifiable nor deducible from frequency of use. What's more, he pointed out to my source, *"ee* is a vowel made in the highest position of the front of the tongue, *o* in the midback area. Since *e* is mid-front, there's less distance to travel in 'e-mo.' Should be easier, eh? ... When the phonetics is put into more objective terms, the argument disappears."

Then Professor Teeter made a more general point that addresses (indeed, stamps and mails) a concern I have, as I issue my own ukases to a public avid for correctness. "Linguistics is a study which in certain areas, such as phonetics, has accumulated some simple and incontrovertible facts. Yet these have not noticeably penetrated to the public. Ha, linguists are lousy teachers, you say. Could be, but we're also few, and greatly outnumbered by those who speak from within a normative tradition which is largely based on social snobbery and careless of fact.

"My friend Mr. Safire, whom I regularly castigate by letter, often transcends this tradition, and I find he purveys a sufficient degree of truth to make his error worth pointing out. A large number of these errors of his, perhaps the majority, come from not knowing basic linguistic facts. . . . When I reflect on the general ignorance of the public, which may be the fault of us linguists but is nevertheless frustrating, and find it deepened and confirmed by this sort of negligence of fact . . . I get quite explicably irascible."

What bothers Professor Teeter most are the guesses, hunches, speculations, and fancies in which many language shamans like me indulge as we grope for explanations that the language scientists often do not have. Are these shots in the dark really stabs in the back? Is a subjective reach a disservice?

As every asker of rhetorical questions knows, the answer is no. Or at least I think not. For example, in reporting in "V-Hicks" that the southern pronunciation of *vehicle*—as "vee-HICK-el"—was growing, I speculated that the Army field telephonists liked that pronunciation, since it was easier to shout. I predicted that the "hick" would triumph because the word sounded "punchier and more authoritative than vowel-joined 'VEE-uh-cul.' "

Here comes the news clerk with the tongs and the Teeter letter.

"You're reaching again. . . . For 'vee-HICK-el' there is a perfectly good pseudoderivative in my speech, and I dare say yours, namely *vehicular.* The word *vehicle* is quasi-learned vocabulary anyhow, and the 'southern' pronunciation you cite is easily explainable as a back-formation.

"True or not, I object once again," writes the nearest we have to a Mr. Pronunciation in America, "to your speculative explanations, which really don't explain. That the pronunciation with the accent on the second syllable 'sounds punchier and more authoritative' sounds like self-hypnosis to me, though it may just be that you're more sensitive at such judgements than I am. . . . As usual, I do not see that subjective impressions, even those of clever people, are any help at all to explain matters of this sort. Furthermore, they are often not needed, for data relevant to an explanation is frequently found in the grammar or structure of the language, as in this case. Same old tune, I know. Cheers."

I think that is a lot of objective fiddle-faddle (a reduplication of *fiddlesticks*). Professor Teeter is to be hailed for his willingness to accept "data . . . is," and it is not for the likes of me to prescribe an old-fashioned spelling of *judgment* to the denizens of the great academy on the Charles River, but to be faulted for an outasight insight like the southern usage of "vee-HICK-el" based on military dissemination is to be wounded to the quick. (That sentence would have been much stronger had I avoided the passive construction, but the powers that be are forcing me to write on a video screen and I have not yet found the "simple declarative sentence" button, which accounts for all the parenthetical corrections in this piece.) In the language dodge, a cat can look at a king; hunches, or hypotheses, should be a stimulus to scientists.

I do not make all that many mistakes, Professor Totter, thanks to my own care and the assiduous cross-checking of Blunteye, my copy editor. But if I err (pronounced "air" because the "err" in *error* makes the speaker look like a duck), let it be in the cause of pushing beyond the horizons of the linguistic empire's empiricism.

A final word, Tooter: Belay those nice little notes you send about my investigations of such lingo as *cosmeticsese*. Don't start going soft now. Remember that the only acceptable mood for a curmudgeon is dudgeon, and the higher the better.

Further on your theory about the rejection of "VEE-uh-cul" for vehicle: *English-speakers don't like vowels without consonants between, and are constantly reshaping words to avoid such combinations; hence the spelling pronunciation with* h *is to be expected. Some current examples:*

> *nuclEAr becomes nucular*
> *medIEval becomes medevial*
> *famillArity becomes famililarity*
> *peculIArity becomes peculularity*
> *reALtor and reALty become relator and relaty*

Here's an item from your usage that's worth a note: "What BOTHERS Teeter most ARE the guesses" etc. That what *doesn't seem to be able to make up its mind whether it is singular or plural. If* what (that which) *is the subject of the verb, then whether the predicate nouns are singular or plural shouldn't make any difference. In Spanish and French it does make a difference—a plural to either side of the copula almost always forces plurality in the verb, and that practice is gaining ground in English. People who would probably not write or say "What succeeds are computers" will, when enough foreign matter intrudes between subject and verb, make the verb plural. You can argue of course that there is an inversion here: "The guesses are what bothers"; but I'm doubtful.* *

> *Dwight Bolinger*
> *Palo Alto, California*

*Better examples:
  What he prefers is oranges.
  What I need only one of is pennies.
Francis Christensen has a piece on this, American Speech *30 (1955) 30–37, "Number concord with 'what' clauses."*

And I always thought that ERR *rhymes with* FUR*!*

> *Dr. Arnold Gallub*
> *New York, New York*

> *You seemed to tĕtter-totter*
> *In Sunday's mention of Karl Teeter.*
> *Did you mean to tut-tut(er)*
> *This learned Harvard tutor*
> *And his erudition tatter*
> *To make your readers titter?*
> *Or are you really his academic touter?*

> *Fred Jacobson*
> *Flushing, New York*

Although a physician by profession, I have a long-standing interest in languages and linguistics and I am au courant with developments in modern, scientific syntax and phonology. I doubt I could "chew up Chomsky" but I am conversant with both his work and other studies in the spirit of generative grammar.

Teeter ridicules your suggestion that the pronunciation vèhícle arose because it sounds more "authoritative" or "military" than véhicle, calling your idea "unscientific." I should like to point out that Teeter's own explanation as a back-formation from vehicular is 1) based on a discredited concept of historical change and 2) unsupportable when viewed from the perspective of current phonological theory.

English phonology is quite intricate, and many derivational paradigms involve shifts of stress and changes in vowel quality. In this regard, véhicle-vehicular is a regular manifestation of the same phonological processes which produce

corpuscle	*corpuscular*
ventricle	*ventricular*
peduncle	*peduncular*
testicle	*testicular*
oracle	*oracular*
spectacle	*spectacular*
vesicle	*vesicular*

The changes in the quality of the vowels are direct, automatic consequences of the "stress shift" by virtue of regular rules which I will not go into here. How is the "stress shift" accounted for? Oversimplifying greatly, English stresses the penultimate syllable of polysyllabic nouns. (I ignore the distinction between primary and lower degrees of stress—these are determined by other regular rules which have no bearing on the matter at hand.)

I will refer to this generalization (though it is obviously incomplete as stated) as the Noun Stress Rule. Before the Noun Stress Rule can apply, however, certain suffixes are declared "extrametrical." That is a fancy way of saying that they are ignored by subsequent stress placement rules. Many languages exhibit extrametrical affixes. It appears to be a linguistic universal that such extrametricality applies ONLY when the affix appears in final position, NOT when followed by another affix. And the extrametricality does NOT apply to the same syllable when it is part of the root or stem, rather than an affix. The words in (1) demonstrate that the suffix /kul/ (from a Latin diminutive, historically) is extrametrical, as is the adjective-forming suffix /ar/. The working of these rules, and a demonstration of how extrametricality works, is shown in the following derivations:

> (2)   a. /testi-kul/   b. /testi-kul-ar/   c. /pumpernikul/

Extrametricality applies to the suffixes /kul/ and /ar/ when in final position, but not to the syllable at the end of "pumpernickel" where it is not an affix but part of the root. The results of extrametricality are:

> (3)   a. /testi-(kul)/   b. /testi-kul-(ar)/   c. No Change

Now the noun stress rule applies, giving penultimate stress but ignoring parenthesized material:

> (4)   a. /tésti-(kul)/   b. /testí-kul-(ar)   c. /pumperníkul/

Later, regular rules which are not relevant to our discussion, then supply and adjust primary and secondary levels to the stress contours and specify the exact articulation of the vowels, producing the correct results.

It is clear by analogy with the above derivations that if one truncates the suffix /-ar/ from vehicular and applies the usual rules, the resulting pronunciation is véh-

icle, analagous to téstícle. *To justify* vèhícle *as a truncated form of vehicular, one would have to postulate that the regular application of extrametricality and the noun stress rule were, miraculously, suspended. If this were true, it would be the first attested instance of such a change.*

Having debunked Teeter's "back formation" analysis and replaced it with a better explanation, what can I say about "authoritativeness" and "militariness"? Linguists have always noted the arbitrary, idiosyncratic nature of morphological reanalysis: why "vehicle" but not "spectacle"? There is nothing semantically diminutive about the latter. Currently, no "scientific" explanations are available.

In Isaac Newton's day, acceptable science did not include any theoretical equipment to handle abstract action at a distance of the kind Newton postulated in his law of gravity. Progress in science comes from finding ways to make intuitive hunches "precise." As it stands, your "authoritative" concept has no meaning: one could not even begin to argue its merits. But it may contain the seed of a sociolinguistic idea. Perhaps "authoritative" or "military" could be defined objectively (somehow). And with proper investigation it might indeed turn out that such factors can be shown to explain why re-analysis occurs in vehicle but not spectacle. So Teeter's condemnation of your suggestion is unwarranted. Granted, what you say is not "scientific." But it certainly could provide the impetus for a program of scientific investigation. All important scientific concepts began as vague intuitions!

Clyde B. Schechter, M.D.
New York, New York

As a child, I learned to spell "judgement" with two "e"'s—one before the "m" and one after. Despite frequent arguments with friends and teachers, I have continued to use this spelling because I believe it to be the better of the two.

You attack this spelling on the grounds that it is new and, hence, inferior. In your words, "it is not for the likes of me to prescribe an old-fashioned spelling of judgment.

"Old-fashioned," Mr. Safire? In Paradise Lost, *Milton writes,*

> *But whom send I to judge them? whom but thee*
> *Vicegerent Son, to thee I have transferr'd*
> *All Judgement, whether in Heav'n, or Earth, or Hell.*

John D. Jump, the editor, notes that "Milton carefully controlled the spelling and punctuation in the printed versions of his poems—especially Paradise Lost. *The seventeenth-century spelling and punctuation have therefore been preserved in this edition." Christopher Marlowe, in the opening scene of* The tragicall History of Doctor Faustus, *writes,*

> *To patient Iudgements we appeale our plaude,*
> *and speake for Faustus in his infancie:*

His editor, C.F. Tucker Brooke, also states that "the text reproduces faithfully, it is believed, that of the most reliable version of each work, except as regards punctuation and capitalization." Chaucer, in the Canterbury Tales, *writes,*

> *In heigh and lowe; and thus, by oon assent,*
> *We been accorded to his jugement.*

In his case, various editions disagree on the spelling, but with regard to the number of "g"'s not "e"'s.

Need I say more? Forgive me if you are indeed quoting Beowulf, *but in my judgement the "old-fashioned spelling" has two "e"'s.*

David Millar
South Plainfield, New Jersey

I understand and applaud the give-and-take relationship between you and Dr. Teeter—you are both worthy symbiotes.

Yet I would remind the doctor that it is "subjective impressions" that originally impel "clever people" to investigate areas in which they're ignorant, and that as long as they are conscientious, such people's initial errors will be corrected by the results of their inquiries, which may even eventually furnish knowledge that is scientifically *valid.*

Maybe the doctor didn't "mean" or "intend" to discourage a compulsion that is one of the bases of science itself; maybe he only meant to inhibit overzealous amateurs from prematurely ejaculating their findings, in which case he's guilty of nothing more than not having rigorously thought through his concepts, *a failing which he may be able to improve through consultation with a good syntactician.*

If he doesn't watch it, Dr. Teeter could even put himself in jeopardy of being a word-doctor who is also a tongue-depressor, which amounts to a confusion of objectives (probably resulting from subjective impressions), and in his line of work, that is almost certainly a no-no.

Don Thompson
Rolling Hills Estates, California

Dear Bill:

It's lucky for you you finally found a case among my thundering condemnations where you had a leg to stand on. I really don't object to subjective hunches, and I did allow for usage as a factor in the vee-HICK-el case. But the former ought to be disciplined (as you appear to agree), and the latter will do nothing to tell us how the pronunciation might have originated. In both cases, linguistics can be useful.

Anyhow, thanks for the plug. I'll stop there before this becomes a "nice little note."

> *Karl [Karl V. Teeter]*
> *Professor of Linguistics*
> *Harvard University*
> *Cambridge, Massachusetts*

virgule violation

The integrity of the virgule has been slashed.

At the bottom of most stories in *Time* magazine, bylines appear, looking something like this: "By Edwin Warner. Reported by Anne Constable/Atlanta and Neil MacNeil/Washington."

The virgule is that diagonal line, usually called a slash, that has three meanings: (1) "either," as in *and/or,* or, in tests, *is/is not,* or, in invitations, *will/will not;* (2) "per," as in *feet/second* or *miles/hour;* (3) as the separator of numerals in fractions, such as *1/8.*

Thus, in *Time*'s use of the virgule, "MacNeil/Washington" means "Either MacNeil or Washington," or "MacNeil per Washington" or "MacNeil divided by Washington."

Philip Shaver of Princeton, New Jersey, who noticed this violation of the virgule, asks: "Can you help stamp out/cure this malady before it spreads?"

Sure/gladly. The virgule (pronounced "vur-gyool," from the Latin *virga,* a slender branch) has been seized upon by typists and typesetters as a great space saver—who likes to use a whole comma or a long word like *or* when a virgule will do? The path was cleared for the substitution of the verbalizable *or* by the unspeakable / in the legalistic term *and/or,* which would be hard to say as "and or or." Now we are afflicted by the promiscuous use of virgules.

This has resulted in a case in the New York Supreme Court in Ulster County over the meaning of a virgule. A man made a check payable to "Revel/Miron Ready Mix"; it was endorsed and cashed by Revel and not by Miron Ready Mix. The issue: Could the check be cashed without the endorsement of the co-payee?

The court held that "the symbol (/), or virgule, denotes the disjunctive or alternative. . . . A check made payable to the order of two payees whose names are separated by a diagonal slash . . . [is] properly paid by a bank with the endorsement of only one of the named payees."

In a similar case, the virgule reached a Georgia appellate court and the same decision—that the virgule meant "or"—was upheld. Judge Harold Banke wrote: "During oral argument of this case, appellant's counsel was asked by the court why the maker of the checks did not write the word 'and' between the names of the payees if that was its intention. Counsel's reply was that the checks were written by computer. The court makes no suggestion about changing computers, but it does bring to mind the following: 'To err is human but to really foul things up requires a computer.' Judgment affirmed."

When a diagonal line, or slash, is used to separate numerals, as in ⅛, it is defined as a solidus in both the Oxford English Dictionary *and* Webster's New World Dictionary. *The virgule separates words.*

While others violate the virgule, is it possible that in definition (3) you have slighted the solidus?

Raymond E. Lafferty
Parsippany, New Jersey

In defense of Time *magazine, since the lower portion of a fraction is known as the "denominator," it is not farfetched to use it as a locater, "denominating" the correspondent geographically; the correspondent becomes the "numerator" in this equation, which seems to me not linguistically malaprop, since he can be seen as the "one who counts" in this example.*

Further, in many cases the virgule may stand for the words "out of," as in "4/5 doctors recommend" etc. It implies a relationship but not necessarily a division. This linguistic substitution is entirely appropriate in your citations.

The virgule suffers greater abuse, I feel, in the logo of the "McNeill/Lehrer Report," where it substitutes for a dash. Maybe they were afraid a dash would be taken for a hyphen, inducing some unwary observer to conclude they were one and the same, siamese twins of Scottish-German ancestry.

Dr. Michael Riesman
New York, New York

On virgules: w/ . (from speedwriting?) I've used it notetaking for years, and it's been cropping up in print.

An Anecdote: When I was setting type (by hand—from a case) at the London College of Printing two years ago I needed a virgule (I was in Britain as "US/UK Bicentennial Fellow") and, finding none in the type case, I said to the printsbox supervisor, "I need a slash," to which he replied, "Down the hall and to the right," where I found the men's room. In London "slash" is slang for "piss."

Richard Minsky
Kew Gardens, New York

I must point out what seems to me a serious error in your disquisition on the misuses of the "virgule." Though the word ultimately derives from the Latin virga, *it is already used in the diminutive form as the name of an editorial mark by Tertullian's time. The term* virgula censoria *refers to a possibly spurious passage in an MS.*

To the best of my knowledge, the name "virgule" is used in English only when referring to the figure "/" which appeared in medieval MSS and had the value of either a comma or a caesura. The only specifically modern usage of that term which I recognize, after years of editorial work in trade publishing and newspapers, is the French virgule, *where it is either a comma or a decimal point. "2.2" is read aloud as* deux virgule deux.

A Manual of Style *(University of Chicago Press), the Bible of trade publishing in these matters, refers to the figure "/" only as a solidus and has no entry for virgule. The* OED *mentions only the medieval usage. I grant that I have sometimes received blank stares in return for my using the term "solidus," even among professional editors, but the only alternate term I have found by asking editors, copy editors, proofreaders and compositors in both publishing and newspaper work is "slash." Though the New York Superior Court may employ a former medievalist as informant to the presiding judge in this case, I doubt that the word would make much sense to anyone not trained in French or in advanced Latin or medieval studies.*

Bernard J. Hassan
Jersey City, New Jersey

Your discussion of the virgule brings to mind the fervid discussions of that little mark and of even smaller marks of punctuation among writers and professors (not to speak of writer/professors) in the late 1960's and early 1970's.

The sufficient cause for these discussions was poet Charles Olson's virgule in the opening line of "The Kingfishers":

What does not change / is the will to change.

What the virgule meant, and how it was adopted by Olson's readers/disciples, and how it came to be substituted for the hyphen, dash, colon, or double space in poems great and small, would make a worthy chapter in the history of literary solemnity. (e.e. cummings's virgules, by the way, were used no more idiosyncratically than his other punctuation marks, and therefore his influence cannot be studied so single-markedly as Olson's.)

I have been referred to in print as a poet/teacher, a poet/bureaucrat, a teacher-writer, a hyphenated poet (the word hyphenated *is used in these contexts even by folks who when preparing manuscripts use virgules, e.g., "the hyphenated poet Iamb Trochee and his poet/scoundrel friends." I am now working as Information*

*Officer/Grantsman for a community action agency. I suppose the whole vir-
guling/hyphenization of occupations started with the Industrial Revolution when
moonlighting as a Luddite/miller (or whatever) became possible. At least that is
when Robert Burns, the shepherd-poet, became so beloved that Burns societies
published lists of hyphenated members.*

> Marty Cohen
> Poughkeepsie, New York

*Although you claimed three meanings for the slash, you gave only two: "either"
(although I am sure others will already have pointed out that you meant "or," the
"either" being implied before the entity preceding the slash) and "per." Your third
example, using fractions, still means "per." ⅛ has the same meaning as 1 per 8.
A more precise definition would be "divided by" and I imagine this use of the slash
resulted from the inability of fonts to contain all available fractions (my typewriter
has ½ and ¼ but not $\frac{37}{59}$ and you will note that I now have to skip a line even*

*to accommodate it). "Miles/hour" means miles divided by hours—actually num-
ber of miles divided by number of hours—just as "¼," or "1/4," means 1 divided
by 4.*

*But there is indeed a third (at least) legitimate use for the virgule, and that is
to separate complete entities, indivisible entities, that make up another entity—
and here, I am afraid, the concept is "both/and" (sic) rather than "either/or"
(ditto). Thus, I have a blue-gray tie. It is sort of slate-colored. I also have a
blue/gray/black tie. It is not simply a darker color of slate; the tie's colors are
separate, unblended, and form a pattern.*

> Leonard Marcus
> Lenox, Massachusetts

*You listed three secondary meanings of the virgule and then you heaped ridicule
on* Time *magazine by conforming its byline to those meanings. No defender of
Timestyle I, yet fair is fair: This is strawmanship run amok. / The* Oxford English
Dictionary *reports that in medieval manuscripts, the virgule indicated a caesura
(a sense pause), and it notes that Chaucer, among others, used virgules where
modern editions insert commas. The* American Heritage Dictionary *says the
virgule is used "to indicate the ends of verse lines printed continuously, as in*
Candy / Is dandy*"—surely, an extension of the earlier meaning of a caesura. In
my usage and that of people with whom I associate (editors and English teachers)
the virgule is in fact understood and used today as a caesura, except I think we
would not use that language; we would say, less pretentiously, that a "slash" means
"start a new line" not only in poetry but generally. / Thus here in this letter the*

virgule has a self-evident meaning of "Here is a new paragraph," and in the case of your example from Time, *just as self-evidently at least to me, the byline should be read as follows:*

> Reported by Anne Constable
> Atlanta
> and Neil MacNeil
> Washington

If this meaning is not self-evident to you, I suspect that is because you are too close to your topic and it went out of focus./ I am more surprised that you should cite legal decisions in support of usage. Surely one knows prima facie *that lawyers and judges are incompetent on matters of English usage.*

> R. W. Tucker
> Philadelphia, Pennsylvania

Virgule, indeed. Quit showing off in front of your Princeton readers! Slash/slant say it more graphically. Solidus is impressive, if you must impress. Diagonal is the bed rock noun. Synonyms are not in short supply. Most need no pronunciation guide.

> Howard Kahn
> Managing Editor, School Shop
> Ann Arbor, Michigan

Very funny, those virgules! Below are some more uses of it that are also appropriate in these United States:

normal use	understood meaning
5/28/81	May 28th, 1981 May twenty-eighth, nineteen eighty-one
t/a	trading as
a/k/a	also known as
c/o	care of

> Peter A. Cohn
> Syosset, New York

Aha! I finally got you!
I, my dear sir, am a TYPOGRAPHER. *The machine I use to do my work is called*

a typesetter. *(You would not call a typist a typewriter, nor a machinist a machine —and somehow, "typesetterist" doesn't sound right.)*

There is much precedent for other uses of the virgule than those you mentioned. For instance 212/555-1212 does not *mean "two hundred twelve divided by five hundred fifty-five minus one thousand two hundred twelve"; it is a phone number.*

7/2/81 is not a bi-level equation; it is a date (July 2, 1981, here; February 7, 1981, in Europe).

"How are things in Glocamorra/is that little brook still . . ." does not mean "How are things . . . or is that little brook. . . ." It indicates the verse form for matter being presented in another format.

In the last example only would I grudgingly accept a complaint against my profession—but only because we charge by depth of type, and it is for that reason editors are loathe to set verse line-for-line in text.

Last but not least, you're wrong when you imply (you didn't quite say it) that a comma takes up more space than a virgule. In most alphabets—which we call "fonts" when we want to include the digits and symbols ("pi" characters)—the virgule takes up approximately 25% more horizontal space than a comma.

> *T.H. Richards*
> *President, ILNY Communications & Media Corp.*
> *New York, New York*

---

volunteerism not compulsory

"Mr. Reagan has called for increased volunteerism," goes a U.P.I. story, ". . . and he recently created a 36-member Presidential commission to study volunteerism."

On the other hand, in an A.P. interview with Saul Pett, President Reagan was quoted directly as saying: "Voluntarism . . . more in the sense of the ability at the community level, whatever level, to get together to solve a problem, a community problem—the community charity drives and so forth."

Which is right, *volunteerism* or *voluntarism*? "The two words are used to describe the same concept," writes Emilie Hauser of Flint, Michigan, "that is, that Americans should volunteer more of their time to social services. Perhaps *voluntaryism* is the more correct term."

Voluntaryism, over a century ago, meant the doctrine that churches should be supported not by the state but by voluntary contributions from individuals. *Voluntarism,* first used in 1838, was a variant of that word describing a philosophy; those old meanings remain.

Today, the primary meaning of *voluntarism* is "the maintenance of social-welfare programs through nongovernmental means." Says David Guralnik, editor of the *New World Dictionary:* "These programs are more and more today carried out through a program of *volunteerism,* the use of volunteers who are not paid for their services." *Volunteerism* is the newest coinage; to keep the meanings of related words clear, remember Guralnik's rule:

"*Voluntar(y)ism* is concerned with financial support; *volunteerism,* with the voluntary offering of one's time and services."

Both isms are good. When it comes to correcting your friends on this usage, however, the old Army sergeant's advice may well be taken: Keep your mouth shut and don't.

Walesa's pronunciation

"Help! I must get an answer before I go crazy!" expostulates Matthew Haines of New York. "Ever since Solidarity has been in the news, people in the media keep pronouncing Lech Walesa's name as though there were an *n* in it. Is this correct? Is Walesa's name pronounced 'Walensa'?"

No. It is pronounced "Vawensa."

Start with the *w:* As in many languages, the *w* is pronounced as a *v.* (What is the question to which "9-W" is the answer? "Do you spell your name with a *v,* Mr. Wagner?") Now take the *l:* In Polish, this is an irregular letter with a slash through it that does not exist in English; it sounds like the English *w,* "weh." That gives us "va-weh," and we haven't even finished with the *l.* Wiktor Weintraub, professor emeritus of Polish language and literature at Harvard University, tells me that when followed by an *e,* the nasal quality of the *l* makes the *e* sound like a French *un.*

That takes you to "va-wens," hinting at an *n* but not coming down hard on it. Add a normal *a,* and you have "Vawensa," spelled *Walesa.*

The first irate communication about this will be: "Of course, I know how to pronounce *Walesa,* but what about the hard part—his first name?" That should be easy. That *l* is handled in a manner familiar to speakers of English, and the first part of the name is "leh." The ending is a voiceless velar fricative, according to Mrs. Grazyna Slanda, of the Harvard University Slavic department, whose name is pronounced as spelled. That means that it sounds like the *ch* in Loch Lomond, and if you pronounce that as "lock," drop English immediately and start learning Polish.

You quote Prof. Wiktor Weintraub as saying that, in the Polish name Walesa,
"when followed by an e, *the nasal quality of the* l *makes the* e *sound like a French*

un." This statement, as it stands, is inaccurate on two counts: (1) The sound "l" is classified by phoneticists as a liquid, not a nasal; (2) the Polish nasal "e" (written "ę") is an independent phoneme, is etymologically distinct from oral "e" and is in no sense conditioned by its phonetic environment.

I am the author of A Dictionary of Slavic Word Families *(Columbia University Press, 1975) and am a former senior translator at the United Nations.*

Louis Jay Herman
New York, New York

Your treatment of the pronunciation of Lech Walesa's surname does not quite end it. There are two "e's" in the Polish alphabet; one the conventional "e" which you find in these sentences, the other has a marking beneath it similar to the Spanish cedilla, *or French* cedille, *thus "ę". It is this "ę" in Walesa's name which follows the "w" sounding ł, and which gives it the nasal sound. The closest thing to it in the English language would be the "en" sound in spending.*

Ted Humes
Phoenix, Arizona

I fear that Professor Weintraub was pulling your leg just to see if you would publish a Polish joke in a major newspaper. No doubt, Poles are still laughing their heads off all over the country. The nasal quality of "ł": indeed!

Actually, Walesa *is really* Wałęsa, *with the bar through the l and a hook under the e. The hook indicates a nasalized vowel before a fricative, a homorganic nasal consonant before other consonants, or nothing before l or ł. Since s is a fricative, the ę indicates the sound of in in French: [ē]: [vawēsa]. The n is pronounced only because American speakers seem incapable of producing a simple nasalized vowel without "resolving" it.*

Michael C. Fuller
Associate Professor, French
Department of English, Foreign
    Languages and Philosophy
California State College, Stanislaus
Turlock, California

Regardless of what Professor Weintraub (is the seeming metathesis in his first name a fact or a typo?) may have told you anent Wałęsa, the crucial reason for the mysterious "n" that drives Mr. Haines to desperation (are there no Poles, no libraries in New York?) is absent from your explanation: it is the "inverted cedilla" at the bottom of the "e" which betokens the nasal quality of the vowel and which, in certain phonetic contexts, is tantamount to an added "n." This "nasalization hook" is known to the Poles as "ogonek," i.e., "little tail." It also occurs under "a," which then tends towards the French "on." Most non-Polish printers obviously lack the fonts (and funds) correctly to print Wałęsa and a host of other Polish names and words, and I have often wondered, once even in print, why the Poles don't abandon the ogonek and replace it with a postscript "n." Doing it across the board would leave them stuck, in other phonetic contexts, with a "silent n," so the substitution would have to be selective.

Louis Marck
New York, New York

we wuz robbed

Willie Sutton, the bank robber—known as "Slick Willie" and "Willie the Actor" because of his skillful use of disguises—made an observation of great psychological import toward the end of his career: "I was more alive when I was inside a bank, robbing it, than at any other time in my life."

Was Willie guilty of misusage? Legally speaking, can anybody "rob" a bank or any other place?

"The other night," writes Sybil Hart Kooper, justice of the Supreme Court of New York, "a television commentator said that Robert Redford's apartment had been 'robbed.' Not true. His apartment had been burglarized."

What's the difference? "Robbery is forcible stealing from a person," opines Justice Kooper in an obiter dictum. "Burglary is entering a premises unlawfully for the purpose of committing a crime. As they say in my home town, Brooklyn, 'You can't boigle a poison.' "

It is argued that, in law, *robbery* is a crime against a person while *burglary* is a crime against property (from the Teutonic word for "a fortified place," expressed in Latin as *burgus,* with a possible addition of *latro,* "thief").

That seems like a neat distinction, but what happens when you put your head in a stocking mask, break into somebody's premises with felonious intent, and run smack-dab into the resident? The victim is entitled to claim that he was not only burglarized but robbed, since you committed a crime against his property and himself.

The trick is to remember that the language of law is not necessarily the language of life. In law, *burglary* is limited, as Justice Kooper notes, to unlawful entry with a crime in mind, whether that crime is larceny or some other, and whether or not the attempt is successful; but in layman's language, which is not to be sneered at by lawyers, the word means the successful attempt to steal something. In law, *robbery* is limited to what psychologists like to call hostile interpersonal communication, but in life, that term spreads over both burglary of an empty house and the more personal "yer-money-or-yer-life" action.

"In popular usage," reports David Guralnik, Simon & Schuster's dictionary chief, "the verb to *rob* is used with reference to any kind of theft, including burglary, embezzlement, etc., and, of course, in extended use, it can mean 'to deprive of any thing or right in an unjust way,' so that the manager of a fighter who loses a decision might shout, 'We was robbed.' "

So the language of life follows the law in limiting *burglarize* to theft of property from a place without the owner's knowing it, but it leaves the law in using *rob* to mean stealing from both a person and a place. Slick Willie was correct: Though his crime against the bank may have been legally termed burglary, in proper English he robbed the bank. He was a bank robber, not a bank burglar. I am pleased to be able to exonerate him posthumously.

While at it, let me put in a good word for a back-formation from *burglar,* to *burgle,* which purists have tried to pilfer, steal, purloin, filch, and rifle from the language for more than a hundred years. True, it has a humorous connotation, perhaps because it sounds like *gurgle,* a funny sound unless you're drowning, but *burgle* gets across its message more succinctly than *to enter unlawfully intending to commit a crime,* and it avoids letting the *ize* have it. So let's prioritize *to burgle.*

Justice Kooper had another linguistic beef: "Later in the week, another *doyenne* of the airways referred to a man and his 'common-law wife.' Again, wrong. Common-law marriage ended in New York in 1932. The lady may have been his mistress, his paramour, or even his tootsy, but she was not his common-law wife. . . . Precision in terminology is a requisite in legal pleading. Why not in the media?"

I'll take that case. Why have lawyers killed the distinction between *lawyer* and *attorney*? Writes Gwinn Owens, editor of the Op-Ed page of the *Baltimore*

Evening Sun: "Lawyers are insecure. When I was with the *Providence Journal,* many years ago, there was a proscription on the word *attorney,* unless it applied to *a lawyer who was representing someone.* ('I am his attorney.') But a lawyer is incorrect if you ask him what he does and he says, 'I am an attorney,' and, of course, that is precisely what most lawyers say.

"My own interpretation of the word," holds Mr. Owens, warming to his role before the bar of usage, "is that it is like *friend.* I cannot be a friend, standing alone (unless I'm a Quaker), but I can be a friend of John or Mary. In any case, what is wrong with the word *lawyer* that the entire law profession eschews it?"

Before every new partner of Null, Null & Void is moved to write an impassioned response, think about it: How many business cards of lawyers say *lawyer* and how many say *attorney* or the even more deliciously archaic *attorney at law?* In Shakespeare's *King Henry VI, Part Two,* Dick the butcher did not suggest, "The first thing we do, let's kill all the attorneys." Rarely do I see a candid self-description like "the Lawyers of Hufstedler, Miller, Carlson & Beardsley," in an invitation to a reception for Susan Schaefer, a new partner; most often, somebody hanging out a shingle announces his ascension to "Counselor-at-Law."

At the risk of causing another explosion in Prof. Karl Teeter's class at Harvard, let me suggest that the "oi" sound in *lawyer* may annoy some hoity-toity practitioners.

If precision is the goal, lawyers should confine *attorney* to one who acts for a client: Thus, a lawyer *is* not an attorney, but only *acts* as attorney. Mark Sullivan, who identifies himself as a Public Service Representative for the Harvard Law Library (who wants to be called a *law librarian?*), offers a synonymy that differs from mine and Mr. Owens's: "A lawyer is one who is learned in the law. An attorney is one who has been admitted to the bar and can practice. Therefore, a graduate of a law school is a lawyer, but not necessarily an attorney. The graduate must first pass the bar to be considered an attorney. However, in common usage there is no distinction between the two."

Seems to me that lawyers should be in the business of distinctions. In England, *attorney* has been replaced by *solicitor,* who does all sorts of legal work for clients but does not plead in court, that activity reserved for the *barrister,* a term derived from the railing, or bar, in a courtroom. In America, the barrister is sometimes called a *trial lawyer* or *counselor,* and the nomenclature about the people learned in the law is, as we see, pretty sloppy, but proponents of reform lack advocates.

Samuel Johnson to a friend as quoted by Boswell: "While I do not like to speak ill of any man behind his back, I believe the gentleman is an attorney."

Wm. C. Schneider
Paramus, New Jersey

During six years of living, and listening, in South Brooklyn, an old Italian nabe, I have never once heard anyone, young or senior, use the word "steal." It is always some form of "rob," as in "His radio was robbed last week out of his car" or "Two kids jumped him and robbed his watch and money." I suspect that the reason for this is that "steal" has heavier, religious overtones. Stealing is what thou shalt not do; the very thought becomes anathema. But robbing goes on every day and carries no big shock value. I haven't yet heard anybody speak of robbing a kiss, but maybe that's up ahead.

As for Willie Sutton, what he was robbing was actually the people in the bank. He pointed a gun at them, gave them orders, and so on. Nobody was being boigled. When a bank break-in occurs at night, in the absence of homo sapiens, some newspapers use the term "burglarized." And some content themselves with "broken into." In the eyes of a court, there's a big emotional difference between being robbed and being burgled. The former is assumed to be traumatic, worthy of Class A sympathy. Burglary is a lesser phenomenon, hardly worth the notice of the cops.

Calvin K. Towle
Brooklyn, New York

You stated that since 1933, there have been no common law marriages recognized in New York. This is not completely accurate. The law in New York is that a marriage which is valid where celebrated will be valid in New York. Thus a common law marriage which is celebrated in one of the handful of states that recognize common law marriage will be recognized when that couple resides in New York. Thus each party is afforded all the rights and duties of a party who was married in a traditional ceremony.

Please be advised that since my admission to the bar is still a few weeks away, I am not an attorney licensed to practice law in New York. Therefore, this is only for your information and is not intended as legal advice.

Mark Levine
Attorney
Brooklyn, New York

Perhaps "lawyers should be in the business of distinctions," but columnists claiming to be experts in English usage should be experts in correct English usage. You, of all people, should know that common usage is not synonymous with correct usage. Neither the words of Willie Sutton, nor the lamentations of countless Americans that their houses have been robbed, nor the carefully enunciated fuzzy English of television newscasters can change the meaning of the words robbery and burglary.

These words are legal words, and as such their correct definitions are their legal definitions. People get robbed. Places get burglarized. Things get stolen. Willie

Sutton robbed banks because he committed robberies (forcibly stole property from people) in banks. If Willie did his work at night, when the bank was empty, he would have been a bank burglar, not a bank robber.

The same goes for your masked burglar friend. When he was suddenly confronted by the resident of his target premises, he graduated from mere burglar to burglar-robber.

Language is only of use if it is precise. Burglary and robbery have precise meanings. Do not let precision be obfuscated by incorrect "popular usage." Students in my class have momentarily lost their hearing for less.

> Lawrence A. Vogelman
> Assistant Professor of Clinical Education
> Benjamin N. Cardozo School of Law
> Yeshiva University
> New York, New York

Justice Kooper should be benched for writing "another doyenne of the airways," as quoted in your column.

A doyen, or doyenne, is the senior member of a group, such as a diplomatic corps. Obviously, there can be only one in any group, so there could not be "another doyenne of the airways."

As for airways, it means the routes followed by airplanes. Obviously, Justice Kooper was groping for airwaves.

> Richard P. Hunt
> New York, New York

Your discussion of "lawyer" vs. "attorney" deviates somewhat from the distinction made by Dean Vanderbilt of NYU Law School when he addressed the freshmen class in 1947 (and, presumably, in other years as well): "If you study diligently [or words to that effect] you will become lawyers; those who do not will just be attorneys."

> Karl F. Ross
> New York, New York

I went to law school, not attorney school, but when I was admitted to the bar to practice law it was not as a "lawyer." The certificate of admission states that I was "duly admitted and Licensed to practice as an Attorney and Counsellor in all the Courts of this State."

> Robert M. Cohen
> Ballston Lake, New York

When I was first called to the bar, I received a very large certificate bearing the Governor's signature evidencing my appointment as Attorney at Law and Solicitor in Chancery. I thereupon studied assiduously for three more years and was rewarded by another large certificate declaring me to be a COUNSELLOR AT LAW. (The caps are quoted.)

It should be emphasized that this is not a distinction without a difference. In those days, an attorney could not practice in an appellate court unless he was also a counsellor. The difference has since been eliminated. Along with my second certificate, I received smaller documents averring that I was then a Master in Chancery, Proctor in Admiralty, and several other things which I fail to recall.

But nowhere was I certified as a Lawyer!

Perhaps the change which you appear to Advocate (that was another of my secondary titles) is on the way. Some midwestern states refer specifically to us guys as Lawyers—Wisconsin, for one. And now, of all things, the Journal of the New Jersey State Bar Association *is styled "New Jersey Lawyer." When the chief legal officer becomes known as the Lawyer General, I may be convinced.*

Stuart B. Rounds
Hopewell, New Jersey

It is interesting to note that Tom Sawyer, in The Adventures of Huckleberry Finn, *agrees with Willie Sutton's use of the term "to rob."*

After pricking his fingers and signing his name in blood to make official his membership in Tom Sawyer's Gang, Ben Rogers asks:

"Now, what's the line of business of this Gang?"

"Nothing but robbery and murder," Tom said.

"But who are we going to rob?—houses, or cattle, or—"

"Stuff! Stealing cattle and such things ain't robbery; it's burglary," says Tom Sawyer. "We ain't burglars. That ain't no sort of style. We are highwaymen. We stop stages and carriages on the road, with masks on, and kill the people and take their watches and money."

"Must we always kill people?"

"Oh, certainly. It's best. Some authorities think different, but mostly it's considered best to kill them—except some that you bring to the cave here, and keep them till they're ransomed."

Willa M. Stackpole
Princeton, New Jersey

"Lawyer" is the correct usage. "Attorney" is simply one who assumes a responsibility for another, such as "attorney in fact," and acts under a license known as

a "Power of Attorney," derived from the root "attorn"—to turn over to another. No legal education or further license is necessary.

Today, the distinction is lost as lawyers have preempted the use of "attorney" for whatever reason (perhaps to draw some distance between themselves and lawyers of old who were not required to have formal legal education or training in ethics, or perhaps to avoid confusion with the Bowfin, also known as lawyer, a dogfish; a sluggish and voracious species usually remaining in deep water by day and found in the freshwater swamps of North America).

In any event, I submit "lawyer" is quite correct and preferred, at least by me, and on the verge of extinction but for the existence of law schools (as opposed to attorney schools) and relegated to the Miranda warning and for describing others, perhaps derogatorily, who profess to practice law.

"Attorney" is quite incorrect but in common misuse, increasingly, and "attorney at law" is technically correct, but a bastardization in search of an improved image.

Interestingly, in the yellow pages of the Phoenix phonebook, under "lawyer," most lawyers who run private ads who do not use the cop-out of "law offices of ——" advertise themselves as "attorney at law."

I disagree with Mark Sullivan of Harvard. A graduate of a law school without bar admission is just that; neither an attorney nor lawyer. And one admitted to the bar without graduating from a law school (we still have some) is both, to the extent of any other lawyer/attorney.

> Matthew W. Borowiec
> Judge, Superior Court
> Bisbee, Arizona

I read with interest your column which included a dissertation on the difference between lawyers and attorneys. Since no one else seems to want it, we have adopted The Lawyers as a trademark, and have filed a registration with the trademark office. We must advise that your column comes dangerously close to an infringement of that trademark. If you're not careful, you may have to consult your attorneys (we refrain from saying you might have to consult your lawyers since obviously we can't represent you). We trust you will govern yourself accordingly.

> Roger Scott
> Syracuse, New York

I believe that Mr. Sullivan is right or nearly right. I think the traditional expression was "Attorney and Counsellor-at-law." That at least was what was engraved on my father's stationery when he began to practice law in 1903. What it was intended to signify was that the person concerned was licensed to represent others in legal matters and also to give legal advice. A "lawyer" is anyone who has received a law degree, whether or not he has been admitted to practice law. You *can have a practicing lawyer and a nonpracticing lawyer. But only someone who has been licensed to practice can represent himself to be an "attorney [i.e., permitted to represent others in legal matters] and counsellor-at-law [i.e., permitted to give legal advice]."*

Lawrence R. Eno
New York, New York

I call your attention to the definition and attitude of Halakha *(Jewish jurisprudence) towards Theft and Robbery. Theft (*Genevah*), prohibited in Lev. 19:11, is the act of stealing in a clandestine, furtive manner. Robbery (*Gezelah*), prohibited in Lev. 19:13, is defined as the act of stealing openly and forcefully (Maimonides,* Mishneh Torah, Genebah *1:3;* Gezelah *1:3).*

The distinction between theft and robbery is of practical significance within criminal law. The theft of chattel carries a penalty of double payment (Ex. 22:6). Robbery, on the other hand, has only the civil remedy of restoration in statu quo ante *(Lev. 5:23).*

Why does halakha *impose double payment on the thief and only restoration of the robbed item on the robber? The words of the* Tosephta's *analogy (B.K. 7:1) speak for themselves:*

> *"To what is the difference between the thief and the robber comparable?" It is comparable to two who made a party in the city; one invites the residents of the city but not the King, and the other invites neither the King nor residents of the city. Whose punishment will be more severe?—the one who invited only the residents but not the King!*

Making no attempt to conceal his act of stealing, the robber evidences no greater fear of man than of God. In fact, he evidences equal disregard for both man and God. The thief, on the other hand, by acting clandestinely says in effect, "who sees us, who takes note of us?" (Isaiah 29:15). For this expression of "the Lord does not see us" (Ezekiel 8:12), the thief is punished with double payment. The 14th-century Provencal scholar Menahem ben Solomon Meiri writes, "although all sin is despicable, the clandestine sinner, so to speak, presses the feet of the Divine Presence i.e. repudiates Divine Providence from the site of his sin and therefore the Torah treats the thief more severely than the robber."

Menahem Meier, Ph.D.
Teaneck, New Jersey

Will you please run that by about the "oi" sound in "lawyer" again? According to my dictionary, the sound is "ô," like the "aw" in "awful." Or have I missed a funny? Perhaps you're trying to superimpose a little Yiddish on the word, to suggest a lower-class Jewish lawyer!

> Carl Bowman
> New York, New York

Justice Kooper did not "opine" that "Robbery is forcible stealing from a person." That statement is not an opinion, it is the legal definition in every state and country that I am aware of and, as such, the statement is fact. Furthermore, that statement is not an "obiter dictum." Obiter dicta are opinions (not facts) contained in judicial decisions (not letters, though I cannot fault you particularly on that error) that have "no actual bearing on issues involved" (Black's Law Dictionary, Fourth Edition). *The Justice's definition of robbery went to the core of her letter and was not a collateral or tangential opinion. Even my* Webster's New World Dictionary *(College Edition) recognizes that distinction. Tsk! Tsk!*

> John S. Jenness, Jr.
> South Paris, Maine

Willie Sutton was right, in the eyes of the law as well as of the public, when he called himself a bank robber, since he used force or the threat of force to compel another person to give him money. For example, on one occasion described in his autobiography Where the Money Was *(p. 94), Sutton entered a bank surreptitiously and told the manager to "open the vault in one minute flat or they'll be reading your obituary in that newspaper tomorrow." This is robbery just as much as is a mugging.*

In fact, the Federal bank robbery statute, 18 U.S.C. §2113(a), contains separate paragraphs covering bank robbery and burglary and making the distinction between them clear. Written in a style that only a counsellor-at-law could love, the statute punishes anyone who:

> *by force or violence, or by intimidation, takes or attempts to take, from the person or presence of another any property or money or any other thing of value belonging to, or in the care, custody, control, management or possession of, any bank, credit union, or any savings and loan association.*

It also punishes anyone who

> *enters or attempts to enter any bank, credit union, or any savings and loan association, or any building used in whole or in part as a bank, credit union, or as a savings and loan association, with intent to commit in such bank, credit union, or in such savings and loan association, or building, or part thereof, so used, any felony affecting such bank, credit union, or such savings*

and loan association and in violation of any statute of the United States, or
any larceny.

(The exquisite syntax of this statute perhaps helps to explain the movement for a
new Federal criminal code.)

However, as we lawyers say, from the point of view of the poipetrator the
difference between robbery and burglary may be a "distinction without a differ-
ence": each can get him twenty years in the slammer, or twenty-five if he uses a
loaded gun.

> Robert S. Litt
> Assistant United States Attorney
> New York, New York

whomp, *see* boll weevils whomp gypsy moths

window shopping

A plaintive, if syntactically convoluted, message has come to this department
from a United States senator.

"My previous occupation, prior to coming to Washington, having been a
farmer from South Dakota, I have been curious about two new expressions
Washington bureaucrats have expressed to me in the past week."

I am withholding his name to spare him the scorn and obloquy of the Squad
Squad, which will quickly leap on the previous prior and the expressions ex-

pressed. After that shaky start, the senator, whose identity I shall fiercely protect (it was not James Abdnor of South Dakota), went on to pose a legitimate question:

"On Tuesday, during the Law of the Sea hearing, a witness described the new Law of the Sea Treaty as a 'window of opportunity.' On Thursday, during Awacs hearings in the Foreign Relations Committee, a State Department official told me we had a 'window of vulnerability.' Where," asks the hyperfenestrated solon, "did all this window talk come from?"

From outer-space lingo, that's where. *Launch window* was a phrase that came off the pad in the late 1960's. "The Soviet and American vehicles flew to Venus close together," wrote Walter Sullivan of *The New York Times* on October 18, 1967, "because both were fired during one of the periodic 'windows' for such shots. These are brief periods of time when Venus is overtaking the earth and relative positions of the two planets are propitious."

A second metaphoric root can be found at the nearest bank. Most tellers no longer work behind windows, as "thrift institutions" and "full-service financial institutions" vie for depositors' dollars with a new, open look; soon I expect depositors and tellers to work out their transactions on a cozy love seat. In the old days of fishy-eyed stares, however, you went to a barred window; accordingly, the Federal Reserve's willingness to extend or contract credit became known as the nation's *credit window,* and the United States Treasury's willingness to convert gold to dollars became known as *the gold window.*

Thus, the word *window* gained a connotation of a small space or short time in which something important could be accomplished. The old panoramic, openness meaning remained—a new restaurant called Windows on the World opened atop New York's World Trade Center—but suddenly *window* had a new vista on which to look.

John Newhouse, a former arms-control official, says that the *window of vulnerability* phrase crept into the Senate's hearings on the SALT II treaty in the summer of 1979. (Others suspect an early 1970's origin.) "The phrase describes a time just ahead," writes Mr. Newhouse, "when improved Soviet missile forces will, in theory, be able to destroy most of America's silo-based Minuteman ICBM's in a literal bolt from the blue."

As *window of vulnerability* was bruited about in the summer of 1979, it was natural for the view to be described from the other side of the window: "Frank Barnett of the National Strategy Information Center, a hawkish think tank," reported *Time* magazine on November 12, 1979, "warned of a 'Soviet window of opportunity' in the 1980's." Sol Steinmetz of the *Barnhart Dictionary of New English* gives this interpretation: "What is a window of opportunity for the Soviets is a window of vulnerability for the United States and vice versa."

But no political or strategic phrase carries real authority unless it has passed the lips of the Highest Authority. On September 24, 1981, our little window made a breakthrough: "I'll confess, I was reluctant about this," said President Reagan in explanation of a cut in defense spending, "because of the long way we have to go before the dangerous window of vulnerability confronting us will be appreciably narrowed."

Careful users of metaphors will note that these windows are not open and closed, as are gold windows and credit windows, but are "narrowed" and "widened." Although the window refers to time—a period of years—it cannot be used with *lengthened* or *shortened*, because those words do not fit the idea of a window.

I have a hunch that there is still mileage in windows. We have yet to deal with the window pot of marijuana and the window dressing of media manipulation, as the storm window of outrage forces us to fling wide the French doors of recession.

I believe that "window" was used at the Democratic National Convention in 1972.

The McGovern forces needed to win an early procedural fight. But they also needed to win it with a total that fell between two other totals. That is, Senator McGovern needed—and got—more votes than one number and fewer than another.

Television reporters called the range between the two numbers the "window."

> Marie Shear
> Brooklyn, New York

Without becoming window-silly, let me pass on the following usage.

The pay television industry has a "window," and it is not the window on the world commonly attributed to the tube. Instead, the period of time between a motion picture's withdrawal from theatrical distribution and its premiere on network television is referred to as the "pay window," the period during which the movie, i.e., "film," is available to pay TV.

I wonder if medicine has a similar construction. The period between surgery and healing, for example, might be known as the "pain window."

> Dennis P. Waters
> Binghamton, New York

You might be interested to know that it is very fashionable in medicine these days to speak of a "therapeutic window." This refers to the utility or maximum effectiveness of a medication at a precise dosage range. Above and below this range the drug is either less effective or its efficacy is vitiated by side effects. The term "therapeutic window" has been current, I would estimate, for about 3 to 5 years in medicine and has been particularly used in relation to the medications used in psychiatry.

> L. D. Hankoff, M.D.
> Elizabeth, New Jersey

Prior to entering the Gospel ministry of our Lord Jesus, I was a Forensic and Casualty Photographer in the New York City area and photographed many windows for attorneys and insurance companies. In the Old Testament the "windows of heaven" are opened on several occasions. In Genesis 7:11 they bring rain to Noah's times. Later in Malachi 3:10 they bring blessings to good stewards who bring the full tithe to the Lord's house. The idea of windows in the skies is an ancient theme. (See page 703, Volume 1 of the Interpreter's Dictionary of the Bible *where it is called a "sluice.")*

> James E. Minor, Pastor
> Oakland & Moscow Lutheran Churches
> Alberta Lea, Minnesota

In this day of soaring interest rates, how could you have missed the bankers' demand to "go to the window" or to pay a "window rate" meaning, of course, an increase in your mortgage which the teller at the "window" will now charge you?

> Mark Schwarz
> New York, New York

On "window of vulnerability": I think the etymology is straightforward. A "window" is a range of acceptable values around a variable. In the jargon of statistics, the window can be defined in terms of the standard deviation. In practice it means that as a variable takes on different values, the safe "window" is the range between the upper and lower limits, safe in the sense that something dreadful would happen if the system took on values beyond this range. Temperature of the core of a nuclear reactor might be an example. The temperature must be kept steady (more or less) but will change with the electric load the generators are to produce. Thus as the power produced changes, the temperature of the core will change; but for each change there is nevertheless a safe window, an acceptable range.

> Robert N. Ross
> Director, School of Public Communications
> Boston University
> Boston, Massachusetts

While you correctly state that the term "window" has its roots in the space program, you completely lose the flavor of the usage. While the "window" may be expressed as the period of time when celestial bodies are in correct orientation for a shot, the "window" is really an imaginary "hole" in the sky through which the rocket is fired at its target. In reality, therefore, there is a "window" that opens when the alignment is correct.

Your second reference to "window" as a metaphor for banks also falls short of the mark. The Federal Reserve Bank exercises its function as lender of last resort by allowing banks to borrow against or "discount" their loan portfolios. In order to do this, a messenger from the bank literally goes to the window at the Fed with the documents evidencing the loan and which will serve as the Fed's collateral. By changing the rules under which member banks can do this or by changing the rates at which banks can borrow, the Fed is literally carrying out credit policy by the opening and closing (read: availability) of the window.

> Brian H. Saffer
> Summit, New Jersey

Dear Bill—

The Seattle Times *was half-owned, and entirely run, in my time by Colonel Clarence Brettun Blethen. Memos passed along to us underlings by those higher on his staff, and our resultant copy, were flagged with the drawing of a window, meaning that the subject was dear to him. Originally he had looked down and out from his penthouse on the Olympic Hotel and seen something that the paper should pay attention to. Hence,* ⊞

> Dick [Richard L. Williams]
> Smithsonian Magazine
> Washington, D.C.

Dear Bill—

Let me suggest that "window of vulnerability" did in fact spring from "window of opportunity," and the time frame suggested by John Newhouse is probably correct—summer.

My recollection (sometimes albeit known to be faulty) is that Bill Van Cleave and I, and perhaps Fred Ikle, converted "opportunity" into vulnerability because it seemed to suit the tack our candidate was taking. In any event, I recall that we were using the term as often as we could to promote its general acceptability among folks commenting on the SALT II treaty.

While claims are being made, and for your future files, I am registering with you now my exclusive patents on the following:

- *"Margin of safety," as in "restoring the margin of safety." In the days immediately following the Detroit Convention, during which we had adopted a Platform calling for "military superiority" (thus awakening and enraging the media and our opponents), we had need of a less provocative substitute term. I hit upon the tactic of having the candidates (and us) respond to each question about "superiority" by responding: "What we're really talking about here is the need to restore our margin of safety, that vital margin that has kept us free over the past 35 years." By using the formula religiously when confronted with hostile questions about the meaning of superiority, we were uniformly successful in deflecting the question without repudiating the phrase used in the Platform.*
- *"Reaganaut"—as in astronaut, intrepid and bold (not as in Argonaut). This is one accepted term, as you have acknowledged.*
- *"Reagoon"—a hard-line Reaganaut. Never quite made it, but O.K. for cocktail party talk.*
- *"Reaganinny"—former Reaganaut who has fallen into "centrism" and accommodation with the prevailing orthodoxy. A failure for now, but I predict a comeback for this needed word.*
- *"October Surprise"—a term designed to heighten expectations that Carter was planning to pull off something spectacular in October 1980 to win the election. While I had in mind a second hostage rescue attempt in Iran, we deliberately allowed other far-out ideas to become candidates for the "surprise" (e.g., "Stealth"). The theory was to begin accusing Carter early, arousing fears and expectations of a desperate, election-winning gamble, and then claim that we backed him off by premature exposure. In this way, we were guaranteed the opportunity to respond to anything he did in October by saying "we told you so all along." Dick Wirthlin was of initial assistance in planting the concept, and gradually all campaign staff came to use it. As with any respectable social disease, the press caught it after repeated contact.*

For the definitive archives, let's make sure no one invades the credit territory of these very proprietary terms.

With best regards,

> *Sincerely,*
> *Dick [Richard V. Allen]*
> *Washington, D.C.*

winged words

A miss used to be as good as a mile. Under the pressure of airline euphemism (which turned *safety belts* to *seat belts,* and "Life Savers?" to "Mints?"), a moment of danger to two aircraft was dubbed a "near miss."

"One striking air traffic controller told me," reports David Shaffer, of the *Express* in Easton, Pennsylvania, "that *near misses* was coined because it sounds better than *near collisions.* He also told me that air traffic controllers refer to such events as *deals.* Presumably, a *near miss* by two 747's would be a *big deal."*

Since it is now in the interest of the unemployed controllers to cast aspersions on airline safety, their union's press releases reject the euphemism and issue "reports of near midair collisions." Whatever you think of the union's cause, you have to agree with its terminology: The event described is "nearly a collision," and not "nearly a missed collision."

Language never stays the same in the airline world. I had finally talked myself into calling the stewardess a sexless "flight attendant" when the nice young woman on New York Air crossed me up and renamed herself a "customer-service attendant." Since that verges on the redundant, many of us in the Squad Squad have returned to calling her a stewardess, or, if we are unafraid of getting coffee in our laps, a "stew."

Again, union terminology is in the air: With unionized air carriers, the term *customer-service representative* is usually applied to people who provide special services on the ground, like writing tickets or meeting mean little kids; *flight attendant* is reserved for those who have extra training in safety or food handling, and who fly. Eastern Airlines, which is unionized, looks askance at non-U New York Air and sniffs that the newcomer's "customer-service attendants" are not specialists in stewardessing. New York Air responds by calling its flight attendants "in-flight customer-service representatives," which may be difficult to fit on a call button.

Perhaps airline experience causes the affliction among executives known as flying grammar. The ailment travels: When Robin H. H. Wilson left his wings behind to become chief executive of the Long Island Rail Road, he wrote a letter to his riders beginning, "As the media was making much fanfare . . ." He meant "media were," and fanfare is not "made"—a fuss or big deal is "made," a fanfare accompanies or precedes. The grounded executive went on to observe: "Many of you questioned the qualifications of an airline executive to running a railroad." (Many riders question his qualification to writing a letter.)

On occasion, airlinese triumphs. I am caving in on "We will be taking off momentarily." Time was, *momentarily* meant *"for* a moment," and not *"in* a moment." I pause momentarily in respect for a word that has changed its meaning. The current meaning of *momentarily* is "very soon," or "it won't be long now, folks," or "as soon as the stew finds the handle on the rear door." Straight talkers prefer *in a moment* or the slightly more delayed *soon,* but if you're in a hurry for a multisyllabic affectation, you may use *momentarily.*

Lest permissiveness proliferate, let us take a stand on that favorite airline sign: "Fasten Seat Belt While Seated." Writes Margaret Goodman of New York: "I've seen a few inebriated passengers in my time, but never one so far gone that he tried to fasten his seat belt while standing!" She recommends the more prosaic "Keep Seat Belt Fastened While Seated." The airline's version is a near miss.

I was surprised to see the common term "near miss" remarked on as a novelty. "Near miss" has been around for at least as long as I can remember. (I am 51.) I think I first clearly remember it in connection with accounts of bombing and artillery in World War II, but I think it must go far back beyond that. Very likely it's an old firing-range and artillery term. Gunnery is a trade where things are either hits or misses, but a miss may be a near one.

A random check turned up in about 2 minutes: "Just heard a report that there are a number of small fires below, owing to near misses." That's Cecil Brown describing the sinking of H.M.S. Repulse *in* Suez to Singapore, *p. 316 (Random House, 1942).*

> *Thaddeus Holt*
> *Washington, D. C.*

Dear Bill:

Your recent "near-miss" piece took me back at least thirty years to a Buffalo city room and a deathless lead which began: "A near-riot was narrowly averted . . ."

> *Mike [Michael Horton]*
> *Brussels, Belgium*

Your comments on "near miss" seem to me to rest on a shaky foundation.

You appear to be reasoning by analogy from locutions such as "a near-fatal" accident—i.e., one which was not quite fatal. But these are American neologisms, where a hyphen is used to conscript an unwilling adjective into service as an adverb.

Absent a hyphen, the epithet must be taken at face value. One derivation is from archery, where a "near miss" is a miss that came near the target.

Or, what about the contumacious defendant who, according to a seventeenth-century court reporter, became so incensed at the judge that he "jetait un brickbat, que narrowly mist"?

Maxwell R.D. Vos
New York, New York

Unintentionally, I believe, you cavil. In air traffic control, as in gunnery, the term invokes "near" as an adjective (meaning nearby), not as an adverb (meaning nearly or almost).

My unabridged Webster's *includes: "near, a. . . . 7. Close; narrow; such as barely avoids, passes or misses something;—usually in reference to injury or loss; as, a near escape." Are we constrained, then, to refer only to "near capture"?*

Disgruntled ones will prefer "near collision." But the glass is no more accurately half empty than half full.

Fred H. Battle
Dix Hills, New York

By the way, planes are never late anymore, only delayed.

Stanton Frazar
New Orleans, Louisiana

In Atlanta's new airport, travelers are whisked from one airline's concourse to another's by a subway or a moving sidewalk. All along the way travelers are warned to keep moving, to follow colors, etc. by a ubiquitous disembodied voice. When I was there last, the subway was on the fritz, and the disembodied voice urged me to "refer to signage for further instructions." I suspected that she wanted me to read the signs, but I could not be sure.

J. Barron Boyd, Jr.
Associate Professor, Department of Political Science
Le Moyne College
Syracuse, New York

Your recent piece on flying grammar omitted any examples of pilot fly-speak.

The second day of the controllers' strike I was flying, bravely, through an overcast on a flight from Denver, when the TWA pilot announced, "Due to the clouds and haze, your visual reference to the ground will be considerably restricted."

My perceptual reference to this statement was not restricted to puzzlement. I wondered whether the airlines routinely teach all new employees how to speak their language.

Mary Ann Laurans
Providence, Rhode Island

Your attack on "near miss" is wide of the mark. The term does not derive from airline jargon, but rather from naval warfare.

Since water is incompressible, the effect of an explosion in it is magnified. For this reason, a bomb exploding in the water near a ship may do as much, or more, damage than one that hits it.

Bombers, therefore, reported not only the hits that they scored on enemy ships, but also the near misses, meaning, of course, misses that were near the target, not "nearly a miss."

"Nearly a miss." Forsooth! It sounds like a partial virgin! Whatever the sins of airline prose may be, this expression is concise and accurate.

Stuart O. Landry, Jr.
Endwell, New York

woodshed blues

"My visit to the Oval Office," said budget director David Stockman last month, after receiving the dressing-down reserved for inveterate leakers by President Reagan, " . . . was more in the nature of a visit to the woodshed after supper."

Woodshed entered the American language in 1844, to describe a place to put odds and ends; it was used mainly by people who had moved from farm to city and no longer had a large barn out back. The woodshed took on its current meaning of a place of punishment—where Paw could whop the errant son with Maw out of earshot—in 1907. It had a secondary meaning of a place of privacy, where kids could sneak corn-silk smokes, which reappeared, and remains, in the slang of jazz musicians: *Woodshedding* means "rehearsing alone."

Before Mr. Stockman shrewdly reached back for that rural metaphor to describe his session with an irate President, a similar term had been growing in Washington use: *horseshedding.* I have not spotted a written use, but have often heard lawyers and lobbyists speak of "getting to the witness and horseshedding him before the hearing."

This is the rebirth of a favorite old Americanism. H. L. Mencken traced the verb *to horseshed* to Kansas, and defined it as "to wheedle, cajole"; in his *Dictionary of Americanisms,* Mitford Mathews cited a use by James Fenimore Cooper in his novel *The Redskins:* "Your regular 'horse shedder' is employed to frequent taverns where jurors stay, and drop hints before them touching the merits of causes known to be on the calendars." In the days of circuit-riding judges, those who sought special favors did their work before the judge entered the courtroom—out in the horse shed, a synonym for *stable.*

According to Stuart Berg Flexner, editor of Random House's reference department, a 1901 Congressional Record cites Abraham Lincoln as using the verb, but he can find no specific Lincoln quotation with *horseshed* in it.

Perhaps because of its similarity in sound to what copy editors like to call "a barnyard epithet," the colorful verb declined in use in the first half of this century, but is making a comeback now that its sound-alike is generally less offensive.

The shed image is back in style, thanks to Mr. Stockman, who equated *supply-side economics* (a coinage of Herbert Stein, in derogation) with *trickle-down theory** (a concept used by William Jennings Bryan in his "Cross of Gold" speech, though the orator did not use the specific phrase). He also used *Trojan horse,* which has always meant deception, but sought to make it mean "brainless" in subsequent explication. He should have stayed in the woodshed.

As a musician of many years, woodshedding *has always meant "to learn a piece of music without benefit of written music—listening to something over and over and learning by ear—trying again and again until the right notes are come by and the piece memorized."*

Mary Monica Potanas
New York, New York

*See "trickle-down carrotsticks."

In reference to your jazz definition of "woodshedding" as "rehearsing alone"
—I'm sure by now you've heard from many in the world of barbershop quartets
to which I belong.

We use the term "woodshedding" to mean improvising barbershop quartet
harmony without the aid of written arrangements. Woodshedding is usually done
for our own pleasure rather than for the critical ears of an audience. It's analogous
to the after-hours "jam sessions" of jazz musicians.

> Robert S. Rouffa
> New York, New York

You may have erred in defining horse shed as "a synonym for stable."

A stable, as commonly understood in upstate New York and New England at
least since 1920, is a place where horses or cattle are sheltered and fed. A stable
has a door or doors, stalls, and mangers. A shed, however, is open on at least one
side and is used for shelter or storage.

Note that John Heywood observed (c. 1546): "When the steede is stolne, shut
the stable durre" (Familiar Quotations, John Bartlett, 11th ed., 1938, p. 14). Not
the shed door.

Upstate New York horse sheds most commonly were "parking garages" at rural
churches. They were built in units, each with perhaps 10 sections, each section wide
and deep enough to shelter a horse and buggy, surrey or carriage. There were no
dividing partitions, simply framing members to separate the tie-ups. They were
used only during "divine worship" and decorated with advertisements for chewing
tobacco, colic and spavin cures, and the like.

No God-fearing parent would discipline a child in such a public place before
or after divine worship. That came later, in the barn at home. The dirt floor of the
horse sheds, with accumulations, was not conducive to juvenile amours and other
clandestine activities. But "after hours" and behind the horse sheds, weather
permitting, I am not about to say what went on.

> Bruce B. Miner
> Cheshire, Connecticut

I was surprised at your date of 1907 for the use of woodshed as a place for
chastisement, since it is mentioned in chapter two of Peck's Bad Boy. The earliest
copyright on the book I have is 1883, and these stories would have appeared earlier
in the Milwaukee Sun. In this story the bad boy had cut up some small white rubber
hose and added it to his father's plate of macaroni. Watching his father trying to
chew the rubber macaroni became too much for the bad boy, so he left the table:

> *Then the (servant) girl came in and was put on the confessional, and told all,*
> *and presently there was a sound of revelry by night, in the wood shed, and*

the still, small voice was saying, "O, Pa, don't! you said you didn't care for innocent jokes. Oh!" And then the old man, between strokes of the piece of clapboard would say, "Feed your father a hose cart next, won't ye?"

This suggests to me that this use of the word woodshed *was already a familiar one. The words are separated in the story—*wood shed—*but in the chapter sub-headings describing parts of the story it is printed as one word: "Music in the Woodshed."*

David A. Gibson
Hamlin, New York

I was as surprised that no one has written to you regarding "horseshedding" as I was to learn that it was more than a family expression. Every Sunday morning that I visited my great Aunt Martha, she admonished—advised—pleaded—commanded—her son to refrain from horseshedding just for once, but always in vain.

Until the Thirties, country churches had horsesheds. Town leaders were apt to be regular church-goers, or, in the instances where men of power did not attend "meeting," their opposition did. Horsesheds were the "smoke-filled rooms" of far-flung communities before mechanical communication came into being; they served as clearing houses of information and hatcheries of intrigue as long as they stood. Horses were a thing of the past when I first heard the term "horseshedding," but the sheds lingered on for another generation while knots of conspirators gathered among parked cars carrying on a tradition as old as man and his horse.

Doris H. Wackerbarth
Granville, Massachusetts

word order

Always watch the order of your words. "I have only eyes for you" is not "I have eyes for you only," and is a far cry from "Only I have eyes for you."

Said Senator John Glenn, upon getting the Reagan treatment over a Senate vote: "Some of it is sitting down with the most powerful single person in the free world. . . ."

He meant, of course, "the single most powerful person in the free world." Roger Angus Brooks, of Washington, sets him straight: "The real question is: If President Reagan is the most powerful single person in the free world, who is the most powerful married one? And besides, I thought that the honor of being the most powerful single person in the free world would be more appropriately bestowed upon Pope John Paul II."

Unlike you and I, Senator Glenn spent a bit of time in a small capsule orbiting the Earth, with his words his only means of making the link with Earthbound NASA workers on whom his safe return depended. So his syntax is entitled to some presumption of precision.

The phrase you criticized, "most powerful single individual," connotes the singular concentration of power in one individual, as contrasted with the power of the Senate, which is not divisible into portions which can be carried into the meeting with the president in one's suit pocket. Glenn's phrase loses this connotation when the word single *is moved farther from* individual, *whatever false hopes are created in the hearts of young Republican misses with single-track minds.*

Aaron Frishberg
New York, New York

While we are at it, is it necessary to qualify "most powerful" with "single"?

Florence Temko
Lenox, Massachusetts

---

word-watchers at work

ERIC PARTRIDGE IN HIS OWN WORDS, edited by David Crystal
(New York: Macmillan, 1981), and

WORDS FAIL ME, by Philip Howard,
(New York: Oxford University Press, 1981).

"Slang," wrote Carl Sandburg, "is language which takes off its coat, spits on its hands—and goes to work." (The colloquial speaker would change "language which" to "lingo that.") Where does slang begin? "The downtrodden, who are the great creators of slang," writes Anthony Burgess, the novelist-linguist, "hurl pithiness and color at poverty and oppression."

Eric Partridge taught the English-speaking world to treat slang with respect. This sampler of his writings on lexicography and etymology is unified by his fascination with the underside of the language. The disrepute of his subject matter rubbed off on him: Partridge was caught in the web of "dirty words." Hifalutin linguists looked down on his labor, and the popularity of his books was misjudged to be evidence that his work was not serious scholarship.

He was a one-man band, which he defined as "a person that takes rather too much on himself," and he opined that the term originated in the French *l'homme orchestre.* (A "person *that?*" Yes; Partridge went along with Henry Fowler on dispensing with "a person who.") In an age of computerized dictionary-making, with teams of lexicographers seeking public and private grants, it is hard to find one man alone willing to undertake a great dictionary: In that, Partridge—with his monumental *Dictionary of Slang and Unconventional English*—was a modern Samuel Johnson.

Like that self-described "harmless drudge," Partridge occasionally went off half-cocked. (He defines *go off at half-cock* as premature ejaculation; a separate entry, *half-cocked,* means slightly drunk; both terms are derived from gunnery.) When he could not find a word's provenance, rather than list the origin as "obscure," he often took a guess, exercising what he called "that flair without which the delver into the byways of language would do better to refrain from delving at all." Although he eschewed fancy, he embraced an informed speculation: "Imagination, if carefully controlled, will occasionally solve problems that phonetics cannot touch. . . ."

That self-confidence led him to guess that *jerkwater town* came from the jolting of a train passing through, when it actually refers to the scooping of water for the steam engine from a pan between the tracks. In his *Dictionary of the Underworld,* a seminal work, he assumed that calling a man a *heel* was traceable to *down at the heels* or to one who follows at the heels of another; modern scholarship regards it as a shortening of a vulgarism about the portion of a shoe that has been befouled.

His innocent dirty-mindedness found a treasurehouse of bawdiness in Shakespeare, although his assumption that "the Netherlands" in *The Comedy of Errors* refers to "the nether limbs" seems to me to be out of left field. (Why *left field* to denote far-outedness?* Is right field shallower in most ballparks? Partridge, who never came to America, does not address this in his dictionaries.)

Cliché collection was a Partridge speciality, which the lexicographer liked to *lay on with a trowel* (from *As You Like It,* Act I, Scene 2). "To allow oneself one of these," he wrote about the stereotyped phrases, "whether in writing or even in speech, is tantamount to resigning from the human race and to allying oneself with the monkeys and the parrots. . . . Somewhere along the way, everyone must *call a halt* and *take a stand* and *resist to the bitter end.*"

One reason Partridge was liked by philologists was his generosity to others in the field. He invited us all to cannibalize his work, as he did his predecessors. Working on a political dictionary, I went to the British Museum (O.K., it is officially the British Library, but that's like calling the newspaper morgue "the library") and asked for a selection of his books. The answer was, "If you'll wait

*See "left field."

until ten o'clock, you can find him in seat K-1." Sure enough, he took his place in the reading room to play the great library like his personal instrument, and delighted in whispering advice to students.

Who is working in England now to collect clichés and notice the neologisms and nonce words? Robert Burchfield, a New Zealander like Partridge, edits the Oxford dictionaries and meticulously documents the entire language, from Queen's English to vulgarism. (In the U.S., Stuart Berg Flexner has become the resident Partridge.) A relative newcomer is Philip Howard, literary editor of *The Times* of London, who writes a lively column about language. In precise prose, he dissociates himself from "the determined doom-watcher who can find the gloomy satisfaction of 'I told you so' in every issue of his newspaper" and the purist drawn to "misprint, catachresis, misspelling, solecism, barbarism and other evidence that English ain't what it used to be. It never was." While exhibiting his tolerance, he strikes a blow for useful distinctions and gently ridicules jargon.

In this collection of his columns on "new words and new meanings," Mr. Howard displays an ear for the wandering meaning: The noun *alibi,* for example, used to mean "proof of being in another place," but now has shifted to a synonym for *excuse.* Howard objects: "It has spoilt a useful little word and reduced the number of tools in the great box of English."

In the same way, he notes that *in fact* has proliferated to a triple meaning: (1) indeed, (2) in the event, and (3) in truth. *Ongoing* bothers him: "What's wrong with *continuing?*" And he takes offense at what he calls "the barbarous *these,*" as in "these kind of problems" and "these sort of men."

With too much certainty, he attributes the coinage of the neologism *stagflation* (the combination of inflation and industrial stagnation) to Chancellor of the Exchequer Iain Macleod in 1970. I wonder about that; we will have to wait for Volume 3 or 4 of Burchfield's *Supplement to the OED* for the citation that will reveal the coiner. On the minting of "cold war," Mr. Howard says that George Orwell was "an early user"; in fact (sense 3), the coiner was Herbert Bayard Swope, ghostwriting for Bernard Baruch.

On metaphors, however, Mr. Howard may turn out to be a Partridge in a pear tree. His investigation of a hyphenated adjective now in vogue on both sides of the Atlantic—*low-key*—is illuminating. I always assumed *low-key* to be a musical term, akin to *sotto voce,* but musical keys are neither low nor high, only major or minor. "The key to the mystery," writes Mr. Howard, "is that the metaphor is not musical at all. . . . In animated cartoon production *key drawings* indicate situations at special instants, such as at beats in the bar of music, after which the inbetween drawings are made to fit with the timing. And in the lexis of cinematography *low-key* is the term applied when a majority of the tones in the subject or image lie at the dark end of the grey scale."

The London word-watcher is especially critical of his literary sidekicks. In a piece called "Lit Crit," he surveys the taut and luminous world of reviewers, collecting their clichés in a way that would delight Partridge: *"Ambience:* Does this mean any more than atmosphere, surroundings or environment? . . . I think

it means 'I am a man of culture rare who uses the right passwords and shib-
boleths.' "

Emotive: . . . no more than a pretentious synonym for emotional or moving.

Evocative: A laudatory epithet for creative writing, though its context does
not always make clear what images, memories, feelings, associations, allusions, or
symbols the passage so praised tends to evoke.

Oeuvre: Often used in arty periphrasis. . . .

Overview: Much favored recently by the more modish sort of academic reviewer as an apparently exact synonym for survey.

Seminal: Highly influential, original, important, and likely to propagate like
a seed or seminal fluid. . . . a trendy word, the figurative extension of which has
recently grown in a seminal way.

(My own lit-crit favorite is *one-dimensional.* If the critic wants to say "lacks
depth," the correct term would be *two-dimensional.*)

Both Partridge in retrospect and Philip Howard today put needed pinpricks
in ballooning clichés and usefully jab jargon, but keep their eyes on the enrich-
ment of the mother tongue. "The language is in rude health," writes Howard,
"so long as we can go on using it, abusing it, complaining about it, and changing
it in so many rich and varied ways."

When President Charles de Gaulle faced a group of French generals reluctant
to defer to national authority, he told them, "You are not the army's army, you
are France's army." The English language is not the King's English, or the
grammarian's English, but the English-speaking world's English—to be fought
for and fought over by all who find joy in the world of words.

*You mention your lit-crit favorite "one-dimensional" which should be "two
dimensional." A good point.*

*I have one that goes the other way. One sees quite frequently "He has two
choices, either A or B." Of course there is only one choice.*

*William Lang
Southbury, Connecticut*

*I think William Safire does Dr. Robert W. Burchfield [editor of the Oxford
English Dictionary] an injustice by comparing him implicitly with Eric Partridge
when he asks, "Who is working in England now to collect clichés and notice the
neologisms and nonce words?" There is a great contrast between Dr. Burchfield*

and Partridge—or between the scholar and the dilettante. Mr. Safire himself pointed to some errors committed by Partridge and noted that he cannibalized the work of his predecessors. In addition, I do not think that Partridge has contributed much that is new or presented his work properly or correctly, as has Dr. Burchfield. As a popularizer of language Partridge failed to match H. L. Mencken, who even as a dilettante followed good scholarly methods by including specific references and footnotes in his masterpiece The American Language.

I hope William Safire will come out of "left field" in this, re-evaluate the work of Eric Partridge and conclude that although Partridge was a prodigious collector of compendia of words, clichés, slang and so on, Dr. Burchfield, the successor to Murray, Skeat and Onions of the Oxford English Dictionary, *is a a scholar in the best tradition with his lexicographic work. The first two volumes of the* Supplement *have been completed, a long and arduous task, up to and including the letter N. Let's hope he continues and completes the rest of the work.*

David Shulman
New York City

What in the world is the "world of words"? How about the wordsmith community? No? Then why not simply: ". . . and fought over by all who find joy in words"?

Richard Dresselhuys
New York, New York

Surely one-dimensional *is the preferable term if the critic wishes to imply a serious limitation. One-dimensional, with only length and no breadth, let alone depth, would seem to me to be far more expressive of deficit than two-dimensional, which implies at least a breadth.*

Cyril M. Franks
Princeton, New Jersey

I always assumed that low-key *referred to the placement of one lamp—the "key" light—in still photography. The key light was, I believe, to one side of the camera facing the subject. Its position above or below the subject's face affected the shadowing in the portrait—hence high-key or low-key. If I understand the jargon accurately—which I doubt—the term has since been corrupted within photography to mean "high-fashion, brassy" or "subdued."*

Bruce Hyman
Short Hills, New Jersey

You were most firm in stating that "jerkwater town" is derived from the practice of a steam locomotive tender taking water on the fly from track pans.

Know, sir, that track pans are (or were) installed on heavily traveled, high-speed rail lines where the velocity of the trains was sufficient to force the water to travel from the track pans up a scoop into the tender tank. Track pans were not usually featured in settled areas, if only because of the danger of man-made junk turning up in the track pans and damaging or derailing the train.

Now, sir. In olden days slower trains (of which there were many more) often took water in small towns from a tank beside the rails. The spout of the tank was movable. It could be, and was, pulled over (or jerked) from its resting place by a trainman and positioned above the tender, therein to pour the water for the iron horse to make steam of.

Hence, a "jerkwater town," a town about big enough to have a water tank.

The ritual of a locomotive taking water is still bright in the memories of A.K.s like the undersigned. You, unfortunately, were born 30 years too late.

Richard K. Bellamy
Cleveland, Ohio

I would like to add this bit of explanation about Eric Partridge's guess on a railroad term, "jerkwater town."

I worked on the old Chicago and Northwestern R.R. in Iowa in the early 30's, and know whereof I speak. The term "jerkwater town" did not derive from the action of the engine scooping water from between the rails, although this was often done to eliminate stopping the train for water. The term was used to refer to a small town where the only railroad-associated item was the water tower. A train would pull in next to the tower and the fireman would swing out a 6- or 8-inch pipe from the tower and lower it over the water tank on the tender behind the engine. The fireman would then jerk the release chain on a valve to start the gravity flow of the water. Thus the term "jerk water." A jerkwater town meant a town so small it only had a water tower for the railroad and possibly one or two houses.

The scooping method of taking on water was abandoned in favor of the tower. The scooping of water from between the rails invited too many unwanted objects being scooped up and flung into the tank on the tender.

Edward M. Myers
Hampton Bays, New York

I'm interested in the word "key," specifically, "low-key." You're surely right to point out that "low-key" doesn't derive from the music sense of "key." But you neglect another, common-language sense of "key" that would seem a much more likely source for "low-key." Just guessing now, but mightn't the expression come from toys—toy cars, but even more promisingly, toy soldiers and the like—that are wound up with a key. A mechanistic view of humans: someone who is "low-key" is someone who is not "wound up" or—and here's the proof to me—"keyed up." In other words, "low-key" as "running low on 'key.'" I'd love to see a citation for my argument—you'd expect the term to appear around the same time as the toys. . . .

Adam Gussow
New York, New York

You essayed a little joke. "On metaphors, however, Mr. Howard may turn out to be a Partridge in a pear tree," you wrote.

Now, I hate to snipe but, brace yourself, I have a grouse. These word-plays (pheasant and unpleasant), than which nothing could be Fowler, are enough to curlew hair. You have plainly gone off the rails.

Even though I quail before your wrath, still I woodcock a snook at you. You should be thrushed widgeon an inch of your life, condemned to the gallinules and covert in ptarmigan and pfeathers again.

Still, the squib was not worth a squabble. It's all a lark. The game's acoot!

However, in a less serious vein, may I remind you of the origin of the word "partridge"? As I am sure you recall, it is derived from the Old French "pertri" (a female partridge). This surely adds a certain piquancy to the line "And a partridge in a pear tree"; to say nothing about casting some doubt on the activities of the "geese a-laying," the "lords a-leaping," the "maids a-milking," the "drummers drumming" and, hélas, the "French hens."

Ah, how soon is our childhood innocence blown to grots.

Paul Freeman
New York, New York

world-class

First-class has had it. *World-class* is in. Richard Dudley of Guilford, Connecticut, writes: "All of a sudden, world-class runners, entertainers (supersuperstars?), chefs, auto racers ad nauseam. Where do we go from here?" And from Norman Hoffman of Yonkers: "Even in today's 'Market Place' column in *The New York Times*—'Clorox is a world-class household products manufacturer.' I say!"

Early on, it started as a Britishism (and have you noticed that *trendy* isn't trendy anymore?). The earliest citation that Sol Steinmetz can dig out of the Clarence L. Barnhart files is this soccer item from *The* (London) *Sunday Times* of April 14, 1963, from a sports column by Brian Granville: "But Charlton and

Greaves are world-class players and, for a match like this, both must stay."

"Since soccer players participate in international competitions for the *World Cup*," ruminates lexicographer Steinmetz, "top-seeded players were viewed as more than 'first-class'; they were 'world-class.' The term proved to be very useful for describing the top-drawer athletes or superstars of international competitions."

The key is "competitor for an international prize," whether it be the Olympics or chess tournaments. I would approve its extended use to international competition where the prize is fame or fortune, but would frown on its extension to a synonym for *international,* as in "a world-class household products manufacturer." (And who am I to approve or frown? I'm a world-class language maven, that's who.)

This points up the "honeymoon effect" of superlatives. A honey, or full, moon begins to wane as soon as it appears; similarly (in what is known to first-class writers as a "labored simile"), *world-class* began to lose its international-prize eminence as soon as it hit the top. Superlative hounds quickly applied it to bleaches being shipped across town.

World-class has done to *first-class* what *superstar* has done to *star*. Who wants to go to a lousy first-class match or see a mere star? The language always needs a word one rank higher, and as soon as we get it, we start dragging it down. (So he's a superstar—but is he a *world-class* superstar?)

Just when did "honeymoon" become a full moon? After impregnation by the sun perhaps? In what dictionary is it so defined? The "-moon" means month. The term refers to the obligation of the newly married German tribesman to provide his bride with honeyed wine for the first month.

Victor Fox
New York, New York

Thanks to Mr. Barry Newman of The Wall Street Journal, *your "world superstars" have been outclassed by Pope John Paul II. According to Mr. Newman, some Britons think of the Bishop of Rome as the antichrist, while others view him "more as an international megastar." I suppose an "international megastar" is more important than a mere "world-class superstar."*

Jackson L. Blanton
Richmond, Virginia

You discussed the phrase "world-class." I was intrigued by the earliest reference so far discovered being 1963. In my ignorance I had always assumed that "world-

class" had been in use much longer than that. This feeling had been reinforced by two viewings of the John Huston film Victory—*escapist fare about WWII POWs (mostly British, with Pele and Sylvester Stallone thrown in for box office appeal). In that film international soccer players (ca. 1944) are referred to both as "world-class" and "first-class." After your column I searched the Trinity library, and came up with two English books, both published in the 1930s. One was on soccer, the other about cricket. I could not find one reference to "world-class," only first-class players traipsed through their pages.*

The reason for this, it seemed to me, was an overwhelming arrogance on the part of the two English authors (which might or might not have been justified, at least in the case of cricket), who devoted each a chapter to the game played outside of England, and then asserted that the English players were the best. I am sure that "world-class" came into vogue initially in these circles, as soon as the non-English players gained more respect among English players. This may have happened before 1964, but certainly after WWII, and thus the dialogue in Victory *was anachronistic. While I expect a measure of anachronism in film sets, costumes, music, etc., and while anachronistic dialogue in a film about medieval England is essential for contemporary audiences, I was somewhat disappointed with the shoddy research in the preparing of a relatively modern story. Ah, well . . .*

Nick Noble
Sports Information Director
Trinity College
Hartford, Connecticut

yet, *see* and yet

zapped again

When you push somebody out of a window, how would you describe the sound the person makes as he heads for the asphalt forty stories below?

The answer, as any reader of old comic books will quickly tell you, is *Aieeeee!* —sometimes spelled *Aiiieeeee!* It is the nearest written approximation of a scream—not perfect, but an improvement over *Eek!*, which is now used exclusively by people leaping on chairs to escape mice. A strangled scream is spelled *Arrgh!*

These thoughts on how to transmit grunts *(ugh!)* and sounds that make sense but are not words *(hunh?)* come to mind in an investigation of the origin of a sound word that is beginning to make it as a real word: *zap*.

To zap someone is "to let him have it"—to strike as if by thunderbolt. The verb has been used to mean "to increase speed," as in this citation from *Time* magazine in 1967: "Nickel-cadmium batteries . . . could zap the car from a standstill to 50 miles per hour in 20 seconds." As a noun, *zap* is sometimes confused with *zip*, which means "pep, sparkle, vivacity," but since the mid-1970's, both noun and verb have denoted the action of a swift shot in the teeth, actual or metaphoric.

The word's recent popularity stems from the comic strip "B.C.," by Johnny Hart, in which the word is often accompanied by a lightning bolt; the *z* in *zap* reinforces the sharp angles of the stylized lightning. In the *Barnhart Dictionary of New English Since 1963*, an older origin is indicated: "*zap!*, interjection used in the comic-strip balloons of Buck Rogers and Flash Gordon to render graphically the blast of space guns."

The novelist Ray Russell, who lives in Beverly Hills, caught my reference to the adoption of *zap* as a useful and colorful bit of informal English, and informs me that the word's coiner was Philip Francis Nowlan, not "the man without a country," but the man who originated the character of Buck Rogers.

Buck Rogers, a man of our time thrust forward in time (actually, back in time, when you think about it) to the twenty-fifth century, was introduced in the

August 1928 issue of *Amazing Stories*. Nowlan teamed up with Dick Calkins, an artist, to produce the comic strip the next year.

"Nowlan also coined the now-common word *zap!*—the sound emitted by the 'paralysis gun,' " writes Russell, "a handy little gadget that foreshadowed today's tranquilizer rifle."

Such specific coinage deserves recording here. When you are mildly zapped, it is correct to say, "Arrgh!"; a more forceful zapping rates an "Aieeeee!"; when the zapping causes vibrations, the only thing to say is: "Boinggg!"

Aieeee!! You obviously don't follow "B.C." It's "zot," not "zap."

> Craig Whitney
> *Foreign Editor*, The New York Times
> *New York, New York*

You are quite right about the Buck Rogers origin of zap, *but quite wrong in attributing its current popularity to "B.C." The sound of a lightning bolt in "B.C." is always ZOT. In fact, this is one of the three quintessential sound effects of Johnny Hart's comic strips, the others being GRONK (a dinosaur bellow) and non-onomatopoeia, as in the sound of a snake biting itself (BITE BITE BITE BITE BITE) or of a printing press (PRINT PRINT PRINT).*

> Philip M. Cohen
> *Aliquippa, Pennsylvania*

You missed a current culinary use of zap.

In our house, if you need something cooked quickly, you "zap it in the microwave."

> Ann Robison
> *St. Louis, Missouri*

You say the Barnhart Dictionary *suggests an origin older than Hart's "B.C." What about an origin even older? Would a B.C. origin please you? Maybe that's too romantic. Could it possibly go back to the Romans of the Empire, though, or to the medieval period, when they constructed saps or tunnels to reach under walls, or beyond, to approach, undermine or explode fortifications? Then it would be correct to say those fortifications were sapped. Or zapped.*

The dictionaries suggest a source word in the Italian, zappare. *The* OED *lists an English word "zappe" used as n. and v. and quoted as early as 1600 from*

Dymmok's Ireland: *"When that rampart which is, shall either be beaten or zapped."*

It seems so simple to start from "sap" to get to "zap." But we all know that in etymologies, as in other kinds of traffic or communication, green is for danger, and no one wants to be sap enough to be sapped—or zapped—by the obvious. However, the above does consist of facts.

Hy Gordon
Hewlett Harbor, New York

In the late sixties, there was an underground comic book called Zap Comix. *I was going to ascribe the current popularity of the "z" word to a cabal of* Zap Comix *worshipping, old hippies bemoaning the loss of status of the word "groovy." But overwrought satire is out of place in a short pedagogical letter.*

Michael J. Simmons
Palo Alto, California

Dear Bill:

Did these excited people begin their leaps on chairs or jump onto the chairs from the floor?

If usage has changed, I'll throw myself in the ocean (rather than into it).

Don [Don Janson]
The New York Times
Swarthmore, Pennsylvania

Acknowledgments

In the standard thank-yous at the end of a scholarly work, the author lists all the people who helped him, throws in a couple of relatives, old flames, and hosts he owes dinner parties to, and then graciously absolves them from any responsibility for errors. That is not my way.

Colleagues at *The New York Times* who have not usually led me astray or caused me embarrassment (somebody had better check the spelling of that last word) include Phyllis Shapiro and Sherwin Smith at the *Magazine,* Stephen Pickering and Mary Drohan at the Op-Ed page, and Ann Rubin, Angela Hoover, and Sunday Fellows at the Washington Bureau. If the wrong number of *r*'s appear in *embarrassment,* Pam Lyons, Elizabeth O'Brien, Ted Johnson, and Sharon Kapnick of Times Books are to blame, not me, because I know my limitations.

In the Land of Linguistics and Lexicography, I salute and lean on John Algeo, Jacques Barzun, Clarence Barnhart, Robert Barnhart, Robert Burchfield, Ron Butters of *American Speech,* Frederic Cassidy and Joan Hall of *DARE,* Stuart Berg Flexner, David Guralnik, James McCawley, Fred Mish, Allen Walker Read, Anne Soukhanov, Sol Steinmetz, and Karl Teeter.

Credit is grudgingly given to the Lexicographic Irregulars, that easily infuriated band of language lovers who have assembled themselves into groups like the Squad Squad, which sails into the lists against redundancy, and the Nitpicker's League, which is torn between those who insist it should be spelled that way and those who get all red-faced about their preference for Nitpickers' League. To all, my gratitude; I have found "standing corrected" to be more rewarding than embarrassing. (Check sp.)

Index